Photoshop® CS For Dummies

Windows Version

Cheat Sheet

Toolbox Shortcuts

Note: To access the tools, press the key(s) listed. If you uncheck the option Use Shift key for Tool Switch in Preferences, you can eliminate the need to press the Shift key to change tools.

M				V
Shift+M				W
None				K
None				Shift+K
L				B
Shift+L				Shift+B
Shift+L				Y
C				Shift+Y
J				G
Shift+J				Shift+G
Shift+J				O
S				Shift+O
Shift+S				Shift+O
E				T
Shift+E				Shift+T
Shift+E				Shift+T
R				Shift+T
Shift+R				U
Shift+R				Shift+U
Shift+A				Shift+U
Shift+A				Shift+U
P				Shift+U
Shift+P				Shift+U
None				I
None				Shift+I
None				Shift+I
N				Z
Shift+N				X
H				
				Q
D				F
				Ctrl+Shift+M

Selections

Note: Most of these tasks are performed with selection tools. (There's a shocker.)

Draw straight lines	Alt+click with Lasso tool
Add to selection outline	Shift+drag
Deselect specific area	Alt+drag
Deselect all but intersected area	Shift+Alt+drag
Deselect entire image	Ctrl+D
Reselect last selection	Ctrl+Shift+D
Select everything	Ctrl+A
Hide extras	Ctrl+H
Move selection outline only	Drag or press an arrow key

More Fun with Selections

Fill selection with foreground color	Alt+Backspace
Fill selection with background color	Ctrl+Backspace
Display Fill dialog box	Shift+Backspace
Cut selection	Ctrl+X
Copy selection	Ctrl+C
Paste image last cut or copied	Ctrl+V
Reapply last filter	Ctrl+F
Adjust levels	Ctrl+L
Free Transform	Ctrl+T
Transform Again	Ctrl+Shift+T

Painting and Editing Tricks

Increase brush size	]
Decrease brush size	[
Change opacity or flow of tool in 10% increments	1, ... , 9, 0
Paint or edit in straight lines	click, Shift+click
Erase to History	Alt+drag

For Dummies: Bestselling Book Series for Beginners

Photoshop® CS For Dummies®
Windows Version

Cheat Sheet

Layer Tricks

New Layer	Ctrl+Shift+N
Clone selection to a new layer	Ctrl+J
Cut selection to a new layer	Ctrl+Shift+J
Rename a layer	Double click layer name in Layers palette
Activate layer that contains specific image	Ctrl+click with Move tool
Activate next layer up	Alt+]
Activate next layer down	Alt+[
Hide all layers but one	Alt+click on eyeball
Show all layers	Alt+click on eyeball
Select the contents of active layer	Ctrl+click on layer name in Layers palette

Palette Shortcuts

Brushes palette	F5
Color palette	F6
Layers palette	F7
Info palette	F8
Actions palette	F9
Step forward in History palette	Ctrl+Shift+Z
Step backward in History palette	Ctrl+Alt+Z
All palettes, status bar, options bar, and Toolbox	Tab
Just palettes	Shift+Tab
Raise value in option box	Up arrow
Lower value in option box	Down arrow

Navigation Tricks

Scroll image	Spacebar+drag
Zoom in	Ctrl+spacebar+click
Zoom in and change window size	Ctrl++(plus sign)
Zoom out	Alt+spacebar+click
Zoom out and change window size	Ctrl+-(minus sign)
Scroll up or down one screen	PgUp/PgDn
Scroll left or right	Ctrl+PgUp/PgDn
Move to upper-left corner	Home of image
Move to lower-right corner	End of image
Zoom to 100%	Double-click Zoom tool
Fit on Screen	Ctrl+0
Cycle through all open image windows	Ctrl+Tab

Daily Activities

Cancel operation	Esc or Ctrl+. (period)
Close image	Ctrl+W
General preferences	Ctrl+K
Display last preferences panel used	Ctrl+Alt+K
Open image	Ctrl+O
Print image with preview	Ctrl+P
Page setup	Ctrl+Shift+P
Quit Photoshop	Ctrl+Q
Save image to disk	Ctrl+S
Save As	Ctrl+Shift+S
Save for Web	Ctrl+Alt+Shift+S
Undo last operation	Ctrl+Z

For Dummies: Bestselling Book Series for Beginners

Photoshop® CS For Dummies®
Mac Version

Cheat Sheet

Toolbox Shortcuts

Note: To access the tools, press the key(s) listed. If you uncheck the option Use Shift key for Tool Switch in Preferences, you can eliminate the need to press the Shift key to change tools.

M		V
Shift+M		W
None		K
None		Shift+K
L		B
Shift+L		Shift+B
Shift+L		Y
C		Shift+Y
J		G
Shift+J		Shift+G
Shift+J		O
S		Shift+O
Shift+S		Shift+O
E		T
Shift+E		Shift+T
Shift+E		Shift+T
R		Shift+T
Shift+R		U
Shift+R		Shift+U
Shift+A		Shift+U
Shift+A		Shift+U
P		Shift+U
Shift+P		Shift+U
None		I
None		Shift+I
None		Shift+I
N		Z
Shift+N		X
H		
D		
		Q
		F
		Ctrl+Shift+M

Selection Tricks

Note: All selection tricks are performed with selection tools. (There's a shocker.)

Draw straight lines	Option+click with Lasso tool
Add to selection outline	Shift+drag
Deselect specific area	Option+drag
Deselect all but intersected area	Option+drag
Deselect entire image	⌘+D
Reselect last selection	⌘+Shift+D
Select everything	⌘+A
Hide extras	⌘+H
Move selection outline only	Drag or press an arrow key

More Fun with Selections

Fill selection with foreground color	Option+Delete
Fill selection with background color	⌘+Delete
Display Fill dialog box	Shift+Delete
Cut selection	⌘+X
Copy selection	⌘+C
Paste image last cut or copied	⌘+V
Reapply last filter	⌘+F
Adjust levels	⌘+L
Free Transform	⌘+T
Transform again	⌘+Shift+T

For Dummies: Bestselling Book Series for Beginners

Photoshop® CS For Dummies®
Mac Version

Cheat Sheet

Layer Tricks

New Layer	⌘+Shift+N
Clone selection to a new layer	⌘+J
Cut selection to a new layer	⌘+Shift+J
Rename a layer	Double-click layer name in Layers palette
Activate layer that contains specific image	⌘+click with Move tool
Activate next layer up	Option+]
Lower value in option box	Down arrow

Painting and Editing Tricks

Increase brush size	]
Decrease brush size	[
Change opacity or flow of tool in 10% increments	1, ..., 9, 0
Paint or edit in straight lines	click, Shift+click
Erase to History	Option+drag

Navigation Tricks

Scroll image	Spacebar+drag
Zoom in	Ctrl ⌘+spacebar+click
Zoom in and change window size	⌘++(plus sign)
Zoom out	Option+spacebar+click
Zoom out and change window size	⌘+-(minus sign)
Scroll up or down one screen	PgUp/PgDn
Scroll left or right	⌘+PgUp/PgDn
Move to upper-left corner	Home of image
Move to lower-right corner	End of image
Zoom to 100%	Double-click Zoom tool
Fit on Screen	⌘+0
Cycle through all open image windows	⌘+Tab

Daily Activities

Cancel operation	⌘+. (period)
Close image	⌘+W
General preferences	⌘+K
Display last preferences panel used	⌘+Option+K
Open image	Ctrl [⌘]+O
Print image with preview	⌘+P
Page setup	⌘+Shift+P
Quit Photoshop	⌘+Q
Save image to disk	⌘+S
Save As	⌘+Shift+S
Save for Web	⌘+Option+Shift+S
Undo last operation	⌘+Z

For Dummies: Bestselling Book Series for Beginners

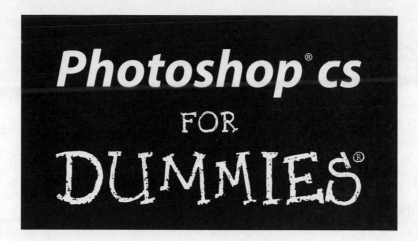

by Deke McClelland and Phyllis Davis

WILEY

Wiley Publishing, Inc.

Photoshop® cs For Dummies®
Published by
Wiley Publishing, Inc.
111 River Street
Hoboken, NJ 07030
www.wiley.com

Copyright © 2004 by Wiley Publishing, Inc., Indianapolis, Indiana

Published by Wiley Publishing, Inc., Indianapolis, Indiana

Published simultaneously in Canada

For general information on our other products and services or to obtain technical support, please contact our Customer Care Department within the U.S. at 800-762-2974, outside the U.S. at 317-572-3993, or fax 317-572-4002.

Wiley also publishes its books in a variety of electronic formats. Some content that appears in print may not be available in electronic books.

Library of Congress Control Number: 2003113613

ISBN: 0-7645-4356-3

Manufactured in the United States of America

10 9 8 7 6 5 4 3 2 1

1O/RW/RQ/QT/IN

About the Authors

Pioneering electronic publishing expert **Deke McClelland** is the author of *Photoshop 7 Bible* (Wiley Publishing, Inc.), the best-selling guide on digital imaging. Having written more than 60 titles in 20 languages, with 3 million copies in print, Deke is one of the most award-winning writers in the business, including a total of seven honors from the Computer Press Association. In addition to designing and editing the *Look & Learn* visual learning series (Wiley Publishing, Inc.), Deke hosts the in-depth training videos, *Total Photoshop, Total Illustrator,* and *Total InDesign* (all Total Training). He is a contributing editor for *Macworld* and *Photoshop User* magazines, and a member of the PhotoshopWorld Instructor Dream Team.

Phyllis Davis is a writer, graphics and Web designer, teacher, and graphics software expert. Her professional design credits include many books, fine art posters, and advertisements.

In addition to being co-author of Photoshop CS for Dummies, Phyllis is also the author of *The GIMP: Visual QuickStart Guide* (Peachpit Press), *CorelDraw: Visual QuickStart Guide* (Peachpit Press), and many other highly regarded books about graphic and photo-manipulation software.

When she isn't writing and designing books and creating Web sites, Phyllis can be found developing and teaching computer courses, digging in her garden with her husband, Harold, and playing with her wonderful boys, Julian and Nicholas.

Dedication

For my men, Harold, Julian, and Nicholas. You guys keep life fun!

Author's Acknowledgments

Special thanks to Matt Wagner and Bob Woerner for entrusting me with this great project. I also owe a debt of gratitude to Nicole Haims, who untwisted my gnarled sentences and kept me to the point. Without Nicole this book would have never gotten out the door on time.

Many of the beautiful photographs in this book were created by my husband, Harold Davis. These photographs are copyright © Harold Davis and are used with his permission. Thanks, Harold!

Publisher's Acknowledgments

We're proud of this book; please send us your comments through our online registration form located at www.dummies.com/register/.

Some of the people who helped bring this book to market include the following:

Acquisitions, Editorial, and Media Development

Project Editor: Nicole Haims

(Previous Edition: Christine Berman)

Acquisitions Editor: Bob Woerner

Copy Editor: Nicole Haims

Technical Editor: Dennis Cohen

Editorial Manager: Carol Sheehan

Media Development Manager:
Laura VanWinkle

Media Development Supervisor:
Richard Graves

Editorial Assistant: Amanda Foxworth

Cartoons: Rich Tennant
(www.the5thwave.com)

Production

Project Coordinator: Ryan Steffen

Layout and Graphics: Joyce Haughey,
Barry Offringa, Heather Ryan,
Shae Lynn Wilson

Proofreaders: John Greenough, Susan Moritz,
Carl William Pierce, TECHBOOKS Production
Services

Indexer: TECHBOOKS Production Services

Publishing and Editorial for Technology Dummies

Richard Swadley, Vice President and Executive Group Publisher

Andy Cummings, Vice President and Publisher

Mary C. Corder, Editorial Director

Publishing for Consumer Dummies

Diane Graves Steele, Vice President and Publisher

Joyce Pepple, Acquisitions Director

Composition Services

Gerry Fahey, Vice President of Production Services

Debbie Stailey, Director of Composition Services

Contents at a Glance

Table of Contents

Introduction

● ●

Why in the world is Adobe Photoshop such a popular program? Normally, graphics software is about as much of a hit with the general public as an alternative rock band is with the senior citizen set. And yet Photoshop — a program that lets you correct and modify photographs on your computer — has managed to work its way into the hearts and minds of computer users from all walks of life. What gives?

Wouldn't you know it, I just happen to have a couple of theories. First, when you work in Photoshop, you're not drawing from scratch; you're editing photos. Sure, tampering with a photograph can be a little intimidating, but it's nothing like the chilling, abject fear that seizes your soul when you stare at a blank screen and try to figure out how to draw things on it. Simply put, a photograph inspires you to edit it in precisely the same way that an empty piece of paper does not.

Second, after Photoshop hooks you, it keeps you interested with a depth of capabilities that few pieces of software can match. Okay, so a couple of stinky minutes sneak themselves in every once in a while, but that's to be expected. Photoshop is a computer program, after all, and we all know that computers are cosmic jokes whose only reason for being is to frustrate us, mock us, ignore our requests, and crash. This book comes in handy for just those moments.

About This Book

Just because Photoshop is a pleasure to use doesn't mean that the program is easy to learn. In fact, it's kind of a bear — a big, ornery, grizzly bear with about 17 rows of teeth and claws to match. This program contains so much that it honestly takes months of earnest endeavor to sift through it all. By yourself, that is.

I wrote this book with the following specific goals in mind:

✔ To show you what you need to know at the precise pace you need to know it.

✔ To show you how to do the right things in the right way, right off the bat.

- To distract you and shove little facts into your head when you're not looking.

- To make the process not only less painful, but also a real adventure that you'll look back on during your Golden Years with a wistful tear in your eye. "Oh, how I'd like to learn Photoshop all over again," you'll sigh. "Nothing I've done since — whether it was winning the lottery that time, or flying on the inaugural commuter shuttle to the moon with the original cast of *Star Trek* — seemed quite as thrilling as sifting through Photoshop with that crazy old *For Dummies* book."

Okay, maybe that's an exaggeration, but prepare yourself for a fun time. In a matter of days, you'll be doing things that'll make your jaw hang down and dangle from its hinges.

While you were browsing the bookstore shelves deciding which book on Photoshop to buy, you may have noticed another book by yours truly (published by Wiley Publishing, Inc.): *Photoshop Bible*. There's a version for Windows and one for Macs. Those 800-page tomes cover just about everything there is to know about Photoshop. This book's a little more manageable than that tome, but when you're ready for the big leagues, check it out. Becoming comfortable and productive with Photoshop is what this book is all about.

How This Book Is Organized

This book comprises a bunch of independent sections designed to answer your basic Photoshop questions. Oh, sure, you can read the book cover-to-cover, and it will make perfect sense. But you can also read any chapter or section out of context.

Also, this book is a cross-platform book, meaning that it tells you how to do things in Photoshop on both a PC and a Macintosh computer. You'll notice commands for both PCs and Macs, and sometimes text is specific to one platform or another.

To help you slog through the information, I've broken the book into eight parts. Each of those parts contains chapters, and those chapters are divided into sections and subsections. Graphics abound to illustrate things that would take 1,000 words to explain, and you'll even find glorious color plates — 16 pages in all — to show off techniques and effects in living color.

To give you an overview of the kind of information you're likely to find in these pages, here's a quick rundown of the eight parts.

Part 1: Getting the Basics Down

The first stage of using any computer program is the worst. You don't know what you can do, you don't know how good the program is, and you don't even know how to ask a reasonably intelligent question. These first three chapters get you up and running in record time.

Chapter 1 introduces you to image editing, explains where to find images to edit, and provides a quick glimpse of what's new in Photoshop CS. Chapters 2 and 3 take you on a grand tour of the Photoshop interface and image window and give you all the information you need to navigate both.

Part 11: The Care and Feeding of Pixels

Before you can edit a digital photograph, you have to know a few things about the nature of the beast. What's a pixel, for example, and why is getting rid of one so dangerous? What's the difference between a color image and a grayscale image — other than the obvious? And how do you save or print your image after you finish editing it? All these questions and many more are answered in Chapters 4 through 6.

Part 111: Selections and Layers

The selection tools let you cordon off the portion of the photograph you want to edit. Select the face, for example, and Photoshop protects the body, no matter how randomly you drag or how spastic your brushstrokes. Chapter 7 helps you understand how selections work and how to use them to your advantage. In Chapter 8, I give you a full run down of layers, a Photoshop feature that adds flexibility, creative opportunity, and security to your image-editing life.

Part 1V: Basic Editing

Chapters 9 through 11 are all about image editing — a body of skills that comes in very handy when you want to retouch, change, or improve photographs. Chapters 9 and 10 tell you all you need to know about correcting image colors and imperfections. Chapter 11 goes into all those cool filters that can magically transform your images into anything you can imagine — watercolor paintings, mosaics, or chrome, just to name a few. (When you're done with Chapter 11, check out Chapter 21 for more about filters.)

Part V: Using Your Virtual Paint Brush

Photoshop offers amazing brushes and pencils that are remarkably capable, allowing you to perform pages and pages of tricks while expending minimum effort. Find out how to smear colors, get rid of dust specks, fill areas with colors and patterns, erase mistakes, and do a whole lot more in Chapters 12 through 14.

Part VI: Heavy-Duty Photoshop

Just what is a layer mask? Chapter 15 answers these questions and more as it plumbs the depths of creating fade outs, saving intricate selections, and more. Chapter 16 takes you to the world of paths and shapes where you'll discover how to add *vector graphics,* to your Photoshop images. Chapter 17 moves on to creating type and how to manipulate it as well as warp it into incredible shapes. In addition, you'll find out how to place type on a path, a new Photoshop cs feature.

Part VII: Photoshop for Webbies

Web graphics differ in many respects from real-world images. For starters, the color palette is different, Web graphics use specific file formats than image files meant for print, and Web graphics are *dynamic,* meaning they can move and change on the Web page. Chapters 18 and 19 give you the lowdown on Web graphics and Photoshop's sister program, ImageReady. Check out the bonus chapter (www.dummies.com/go/photoshop_cs_fd) for more Web graphics details.

Part VIII: The Part of Tens

Chapters 20 and 21 contain the ultimate Photoshop Top Ten lists. In Chapter 20, find out more about just a few of Photoshop's essential filter effects, and in Chapter 21, find answers to that age-old question, "Now that I've finished mucking up my image in Photoshop, what do I do with it?"

Conventions Used in This Book

If I'm showing you how to access a menu, you see a command arrow like this: ⇨. For example, if I say choose Select⇨Feather, click the Select menu and choose the Feather option. (Incidentally, this menu option enables you to blur a selection outline as I explain in Chapter 7.)

This is a cross-platform book, and in the Mac OS things are called by different names than they are in the Windows OS. For example, on the Mac, a traditional Windows drop-down list box is called a pop-up menu. For the sake of simplicity in this book, I consistently go with the Windows vernacular and call Mac pop-up menus drop-down lists. In all other cases, the Mac equivalent of a Windows operation appears in parentheses, like this:

Press Enter (Return on a Mac).

Press Ctrl+Z (⌘+Z on a Mac).

Press Alt+Shift (Option+Shift on a Mac).

Icons Used in This Book

When you're driving, road signs are always warning you about bad things. Slow, Detour, Stop, Dip — these are all signs that I, for one, hate to see. I mean, you never see good signs like Go Ahead and Speed, No Traffic This Way, or Free Money Ahead.

This book isn't like that. Using friendly icons in the margins, I highlight good things and bad things, and the good things outnumber the bad. So don't shy away from the road signs in this book — welcome them into your reading ritual with open arms. Here's your field guide to icons:

Photoshop has very few obvious shortcuts and a ton of hidden ones. That's where the Tip icon comes in. It says, "Hey, whoa there; here's a juicy one!"

This icon acts as a special reminder of things I've mentioned in the past, or things I want you to bear in mind for the future.

Photoshop is a kind and gentle program. But every once in a while it pays to be careful. This icon tells you when to keep an eye out for trouble.

This icon points out features or commands that have changed or are new in Photoshop CS. If you're upgrading from an earlier version of Photoshop pay attention to this icon.

I hate computer jargon just as much as the next red-blooded computer user. But sometimes, I have to use it because there's no word for this stuff in normal, everyday, conversational English. It's a crying shame, I know, but at least I warn you that something nerdy is coming your way with this icon.

How to Use This Book

When I was in grade school, I don't think a year went by that our teacher didn't show us how to handle our new books. Open the book once in the center and then open the first quarter and the last quarter, each time gently creasing the spine. Never fold the pages or roll them so that they won't lie flat. And be sure to read the words from the beginning to end, just as the author meant them to be read. A book, after all, is a Special Thing to Be Treasured. Here are a couple of thoughts:

- Break the spine first thing out. The pages lie flatter that way.

- When you have a question, look it up in the index. Feel free to shut the book and get on with your life when you're done (though I do my best to snag you and make you read longer).

- If you're just curious about what the book has to offer, skim the Table of Contents and read a few pages about a topic that interests you.

- If you want to learn everything the book has to offer in what I consider the optimum order, turn the page and start reading at your own pace.

- If you come across something important, don't hesitate to fold the page, slap a sticky note on it, circle the text with a highlighter pen, or rip out the page and tack it to the wall.

- And when you've gleaned everything there is to glean, house-train your new puppy with the pages or use them for kindling. Or keep the book handy as a reference as questions arise.

On the Web

This book has a companion Web site. Visit www.dummies.com/go/photoshop_cs_fd to find fantastic filter and blending mode galleries. You can also find links to great Web sites to help you with your Photoshop activities. I even included a bonus chapter that shows you how to create rollovers and animations with your Web graphics.

Want to send me a line of congratulations or a complaint? If so, please feel free to visit my Web site at www.dekemc.com and then click on the Contact Deke button to drop me a line.

Part I
Getting the Basics Down

In this part . . .

1t's true that the best place to start something is usually
the beginning. And, as your mother or father may have
told you, you can't move on to the fun stuff — dessert if
you are five years old, creating stunning imagery in
Photoshop if you are reading this book — until you've
gotten the basics down.

The chapters in the part explain what you need to know
to get the basics of Photoshop under your belt. Chapter 1
explains what Photoshop is and how it works.

In Chapter 2, you discover the menus, palettes, and tools
that Photoshop has to offer. In addition, you'll find out how
to create custom shortcuts, a new Photoshop cs feature.

Scanners and digital cameras are becoming almost as
common as household toasters. But, how do you get the
photos and scanned images into Photoshop? Chapter 3
takes you through the ins-and-outs of importing images
from these types of devices. With Photoshop cs, importing images is easier than ever. And after you import your
image, you'll find out how to save it, what file format it
should be saved in, and how to use the enhanced File
Browser to organize your images.

Chapter 1

Introducing the Two Faces of Photoshop

In This Chapter

▶ Introducing the dual world of Photoshop

▶ Discovering the difference between painting and image editing

▶ Adjusting photographs

▶ What's new in Photoshop CS

▶ Finding images to edit

Adobe Photoshop is arguably the most comprehensive and popular photo editor around. In fact, I don't know a single computer artist who doesn't use Photoshop on an almost daily basis, regardless of what other programs he or she may use.

I assume that you've at least seen, if not used, Photoshop, and that you have a vague idea of what it's all about. But just so that we're all clear on the subject, the primary purpose of Photoshop is to make changes to digital photographic images. (For some clever ideas on acquiring such images, see the sidebar "Finding images to abuse," later in this chapter.)

If you've used Photoshop for only a week or so, you may have mistaken it for a fairly straightforward package. Certainly, on the surface of the program, Photoshop comes off as rather friendly. But lurking a few fathoms deep is another, darker program, one that is distinctly unfriendly for the uninitiated, but wildly capable for the stout of heart. My analyst would no doubt declare Photoshop a classic case of a split personality. In short, Photoshop has a Dr. Jekyll-and-Mr. Hyde thing going on.

This chapter explores both sides of the Photoshop brain. It also introduces you to the personality changes found in the latest incarnation of the program, Photoshop CS. Finally, I get you started on the road to image-editing bliss by explaining where to find images to edit in the first place.

The Two Functions of Photoshop

Generally speaking, the two halves of Photoshop serve different purposes. The straightforward Jekyll tools mostly concentrate on *painting,* and the more complex Hyde capabilities are devoted to *image editing.* Therefore, to tackle this great program, you may find it helpful to understand the difference between the two terms.

Drawing and painting without the mess

To discover the benevolent Dr. Jekyll half of Photoshop, you need look no farther than the standard painting and editing tools. Shown in Figure 1-1, these tools are so simple, they're practically pastoral. The Eraser tool erases, the Pencil tool draws hard-edged lines, the magnifying glass magnifies your images, and so on. These incredibly straightforward tools attract new users just as surely as a light attracts miller moths.

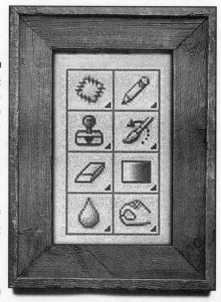

Figure 1-1: Many of the Photoshop tools have an old-world, rustic charm that's sure to warm the cockles of the most timid technophobe.

Likewise, painting is just what it sounds like: You take a brush loaded with color and smear it all over your on-screen image. You can paint from scratch on a blank canvas, or you can paint directly on top of a photograph.

Notice in Figure 1-2 the rather drab fellow drinking a rather drab beverage. (Though you may guess this man to be Dr. Jekyll armed with the secret potion, most scholars consider it highly doubtful that even Jekyll was this goofy.)

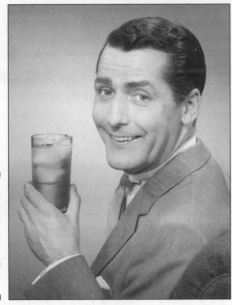

Figure 1-2: The unadorned "I Love My Libation" poster boy of 1948.

I invoked all the changes in Figure 1-3 by using a single tool — the brush — and just two colors — black and white. Suddenly, a singularly cool dude emerges. By saving the original image to disk (as explained in Chapter 3), you don't have to worry about making permanent changes to your images. You can restore details from the original image at whim (the subject of Chapter 14).

Figure 1-3: A few hundred strokes of the brush result in a party animal to rival Carmen Miranda.

You quickly discover that, on their own, the painting tools aren't super-duper exciting. Also, the tools don't work much like their traditional counterparts — a line drawn with the Pencil tool, for example, doesn't look anything like a line drawn with a real pencil. Here's another little issue — the so-called straightforward tools aren't particularly applicable to the job of editing images. Generally speaking, you have to be blessed with pretty major eye-hand coordination to achieve good results using these tools.

Editing existing image detail

The remade man in Figure 1-3 is the life of the party, but he's nothing compared to what he could be with the aid of some image editing. When you edit an image, you distort and enhance its existing details. So rather than paint with color, you paint with the image itself.

Unfortunately, that's when you discover the Mr. Hyde half of the program. You encounter options that have meaningless names such as Dissolve, Multiply, and Difference. Commands such as Image Size and Trim — both of which sound harmless enough — seem to damage your images. And clicking icons frequently produces no result. It's enough to drive a reticent computer artist stark raving insane.

Figure 1-4 demonstrates what I mean. To achieve this grotesque turn of the visual phrase, I was obliged to indulge in a liberal amount of distortion. First, I flipped the guy's head and stretched it a little bit. Well, actually, I stretched it a lot. Then, I further exaggerated the eyes and mouth. I rotated the arm and distorted the glass to make the glass meet the ear. Finally, I *cloned* a background from a different image to cover up where the head and arm used to be. The only thing I painted was the straw (the one coming out of the guy's ear). Otherwise, I lifted every detail from one of two photographs.

Okay, so that's a lot of complicated stuff I did. Unfortunately, many folks return broken and frustrated to the under-equipped and boring, but non-threatening, painting and editing tools that they've come to know. It's sad, really. Especially when you consider all the wonderful things that the more complex Photoshop controls can do. Oh sure, the controls have weird names, and they may not respond as you think they should at first, but after you come to terms with these slick puppies, they perform in ways you wouldn't believe.

In fact, the dreaded Mr. Hyde side of Photoshop represents the core of this powerful program. Without its sinister half, Photoshop is just another rinky-dink piece of painting software whose most remarkable capability is keeping the kids out of mischief on a rainy day.

Figure 1-4:
Image
editing has
no respect
for com-
position,
form, or
underlying
skeletal
structure.

Mind you, you don't have to go quite so hog-wild with the image editing. If you're a photographer, for example, you may not care to mess with your work to the point that it becomes completely unrecognizable. Figure 1-5 shows a few subtle adjustments that affect neither the form nor composition of the original image. These changes merely accentuate details or downplay defects in the image.

It's New! It's Improved!

Someday, the folks at Adobe may come out with an upgrade to Photoshop that completely tames the Mr. Hyde half of the program. But Photoshop CS isn't the upgrade to do it, which is good for me because it lets me continue with my colorful dual-personality analogy.

Photoshop CS is a great upgrade. The whole program is more polished, many existing features have been extended and enhanced, and several new items ramp up productivity 200 percent.

One thing that hasn't changed, however, is the hefty system requirements needed to run Photoshop. Photoshop CS works on PCs running Windows 2000 with Service Pack 3, or Windows XP and later Windows versions (all hereafter referred to as just *Windows*) with 280MB of available disk space. Photoshop CS runs on Macs running OS 10.2.4 or later with 320MB of available disk space. Both platforms require 192MB of RAM (256MB recommended) and a CD-ROM.

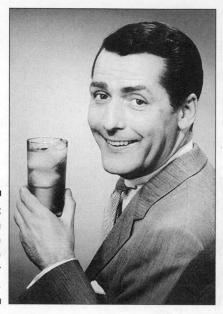 

Figure 1-5:
You can apply more moderate edits to your image.

Please note that these are Adobe's *minimum* requirements. If there's one program that benefits from as much RAM as you can throw at it, it's Photoshop. The more you give it, the better the performance.

Here are some Photoshop CS improvements:

- ✔ **Use the File Browser with ease (see Chapter 3):** Introduced in Version 7, the File Browser is more powerful and easy to use than ever. New Photoshop CS features include the ability to preview high-quality images and create custom-sized thumbnails, drag images around to group or rank them, batch process groups of images, search for filenames, and open images directly to Photoshop or ImageReady.

- ✔ **Customize keyboard shortcuts (see Chapter 2):** This new feature speaks for itself. Although the program has always utilized shortcuts, now you can make up your own.

- ✔ **Use new photography features (see Chapters 9, 11, and 12):** Photoshop 7 introduced a Camera Raw plug-in that shipped separately. Photoshop CS integrates and enhances Camera Raw settings while supporting a wider range of cameras, and includes color calibration controls (see Chapter 9). To enhance photographs quickly, use the new Shadow/Highlight Correction command to quickly correct over- and under-exposed areas (see Chapter 9). Simulating real-world blurring, the

Lens Blur filter creates highlights that take on the shape of the camera lens (see Chapter 11). Create panoramas quickly by using the new Photomerge plug-in (see Chapter 12). The new Crop and Straighten Photos command separates multiple scanned photos into separate image files.

✔ **Utilize digital video enhancements:** Photoshop CS includes new video features including support for video screen formats such as wide-screen and full-screen television sizes. This means that pixels aren't always represented as squares. When a non-square pixel ratio is selected (for instance, a regular image uses a 1:1 pixel ratio, whereas a wide-screen video image uses a 1:2 pixel ratio), Photoshop automatically changes the appearance of shapes, text, and brushes to match the selected ratio. Although this new feature is beyond the scope of this book, suffice it to say that the folks at Adobe are adding exciting new features for video creators.

✔ **Replace Color Brush (see Chapter 12):** Located on the Toolbar in the Brush Tool slot, this new brush lets you replace existing color with the foreground color.

✔ **Brush Tool enhancements (see Chapter 12):** Photoshop CS lets you create brush groups for the Brush Tools.

✔ **New text features (see Chapter 17):** Photoshop CS now includes the capability of putting text on or inside a path and change the starting point of text on a path.

✔ **Create layer comps (see Chapter 8):** This new feature lets you capture document layer states, including layer visibility, position, and blending options. It's like taking a snapshot of layer settings that you can save for later. Using layer comps, you can switch comps while working on a document, cycle through saved comps to select one, and more.

✔ **Create PDF presentations (see Chapter 6):** This new plug-in lets you create Acrobat PDF presentations of your images with just a few clicks of the mouse.

Photoshop's sister program ImageReady is used to create Web images. ImageReady also includes many new features and improvements. You'll find these listed and discussed in Part VII, "Photoshop for Webbies."

Finding images to abuse

Just about any local drugstore has a photo lab that can turn photographs from your camera into colorful pieces of paper that you can slap into albums or frames. But what if you want those photos in a digital form, too? You can find plenty of affordable options if you look in the right places:

✔ You can purchase photos on CD-ROM (prices range from pocket change to several dollars per image). I like Getty Images, which is the parent of the popular PhotoDisc and FPG, Stone, and The Image Bank, among others. I also like Eyewire (also owned by Getty Images) and Corbis. These vendors are all available online. Check them out at: www.gettyimages.com, www.eyewire.com, and www.corbis.com. Prices can be high, so be sure to check *before* you download an image.

✔ You can find zillions of photos to download on the Internet or from online services like America Online. The problem is that images may be of dubious quality. Also, you can't rule out the possibility of running across something pornographic or otherwise distasteful. If you want high-quality, general-purpose images, you have to subscribe to specialized services such as Newscom (visit www.newscom.com or call (800) 601-NEWS). A full membership gives you access to all the a la carte and free content for $10–$20 a month. You are then billed additionally for any other images you download.

✔ Digital cameras are becoming less expensive and better in quality. Downloading images from your camera to your computer is also quick and easy. Photoshop accepts the two file formats, JPEG and TIFF, that most cameras utilize. (For more information on formats, see Chapter 3.)

✔ You can take your own photo into your local copy shop or service bureau, and scan the image to disk. Kinko's charges about $6–$15 per image. If you find yourself using this service frequently, it would be worth your time and money to invest in your very own scanner. The cost of scanners has plummeted in recent years. You can pick up scanners as cheap as $30 for a CIS scanner, to $1500 for a premium CCD scanner by a well-known manufacturer.

✔ A better (and cheaper) method is to scan images to a Photo CD, which costs between $1 and $2 a shot, plus the price of the CD itself, which is usually in the neighborhood of $12–$20. ProCD scans are around $16–$20 dollars per scan, but offer six resolutions instead of five. One CD can hold about 100 images. Some vendors allow you to supply your own media — blank CDs, Zip disks, and so on. They also provide you with a handy Index print of your images for a nominal fee of around $5. Check the Yellow Pages under Photo Finishing — Retail. Service bureaus also provide this service. Prices vary widely from vendor to vendor.

Chapter 2

Getting to Know the Interface

• •

In This Chapter

▶ Launching Photoshop

▶ Taking a look at the Photoshop CS interface

▶ Checking out the Toolbox

▶ Working with the program window

▶ Switching between Photoshop and other programs

▶ Choosing commands

▶ Using dialog boxes and palettes

▶ Customizing your workspace

▶ Creating tool presets

• •

*I*f you're brand new to Photoshop — or to computers in general — this is the chapter for you. You get the basic stuff you need to know before you begin using the program to distort the faces of all your family members.

Even if you're already familiar with the basic interface of Photoshop, give this chapter the once-over to get acquainted with a couple of great new features in Photoshop CS and to make sure that you and I are speaking the same language. Here, you and I calibrate brains, so to speak.

Giving Photoshop the Electronic Breath of Life

Before you can use Photoshop, you have to start up — or *launch* — the program. Here's how:

> **1. Start your computer if it isn't already on.**

2. **PC users, choose Start➪All Programs➪Adobe Photoshop CS.**

   If the Photoshop CS icon is not available on the All Programs menu, take a look at the folder where Photoshop is installed to find the program file (the default location is `C:\Program Files\Adobe\Photoshop CS`). Double-click the Photoshop program icon to launch Photoshop.

    Create a shortcut using the Photoshop program icon and place it on the desktop. That way, you can just double-click the desktop shortcut to launch Photoshop in the future.

    If you're a Windows user and you're not sure where Photoshop is located on your hard drive, choose Start➪Search. On the left side of the Search Results dialog box, click All Files and Folders to search these items. Type Photoshop CS into the text box that appears and then click Search. A list appears with all the folders and files containing the word Photoshop. By default, the Photoshop program should be located in the `C:\Program Files\Adobe` folder. Locate the program icon and double-click to launch the program.

2. **Mac users, locate and activate the Adobe Photoshop CS folder in the Finder.**

   Use the mouse to move the arrow-shaped cursor over the icon and press the mouse button. Then choose File➪Open from the menu bar or press ⌘+O. A window labeled Welcome Screen opens, containing the Adobe Photoshop icon and some other icons. You also can launch Photoshop by using a couple of shortcuts. Either double-click the program icon or select the icon and press ⌘+↓. You can drag the icon to the Dock; that way, you can open it in the future with just one click.

    If you're a Mac user and you're not sure where Photoshop is located on your hard drive, choose File➪Find from the menu bar (or press ⌘+F). Then type the word **Photoshop** and press the Return key. A list appears with all files containing the word Photoshop. By default, the Photoshop program should be located in the Applications folder. Locate the program icon and double-click to launch the program.

   After your computer stops making little shicka-shicka noises and your screen settles down, you see the Photoshop Welcome Screen, as shown in Figure 2-1. You can use the Welcome Screen to access Photoshop resources such as tutorials, what's new in Photoshop CS, and tips and tricks.

3. **Click Close.**

   The Welcome Screen closes and you see the Photoshop program window, as shown in Figure 2-2.

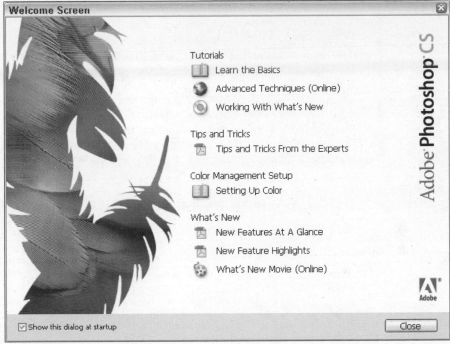

Figure 2-1:
The
Photoshop
Welcome
Screen
gives
access to
Photoshop
resources.

Working with Windows

This section is relevant to PC users only. Mac people, skip down to the following section, "Switching between Photoshop and the Finder." In Photoshop, as in most other Windows programs, you have two kinds of windows: the program window, which contains the main Photoshop work area; and image windows, which contain the images that you create and edit. To see the program window and image window, take a look at Figure 2-3.

Photoshop windows — both program and image — contain the same basic elements as do other Windows program windows. But just in case you need a refresher or you're new to this whole computing business, here's how the Photoshop program window works with Windows:

✔ Click the Close button in the upper-right corner of the program window to shut down Photoshop. Photoshop prompts you to save open, unsaved images before it lets you exit. (For details on saving images, see Chapter 3.) Another way to shut down Photoshop is to press the keyboard shortcut Ctrl+Q (as in Quit).

✔ Click the Minimize button to reduce the program window to a button on the Windows taskbar. To redisplay the program window, just click the button on the taskbar.

✔ The Restore/Maximize button changes depending on the current status of the window. If you see two boxes on the button, as in Figure 2-1, the button is in Restore mode. Click this button to shrink the window in order to see other open program windows. You can resize the window by placing the mouse cursor over a corner or edge of the program window. A double-headed arrow appears, letting you drag the window to resize it. To move the window around, drag the title bar. To restore the Photoshop program window to its former size, just click the Restore/Maximize button.

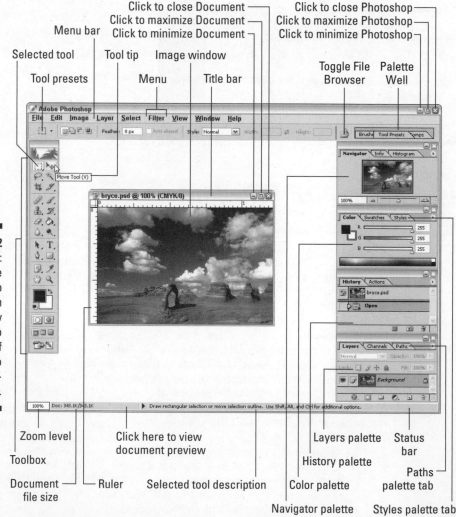

Figure 2-2 (Windows): The Photoshop program window opens onto a world of photo manipulation wonder.

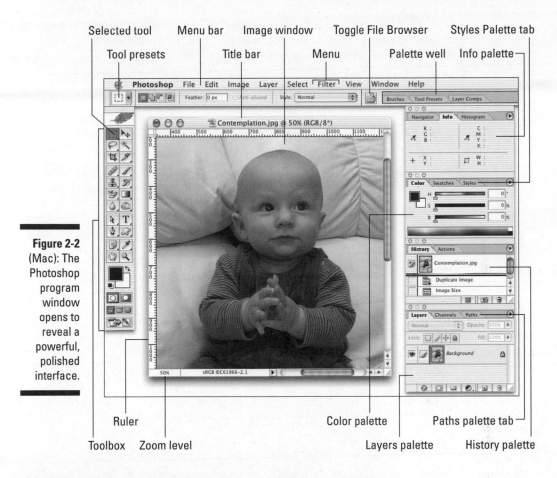

Figure 2-2 (Mac): The Photoshop program window opens to reveal a powerful, polished interface.

Labels around figure:
Selected tool · Menu bar · Image window · Toggle File Browser · Styles Palette tab
Tool presets · Title bar · Menu · Palette well · Info palette

Ruler · Color palette · Paths palette tab
Toolbox · Zoom level · Layers palette · History palette

Switching between Photoshop and the Finder

In back of the myriad desktop elements of Photoshop, Mac users can probably see the icons and open windows from the Finder. If you click a Finder element or anywhere on the desktop, you're taken back to the Finder, and the Photoshop desktop elements disappear. If an image is open, however, the image window remains visible. Here are some tips to help you manage working between the Finder and Photoshop.

✔ If you inadvertently click yourself out of Photoshop, click the Photoshop icon in the Dock, located at the bottom, left, or right side of your screen (depending on where you positioned it). Or just click the Photoshop image window. The Toolbox and palettes return to the screen to show you that Photoshop is back in the game.

✔ When using Photoshop, you may find that the clutter from the Finder gets somewhat distracting. Choose Photoshop➪Hide Others to hide every Finder element except the icons.

✔ You can hide the Dock by choosing Apple➪Dock➪Turn Hiding On.

Opening Up Your Toolbox

Now it's time to move on to the incredible world of the Toolbox. As shown in Figures 2-3 and 2-4, the tools in the Toolbox cover a myriad of functions.

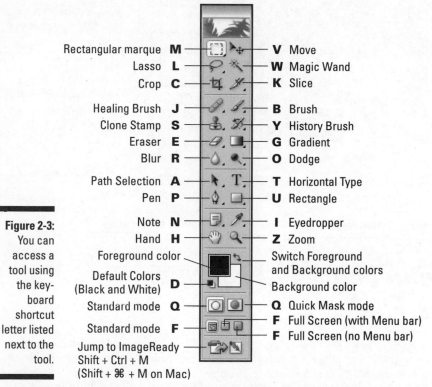

Rectangular marque **M** — **V** Move
Lasso **L** — **W** Magic Wand
Crop **C** — **K** Slice
Healing Brush **J** — **B** Brush
Clone Stamp **S** — **Y** History Brush
Eraser **E** — **G** Gradient
Blur **R** — **O** Dodge
Path Selection **A** — **T** Horizontal Type
Pen **P** — **U** Rectangle
Note **N** — **I** Eyedropper
Hand **H** — **Z** Zoom
Foreground color — Switch Foreground and Background colors
Default Colors (Black and White) **D** — Background color
Standard mode **Q** — **Q** Quick Mask mode
Standard mode **F** — **F** Full Screen (with Menu bar)
— **F** Full Screen (no Menu bar)
Jump to ImageReady Shift + Ctrl + M (Shift + ⌘ + M on Mac)

Figure 2-3: You can access a tool using the keyboard shortcut letter listed next to the tool.

✔ Photoshop CS adds the Color Replacement tool which is discussed in detail in Chapter 12.

✔ The top two-thirds of the Toolbox is devoted to an assortment of tools that you can use to edit images, just as you might use an assortment of pencils and brushes to paint a picture.

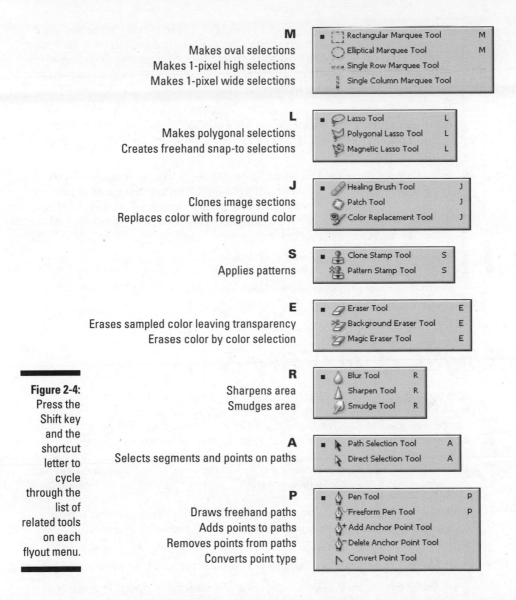

M
Makes oval selections
Makes 1-pixel high selections
Makes 1-pixel wide selections

L
Makes polygonal selections
Creates freehand snap-to selections

J
Clones image sections
Replaces color with foreground color

S
Applies patterns

E
Erases sampled color leaving transparency
Erases color by color selection

R
Sharpens area
Smudges area

A
Selects segments and points on paths

P
Draws freehand paths
Adds points to paths
Removes points from paths
Converts point type

Figure 2-4:
Press the
Shift key
and the
shortcut
letter to
cycle
through the
list of
related tools
on each
flyout menu.

✔ The bottom third of the Toolbox contains color selection options, masking icons, and viewing icons. These icons respond immediately when you click them. Click the bottom-most icon to jump to ImageReady, a Web graphics program (for details see Chapter 18).

✔ If you see a tiny triangle in the bottom-right corner of a tool icon, that means that the button is associated with a *flyout* menu (refer to Figure 2-4 for the complete set of flyout menus and descriptions of all the tools).

✔ To display the flyout menu and reveal the hidden tools, press and hold the mouse button on the tiny triangle. Notice that the currently selected tool has a black square next to it. Drag over and down the column of tools until your cursor is hovering over the tool you want to use, and then release the mouse button.

✔ If you've been clicking away on the Toolbox icons and haven't seen any results, don't worry! Your copy of Photoshop isn't broken; the icons just don't do anything unless you have an image open. To find out how to open images, see Chapter 3.

✔ To find out the name of a particular tool, pause your cursor over its icon for a second or two. A tool tip will appear, telling you the name of the tool and its keyboard equivalent. This feature can be turned off by choosing Edit➪Preferences➪General (Photoshop➪Preferences➪General on a Mac). Uncheck the Show Tool Tips option.

✔ If you grab a tool, try to use it, and all you see is the Cancel icon — a circle with a diagonal line — simply click anywhere on the image window. An error message appears in the status bar at the bottom of the screen to explain why Photoshop can't perform the operation.

Talking Back to Dialog Boxes

Photoshop reacts immediately to some menu commands. But for other commands, the program requires you to spell out your exact needs before it processes your request. If you see an ellipsis (three dots, like so . . .) next to a command name, that's your clue that you're about to see a *dialog box*.

Figure 2-5 shows a sample dialog box. As the figure demonstrates, a dialog box can contain any or all of six basic kinds of options. The options work as follows:

✔ Use a *text box* to enter text or numbers. Double-click in a text box to highlight its contents, and then replace the contents by entering new stuff using the keyboard.

✔ *Slider bars* are used to increase or decrease a numerical value in text boxes.

✔ *Radio buttons* let you select only one option from a group. The selected radio button is filled with a black dot; unselected radio buttons are hollow.

✔ Although you can select only one radio button at a time, usually you can select as many *check boxes* as you want. To select a check box, click in the box or on the option name that follows it. A check mark fills the box to show that it's selected. Removing a check mark (by clicking again) turns off the option.

✔ Some multiple-choice options appear as *drop-down list boxes*.

Title bar   Drop-down list box   Text box   Close button

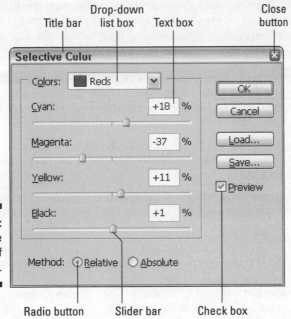

Figure 2-5:
The anatomy of a dialog box.

Radio button   Slider bar   Check box

On the Mac drop-down list boxes are called pop-up menus. For the sake of simplicity in this book, we call this feature a drop-down list box.

Click the small down arrow to display a list of options and then click the desired item. As with radio buttons, you can select only one option at a time from a drop-down list box.

If you change your mind about settings you made in a dialog box, you can quickly revert to the default settings by pressing and holding the Alt key (Option key on a Mac). The Cancel button magically changes to a Reset button. Click the Reset button to return to the original default settings.

Maneuvering through Menus

Like all Windows and Macintosh programs, Photoshop sports a menu bar (refer to Figure 2-2) at the top of its window. Each word in the menu bar — File, Edit, Image, and so on — represents a menu. A *menu* is simply a list of commands that you can use to open and close images, manipulate selected portions of a photograph, hide and display palettes, and initiate all kinds of mind-boggling, sophisticated procedures.

Most of the essential Photoshop commands are explained throughout this book. But before I send you off to cope with a single one of them, I feel compelled to provide some background information on how to work with menus:

- ✔ To choose a command from a menu, click the menu name, and then click the command name. Or you can press and hold the menu name, drag down to the command name, and release the mouse button at the desired command.

- ✔ You can access commands by pressing keyboard shortcuts. For example, to initiate the File➪Open command, press the keyboard shortcut Ctrl+O (⌘+O on a Mac).

  You also can create sets of custom keyboard shortcuts. This new feature is described in the next section "You take the high road; I'll make a new shortcut."

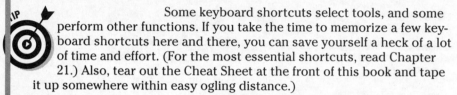

Some keyboard shortcuts select tools, and some perform other functions. If you take the time to memorize a few keyboard shortcuts here and there, you can save yourself a heck of a lot of time and effort. (For the most essential shortcuts, read Chapter 21.) Also, tear out the Cheat Sheet at the front of this book and tape it up somewhere within easy ogling distance.)

- ✔ Photoshop offers yet another way to access some commands. Right-click (Control+click on a Mac with a one-button mouse) inside an image window to display a *context-sensitive* menu. In nongeek-speak, a context-sensitive menu, also known as a shortcut menu, is a mini-menu that contains commands related to the current tool, palette, or image, as shown in Figure 2-6.

You take the high road; I'll make a new shortcut

If you're partial to particular keyboard shortcuts that you use in other programs, you can customize Photoshop CS to do it your way. To access current shortcuts and create new ones (as well as to delete the ones you don't like), here's what you do:

1. **Choose Edit➪Keyboard Shortcuts.**

   Of course, you can always press Shift+Alt+Ctrl+K (Shift+Option+Cmd+K on a Mac).

   The Keyboard Shortcuts dialog box appears, as shown in Figure 2-7.

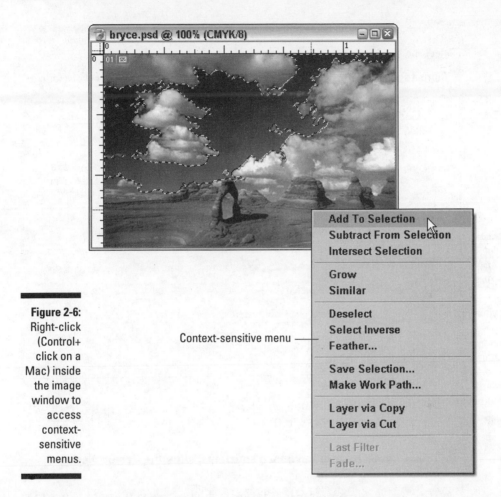

Figure 2-6:
Right-click
(Control+
click on a
Mac) inside
the image
window to
access
context-
sensitive
menus.

Context-sensitive menu

2. **To change an existing keyboard shortcut, use the Shortcuts For drop-down list to select where the feature is located in Photoshop: on a menu in the Menu Bar, on a palette menu, or in the Toolbox.**

3. **Select the item you want to change from the list box.**

   A text box appears, with the default shortcut selected.

4. **Type in the new shortcut you want to associate with the command, and then click Accept to make the change.**

   If you don't like the change you made, you can always click Undo.

   If the keyboard shortcut you want to use is already used by another function, tool, or command, Photoshop gently warns you that you are about to override the other command.

Change shortcuts here   Information pane   Create a new set of shortcuts

Select shortcut location

Current shortcut set   Save all changes to   Delete the
current set of shortcuts   current set of shortcuts

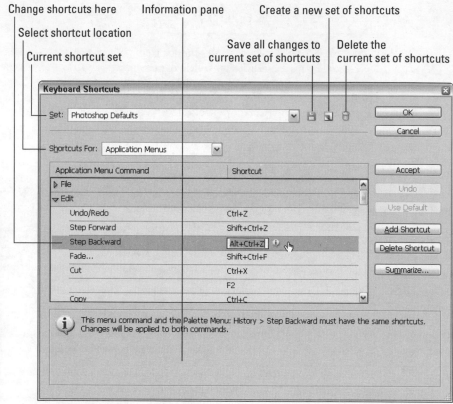

Figure 2-7:
Get your
fingers
snapping
and your
keyboard
tapping by
creating
custom
keyboard
shortcuts.

5. **To save your custom keyboard shortcuts, click the Create New Set button.**

   The Save dialog box appears. Select a folder where you want to save the custom shortcuts file (Photoshop saved the default shortcut file in `C:\ Program Files\Adobe\Photoshop CS\Required`). Enter a name for the shortcut file in the File Name text box. Then click Save and close the Save As dialog box.

   Creating custom shortcuts that are easy for you to remember can help you work more efficiently. For instance, if you find yourself constantly jumping back and forth between Photoshop and ImageReady when creating Web graphics, pressing Shift+Ctrl+M (Shift+⌘+M on a Mac) isn't very convenient. Instead you could assign F2 to the File⇨Edit in ImageReady command. Then, when you want to jump to ImageReady, all you need to do is press F2.

6. **When you're finished assigning new keyboard shortcuts, click OK to close the Keyboard Shortcuts dialog box.**

Playing Around with Palettes

Photoshop CS offers free-floating *palettes* that you can hide or leave on-screen (see Figure 2-8). The palettes provide access to options that affect the performance of tools, change the appearance of images, and otherwise assist you in your editing adventures. I cover the specifics of using the most popular palettes in later chapters, but here's a brief introductory tour of how palettes work:

- ✔ Open a palette by choosing its name from the Window menu.

- ✔ Palettes are displayed as *groups* to save screen space. Some of these groups include Navigator/Info/Histogram and Layers/Channels/Paths. Each group contains individual palettes. For instance the Layers/Channels/Paths group contains the Layers palette, the Channels palette, and the Paths palette.

- ✔ To bring a palette to the front of its group, click the palette's tab.

- ✔ Palettes can be docked on the right side of the Options bar in the Palette Well (see Figure 2-2).

Palette group   Collapse button

Palette tab   Close button   Click to choose palette commands from a menu

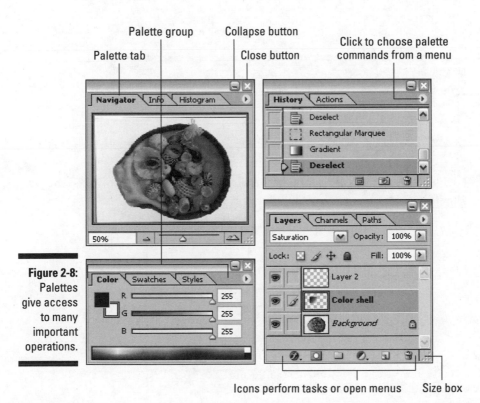

Figure 2-8: Palettes give access to many important operations.

Icons perform tasks or open menus   Size box

✔ You can shrink or expand a palette by double-clicking its tab or by clicking the Minimize/Maximize button.

✔ You can break any palette into its own window by dragging the palette tab out of the current window, as shown in Figure 2-9. You can create your own customized palette groups, combining multiple palettes into a single palette window by dragging a tab from one palette into another.

✔ Press Tab to show or hide all open palettes, including the Toolbox, Options bar, and *status bar*. The status bar shows information about an image you are working on and is the place that Photoshop uses to give you information. For instance, if you select a tool, the purpose of the tool and how to use it is displayed in the status bar.

✔ You can ensure that your palette setup doesn't change. Simply choose Edit⇨Preferences⇨General (Photoshop⇨Preferences⇨General on a Mac). In the Preferences dialog box that appears, make sure that Save Palette Locations is checked. Now Photoshop will remember which palettes are open when you exit Photoshop, and those palettes will appear on-screen (and in the same location, no less) the next time you launch Photoshop.

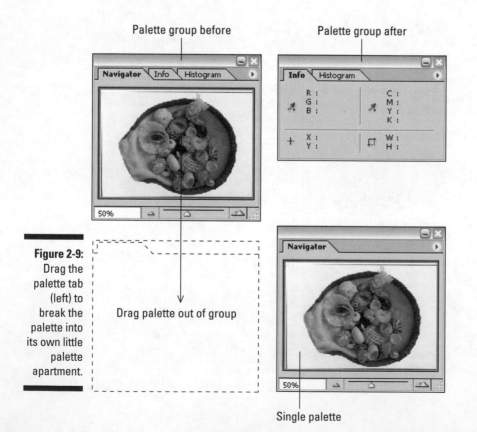

Palette group before

Palette group after

Figure 2-9: Drag the palette tab (left) to break the palette into its own little palette apartment.

Drag palette out of group

Single palette

Original image

Color palette borrowed from this image

After applying desert color palette to original image

Color Plate 5-1: Using the new Photoshop CS Match Color command, the color palette from the desert image was applied to the mountain lake image, adding a warm, rosy color to the clouds and bringing back the sky and lake to a more true blue.

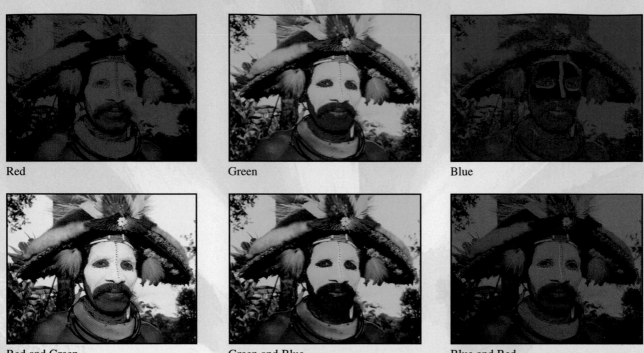

Red

Green

Blue

Red and Green

Green and Blue

Blue and Red

Image with all color channels

Color Plate 5-2: The RGB color mode represents the colors that make up light — red, green, and blue (top row). When combined with another channel, new colors are created (middle row). It's hard to believe that these three primary hues mix together to create so many colors (bottom image).

Cyan

Magenta

Yellow

Cyan and Black

Magenta and Black

Yellow and Black

Cyan and Magenta

Cyan, Magenta, and Yellow

CMYK

Color Plate 5-3: The Cyan, Magenta, and Yellow channels as they appear when inked in their proper colors (top row). Each color channel takes on new depth and detail when combined with black (middle row). During the commercial printing process, the cyan image is first combined with magenta (bottom left), and then yellow (bottom center), and then black (bottom right).

Color Plate 8-1: The composition at the top of the page was created using four images copied to separate layers. First, the Watercolor filter was applied to the turtle layer. Next, the Ink Outlines filter was applied to the Buddha layer, opacity was set to 65%; a layer mask was created and a gradient was used to fade out the layer. The Pin Light blending mode was applied to the people layer and a layer mask was used to hide the portion of the layer that covered the turtle. Finally, the Dark Strokes and Lighting Effects filters were applied to the goddess layer, and opacity was set to 43%.

Original image

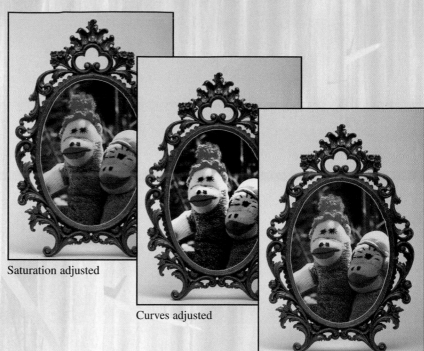

Saturation adjusted

Curves adjusted

Photo filter applied

Color Plate 8-2: Adjustment layers are great for quickly adding color, tonal corrections, fills, gradients, and patterns to an image.

Original image

Pillow Emboss

Inner Shadow

Drop Shadow

Gradient Overlay, Difference mode

Color Plate 8-3: You can apply layer styles to an entire layer or to the masked portion of a layer. Using layer styles, you can add bevels, shadows, glows, textures, patterns, and strokes to create special effects.

Normal mode, 80% opacity

Color Burn mode

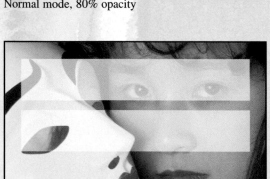

Color Dodge mode

Overlay mode

Soft Light mode

Hard Light mode

Hard Mix mode

Difference mode

Normal mode, 80% opacity

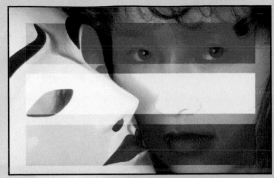

Overlay mode

Hue mode

Saturation mode

Color mode

Luminosity mode

Color Plates 8-4 and 8-5: Blending modes work by changing the light and dark pixels in a layer. The images on these two pages are composed of two layers. The bottom layer contains the woman. The upper layer contains shaded rectangles. The blending modes are applied to the upper layer and affect the pixels on the lower layer. In Color Plate 8-4, the upper layer contains white, gray, and black rectangles. In Color Plate 8-5, the upper layer contains red, yellow, and blue rectangles. Look carefully at the way the lights and darks in each image are affected by the different blending modes.

Original image

Shadows adjusted

Highlights adjusted

Color Correction and Midtone Contrast adjusted

Color Plate 9-1: Using the new Photoshop CS Shadow/Highlight command, the Shadows setting was increased by 15%; the Highlights setting was increased by 41%; the Color Correction setting was set to 14; and the Midtone Contrast setting was adjusted to 18.

Original image

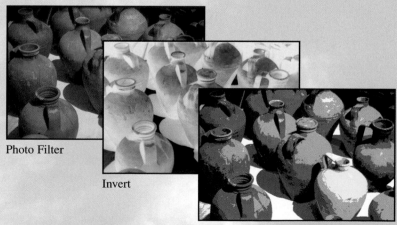

Photo Filter

Invert

Posterize

Color Plate 9-2: The commands found in the Image⇨Adjustments menu enable you to adjust color and tonal range, brightness, contrast, and saturation. Image adjustments can be quite subtle or very pronounced.

Original image

Color Plate 9-3: First, the area of the basket containing the red peppers and the area containing the "Hottest" sign were selected. Then, after the Replace Color command was chosen, red was sampled as the color to be replaced. Fuzziness was set high to select more of the reds. Then the Hue and Saturation sliders were used to create blue peppers and yellow peppers.

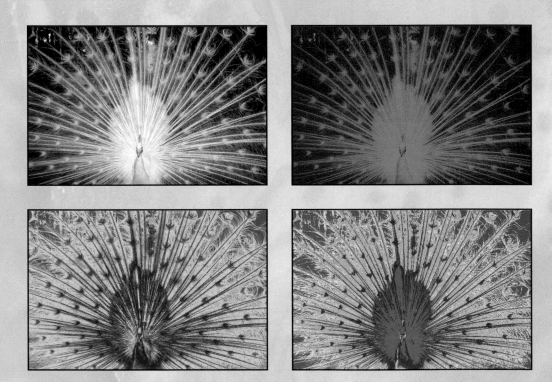

Color Plate 9-4: The Gradient Map command was applied to three duplicates of the white peacock image. The first duplicate was mapped with a Violet-Orange gradient. The second was mapped with a Copper gradient. And the third was mapped with a Translucent Rainbow gradient.

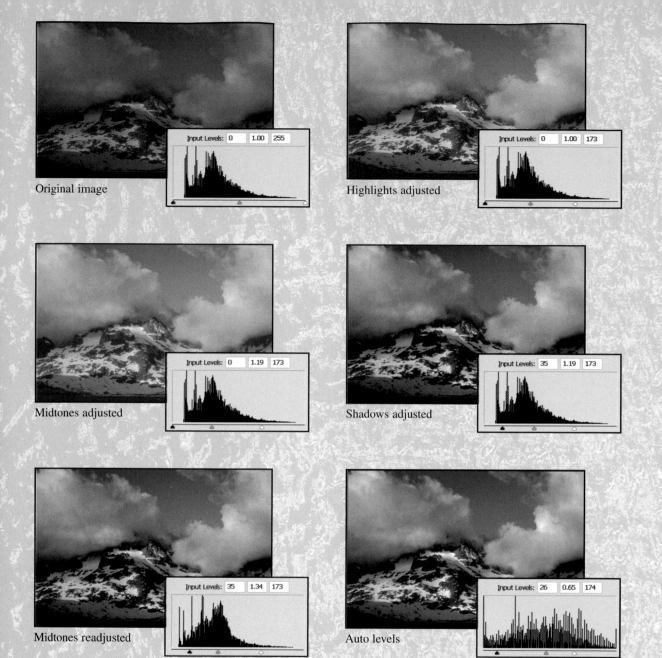

Color Plate 9-5: The Levels command was used to correct colors of the original image. For reference, the histogram and Input Levels from the Levels dialog box are inset with each step. Starting with the original image, highlights were first adjusted using the white slider. Next, midtones were adjusted using the gray slider. Then, the shadows were adjusted using the black slider. Finally, the midtones were readjusted to add more color depth. Compare the results of manually adjusting levels with the results of choosing the Auto Levels command.

Original image

More blue

More red

More yellow

More yellow and more cyan

More saturation

Color Plate 9-6: The original image looked rather drab, so it was enhanced by using Variations. First, three different colors were tried to find the right hue: more blue, more red, and more yellow. Yellow looked best, so cyan was added, and finally, the saturation was raised to give the peacock's feathers more color depth and sheen.

Original image

Cutout

Dry Brush

Fresco

Ink Outlines

Rough Pastels

Sumi-e

Find Edges

Glowing Edges

Color Plate 11-1: Filters quickly add super effects that can turn an ordinary image into something special. There are nearly 100 filters you can use to change an image subtly or dramatically.

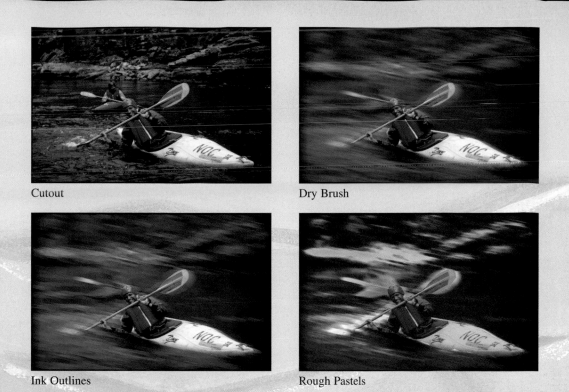

Cutout

Dry Brush

Ink Outlines

Rough Pastels

Color Plate 11-2: Filters can add the appearance of motion to images. Using the Motion Blur filter, a kayaker resting in still water seems to move. Applying the Dry Brush filter or the Smudge Stick filter to the area that appears to move adds another interesting look.

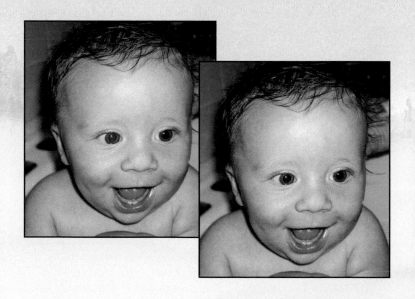

Color Plate 12-1: Besides fixing a case of red eye, you also can use the Color Replacement Tool to put some red in.

Color Plate 15-1: The composition at the top of the page was created using three layers, as shown in the Layers palette. A spotlight was added to the Background layer using the Lighting Effects filter. Then, the Watercolor filter and Accented Edges filter were applied to the Morning Glory layer and the layer's opacity was set at 53%. A layer mask was added to hide the entire morning glory layer except for the moon area. Next, the leaves layer was posterized to 4 levels, the Ink Outlines filter was applied, and the opacity was set at 50%. A layer mask was added to the leaves layer to hide the leaves in the moon area and reveal them in the rest of the layer.

Original image

Red channel

Blue channel

Green channel

Color Plate 15-2: First the Red channel was selected and levels were adjusted to increase highlights and midtones. Next, the Blue channel was selected and the Sponge filter was applied to the channel. Finally, the Green channel was selected and the Watercolor filter was applied to the channel.

Layer mask applied to
create filled type

Fresco filter applied

Craquelure filter applied

Ink Outlines applied to
Red channel

Layer style applied: Emboss
and Stroke: 8 pixels

Dark blue Photo Filter
adjustment layer applied

Chrome Gradient Map
adjustment layer applied

Curves adjustment layer
applied

Color Plate 17-1: After creating type using a layer mask you can quickly enhance it using various techniques.

Color Plate 17-2: First an editable type layer was added above the fish layer; then the text was warped, rotated, and scaled to fit the shape of the fish. Next, using layer styles the text was blended into the fish layer, opacity was set at 63%, and an inner glow and bevel were added to accentuate the text edges.

Saving Palette and Toolbox Locations

Photoshop offers many tools to help you customize your work area and simplify the image editing process. For one thing, you can create a *workspace* so Photoshop remembers the location of where you like to place the Toolbox and palettes on the screen.

To establish a workspace, first get the Toolbox and palettes positioned in the Photoshop window where you like them.

Then, simply choose Window➪Workspace➪Save Workspace. In the Save Workspace dialog box, name your workspace and then click Save. When you want to load a workspace, choose Window➪Workspace. All your workspaces are listed at the bottom of the menu. Click the one you want, and the palettes and Toolbox appear on screen in position.

To delete a workspace, choose Window➪Workspace➪Delete Workspace. In the Delete Workspace dialog box, choose the workspace that you want to delete, and then click Delete.

If you want to return the palettes back to their default settings and positions, choose Window➪Workspace➪Reset Palette Locations.

Getting Productive with Tool Presets

You can save and reuse tool settings, just like any other type of preset. For example, I work with images for both the Web and for print. So I have a few crop settings that I use repeatedly — 144 x 216 pixels at 72 dpi, 3.25 x 4 inches at 300 dpi, 400 x 300 pixels at 72 dpi, 5 x 7 inches at 300 dpi, and so on. I used to have to specify those settings manually each time I wanted to use them. Now, I just save them all as presets, and so can you.

You also can use presets for type, custom brushes, selection tools, gradients, and pattern shape options, to just name a few of the endless possibilities. In addition to being great time savers, presets allow you to replicate certain effects quickly. No more saving sticky notes to remind you how to create a fantastic effect.

The Tool Presets palette is used to manage saved tool presets. Click the Tool Presets tab in the Palette Well on the Options bar to open the Tool Presets palette, as shown in Figure 2-10. You also can access tool presets by clicking the left-most button on the Options bar (refer to Figure 2-2).

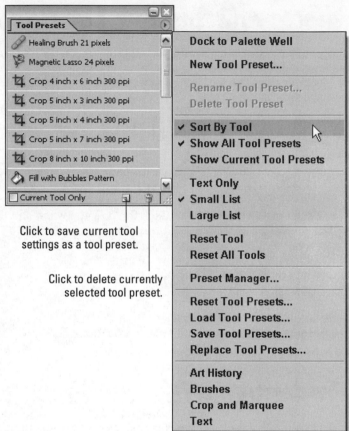

Figure 2-10:
The Tool Presets palette provides quick and easy access to frequently used tool settings.

Click to save current tool settings as a tool preset.

Click to delete currently selected tool preset.

✔ You can pull the Tool Presets palette out of the Palette Well by dragging its tab out to the image window.

✔ To create a new presct, select the tool you want to use to create the preset; then set the tool options using the Options bar. Click the Create New Tool Preset button. Enter a name for your preset in the dialog box that appears, and then click OK.

✔ You can delete a tool preset by clicking the preset, and then clicking the Delete tool preset button at bottom right of the Tool Presets palette.

✔ Put a check the Current Tool Only check box to only see the presets for the tool that is currently selected.

✔ Use the Preset Manager to organize presets by tool type, delete presets, load preset libraries, and to set how the tool presets are displayed in the Tool presets palette. To open the Preset Manager, choose Edit➪Preset Manager.

Chapter 3

Using Photoshop for the First Time

*W*hen you first start Photoshop, you're presented with an amazing array of tools, menus, and palettes, (check out Chapter 2 for an introduction to them). Until you open an image, those interesting features and tools won't do much — it's like having an easel, a full set of brushes, and a whole paint box full of paints, but no canvas.

In this chapter, I explain how to create a new, blank canvas for an image you want to paint from scratch. I also show you how to open existing images using commands and by using the File Browser. Then I explain how to move around an image, zoom in to see details, turn on rulers, grids, and guides, and add notes to an image. Finally, you find out how to save an image, create a back-up copy, close the image, and shut down Photoshop.

Creating a New Image

Creating a new image in Photoshop is like giving a painter a blank canvas. Photoshop CS offers several new options when you create a new image. In the New dialog box you can use *document presets* (Photoshop comes with quite a list all ready for you to use) to select a specific image size, create and save custom document presets, and delete presets. All of these features are discussed in the following steps.

You can also choose the color mode and color depth you want to use, and adjust the color profile to match your monitor type. The color mode and color depth you select depends upon the type of image you're creating. (For more about color mode and depth, look at Chapter 4; to learn about color profiles and color management, turn to Chapter 5.)

To create a new image:

1. **Choose File⇨New or select Ctrl+N (⌘+N on a Mac).**

    The New dialog box, shown in Figure 3-1, appears, displaying many options.

Set size here.

Click here to choose preset document size.

Click to save custom document size, resolution, color mode and background.

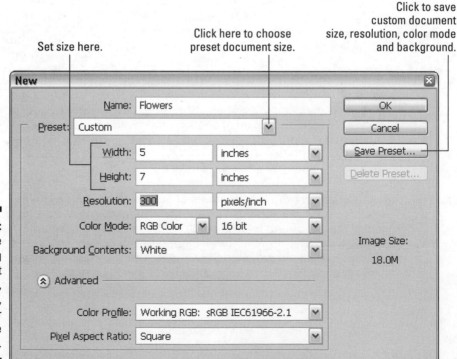

Figure 3-1: Use the New dialog box to set the size, resolution, and color mode of the image.

2. **Type a name for the image in the Name text box.**

   The name you enter appears in the image's title bar, but Photoshop doesn't automatically save the image using that name because you haven't saved the image yet. (To find out how to save an image, check out "Saving a new image," later in this chapter.)

3. **Set the size of the image.**

   You can choose a preset document size using the Preset drop-down list box, or you can enter the image dimensions in the Width and Height text boxes.

   If you have copied an image to the Clipboard, the New dialog box automatically displays the image's dimensions and the Preset drop-down list box displays `Clipboard`.

4. **Enter the resolution you need for your final output.**

   If you are going to print the image you create, you'll want to set this option for at least 300 ppi (pixels per inch); if you are creating an image for the Web, set this option to 96 ppi. (Turn to Chapter 4 for a discussion about image resolution. I cover printing in Chapter 6, and in Part VII I discuss preparing images for the Web.)

5. **Select a color mode and bit depth.**

   Use the Color Mode drop-down list to select a color mode and use the drop-down list to the right of the Color Mode box to select a bit depth. The color mode you select depends upon the type of image you are creating. A good default selection is RGB. You can always convert the image to a different color mode later.

   In addition, a new bit depth feature in the Photoshop cs New dialog box, determines the maximum number of colors possible in an image. Turn to Chapter 5 for a complete explanation of color modes, converting images from one color mode to another, and bit depth.

6. **Select a background color using the Background Contents drop-down list box.**

   In the Background Contents drop-down list box, you have three options to choose from for the image's background:

   - **White:** White creates a new image with a white background.

   - **Background color:** Background color refers to the color currently selected in the Background color square in the Toolbox

   - **Transparent:** Transparent sets a *layer* as the bottom tier of the document (for more about layers and transparency, check out Chapter 8).

   To find the location of the Background color square, look at Figure 2-2 in Chapter 2; for information on selecting a Background color, turn to Chapter 5.

7. **Click the button next to Advanced to expand the New dialog box.**

8. **Use the Color Profile drop-down list to select a color management option.**

   Color management deals with how color is handled between Photoshop and peripheral input and output devices (such as digital cameras, scanners, computer monitors, and printers). Color management is a system that equates colors between these devices, making the input (for instance a photograph from a digital camera) look like the output (a printed version of the photograph).

   If you're not sure what to select from this menu, just use the Photoshop default already selected in the drop-down list. For more information about color management and setting color profiles, turn to Chapter 5.

9. **Click OK.**

   The new image window opens, ready for action, as shown in Figure 3-2.

Creating and Deleting Document Presets

A *document preset* contains custom settings such as the specific width and height, resolution, and color depth of an image. If you find yourself creating the same type of image over and over again, — for instance, you create several CD jewel case covers — you can create your own document preset that automatically creates a new image with the right specifications.

If you create a custom document that you want to save as a document preset, follow the steps in the preceding section, "Creating a New Image," and just before Step 9, click the Save Preset button in the New dialog box. The New Document Preset dialog box opens, prompting you to enter a preset name. At this stage, you can select the settings you want saved. For example, you can set the width, height, and resolution. When you're done, click the OK button to close the New Document Preset dialog box, and click OK to close the New dialog box.

Here's how to set up a document preset for the CD jewel case cover:

1. **Choose File⇨New or press Ctrl+N (⌘+N on a Mac) to open the New Dialog box.**

2. **Enter 4.75 in both the Width and Height text boxes.**

3. **Set the Resolution to 300, the Color Mode to RGB, and the bit depth to 16 bit.**

4. **Set the Background Contents to White.**

5. **Click Save Preset.**

6. **Using the New Document Preset dialog box, type a name (such as** Jewel Case**) in the Preset Name text box.**

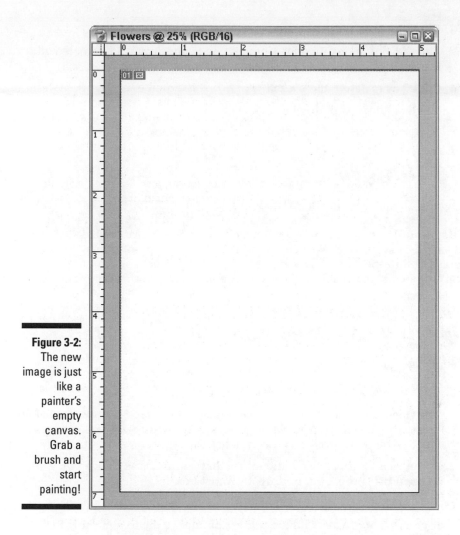

Figure 3-2:
The new
image is just
like a
painter's
empty
canvas.
Grab a
brush and
start
painting!

7. **Click OK to close the New Document Preset dialog box.**

   Notice that the name you selected in the Preset drop-down list appears in the drop-down list from here on out.

8. **Click OK to close the New dialog box and create a new image based on the document preset you created.**

To delete a preset that you don't need anymore, follow these steps:

1. **Open the New dialog box.**

2. **Select the preset you want to delete from the Preset drop-down list box.**

3. **Click the Delete Preset button.**

   A dialog box appears asking whether you're sure you want to delete the preset.

4. **Click Yes to delete the preset.**

5. **To close the New dialog box click OK.**

Opening Images

Opening an image in one of Photoshop's accepted file types is a snap (take a look at the sidebar "What you need to know about file types" for a list of file types). If you want to open an image from a peripheral device such as a camera or scanner, the process is a little trickier, but not much. For details about opening images from a peripheral device, check out the section "Importing Images into Photoshop," a little later in this chapter.

Opening an image using the File menu

To open an image:

1. **Choose File➪Open or Ctrl+O (⌘+O on a Mac).**

   The Open dialog box appears. The two images in Figure 3-3 show the dialog box for both Windows and Mac machines as shown in Figure 3-3, ready for you to move to the folder where the image is stored and select it.

2. **If you're a PC user, locate the folder that contains the image you want to open using the Look In drop-down list box.**

   After selecting folder, the folder's contents will appear in the file list box.

   If you're a Mac user, find the folder containing the image using the Browser pane or the Favorites pop-up menu.

   The scrolling browser list shows folders and images on the disk. Double-click a folder name to open a folder to see a list of all its contents (subfolders and images).

3. **Click the image you want to open.**

   A preview of the image appears in the dialog box so you can see what it looks like.

4. **Click Open.**

   You can just double-click the image file name to open it, skipping the preview mentioned in Step 3 and skipping Step 4.

Using the File Browser

Introduced in Photoshop 7, the File Browser is a special window that lets you search for images using thumbnails, as well as moving, renaming, rotating, and, yes, even opening images (several at a time, if you want!). New Photoshop CS features allow you to flag, sort, group, and rank images, drag images around the File Browser just like it's a light box, and perform *batch* actions. For instance, you can convert a group of images from color to grayscale, instead of performing the task one image at a time. You also can use automated plug-ins from inside the File Browser.

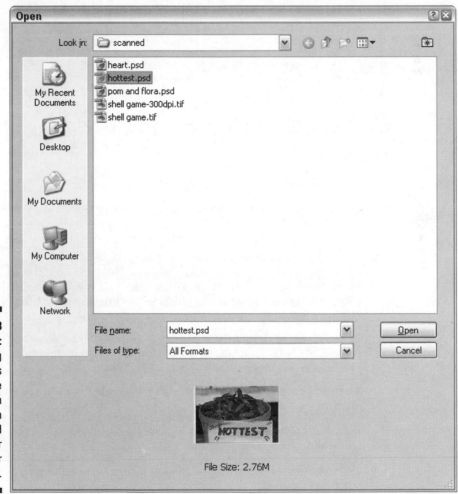

Figure 3-3 (Windows): This dialog box lets you locate and open images on your hard drive or some other disk.

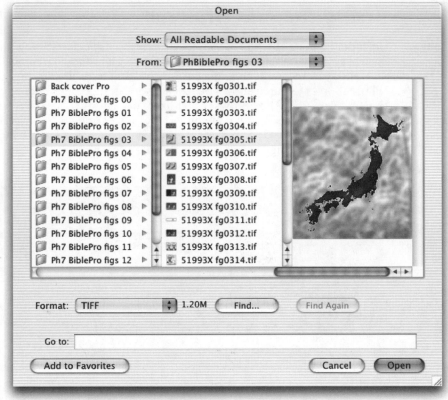

**Figure 3-3
(Mac):**
The Open
dialog box in
Mac OS X
sports a
browser
type display,
allowing you
to easily
locate and
open your
image.

To open images using the File Browser is easy, here's how:

1. **Open the File Browser by choosing File➪Browse or Ctrl+Shift+O
   (⌘+Shift +O on a Mac) or by clicking the File Browser button on the
   Options bar.**

   Located on the right side of the Options bar is a File Browser button
   (see Figure 3-4). This button toggles on and off, meaning that you can
   both open and close the File Browser by clicking this button.

   The File Browser, shown in Figure 3-5, consists of several palettes that
   vertically line up along the left side of the File Browser window, menus
   and buttons along the top that help you perform tasks, drop-down list
   boxes to help locate folders and sort images, and a large pane that lets
   you quickly look at thumbnails of the images.

2. **Use the Folders palette to locate the folder where the image you want
   to open is stored.**

   Thumbnails of the images contained in that folder appear in the view
   pane.

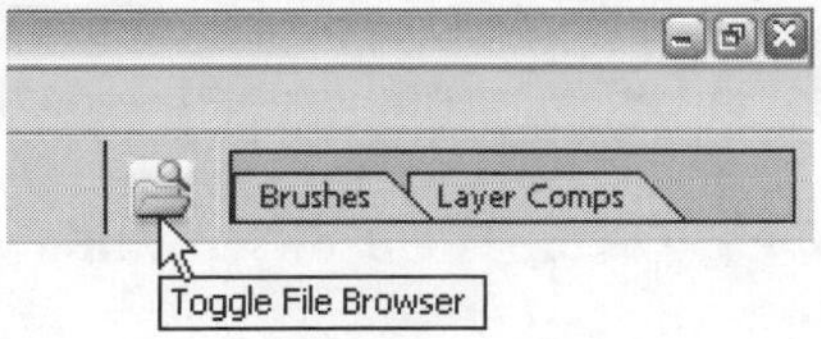

Figure 3-4:
The new File Browser button on the Options bar makes opening and closing the File Browser easy.

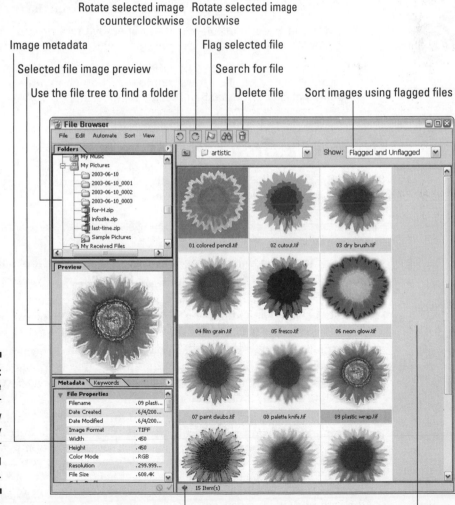

Rotate selected image counterclockwise

Rotate selected image clockwise

Image metadata

Flag selected file

Selected file image preview

Search for file

Use the file tree to find a folder

Delete file

Sort images using flagged files

Figure 3-5:
The File Browser window offers many options for managing image files.

Click to view expanded File view pane

File view pane

3. **Click a thumbnail to select an image.**

   The image you selected appears in the Preview palette. If any *metadata* is associated with the file, that information appears in the Metadata palette. Metadata is information, such as the filename, file creator, image format, date the file was last modified, resolution, and so on, that is associated with the image.

4. **Choose File⇨Open from the top of the File Browser window (not the Photoshop window).**

   The image opens, ready for editing. Photoshop keeps the File Browser open and close at hand in case you want to select another image to open or perform other File Browser tasks.

5. **To close the File Browser either click the Close button in the File Browser window or click the File Browser button on the Options bar.**

   You also can select multiple images to open by Ctrl+clicking (⌘+clicking on a Mac) the thumbnails at the right of the File Browser window.

   Other ways to open images using the file browser include dragging a thumbnail out of the File Browser onto the Photoshop desktop, and double-clicking a thumbnail in the File Browser dialog box.

Other File Browser features

The File Browser makes many important tasks just a mouse click away. With the File Browser open, give these features a try:

- ✔ **Rename files:** Click the filename below a thumbnail, and then type in the new name.

- ✔ **Delete files:** Drag the file to the trash can button at the top of the File Browser or choose File⇨Delete.

- ✔ **Rotate images:** Select the image thumbnail, and then click either the Rotate Counter-Clockwise or Rotate Clockwise button at the top of the File Browser. You also can select a rotation method from the Edit menu.

- ✔ **Sort files:** Click the Sort button at the top of the File Browser window, and then select a sorting method from the menu that appears. Some sorting methods include sorting by filename, width, file size, resolution, and color profile.

- ✔ **View specific images in a particular folder:** Select the thumbnail of the first image you want to view, and then click the Flag File button at the top of the File Browser window. Select the second thumbnail and then click the Flag File button, and repeat this process until you have flagged all the files you want to view. Then, select Flagged Files from the Show drop-down list box. All the unflagged thumbnails disappear, leaving only the flagged image thumbnails for viewing.

✔ **Drag sorted and ranked images:** Drag the thumbnails to your heart's content. To expand the view pane and hide the palettes at the left of the File Browser, click the Toggle Expanded View button at the bottom of the File Browser dialog box.

✔ **Perform batch processes:** To perform the same task on several images at a time, select the image thumbnails in the view pane, and then choose Automate➪Batch from the top of the File Browser window. The Batch dialog box opens. Select a task from the Action drop-down list; for instance you can convert the images from RGB to grayscale, and then click OK. Photoshop opens the images and performs the task. You can then save the changes that Photoshop performed.

✔ **Open files in ImageReady:** ImageReady is Photoshop's sister program for creating Web graphics. Select the thumbnail of the image you want to open, and then choose File➪Edit in ImageReady. For a detailed description of ImageReady and what it can do, turn to Chapter 18.

What you need to know about file types

Photoshop can open and save 35 different file types. This list of file types includes many that you have heard of, such as PDF, TIF, BMP, and GIF, and a few that you probably have never heard of and will never use. You can identify an image's file type by looking at the three or four characters that appear after the period at the end of the filename (for instance, `Flower.eps` is an Encapsulated PostScript, or EPS, file). Check out Table 3-1 to see a list of the most common file types and what they are used for. To learn how to save images in other file formats, take a look at the section "Saving an image in another file format," later in this chapter.

Table 3-1:	Common File Types
File Type	*Uses*
PSD	Photoshop's native file format. This is the default file format and the only one that supports all Photoshop features. Save images that you edit in Photoshop in this format, but if you want to send the files electronically to others, you may want to choose a specialized format such as TIF, EPS, JPG, or GIF that can be viewed by people who don't have Photoshop (you can save a copy of the image in any of these file types).
BMP	Windows Bitmap format. BMP is a standard Windows-only image format. This format supports RGB, Indexed Color, Grayscale, and Bitmap color modes, but it does not preserve layers, editable type, grids, or guides. This is the file format used to save graphics on a Windows computer that become part of the computer's resources, such as desktop wallpaper.

(continued)

Table 3-1 (continued)

File Type	Uses
EPS	Encapsulated PostScript format. Postscript is a page description language used by printers. It is typically used for high-end image reproduction; for instance, you might choose the EPS format if you're creating expert color separations for print. (For details on saving an image in EPS file format, turn to Chapter 6).
GIF	Graphics Interchange Format. Used for Web images and animations (see Chapter 18).
JPG, JPEG	Joint Photographic Experts Group format. Typically used for full-color Web images and photographs (see Chapter 18) because it compresses image file size.
PDF	Portable Document Format. Adobe Acrobat's native file format. This format was developed by Adobe to be a file viewing option that is operating system independent. Saving an image in Photoshop PDF format preserves layers, editable type, grids, and guidelines.
TIF, TIFF	Tagged Image File Format. This format was developed to serve as a cross-platform image format. TIFF is an excellent file format to use for printed images. It can be imported in to almost all page layout and drawing programs. Saving an image in Photoshop TIF format preserves layers, editable type, grids, and guidelines.

Importing Images into Photoshop

Lower prices and better quality have made digital cameras and scanners as common as toasters. Well, maybe not quite *that* common, but they're certainly becoming a popular commodity. Because there are a variety of peripheral devices, I try to make this section as generic as possible. But you may find a few differences between my description and what you experience with your device.

The first thing you should do is thoroughly read the documentation that comes with your device. I know it's dry, but you're sure to glean some useful tidbits in the process. Second, install the software that comes with the device. Most of the software installation is self-explanatory, so you shouldn't have any problems. The software usually includes viewing and image archiving software.

After you have installed the device's software, connect the camera or scanner to your computer using a USB cable or FireWire. (Typically, the connection is a USB cable, but some devices connect using a FireWire. Check the device's documentation for exact information.) You may have to crawl around on the floor a little to find your computer's USB port (it may be located in the back), but many computers nowadays have handy USB ports located right on the front panel.

For Windows Users

To import images from a digital scanner or camera, follow these steps; the figures show download images from both a digital camera and scanner:

1. **Launch Photoshop and choose File⇨Import to view the flyout menu shown in Figure 3-6.**

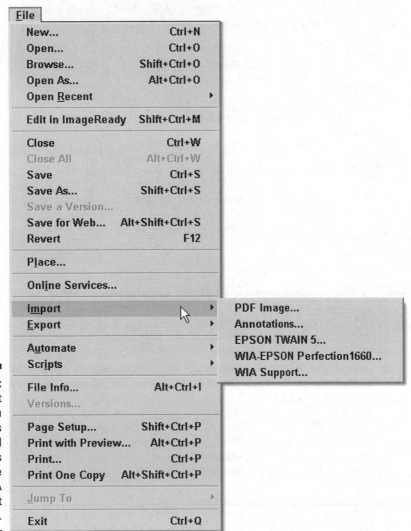

Figure 3-6: The Import flyout menu displays installed devices, as well as the WIA Support menu item.

WIA is short for Windows Image Acquisition. It is a programming standard setup by Microsoft to ensure that devices that obtain images, such as scanners and digital cameras, use the same dialog boxes and interfaces that you see on the screen. This standard works for Windows computers only. A similar option, called TWAIN, works on both Windows and Mac machines. (You may have seen TWAIN if you have a scanner installed.)

If you know which device you want to use, you can select the device and skip ahead to step 7.

 2. **Choose WIA Support from the flyout menu.**

    The WIA Support wizard opens, as shown in Figure 3-7, ready to acquire those images.

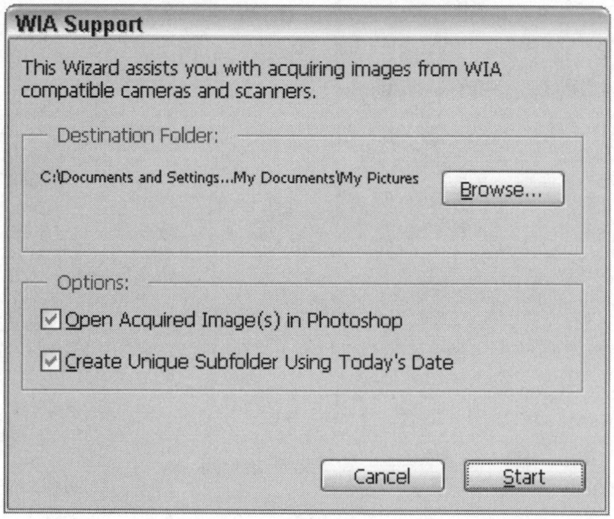

Figure 3-7:
The WIA
Support
wizard helps
you through
the steps
you need to
take to
import an
image from
a peripheral
device.

> **WIA Support**
>
> This Wizard assists you with acquiring images from WIA compatible cameras and scanners.
>
> ┌─ Destination Folder: ─────────────────────
> │ C:\Documents and Settings...My Documents\My Pictures   [Browse...]
> └──
>
> ┌─ Options: ────────────────────────────────
> │ ☑ Open Acquired Image(s) in Photoshop
> │ ☑ Create Unique Subfolder Using Today's Date
> └──
>
>   [Cancel]   [Start]

 3. **Click the Browse button to set the destination where you want to save the images. To open the image in Photoshop, make sure the Open Acquired Image(s) in Photoshop checkbox is checked.**

 4. **Click the Start button to continue.**

    The Select Device dialog box opens, as shown in Figure 3-8. A list of the devices connected to your computer appears in the dialog box. For example, in Figure 3-4 an Epson Perfection 1660 scanner and Canon G3 camera are listed.

 5. **Select the device from which you want to import images, and then click OK.**

Selected device description

Available devices

Click to continue importing image.

Click to view and change selected device properties.

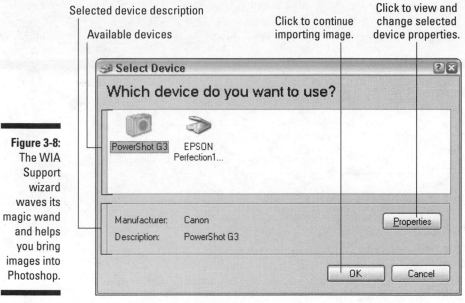

Figure 3-8:
The WIA Support wizard waves its magic wand and helps you bring images into Photoshop.

A Get Pictures from [Your Device] dialog box opens. The WIA Support wizard uses the device's software to help find the images you want to import.

6. **Click OK or Get Pictures (the button changes depending on what kind of device is selected).**

   The WIA Support wizard opens a custom dialog box suited to the selected device. Figure 3-9 shows custom programs for the scanner (on the left) and the camera (on the right).

7. **Click Scan or Import Photo (depending upon the device's software).**

   The image opens in Photoshop. Figure 3-10 shows both the scanned image and photo from the Canon camera.

For Mac users

The directions for Mac users are pretty simple. Basically, your peripheral devices will use TWAIN compliant software to acquire images and import them into Photoshop.

To download images from a peripheral device:

1. **Launch Photoshop and choose File⇨Import to view the flyout menu.**

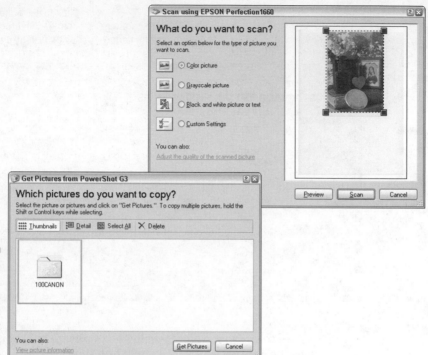

Figure 3-9: Use this custom dialog box to get pictures.

Figure 3-10: When the images are in Photoshop, you can fiddle with them to your heart's desire.

Scanned image

Image from camera

TWAIN is a cross-platform interface used by scanners and digital cameras to acquire images. It ensures that the software you install on your computer works correctly and consistently when you download images using peripheral devices no matter what computer platform you are using. Microsoft has introduced a proprietary standard called WIA for the Windows platform. For more information about the TWAIN standard, check out www.twain.org.

2. **Choose the device you want to use from the Import flyout menu.**

   Photoshop switches to the program that you installed for your device. This program steps you through the process of acquiring an image (refer to Figure 3-5 for examples of custom interfaces supplied by the device's software).

3. **Follow the steps outlined by your device's software to acquire the image.**

   When the device is finished acquiring the image, Photoshop automatically opens it in an image window.

Saving Your Work

Saving your work is *oh-so* important. After all, to say that it's *frustrating* to lose several hours of work because of a program or computer crash is a bit of an understatement, don't you think? So become a member of the frequent savers club.

Saving a new image

Saving a new image is a little bit different than saving an existing image because you need to tell Photoshop where to store the image on your computer, what file format to save the file in, Follow these steps:

1. **Choose File⇨Save.**

   The Save As dialog box opens as shown in Figure 3-11.

2. **Select the folder where your image will be stored.**

   Windows users: Use the Save in drop-down list to locate the folder where you want to store the image.

   Mac users: Use the browser pane to select a folder where you want to store the image, or click New Folder to create a new folder within the currently selected folder.

3. **Enter a name for the image file.**

   If you're a Windows user, type a name in the File Name text box. If you're a Mac user, type a name in the Save As text box.

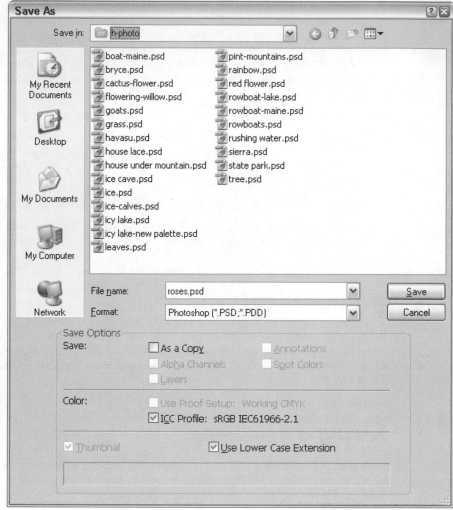

**Figure 3-11
(Windows):**
Use the
Save As
dialog box
to select a
file location
and give the
image a
name.

4. Select a file format.

Choose a file format from the Format drop-down list.

Only native Photoshop, TIF, and Photoshop PDF formats can save files that contain multiple layers and editable type. (For more about file types, see "What you need to know about file types.")

5. Check any options you need in the Save area.

If your image has layers and you want to preserve them, put a check in the Layers check box. Likewise for alpha channels, annotations, and spot colors. (For more information about layers, see Chapter 8; for a discussion of alpha channels and spot colors, turn to Chapter 5; to find out about notes and voice annotations, see "Adding Notes to Your Image," later in this chapter.)

6. Click Save.

Your file is saved on your computer and you're done.

Saving an existing image

Saving an existing image is really easy because you've already done the work of naming the file, choosing its file type, and all the other options described in "Saving a new image."

To save an existing image, press Ctrl+S (⌘+S on a Mac).

Figure 3-11 (Mac): The Save As dialog box lets you select image file format and where the image will be stored.

Saving an image in another file format

If you're finished working on an image and need to save it in another file format, you can do this using the Save As dialog box (refer to Figure 3-11). Or if you would like to save a new version of an image (with the same file format as the original), you can use these directions to do that, too.

To save an image in another file format or to save a new version of an existing image:

1. **Choose File⇨Save As or Ctrl+Shift+S (⌘+Shift+S on a Mac).**

   The Save as dialog box opens.

   In this dialog box, you can change the name of the file and select a different file format.

2. **Select the folder where your image will be stored.**

   Windows users: Use the Save in drop-down list to locate the folder where you want to store the image.

   Mac users: Use the browser pane to select a folder where you want to store the image, or click New Folder to create a new folder within the currently selected folder.

3. **Enter a new name for the file or edit the existing name.**

   Type the new filename in the File Name text box if you're working in Windows or the Save as text box if you're using a Mac.

4. **Change the file format, if you wish.**

   Use the Format drop-down list box to select a new file format if you want to change it. Photoshop lets you choose only from formats that can handle the current image's color mode (Chapter 5 talks about color modes).

5. **Check any options you need in the Save Options area.**

   If your image has layers and you want to preserve them, put a check in the Layers check box. Likewise for alpha channels, annotations, and spot colors.

   If the new file format doesn't support layers, the Layers check box in the Save Options area is grayed out. If you save the image with that file format, the layers in the image will be flattened. When layers are flattened, it's permanent.

6. **Click Save.**

   Your image is saved in the file format you selected and is ready for use. Remember that this image is a copy of the original image. Your original image still exists with its old file format.

Creating a back-up copy

If you want to create a back-up copy of an image, follow the directions in "Saving an image in another file format" above, but in Step 5, in addition to the other Save Options, put a check mark in the As a Copy check box. Photoshop dutifully saves a back-up copy of the image in the selected folder without opening the back-up copy.

Reverting to the last-saved version

If you decide you don't like changes you have made to an image, you can use the Revert command. The Revert command restores a document to its last saved version. To revert to the last saved version of an image, choose File⇨ Revert or press F12 on the keyboard.

Viewing Your Image On-Screen

As you become more accustomed to creating and editing images in Photoshop, you'll find that working on small areas is very difficult if you can't see what you're doing. That's why Photoshop offers many ways to view an image, including using the Navigator palette, and the Hand and Zoom tools, keyboard shortcuts, and the tiny Magnification box at the lower-left corner of the Photoshop window.

The Navigator palette

The Navigator palette, shown in Figure 3-12, is a great navigational aid. You can use the Navigator palette to quickly change the magnification of the image and move the view to another area of the image window for editing.

By default, the Navigator palette is grouped with the Info and Histogram palettes at the right of the Photoshop window. If the Navigator palette is not displayed, choose Window⇨Navigator to open the palette.

With an image open, use the Navigator palette to try these features:

✔ **Zoom in and out:** The Zoom bar at the bottom of the Navigator palette contains buttons, a slider bar, and a text box that are used for zooming. Move the Zoom slider bar right to magnify the image and right to decrease the magnification. Click the Zoom in button to magnify in increments. Click the Zoom out button to decrease the magnification in increments. Click in the Zoom percentage box, enter a magnification percentage, and then press Enter (Return on a Mac) to zoom to that magnification.

✔ **Navigate the nooks and crannies of a magnified image:** If an image is magnified, a red View box appears on the image thumbnail, indicating that only part of the image is visible in the image window. To move around inside the image, just drag the View box around the thumbnail. Ctrl+drag (⌘+drag) the thumbnail, to see a red rectangle, or *marquee*. When you release the mouse button, the marquee turns into the View box, and that portion of the image is magnified in the image window.

Changing the magnification of an image does not change the actual size of the image.

✔ **Manipulate the Navigator palette:** Pull the Navigator palette out of its group with the Info and Histogram palettes, and then make the Navigator palette larger or smaller by dragging the size box.

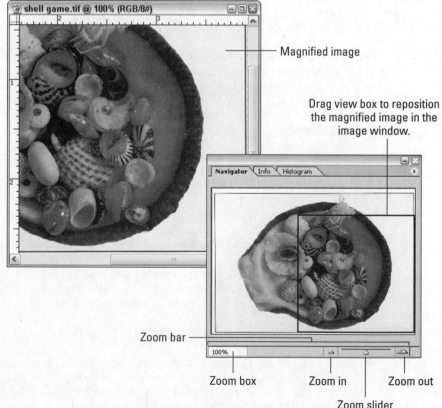

Figure 3-12:
The Navigator palette lets you quickly zoom in and out. You can move the view to another area of the image.

Magnified image

Drag view box to reposition the magnified image in the image window.

Zoom bar

Zoom box   Zoom in   Zoom out

Zoom slider

Using the Zoom tool

 The Zoom tool works in a similar fashion to the items on the Navigator palette's Zoom bar. You can use the Zoom tool to zoom in and out, and use specific magnifications.

Open an image in Photoshop, then select the Zoom tool from the Toolbox, and give these zooming techniques a try:

- ✔ **Zoom:** Click the image in the area you want to magnify, as shown in Figure 3-13.

- ✔ **Zoom to a specific location:** Drag the Zoom tool to create a marquee. When you release the mouse button, the image zooms to the area you selected.

- ✔ **Zoom out:** Hold down Alt (Option on a Mac) when you click with the Zoom tool to zoom out.

- ✔ **Select Zoom options:** With the Zoom tool selected, right-click (Control+click) the image window to access a context-sensitive menu that lets you select one of these options:

    - **Fit on Screen:** Displays the image in its largest possible size.

    - **Actual Pixels:** Displays the image at actual pixel size.

    - **Print Size:** Displays the image at its print size.

Figure 3-13: Clicking with the Zoom tool magnifies the image in preset increments.

✔ **Toggle between tools and the Zoom option:** If you have another tool selected and want to zoom in, press and hold the Spacebar+Ctrl (Spacebar+⌘ on a Mac) keyboard combination. The tool changes to the Zoom tool. Click or *marquee-select* to magnify the image. When you release the keyboard keys, the tool you were originally working with returns. Likewise, if you want to zoom out while another tool is selected, hold down Space-bar+Alt (Spacebar+Option on a Mac), then click or marquee-select. (When you marquee-select an area, you press the mouse button and drag to select a region.)

✔ **Set Zoom magnifications:** To change the magnification to a specific percentage, use the Magnification box at the lower-left corner of the Photoshop window. Double-click the Magnification box to highlight the current percentage, type in a new percentage, and then press Enter (Return on a Mac). The image zooms to the magnification you specify.

Using keyboard shortcuts for zooming

Using keyboard shortcuts to zoom in and out is fast and easy. Table 3-2 lists shortcuts you should know.

Table 3-2	Zooming Shortcuts	
Zoom Action	*Windows*	*Mac*
Zoom in (image window not resize	Ctrl++ (Ctrl and the plus sign)	⌘++ (⌘ and the plus sign)
Zoom out (image does window not resize	Ctrl+- (Ctrl and the minus sign)	⌘+- (⌘ and the minus sign)
Zoom in (image window resizes)	Ctrl+Alt+ (Ctrl, Alt, and the plus sign)	⌘+Option+ (⌘, Option, and the plus sign)
Zoom out (image window resizes)	Ctrl+Alt+- (Ctrl, Alt, and the minus sign)	⌘+Option+- (⌘, Option, and the minus sign)
Zoom to actual pixels, 100% view	Ctrl+Alt+0 (Zero)	⌘+Option+0 (Zero)
Fit image on screen	Ctrl+0 (Zero)	⌘+0 (Zero)

Using the Hand tool

 Imagine putting your hand down on a piece of paper that is on a table, and then sliding the paper around using the flat of your hand. The Hand tool works in just this way. The Hand tool is great for quickly repositioning an image in the image window.

To use the Hand tool, select it from the Toolbox. You'll notice that the mouse pointer turns into a little hand, as shown in Figure 3-14. Then, position the hand over the image, press and hold the mouse button, and drag. The image moves in the image window, corresponding with your dragging movements. When you're finished moving the image around, release the mouse button.

Figure 3-14:
Use the Hand tool to move an image around in its window.

Opening two windows for easier image editing

If you find that you need to do a lot of work at high magnification, seeing the changes as you make them is very important. With Photoshop cs you can open the same image in two windows at the same time, work in the magnified window (suppose it's magnified to 400%), and watch the changes on a window set to actual pixel size (100%). To open a second window, choose Window⇨Arrange⇨New Window.

Using Toolbox buttons to change image view

The three buttons at the bottom of the Toolbox — Standard Screen mode, Full Screen mode with Menu Bar, and Full Screen mode — let you change the way the image fills the screen. They are shown in Figure 3-15.

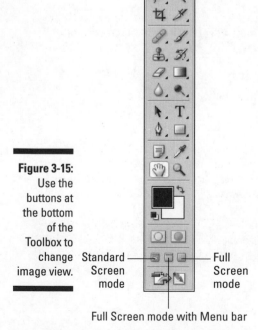

Figure 3-15:
Use the buttons at the bottom of the Toolbox to change image view.

Standard Screen mode

Full Screen mode

Full Screen mode with Menu bar

Try the three buttons out to see how they change image view:

- ✔ To view the image window as you normally see it with scroll bars and title bar, and Photoshop's Menu bar and Options bar visible, click the Standard Screen mode button. (This is the default.)

- ✔ If you want to the image fill the screen without scroll bars or a title bar (but with the Menu bar showing), click the Full Screen mode with Menu Bar button.

- ✔ To view a full-screen version of the image without scroll bars or title bar, and with Photoshop's Menu bar removed, click the Full Screen Mode button.

- ✔ You also can press Tab to hide the Toolbox, Options bar, all palettes, and the status bar. Then press Tab again to redisplay them.

Tools for Precision

Photoshop offers several features to help you position elements in your images very precisely. *Rulers,* which run across the top and left sides of the image window, help you measure distances. *Guides* are horizontal and vertical lines that you can position anywhere in an image. And *grids* are, well, grids (when you print an image that you've applied grids to, the grids don't print).

Assisting with precise placement is the Snap To feature, which acts like a magnet that gently tugs the mouse pointer, path, shape, or selection border to the nearest guide, grid, or document edge, depending upon which Snap To option is selected.

Rulers

To make rulers visible choose View➪Rulers or Ctrl+R (⌘+R on a Mac). Rulers appear on the top and left sides of the image window. The current position of the mouse pointer is indicated by a dotted line on each ruler as shown in Figure 3-16. To hide the rulers, choose View➪Rulers again.

If you want to change the unit of measure displayed on the ruler, position the mouse over a ruler and then right-click (Control+click on a Mac). Select a new measurement unit, such as pixels, centimeters, millimeters, or points, from the context-sensitive menu.

Mouse pointer location   Mouse pointer location

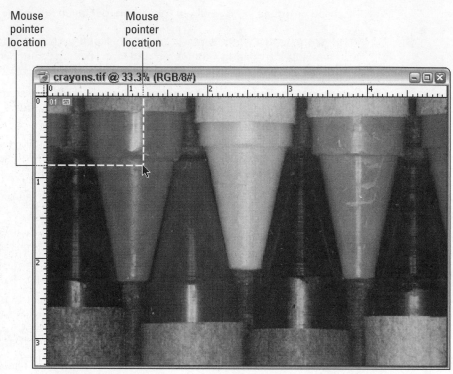

crayons.tif @ 33.3% (RGB/8#)

Figure 3-16:
The dotted
line on each
ruler shows
the location
of the
mouse
pointer.

Grids

In the image window, grid lines look like they are made up of tiny dots as in Figure 3-17. To make a grid visible choose View➪Show➪Grid.

Remember that a grid doesn't print; it is only visible on-screen.

Guides

You can drag guides vertically and horizontally, to any position where you need alignment help, as shown in Figure 3-18. Before you can create a guide, you need to display the rulers by choosing View➪Rulers. To create a guide, position the mouse pointer over a ruler, press the mouse button, and drag. A guide appears under the mouse pointer. Drag it around until you're satisfied, and then release the mouse button.

Remember that guides don't print; they are only visible on-screen.

Grid lines

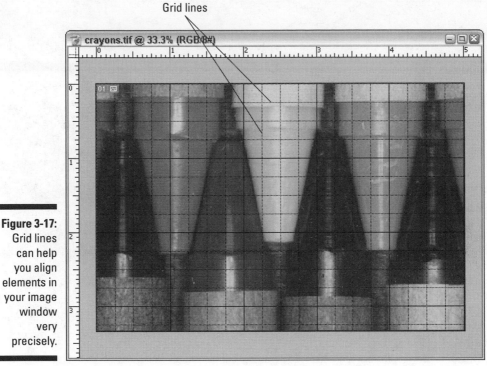

crayons.tif @ 33.3% (RGB)

Figure 3-17:
Grid lines
can help
you align
elements in
your image
window
very
precisely.

Guides are very versatile, so Photoshop offers several other guide features. Create a few guides and try these out:

- ✔ **Select the Move tool to move an existing guide.** Position the tool pointer over the guide you want to move, press the mouse button, and then drag the guide to its new location.

- ✔ **Switch a guide from vertical to horizontal (or vice versa).** Hold down Alt (Option on a Mac) as you drag.

- ✔ **Lock the guides into position.** Choose View➪Lock Guides or Ctrl+Alt+; (⌘+Option+; on a Mac). To unlock the guides, use the same menu selection or keystrokes.

- ✔ **Remove a guide.** Select the Move Tool from the Toolbox, and then drag the guide out of the image window. To remove all guides from the image window, choose View➪Clear Guides.

Guides

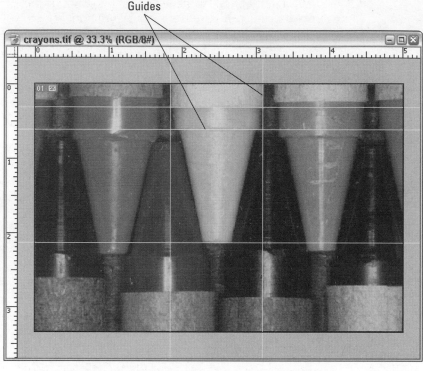

Figure 3-18:
Guides
can be
positioned
horizontally
and
vertically in
the image
window.

Turning on the Snap To feature

The Snap To feature helps you align image elements by gently tugging those elements to grids, guides, or document edges. To turn on the Snap To feature, choose View⇨Snap or Ctrl+Shift+; (⌘+Shift+; on a Mac). To specify what the image elements will snap to, choose View⇨Snap To to open a submenu where you can select guides, grid, or document boundaries.

Adding Notes to Your Image

Besides being a great image editing program that offers so many tools and features, Photoshop even lets you leave virtual sticky notes or voice annotations on your images. After a hard day of work you can leave a reminder for the morning, or you can quickly record the steps for a special effect you created, use a virtual sticky note. Here's how:

✔ To add a note to the image window, select the Notes Tool from the Toolbox, position the mouse in the image window, and then click. A note appears. When you're finished adding text to the note, click the Close button.

✔ If you have a microphone attached to your computer, you can add voice annotations to images. To add a voice annotation, select the Audio Annotation Tool from the Toolbox, and then click the image window. An Audio Annotation dialog box appears; when you're ready to record the annotation, click the Start button. Record your annotation, and then click the Stop button when you are finished.

Closing an Image

When you're finished editing an image, you can close it by clicking the Close button in the upper-right corner (upper-left corner for Macs) of the image. Or, you can choose File⇨Close or press Ctrl+W (⌘+W for Mac users) on the keyboard.

If you try to close a file that has been modified since it was last saved, a dialog box will appear, prompting you to save (see Figure 3-19). Click Don't Save to close the image without saving the changes; click Save to save the changes and close the image; or click Cancel to cancel the entire close operation.

Figure 3-19:
This dialog box appears, prompting you to save changes.

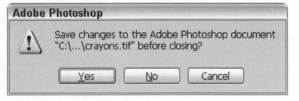

Shutting Down Photoshop

At the end of a work session, Windows users can shut down Photoshop by clicking the Close button in the upper-right corner of the Photoshop window. Mac users can choose Photoshop⇨Quit Photoshop.

 Windows users can also choose File⇨Exit or press Ctrl+Q on the keyboard. Mac users can also press ⌘+Q on the keyboard.

All files open in Photoshop close. If any changes were made to an open file since it was last saved, a dialog box appears, asking whether you want to save the changes (refer to Figure 3-19). Click Don't Save to close the image without saving the changes; click Save to save the changes and close the image; or click Cancel to cancel the entire shutting down operation.

Part II
The Care and Feeding of Pixels

The 5th Wave   By Rich Tennant

"My God! I've gained 9 pixels!"

In this part . . .

Photoshop is all about manipulating *pixels*, the basic unit that you work on in a Photoshop document. Everything in Photoshop is broken down into pixels.

This part explains how to work with pixels and the tools that Photoshop makes available to help you.

In Chapter 4, you learn about images size and image resolution. Your resolution choices depend on your output — a Web graphic looks great at one resolutions, but the same resolution won't look good in print. Find out how to resize images here, too.

Chapter 5 explains color theory basics like why RGB is called RGB. Also, find out about color channels and the Channels palette. Discover Foreground and Background colors, how to define a color, how to use the Color palette and Color picker, how to use the Eyedropper tool, and more.

Chapter 6 explains the mysteries of printing and introduces a new Photoshop cs feature that enables you to create presentations in Adobe Acrobat PDF format.

Chapter 4

Sizing and Resizing Images

• •

• •

*I*mages that you create and edit in Photoshop — or in any other image editor, for that matter — are made up of tiny squares called *pixels*. Every single painting and image-editing function in Photoshop is devoted to changing either the quantity or the color of pixels. That's all Photoshop does. Understanding how pixels work in an image can be confusing at first. Managing pixels correctly is essential to turning out professional-looking images.

This chapter explains everything you need to know to put pixels in perspective, including how the number of pixels in an image affects the image's overall quality, its printed size, and its file size. I also show you how to reduce or enlarge the size of the on-screen canvas on which all your pretty pixels perch. In other words, this chapter offers pages of particularly provocative pixel paragraphs, partner.

Screen Pixels versus Image Pixels

By default, pixels in a computer image is perfectly square, arranged on a perfect grid, and colored uniformly — that is, each pixel is one color and one color only. Put a lot of these pixels together, and your brain perceives them to be an everyday, average photograph. (Photoshop CS can also work with non-square pixels for video and film purposes, but that is beyond the scope of this book.)

The display on your computer's monitor is also made up of pixels. Like image pixels, screen pixels are square and arranged on a grid. The number of screen pixels depends on your display settings; a typical setting is 1024 x 768, which means that the number of screen pixels is 1024 pixels across and 768 pixels down, for a grand total of 788,736 pixels covering the computer screen. These screen pixels are tiny, so you may not be able to make them out even with your nose on the screen.

To understand the relationship between screen and image pixels, all you have to do is open an image — any image. (Choose File⇨Open, select an image, and click the OK button.) After the image appears on-screen, double-click the Zoom tool in the Toolbox, or choose View⇨Actual Pixels. The title bar on the image window lists the zoom ratio as 100%, which means that you can see one pixel in your image for every pixel displayed by your monitor.

To view the image pixels more closely, enter a value of **200** (percent) in the Magnification box in the lower-left corner of the Photoshop window (double-click the box to activate it). A 200% zoom factor magnifies the image pixels to twice their previous size so that one image pixel measures two screen pixels tall and two screen pixels wide. If you change the zoom factor to 400%, Photoshop displays four screen pixels for each image pixel dimension, giving you a total of 16 screen pixels for every image pixel (4 screen pixels tall by 4 screen pixels wide). Figure 4-1 illustrates how different zoom factors affect the appearance of your image pixels on-screen.

The zoom factor has nothing to do with the size at which your image will print — it affects only how your image looks on-screen.

Image Size, Resolution, and Other Tricky Pixel Stuff

A Photoshop image has three primary attributes related to pixels: *file size, resolution,* and *physical dimensions,* as I explain in the following list.

If you just want to get a quick look at the dimensions and resolution of an image, press Alt (Option on a Mac) as you press and hold the mouse button on the status bar in the lower-left corner of the Photoshop window (check out Figure 4-2 if you need a map). Photoshop displays a little box listing the dimensions, resolution, and number of channels.

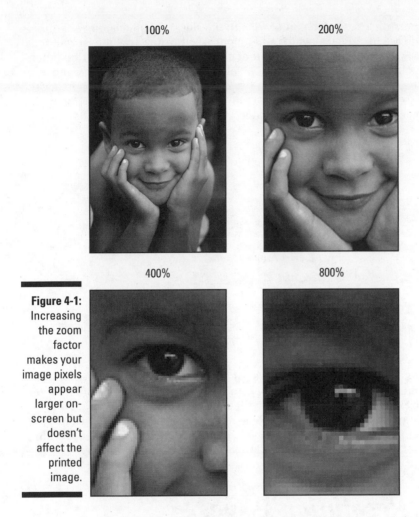

100%   200%

400%   800%

Figure 4-1: Increasing the zoom factor makes your image pixels appear larger on-screen but doesn't affect the printed image.

Here is more information about these three important pixel attributes:

✔ **File size:** The size of an image file depends on how many pixels the image contains. (Photoshop refers to file size as *pixel dimensions.*) The image in Figure 4-1 is 256 pixels wide and 384 pixels tall, for a total of 98,304 pixels. Most of the images you create contain hundreds of thousands or even millions of pixels.

✔ **Resolution:** An image's resolution is the number of pixels that print per inch. For example, the resolution of the first image in Figure 4-1 is 180 pixels per inch *(ppi).* That may sound like an awful lot of pixels squished into a small space, but it's about average.

✔ **Dimensions:** Not to be confused with file size, the dimensions of an image are its physical width and height when printed, as measured in inches, centimeters, or your unit of choice. You can calculate the dimensions by dividing the number of pixels by the resolution. For example, the little boy in Figure 4-1 measures 256 pixels ÷ 180 pixels per inch = 1⅜ inches wide and 384 pixels ÷ 180 ppi = 2⅛ inches tall. Measure him with a ruler, and you see that this is indeed the case.

Figure 4-2:
Click the left side of the status bar to get a quick look at the dimensions and resolution of an image.

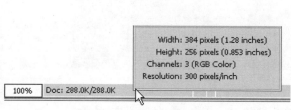

No problem, right? I mean, okay, this stuff is a little technical, but it's not like it requires an advanced degree in physics to figure out what's going on. And yet, the Image Size dialog box may well be the most confusing Photoshop dialog box. You can even damage your image if you're not careful. So be extremely careful before you make changes in the Image Size dialog box. (The upcoming sections tell you everything you need to know to stay out of trouble.)

Resolving Resolution Issues

Although the Resolution text box is positioned unceremoniously toward the bottom of the Image Size dialog box as shown in Figure 4-3, it's one of the most critical values to consider if you want your images to look good.

The Resolution value determines how tightly the pixels are packed together when printed. It's kind of like the population density of one of those ridiculously large urban areas cropping up all over the modern world. Consider Lagos, Nigeria, which is a city of nearly 10 million souls — more than London, Paris, or Shanghai — and continues to grow at a rate of 5 percent each year. Although population explosions in urban environments can have some negative impacts, the larger the number of pixels you have in an image, the better the print quality.

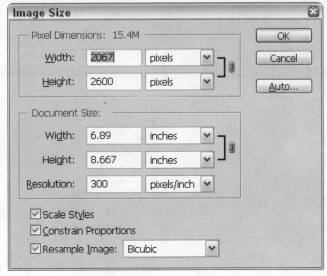

Figure 4-3:
You control
file size,
image
dimen-
sions, and
resolution
with the
Image Size
dialog box.

The rule is simple: More pixels means higher resolution and better print quality. On the other hand, having more pixels also means larger file sizes, which can bog down the transfer of images via electronic formats such as e-mail.

In order to increase pixel population density (thereby improving resolution), you have to either increase the number of people in a city or decrease the physical boundaries of the city and scrunch everyone closer together. If you want a higher resolution (more pixels per inch), you can either decrease the physical dimensions of the image or increase the file size (pixel dimensions) by adding pixels to the image. For example, the two images in Figure 4-4 have the same file size, but the smaller image has twice the resolution of the larger image — 180 pixels per inch versus 90 ppi.

Likewise, when you increase the dimensions of an image or delete some of its pixels, the resolution goes down. Here are some things you ought to know about resolution:

✔ Unlike the population density of a city resolution is constant across the board. It is equally dense at all points.

✔ The boundaries of images are always rectangular.

✔ When you increase or decrease resolution of an image, the image gets bigger or smaller, but it stays rectangular — it grows or becomes smaller.

✔ Population density is measured in terms of area — you know, so many folks per square mile. Resolution, on the other hand, is measured in a line — pixels per linear inch. So an image with a resolution of 180 pixels per inch contains 32,400 pixels per square inch. (That's 180×2.)

Figure 4-4:
Two images
with the
exact same
number
of pixels
but two
different
resolutions.

Changing pixel dimensions

The top two text boxes (the Width text box and the Height text box, which, lumped together, are referred to as Pixel Dimensions) in the Image Size dialog box (refer to Figure 4-4) enable you to change an image's *pixel dimensions* — the number of pixels in the image. Unless you want to risk ruining your image — or you really, really know what you're doing when it comes to pixels — avoid these text boxes like the plague.

If changing the pixel dimensions is so dangerous, you may wonder why Photoshop gives you the option to do so at all. Well, although I don't recommend ever adding pixels to an image, you may need to lower the pixel dimensions on occasion. If your file size is really large — that is, your image contains a ton of pixels — you may want to toss some of the pixels overboard. See the following section, "Dumping pixels," for more information.

In some particularly nerdy circles, changing the number of pixels in an image is called *resampling*. The idea is that you sample the photograph when you scan it — as if that makes a lick of sense — so any adjustment to the quantity of pixels after scanning is resampling. Photoshop uses the term resampling, but I prefer to call it *resizing*, because this gives folks a fighting chance of understanding what I'm talking about.

Dumping pixels

When you delete pixels, you delete detail. Figure 4-5 shows what I mean. The physical size of all three images is the same, but the detail drops off from one image to the next. The top image contains 64,000 pixels and is printed at a resolution of 140 ppi; the middle image contains ¼ as many pixels and is printed at 70 ppi. The bottom image contains only 4,000 pixels and has a resolution of 35 ppi. Notice how details such as the shadows from the girl's eyelashes and the distinction between individual hairs in her eyebrows become less pronounced and more generalized as the pixel population decreases.

Lowering the Pixel Dimensions values can be dangerous because what you're really doing is throwing away pixels. Because pixels = details, tread carefully. When pixels are deleted, you can never get them back.

In an ideal world, you'd want as many pixels as possible because the more pixels you have the greater the image detail. But the more pixels it has the more disk space an image consumes, which can be a problem if you're working with limited computing resources. For one thing, large file sizes can slow down Photoshop substantially. Also, if you're preparing your image for the Web, you need to reduce your file size and/or your resolution so that your image displays properly and loads quickly in the Web browser.

Even when you dump pixels from an image, however, you shouldn't attack the job from the Pixel Dimensions text boxes; I show you a better way in the steps in the section, "Using the Image Size dialog box."

Adding pixels

Increasing the file size (by raising the Pixel Dimensions values) isn't such a hot idea because Photoshop can't generate image elements (pixels) out of thin air. When you raise the Pixel Dimensions values, Photoshop adds pixels by averaging the color of the preexisting pixels (a process computer nerds call *interpolation*) in a way that may result in image softening. Circumstances don't often arise in which the softening of detail is desirable, and I can guarantee that there will never be an occasion in which interpolation results in the miraculous *reconstruction* of detail.

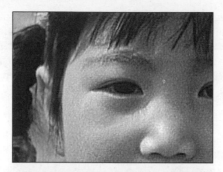

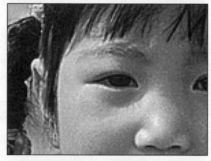

Figure 4-5:
Three
images,
each
containing
fewer pixels
and printed
at a lower
resolution
than the
image
above it.

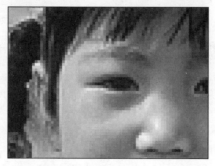

Changing the physical dimensions of an image

The Width and Height boxes in the Document Size portion of the Image Size dialog box reflect the actual printed size of your image and the approximate size of your image when distributed over the Web. (Because users have different sized monitors with different display settings, the actual size of the image may change a little when viewed on different monitors.)

The drop-down list boxes next to the Width and Height options let you change the unit of measure displayed in the text boxes. For example, if you select picas from the Document Size Width drop-down list box, Photoshop converts the Width value from inches to picas. (A pica is an obscure typesetting measurement equal to ⅙ inch.) The percent option in the drop-down list box enables you to enter new Width and Height values as a percentage of the original values. Enter a value higher than 100% to increase the print size; enter a value lower than 100% to reduce the print size.

When you change the document size of the image, either the Resolution value or the number of pixels in the image automatically changes, too, which can affect the quality of your image. For more information, read the "Changing Pixel Dimensions" section earlier in this chapter. And for details on how to change the print size without ruining your image, see the "Using the Image Size dialog box safely" section later in this chapter.

Type of Job	Ideal Resolution	Acceptable Setting
Full-color image for magazine or professional publication	300 ppi	225 ppi
Full-color slides	300 ppi	200 ppi
Color ink jet printers	300 ppi	200 ppi
Color images for laser printing or overhead projections	180 ppi	120 ppi
Color images for multimedia productions and Web pages	72 ppi	72 ppi
Black-and-white images for image-set newsletters, flyers, and so on	180 ppi	120 ppi
Black-and-white images for laser printing	120 ppi	90 ppi

Keeping things proportionate

Both pairs of Width and Height text boxes in the Image Size dialog box list the dimensions of your image in the current unit of measure. If you enter a different value into either text box and click on the OK button (or press Enter), Photoshop resizes your image to the dimensions. Pretty obvious, eh?

Yeah, okay, but what resolution should I use?

The Auto button in the Image Size dialog box is supposed to generate a perfect resolution value based on the line screen that your printer will use. The only problem is that no one knows what a line screen setting is. Rather than bother with trying to explain this arcane bit of printing technology to you at this point I decided to come up with both ideal and acceptable values for certain kinds of print jobs.

But strangely, when you change either the Width or Height value, the other value changes, too. Are these twins that were separated at birth? Is there some new cosmic relationship between Width and Height that's known only to outer-space aliens and the checkout clerk at your local grocery store? No, it's nothing more than a function of the Constrain Proportions check box, which is turned on by default. Photoshop is simply maintaining the original proportions of the image.

When you click to turn off the Constrain Proportions option, Photoshop permits you to adjust the Width and Height values independently. Notice that the little link icon (labeled back in Figure 4-3) disappears, showing that the two options are now maverick independents with reckless disregard for one another. You can now create stretchy effects like the ones shown in Figure 4-6. In the top example, I reduced the Width value by a factor of two and left the Height value unchanged. In the bottom example, I did the opposite, reducing the Height value and leaving the Width value unaltered.

In order to deselect the Constrain Proportions check box, you have to select the Resample Image check box. As explained later, in the section "Using the Image Size dialog box safely," when the Resample Image check box is selected, Photoshop either adds or deletes pixels from your image to compensate for the changes you make to the width and height of the image. Because adding pixels can make your image look like mud, never increase the width or height value with Constrain Proportions deselected. Decreasing the width and height values is okay, as long as the Resolution value stays in the acceptable range. (See the sidebar "Yeah, okay, but what resolution should I use?" earlier in this chapter for recommended resolution values.)

Introducing the Image Size Dialog Box

As mentioned earlier in this chapter, you have three image attributes — size, resolution, and dimension — all vying for your attention and all affecting each other. These attributes, in fact, are like three points on a triangle. Change any one of the points, and at least one of the others has to change proportionately. If you decrease the file size (number of pixels), for example, either the physical dimensions (printed size) or resolution (number of pixels per inch) must also decrease. If you want to increase the physical dimensions, you have to increase the file size — add pixels, in other words — or decrease the resolution.

Figure 4-6: Known to friends and family as Kid Squishums, this versatile little tyke is the result of deselecting the Constrain Proportions check box.

Avoiding mistakes with the Image Size dialog box

Thinking about all the possible permutations can drive you crazy, and besides, they aren't the least bit important. What is important is that you understand what you can accomplish with the Image Size dialog box (refer to Figure 4-3) and that you know how to avoid mistakes.

So, now that I've provided all the background you need, it's finally time for me to offer a modicum of fatherly admonitions and avuncular advice:

✔ **Admonition: Don't change the file size!** Changing the Pixel Dimensions (file size) values can be disastrous, as I explain in the section, "Changing pixel dimensions."

Advice: To avoid changes to file size, deselect the Resample Image check box at the bottom of the Image Size dialog box. When you deselect the option, the Image Size dialog box changes, and the Width and Height options in the Pixel Dimensions portion of the dialog box become unavailable to you. A link icon also connects the Document Size portion's Width, Height, and Resolution text boxes, showing that changes to one value affect the other two values as well.

✔ **More advice: You want the image to look the same on-screen after you get done fiddling around with the Image Size command.** If your image looks different on-screen after you change the Resolution or Width and Height values and exit the Image Size dialog box, you've done something to change the file size.

✔ **Admonition: Don't resample unless you have to!** Turn off the Constrain Proportions check box by checking the Resample Image check box. If you make changes to the image Width and Height values, Photoshop *resamples* (adds pixels by averaging pre-existing pixels) the image.

Advice: If you have to resample, resample down. If you lower the Width and Height values, you'll probably be okay. But if you try to raise the Width and Height values, you're likely to muck things up.

✔ **Admonition: Don't muck up your image!** Above all, make sure that none of the changes you make permanently affect your image.

Advice: You can undo just about anything bad you do. If you manage to mess up everything and change one or more settings in the Image Size dialog box to settings that you don't want to apply, you can return to the original settings by Alt+clicking (Option+clicking on a Mac) the Cancel button. Pressing Alt (Option on a Mac) changes the word Cancel to Reset; clicking it resets the options. Now you have your original settings back in place so that you can muck them up again. If you already pressed Enter (Return on a Mac) to exit the Image Size dialog box, choose Edit➪Undo or press Ctrl+Z (⌘+Z on a Mac) right away to undo your changes.

✔ **Admonition: See, I told you not to muck up your image!** If you performed *another* action after you erroneously resized, you will find, to your dismay, that you can't undo the resize by pressing Ctrl+Z (⌘+Z on a Mac). That command lets you undo only your very last action.

✔ **Advice:** Don't panic. You can undo your mistakes by using the magnificent and powerful History palette (see Chapter 14).

✔ **More advice: Whatever you do, be sure to use the Bicubic setting in the Resample Image drop-down list box.** I'd tell you what *bicubic* means, but you don't want to know. Suffice it to say that it keeps Photoshop running smoothly.

✔ **And still more advice:** If you want to change the unit of measure that displays by default in the Image Size dialog box drop-down list boxes, choose Edit⇨Preferences⇨Units & Rulers (Photoshop⇨Preferences⇨ Units & Rulers on a Mac) and select a different option from the Units drop-down list box.

You may think that changing the image size is something that you never want to do. But you may, in fact, want to reduce the image size on some occasions — to get the image to print at a certain size, to enable your computer to handle the image, or to allow the image to display on the Web properly. The following steps show you how to reduce your image size.

Using the Image Size dialog box

The Image Size dialog box is used to change the dimensions of an image and set image resolution. Use the following steps to resize an image and set the image resolution for your needs. For instance, if you are creating a Web graphic and the image file is set at 300 ppi, you'll use this dialog box to set the image resolution down to 96 ppi.

Before you follow these steps, choose File⇨Save As to save a backup copy of your image. The steps result in Photoshop tossing away pixels, and when you delete pixels you can't get them back after you close the file. (Though you can always undo the action or use the History palette to revert to an earlier history state while the image is open. Check out Chapter 14 for more about the History palette.)

To resize an image and set the image resolution, follow these steps:

1. **Open the image at the highest resolution possible.**

   For example, if you're opening a Photo CD image, select the 2048 x 3072 option from the Resolution drop-down list box.

   If you are opening a non-photo CD image, such as a scanned image, you don't have a choice in resolutions.

2. **Choose Image⇨Image Size to open the Image Size dialog box.**

3. **Note the values in the Pixel Dimensions Width and Height text boxes.**

   You may want to write 'em down — they're important.

4. **Make sure that the Resample Image check box is selected.**

5. **Enter your desired print width and height in the Document Size text boxes.**

   If you want Photoshop to retain the original proportions of your image, make sure that the Constrain Proportions box is checked.

6. **Enter your desired resolution in the Resolution text box.**

   Check the sidebar, "Yeah, okay, but what resolution should I use?" earlier in this chapter for some suggestions on acceptable resolution values if you need help.

7. **Check the Pixel Dimensions values.**

   Did either of the values get bigger? If so, you need to reduce your Output Size Width and Height values or lower the resolution. Otherwise, Photoshop adds pixels to your image, and you probably won't be happy with the results (though minute increases may not change the way the image looks).

   If the Pixel Dimensions values got smaller, on the other hand, proceed to Step 8.

8. **Make sure that the Bicubic option is selected in the Resample Image drop-down list box.**

9. **Click on the OK button.**

   Photoshop resizes — or, if you prefer, *resamples* — your image in accordance with your perfect settings. If you don't like the results, press Ctrl+Z (⌘+Z on a Mac) or choose Edit⇨Undo immediately to put things back to the way they were. Again, if you perform another action after resizing, the History palette (see Chapter 14) is available for undoing.

Playing It Super-Safe: Using the Resize Image Command

The Resize Image Wizard (Resize Image Assistant on a Mac) enables you to do some safe resizing with minimal permanent impact on your images. If you jumped right to this section for the easy way out, definitely read the preceding section first before using this feature.

Find the Resize Image feature on the Help menu on the Photoshop menu bar. The wizard (assistant on a Mac) presents a dialog box (shown in Figure 4-7) that asks you questions regarding your wants and intended use for the image and then steps you through the resizing process.

The great thing about this tool is that if you choose options that it feels are unwise, it warns you that you're lowering your image quality. You can then step back and try another setting. The wizard (assistant on a Mac) creates a new file, calling it `Resize Wizard_1` (`Resize Assistant 1` on a Mac), and that's the version of the file that gets monkeyed around with. Your original file isn't disturbed at all. All in all, the Resize Image Wizard (Resize Image Assistant on a Mac) is pretty smart, but like anything, the more *you* know, the better decisions you can make.

Figure 4-7:
The Resize Image Wizard (Assistant on a Mac) steps you through the sizing process.

Changing Page Size Using Canvas Size

If you've been reading this chapter from beginning-to-end, you may think you've seen it all when it comes to image resizing. Not quite. The Canvas Size command (Image⇨Canvas Size) unlike the Image Size command (which stretches or shrinks the photograph), changes the size of the page — or canvas — on which the image sits. If you increase the size of the canvas, Photoshop fills the new area outside the image with a color that you select. If you make the canvas smaller, Photoshop crops the image.

When you choose Image⇨Canvas Size, the dialog box shown in Figure 4-8 opens.

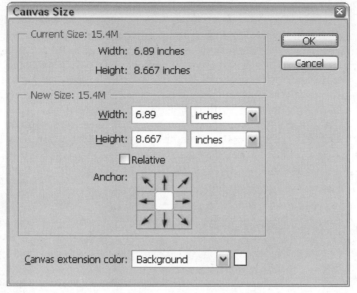

Figure 4-8:
The Canvas
Size dialog
box changes
the size of
the page or
canvas the
image is on.

You can play with the options found in the dialog box:

- ✓ **Enter new values into the Width and Height text boxes as desired.** You can also change the unit of measurement by using the drop-down list boxes, just as in the Image Size dialog box.

   You can't constrain the proportions of the canvas the way you can in the Image Size dialog box. Therefore, the Width and Height values always operate independently.

- ✓ **Use the Relative option to specify an amount of space for Photoshop to add around your image.** This new option is great for adding equal amounts of canvas around images with odd measurements.

- ✓ **Use the Anchor section to see a graphical representation of how the current image sits inside the new canvas.** By default, the image is centered in the canvas, but you can click inside any of the other eight squares to move the image to the upper-right corner, center it along the bottom edge, or place it where you like.

- ✓ **If you are enlarging the canvas, use the Canvas extension color drop-down list to select a color.** When you enlarge the canvas Photoshop automatically fills the new area outside the image with a color. Use this drop-down list to select white, black, gray, the currently selected Foreground or Background color, or a color selected using the Color picker. (To find out more about selecting Foreground and Background colors and using the Color picker, turn to Chapter 5.)

> ✔ **Crop and undo cropping.** If you reduce either the Width or Height value and press Enter (Return on a Mac), Photoshop asks you whether you really want to crop the image. If you click on the Proceed button or press Enter (Return on a Mac) and decide you don't like the results, you can always choose Edit➪Undo or press Ctrl+Z (⌘+Z on a Mac) to restore the original canvas size.

Cropping an Image

When an image is cropped, unneeded edges or portions of the image are cut away. An entire image can be cropped using the Crop tool, Crop command, the Trim command, or the new Crop and Straighten Photos command.

The Crop tool

The Crop tool is used to drag a marquee around the area you want to keep. It's fast and easy to use. Open an image in Photoshop and follow these steps:

1. **Choose the Crop tool from the Toolbox.**

   Before you create the cropping marquee, you can find out the width, height, and resolution of the image you are going to crop by clicking the Front Image option on the Options bar.

2. **To set the Crop tool to create a cropping marquee using specific dimensions, enter the dimensions you would like to use in the Width and Height text boxes.**

   Or you can select preset dimensions using the Tool Presets button on the Options bar.

3. **Drag a marquee over the portion of the image you want to keep.**

   Figure 4-9 shows the selected area of the image. If you want to darken the unselected area outside the cropping marquee as shown in Figure 4-9, put a check in the Shield check box on the Options bar.

   If you're cropping a layer, the Options bar offers you the choice of either deleting the cropped area or hiding it.

4. **Use the radio buttons on the Options bar to make a selection (Delete is the default).**

   For more about layers, turn to Chapter 8.

Cropping   Area that   Cropping   Cropped
shield   will be kept   marquee   image

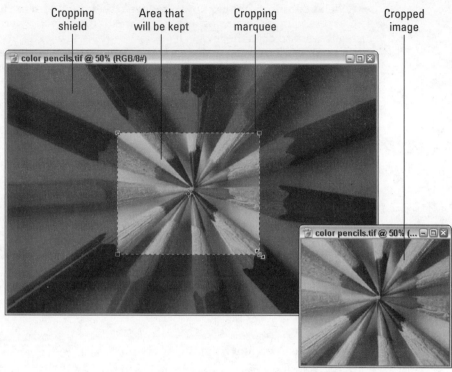

Figure 4-9:
Use the
Crop tool to
select the
area of the
image you
want to
keep (left).
After
cropping,
the
marquee
disappears
(right).

5. **Resize, reposition, or rotate the cropping marquee if you need to.**

   To resize the cropping marquee, position the mouse over a corner, and drag the tiny square handle. If you want to reposition the cropping marquee, position the mouse pointer inside the marquee, and then drag it to its new location. To rotate a cropping marquee, position the mouse pointer outside the cropping marquee, and then drag in a circular direction.

 6. **Click the Commit button on the Options bar to accept the cropping.**

   Instead of clicking the Commit button, you can also double-click inside the cropping marquee, or press Enter (Return on a Mac) on the keyboard.

   Before you click the Commit button, you can cancel the entire cropping process by clicking the Cancel button on the Options bar or pressing Esc on the keyboard.

The Crop command

The Crop command is very simple, but it's also very basic. Use this command if you don't need any of the options — such as a specifically sized cropping marquee, marquee rotation, or cropping only one layer — that the Crop tool offers. Open an image and try out this command:

1. **Choose the Rectangular Marquee tool from the Toolbox or press M on the keyboard.**

2. **Drag a marquee selection around the area of the image you want to keep.**

   To find out more about using the Rectangular Marquee tool to make selections turn to Chapter 7.

3. **Choose Image⇨Crop.**

   The entire image outside of the selected area is cut away and discarded.

You can always undo an action if you decide you don't like it. If you just completed the action, choose Edit⇨Undo or press Ctrl+Z (⌘+Z on a Mac) on the keyboard. If you completed the action a while ago, you can undo it using the History palette. For more about the History palette, take a look at Chapter 14.

The Trim command

The Trim command removes the excess color or transparent areas from around an image. It's easy to use and very basic. Here's how:

1. **Choose Image⇨Trim.**

   The Trim dialog box shown in Figure 4-10 opens.

2. **Select the trim color or transparency that you want to use to trim the image.**

   In the Based On area of the dialog box, set whether the trim color (or transparency) should be selected using the pixel at the upper left corner of the image or the bottom right corner of the image.

Figure 4-10: Use the Trim dialog box to set the trimming color (or transparency) and areas of the image to be trimmed.

3. **Use the Trim Away check boxes to select the areas to be removed.**

   In the Trim Away area, put check marks in the boxes corresponding to the sides of the image you want to remove pixels from.

4. **Click OK.**

   Photoshop samples the pixel color (or transparency) and removes that color or transparency from the sides of the image you selected to remove.

The Crop and Straighten Photos command

If you want to scan several photographs at one time, and then separate them into separate image files, Photoshop CS can help.

The new Crop and Straighten Photos command automatically looks for rectangular areas in an image and then separates each area into a separate image file.

Scan several photographs at one time (see Chapter 3 for more on importing scanned images into Photoshop), and then try out this command:

1. **Open the image file containing the scanned photographs or scan several photos at one time.**

2. **Choose File⇨Automate⇨Crop and Straighten Photos (Photoshop⇨ Automate⇨Crop and Straighten Photos on a Mac).**

   The Crop and Straighten Photos command goes to work, looking for rectangular areas, and quickly extracting the photographs into individual image windows. The images in the separate image windows are only temporary and held in memory, so be sure to save them.

Chapter 5

Introducing Color

• •

• •

This chapter covers the basics of how color works in Photoshop. In order to understand how to use color in Photoshop, you'll need to grasp some basic concepts related to working with color in imaging software. This chapter explains everything you need to know about color models and modes, and how they relate to the tasks you need to perform in Photoshop.

With the basics behind you, you also discover how to use color channels and the Channels Palette, how to choose color settings, how to set the foreground and background colors, how to define colors, how to use the Eyedropper tool, and how to work in grayscale (which used to be called good, old-fashioned black and white).

Introducing Vector- and Pixel-Based Imaging Programs

Computer technology for creating and manipulating images is based on either *vectors* or *bitmaps*. You don't need to understand a great deal about how these concepts work, but you do need to understand the basic distinction between the two approaches toward imaging.

In vector-based programs, such as Adobe Illustrator and the CorelDraw Graphics Suite, the drawing tools make shapes based on mathematical formulas. Vector objects have smooth lines and continuous colors even when you magnify the image (see Figure 5-1). Vector drawings are *resolution independent,* meaning that when you print a vector-based drawing, the quality depends only on the resolution of the printer.

As I mention in Chapter 4, in bitmap-based programs, such as Photoshop, images are made up of tiny pixels that are arranged and colored to form a pattern. Each pixel represents a color. When you view a pixel-based image at its intended size and resolution, the colors and shapes appear smooth, but if you magnify the image, tiny individual squares become more evident (see Figure 5-2). You can edit a pixel-based image pixel by pixel, and pixel-based images depend on the resolution at which they are saved for quality when printing the image.

Understanding Pixel Color Basics

The way Photoshop colors pixels in an image is determined by two things: the color depth of the image and the color mode the image is set in.

Figure 5-1:
A vector drawing looks the same whether viewed at its actual size (left) or magnified (right).

Figure 5-2:
A pixel-
based
image looks
smooth at
its actual
size (left)
but shows
its pixels
when
magnified
(right).

Color depth sets how many colors are available in each pixel. The number of colors available in a pixel can range from two colors to millions. A color mode determines how the channels in each pixel create the colors in an image. And each channel in a pixel represents a primary color.

Getting details on pixel color depth

Typically color information is saved in a measurement called *bit depth* or *color depth*. This color depth measures how much color information is available in each pixel. The more bit depth that an image has, the more colors are available. More color depth translates to more accurate representation of color on-screen as well as on the printed page.

Typical color depth values are 1-bit, 8-bit, 16-bit, and 24-bit. For instance, a pixel with a 1-bit color depth has two possible color values — black and white. An 8-bit pixel has 256 possible color values, and a 24-bit pixel has about 16 million possible color values.

Introducing channels

Every image you create in Photoshop contains *channels*. Channels store an image's color information. Each pixel in an image can have as few as one and as many as four channels. The number of channels in an image depends upon the *color mode* in which the image is set.

To view the channels in a color image, use the Channels palette to display the image's channels as shown in Figure 5-3. Click on one of the channels to display only that channel. For instance, in Figure 5-3, the Red channel is selected. To restore the image to full channel display, click the combined color channel at the top of the channel list in the Channels Palette (in the case of Figure 5-3, clicking RGB would restore the full channel display).

A special grayscale channel that is used to save selections is known as an *alpha channel*. For information on saving selections, turn to Chapter 7. To find out more about using alpha channels, turn to Chapter 15.

Channels

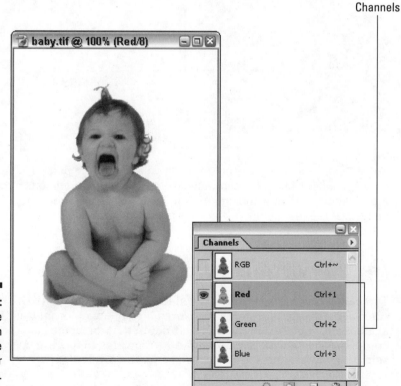

Figure 5-3:
An image
can contain
from one
to four
channels.

Color models and image modes

A *color model* is a scheme used to break colors down into their component primary parts. Color models are used to represent color in images in a standardized way. In Photoshop, color models are applied to images as *color modes*. Photoshop supports eight color modes: Bitmap, Grayscale, Duotone, Indexed Color, RGB, CMYK, Lab, and Multichannel.

Any image can be converted to or edited in any one of the eight color modes. To convert an image to another color mode, choose Image⇨Mode and select a color mode from the submenu as shown in Figure 5-4.

You should know that if your image contains layers and you convert it to bitmap mode the layers will be flattened. So do all your image editing before converting it. Also, it's always a good idea to create a backup copy of a layered image before converting it and flattening the layers.

Figure 5-4: Converting an image to another color mode is easy in Photoshop.

The different color modes contain a different number of channels. Table 5-1 shows the number of channels per mode.

Table 5-1	The Number of Channels in a Color Mode	
One Channel	*Three Channels*	*Four Channels*
Bitmap	RGB	CMYK
Grayscale	Lab	

(continued)

Table 5-1 *(continued)*

One Channel	Three Channels	Four Channels
Duotone	Multichannel	
Indexed Color		

If you want to convert an image to a color mode that is unavailable on the submenu (unavailable options are grayed out), you need to convert the image to another color mode before converting it to the desired color mode. For instance, if you want to convert an RGB color image to Bitmap mode, you have to convert the image to Grayscale first.

RGB model and color mode

The RGB color model (*RGB* stands for Red, Green, and Blue) is used to display a color image on a computer monitor. RGB is an *additive* color model, meaning that every color can be created using red, green, and blue in varying degrees of brightness. At its highest value, RGB creates the color white. For instance, black is represented in RGB mode using the following values Red=0, Green=0, and Blue=0; white is represented using the following values Red=255, Green=255, and Blue=255. Each of these three colors occupies its own *channel* within a pixel, so RGB color has three channels. Photoshop uses the RGB model to create the RGB color mode. Figure 5-5 shows an RGB mode image and its three channels in the Channels Palette.

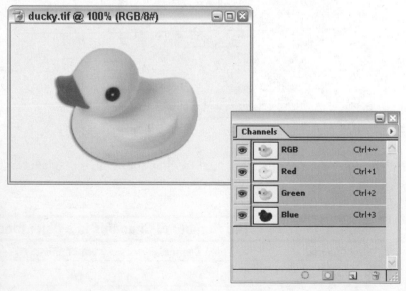

Figure 5-5:
An RGB image contains three channels — red, green, and blue.

All of these color models and modes are interesting, but make more sense when seen in color. Take a look at Color Plate 5-1 for a comparison of the same image in each color mode broken down into its separate channels.

CMYK model and color mode

The Cyan, Magenta, Yellow, Black color model (known as *CMYK* — the K represents black) is used in high-quality offset color printing. Instead of using light to display color as with the RGB model, ink or toner is used. CMYK is a *subtractive* color model, meaning that as the colors are mixed darker colors are created. RGB at its highest value creates white; CMYK at its highest value creates black. For instance, white in the CMYK color mode is represented using the following percentages: Cyan=0%, Magenta=0%, Yellow=0%, and Black=0%; black is represented using the following percentages: Cyan=100%, Magenta=100%, Yellow=100%, and Black=100%.

CMYK color has four channels per pixel, one for each color represented in the model. Photoshop's CMYK color mode is based on the CMYK color model. Figure 5-6 shows a CMYK mode image and its four channels displayed in the Channels Palette.

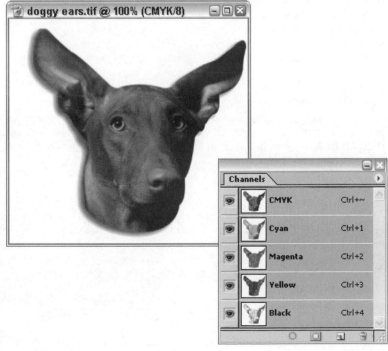

Figure 5-6:
A CMYK image contains four channels: cyan, magenta, yellow, and black.

HSB color model

The HSB color model is based on the way people perceive color with the eye. This color model creates color using three settings:

- ✔ H stands for hue, which is the color of the object.

- ✔ S stands for saturation, which is the strength of the color. For instance, if the hue value is set to red, but the saturation is set to a low percentage, the red appears pink. If the saturation is set to a high percentage, the red is a more true red.

- ✔ B stands for brightness, which sets how dark or light a color is. A red with a high brightness setting appears red. Red with a low brightness setting appears muddier, like brick red.

You can use the Color palette or Color picker to select colors using the HSB color model, but there is no HSB mode available in Photoshop for creating images. (For more about selecting colors, turn to "Choosing Colors" later in this chapter.)

Lab color mode

The Lab color model was introduced to create consistent color between computer devices, such as printers, monitors, and scanners. The Lab color mode contains three channels:

- ✔ L stands for lightness, which can have a value from 0 to 100.

- ✔ A stands for the green-red color axis.

- ✔ B represents the blue-yellow color axis.

When Photoshop converts an image from one color mode to another, it uses the Lab model as an intermediate step in order to keep colors as consistent as possible.

Multichannel mode

An image set in Multichannel mode contains three channels. Each channel contains up to 256 levels of gray. Multichannel images are generally used for specialized printing such as offset printing that uses more than four colors (for more about offset printing, check out Chapter 6). If you delete a channel from a CMYK, RGB, or Lab image, the image is converted automatically to Multichannel mode.

Indexed Color mode

Indexed Color mode sets a specific number of colors used in an image from 1 to 256. When an image is converted to indexed color, Photoshop creates a table that "indexes" the colors in the image. Indexed Color is most often used for applications that require a reduced palette while retaining visual quality. Some examples include graphics intended for use on the Web.

Duotone mode

Duotone mode is used to create specially printed images. Duotone images are grayscale images that include two extra colored inks to increase the richness and depth of the image. The term *duotone* itself comes from photographic and photolithographic processes, and this mode is primarily used when you are interested in creating and printing images reminiscent of these old-fashioned processes.

Grayscale mode

An image set in *grayscale mode* contains no color, only varying shades of gray. There are 256 shades of gray from black (0) to white (255). The median shade of gray on the grayscale spectrum is set at a value of 128. Grayscale has one channel.

Grayscale mode is primarily used when you want to reproduce a color image in black and white (such as the black and white figures in this book).

Bitmap mode

Bitmap mode is the simplest of all. It contains only black or white pixels — no color or shades of gray. Bitmap mode images contain only one channel. To convert an image to bitmap mode, the image must first be converted to grayscale. This mode is used when you need a black-and-white image that contains no grays.

Photoshop Color Management

Every hardware device and software program handles color differently. Try opening an image using several different programs, and you may be surprised to discover that the image looks quite different every time. In fact, you can try scanning an image and opening the scan in all these different programs. I guarantee that none of the output will match the color of the original image.

Photoshop implements color management functions, called *color spaces,* to adjust color so that the same image appears the same no matter what kind of device or program (printer, Web browser, output bureau, and so on) is used for the output. Color management equalizes the colors used by different devices, making the colors appear the same no matter what kind of device is used for input or output.

Color space is just a fancy term for how a device creates color. For instance, a computer monitor uses red, green, and blue light to create color in its color space; a color inkjet printer uses black, red, blue, and yellow inks to create color in its color space; and a digital camera records the colors it sees using the daylight present (which has a yellowish cast) or a flash (which has a bluish cast).

These devices can't create a color match without some type of color correction. That's what color management is all about.

A good color management system solves most of these color problems by acting as a color interpreter. Fortunately, Photoshop comes with extensive color management controls that you can use.

I go into details about what you need do to set up color management for your computer in the following sections.

Calibrating your monitor

The first step in setting up your color management system is to calibrate your monitor. For Windows users, the Photoshop installation includes the Adobe Gamma utility program which is used to define the RGB color space on your monitor. For Mac users, you'll need to calibrate your monitor using Apple's Monitor Display Assistant.

 Before you calibrate your monitor, you should turn it on and let it warm up for 30 minutes. Also, you should make sure that your room lighting is set at a constant level.

Calibrating your monitor in Windows

Follow these steps to calibrate your monitor on a Windows machine:

1. **Choose Start⇨Control Panel.**

   The Windows Control Panel opens, displaying various system utilities.

2. **Double-click the Adobe Gamma icon to open the utility.**

3. **In the Adobe Gamma dialog box, select Control Panel, and then click Next.**

   The Adobe Gamma dialog box opens, ready to help you set monitor calibration. As you can see in Figure 5-7, you can select monitor type, what kind of phosphors your monitor uses (phosphors are the substance that monitors use to emit light), set the red, green, and blue brightness values, and set the *white point* — the coordinates in your monitor's color space where the red, green, and blue phosphors create white.

Light quality

Gamma slider   Monitor model   Check to find your monitor model

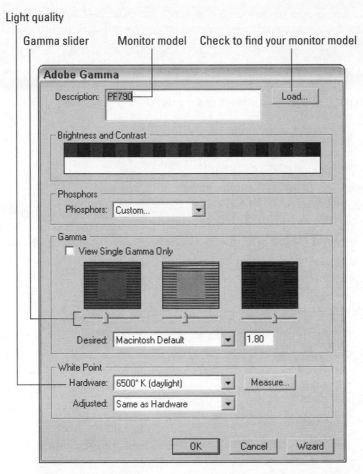

Figure 5-7:
The Adobe
Gamma
dialog box
lets you
save
monitor
color space
settings.

4. **Click the Load button to find your monitor model.**

   The Open Monitor Profile dialog box presents a list of monitor models
   and color profiles followed by an `.icm` file extension. For instance, to
   introduce a ViewSonic PF790 monitor the Adobe Gamma utility, you
   select `PF790.icm` from the list, and then click the Open button, as
   shown in Figure 5-8.

   If you can't find your monitor model in the Open Monitor Profile dialog
   box, click Cancel to return to the Adobe Gamma dialog box, and use the
   default monitor profile provided by the Adobe Gamma utility.

5. **If your monitor isn't listed in Step 4, use the Phosphors drop-down list
   to select your monitor type.**

   If your monitor is not listed (Trinitron is the default and a good basic setting), choose Custom. Then, enter the Red, Green, and Blue phosphors settings. To find these settings, consult the manual that came with your

monitor. (If you selected a monitor model in Step 4, these phosphors settings are automatically entered by the Adobe Gamma utility.)

6. **In the Gamma area, uncheck View Single Gamma Only.**

   This selection allows you to separately adjust the red, green, and blue levels for your monitor. Use the slider bars to adjust each color. For each color, make the inner square match the outer color as closely as possible.

7. **In the White Point area, choose the Hardware setting that the monitor manufacturer recommends, and then choose Same as Hardware using the Adjusted drop-down list.**

8. **Click OK.**

   The Adobe Gamma utility saves your monitor settings. Every time you use Photoshop, these settings will be transferred to Photoshop, so the program will know how to set your monitor's color space.

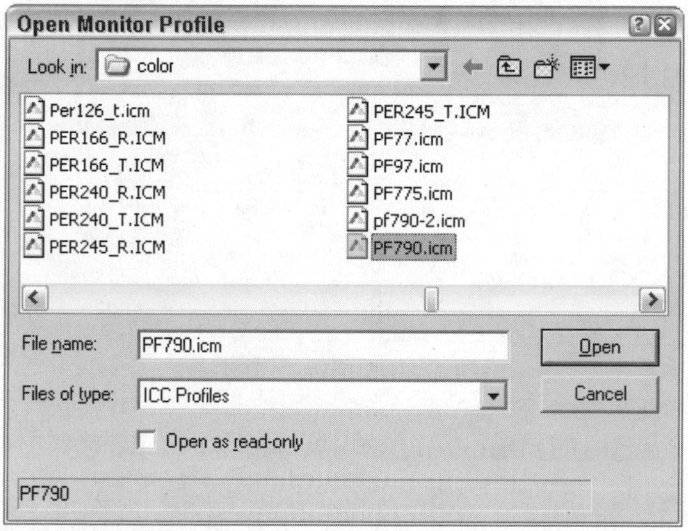

Figure 5-8:
The Open
Monitor
Profile
dialog box
provides
color space
information
for many
monitor
models and
color
spaces.

Calibrating your monitor on a Mac

Follow these steps to calibrate your monitor on a Mac:

1. **Choose Apple⇨System Preferences. Then click Displays, select the Color tab, and then click Calibrate.**

   Apple's Display Calibrator Assistant opens, ready to step you through the monitor calibration process (see Figure 5-9).

2. **Put a check in the Expert Mode check box.**

3. **Click the right arrow button to move to the next Assistant pane.**

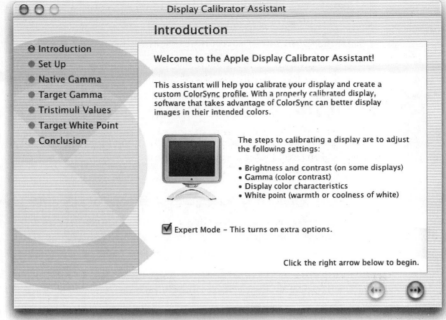

Figure 5-9:
Use the
Display
Calibrator
Assistant to
calibrate
your
monitor.

4. Set your monitor's gamma using the slider bars under the red, green, and blue squares.

Move the slider until the apple in the center matches the striped box as closely as possible.

When you are finished using the sliders, click the right arrow button to move to the next Assistant pane.

5. Use the radio buttons to select the gamma setting you want to use.

You can select from: 1.8 Standard Gamma, the standard setting for Mac OS; 2.2 PC Standard, choose this setting if you are creating images for display on PCs or televisions; or Linear Gamma.

When you are finished using the sliders, click the right arrow button to move to the next Assistant pane.

6. Select a white point that is appropriate for the type of work you do.

Use the slider bar to set the *white point* (color cast) of your monitor. You can move the slider bar through the various light qualities, from warm yellow lighting — which is good for graphics art work — through a cooler setting that is similar to daylight to cool blue lighting — which is similar to television display.

When you're finished using the sliders, click the right arrow button to move to the next Assistant pane.

7. **Name the calibration profile you just set, and then click the Create button to save the profile.**

   Your profile will be saved in `Users/[Current User]/Library/ColorSync or Library/ColorSync/Profiles/Profiles`.

Choosing color settings

The next three steps in setting up color management — setting a color space, setting color profiles, and setting how images will be managed — are all handled in one dialog box in Photoshop.

1. **Choose Edit⇨Color Settings (Photoshop⇨Color Settings on a Mac).**

   Using the Color Settings dialog box shown in Figure 5-10, you can set pre-defined color spaces, individual workspace settings, and how you want Photoshop to deal with images that don't match your color settings.

2. **Using the Settings drop-down list, choose a color setting default for the type of images you primarily create.**

   If you plan to create images both for print and for the Web (and you live in North America), choose North America General Purpose Defaults. This setting ensures consistent color handling across most software that uses color management.

   Choose the Web Graphics defaults if you are a Web designer, primarily creating Web graphics.

   If you are using Photoshop in Europe or Japan, select Europe General Purpose Defaults or Japan General Purpose Defaults, respectively. Both of these settings ensure consistent color handling across most software using color management.

   These default settings select the default options for the drop-down lists in both the Working Spaces area and the Color Management Policies area. If you don't have any special color space needs (such as creating images for high-end printing), use these defaults. Skip down to Step 6 to continue.

3. **In the Working Spaces area, choose RGB, CMYK, Gray, and Spot color settings.**

   For the RGB drop-down list: Use sRGB if you deal with Web graphics only; this setting represents a standard PC monitor display. (The s in sRGB represents *standard*.) If you are going to both print images and create images for the Web, use Adobe RGB (1998).

   For the CMYK, Gray, and Spot drop-down lists: All of these settings are for creating color spaces for images that will be printed by a high-end printer (Gray stands for grayscale). If you are going to do some high-end printing, talk with the print shop for the best setting.

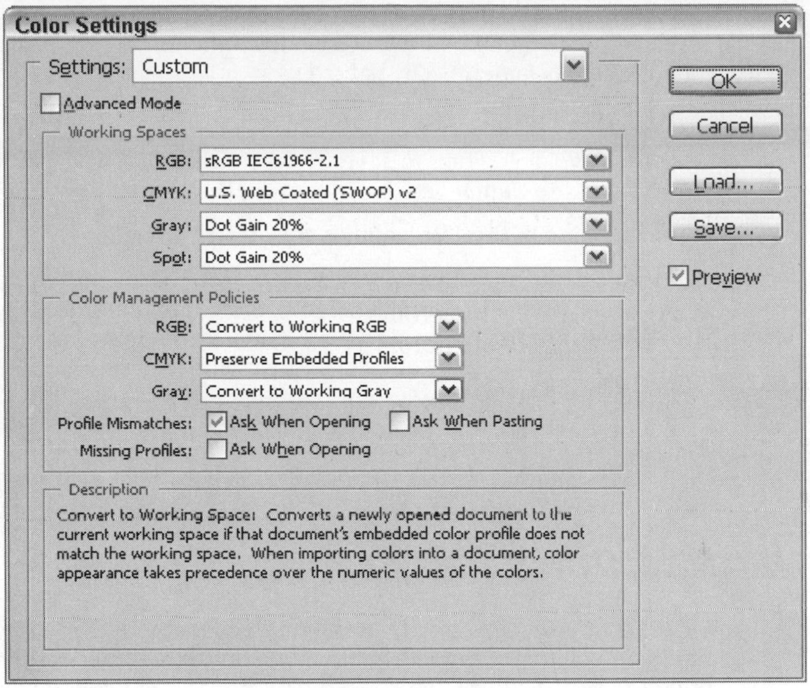

Figure 5-10:
The Color
Settings
dialog box
handles all
the color
space
settings
neces-
sary for
Photoshop.

4. **Set how you want Photoshop to deal with images that don't match your color settings.**

In the Color Management Policies area the RGB, CMYK, and Gray drop-down list boxes all offer the same three options:

- **Convert:** This setting converts a newly opened image to the current profile if the image's profile does not match the working space.

- **Preserve:** This setting saves the color profile embedded in a newly opened image even if the color profile does not match the working space.

- **Off:** This setting turns off color management for new images and newly opened images if their embedded color profiles don't match the working space.

If you aren't sure which settings to choose, good basic settings for these working spaces are:

- **RGB:** Set to Convert

- **CMYK:** Set to Preserve

- **Gray:** Set to Convert

If you want Photoshop to ask you whether to convert an image when it's opened or when it's being pasted in from the Clipboard, put checks in the Profile Mismatches check boxes.

5. **Click Save.**

Use the Save dialog box to save your settings. That way, you will always have access to them even if someone makes changes to your computer.

6. **Enter a name in the File name text box and click Save.**

The Save dialog box closes, returning you to the Color Management dialog box. Notice that the name of your custom color management settings now appears selected in the Settings drop-down list.

7. **Click OK.**

The Color Management dialog box closes and Photoshop will save the color management settings.

Choosing Colors

Now that you've made your way through the conceptual world of color management and color spaces, it's time to move on to the practical topic of selecting the actual colors you use to paint and edit your Photoshop images.

There are several ways to choose colors:

✔ On the Color palette, you can enter red, green, and blue color values or move sliders to create colors.

✔ Using the Swatches palette, you can click a colored square to select a color.

✔ Using the Eyedropper tool, you can pick a color from an image with a mouse click.

✔ Using the Color Picker, you can choose colors from a color spectrum or define the colors manually using the HSB, RGB, Lab, or CMYK color models (see "Color models and image modes" for details about color models).

✔ Using the Custom Colors dialog box, you can select specific colors from color swatches created by companies such as Pantone, Trumatch, and TOYO (more about these color swatches in "Choosing Custom Colors").

✔ Using the new Photoshop CS Match Color command, you can apply the Color palette from one document to another or sample a color.

Before choosing colors, though, you'll need to know how to access the colors you select using the Foreground and Background Color Squares in the Toolbox.

Understanding Foreground and Background colors

In Photoshop, you can work with two colors at a time: a *Foreground color* and a *Background color*. Some tools and commands paint your image with the Foreground color; others paint it with the Background color.

The two colors are displayed in the Foreground color square and the Background color square in the Toolbox. As shown in Figure 5-11, the Foreground color is on top, and the Background color is on the bottom.

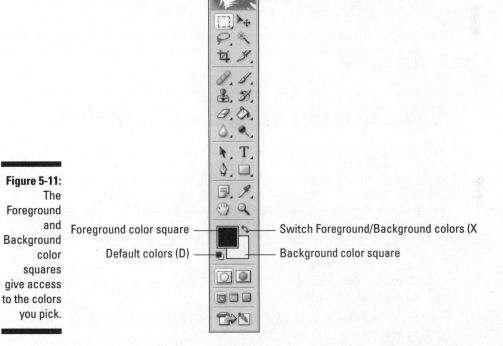

Figure 5-11: The Foreground and Background color squares give access to the colors you pick.

Foreground color square ——— Switch Foreground/Background colors (X

Default colors (D) ——— Background color square

When you select a color, it automatically appears in the Foreground color square in the Toolbox and in the Color palette (for more about the Color palette, turn to "Choosing colors using the Color palette"). To switch between the Foreground and Background colors, click the Switch colors button in the Toolbox or press X on the keyboard. To return to the default Foreground and Background colors (black and white, respectively), click the Default colors button on the Toolbox or press D on the keyboard.

Here are some other ways the Foreground and Background colors are used in Photoshop:

✔ When you use the painting tools, such as the Brush and Pencil Tools, the Foreground color is applied.

✔ When you use the Eraser Tool, the erasure removes the image color and substitutes it with the Background color. (The exception to this rule is that when you're on a layer the erasure reveals transparency instead of the Background color. For more about layers, see Chapter 8.)

✔ If you increase the size of the canvas by choosing Image⇨Canvas Size (as explained in Chapter 4), Photoshop fills the new empty portion of the canvas with the Background color.

✔ If you use one of the shape tools to create a filled shape, the shape is filled and outlined with the Foreground color. (To find out more about creating shapes, turn to Chapter 16.)

✔ When you use the Gradient tool, a rainbow of colors is created between the Foreground and Background colors (the Gradient tool is explained in Chapter 13).

Creating colors using the Color palette

You can use the Color palette, shown in Figure 5-12, to quickly create colors using the slider bars or custom red, green, and blue values. The current Foreground and Background colors are displayed in small color squares in the Color palette. Simply click the Foreground color square in the Color palette to open the Color picker (for more about the Color picker, check out "Choosing colors using the Color picker").

To create colors using the Color palette:

1. **Click the Foreground or Background color square in the Color palette to select it.**

2. **Select a color model for the slider bars using the Color palette menu.**

   Click the small button with the right-facing arrow to access the Color palette menu. To find out more about color models, turn to "Color models and image modes" earlier in this chapter.

3. **Create a color by moving the slider bars, or clicking or dragging on the color bars, or by entering values in the text boxes that correspond to each color channel.**

Foreground color square

Background color square

Color sliders

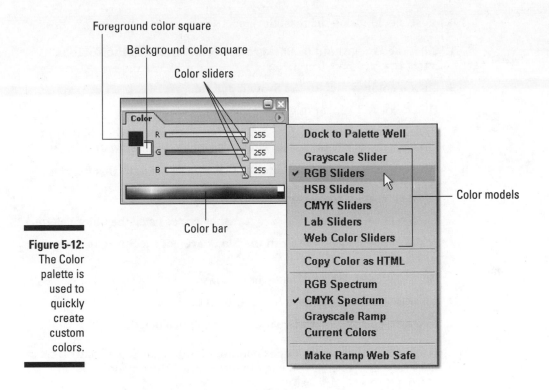

Color bar

Color models

Figure 5-12:
The Color
palette is
used to
quickly
create
custom
colors.

Choosing colors using the Swatches palette

Using the Swatches palette, shown in Figure 5-13, you can quickly choose colors, add colors to the palette, and delete colors as well.

Figure 5-13:
Use the
Swatches
palette to
select
colors and
add custom
colors to the
palette.

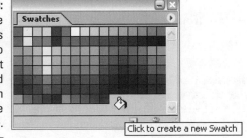

To choose a color using the Swatches palette:

1. **Click the Foreground or Background color square in the Toolbox to select it.**

2. **Click a color swatch in the Swatch palette.**

   That color will appear in the color square you selected.

   To select a color for the color square that is not selected, hold down the Ctrl key (the ⌘ key on a Mac) while clicking on a color swatch.

If you want to add a custom color to the Color palette, follow these steps:

1. **Create a custom color using the Color palette.**

   For details on how to do this, see "Creating colors using the Color palette."

2. **Position the mouse pointer in the blank area of the Swatches palette and click.**

   The Color Swatch Name dialog box appears.

3. **Enter the name for your color, and then click OK.**

   Your new custom color appears in the Swatches palette.

To delete a color from the Swatches palette, simply right-click (Control+click on a Mac) the color swatch you want to remove, and then choose Delete Swatch from the context-sensitive menu.

Picking colors using the Eyedropper tool

With just a click of the mouse, the Eyedropper tool lets you pick colors from an image or the color bar in the Color palette (for the location of the color bar, see Figure 5-12). Here's how:

1. **Click the Foreground or Background color square in the Toolbox to select it.**

2. **Select the Eyedropper tool from the Toolbox or press I on the keyboard.**

3. **Click a color in an open image window, or click the color bar in the Color palette.**

   You can set the Eyedropper tool to sample either a single pixel for color (the default) or to create an average color sample using either a 3 pixel grid or a 5 pixel grid. To set the Eyedropper tool to sample a 3 x 3 pixel or 5 x 5 pixel area, use the sample size drop-down list on the Options bar. Sometimes it's helpful to choose one of the larger sample areas to better match the average color being sampled.

Choosing colors using the Color picker

The Color picker lets you create colors in a way similar to the Color palette. You can select a color using the color slider, click a color in the large color square, or enter values in the color model text boxes.

Try out the Color picker; it's not very hard to use. Here's how:

1. **Double-click either the Foreground or Background color squares in the Toolbox or Color palette to select that color square and open the Color picker.**

   The Color picker appears, shown in Figure 5-14, is handy for specifying exact custom colors. You also can set the Color picker to show Web safe colors — colors that will accurately render in Web images. (To find out more about creating graphics for the Web, turn to Chapter 18.)

2. **Put a check in the Only Web Colors check box if you're creating graphics for the Web.**

   This option sets Photoshop to tell you whether or not the colors you create will accurately render on the Web. If a color isn't safe for the Web, a tiny cube appears next to the New Color box, as shown in Figure 5-14.

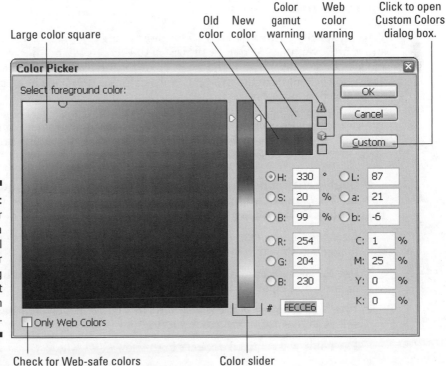

Large color square   Old   New   Color gamut warning   Web color warning   Click to open Custom Colors dialog box.

Figure 5-14:
The Color picker is a great tool for specifying exact custom colors.

Check for Web-safe colors   Color slider

3. **To select a hue, click a color on the color slider, and then click the color you want to use in the large color square.**

   You also can enter specific values in the color mode text boxes.

   If you create a color that won't look so hot in print, a tiny triangle with an exclamation point in it appears next to the New Color box, as shown in Figure 5-14.

4. **Click OK.**

Selecting custom colors

If you're planning on printing an image at a high-end print shop, you may need to specify a special *spot color* for your print job. A spot color is actually special printer's ink mixed using specifications provided by companies such as Pantone, Trumatch, or TOYO.

Companies like Pantone, Trumatch, and TOYO make a business out of creating custom color swatches, which are then published as color swatch books. If you've seen metallic colors on the cover of a book, most likely the color was specified by the graphic artist using just such a swatch book. The benefit, of course, is that these spot colors are WYSIWYG — what you see is what you get, which takes the wiggle room out of choosing colors for print.

You can specify custom swatch book colors using Photoshop. You should know, however, that the colors shown on the screen will not necessarily show the exact color ink. To view the exact color for the brand of ink a printer will use (find this out from the printer), buy a color swatch book at an art or graphic art supply store.

In order to specify custom swatch book colors for your project, you'll need to use the Custom Colors dialog box. The way to access this dialog box is through the Color picker. Here's how:

1. **Double-click either the Foreground or Background color squares in the Toolbox or Color palette to select that color square and open the Custom Colors dialog box.**

   After the Color picker opens, click Custom to open the Custom Colors dialog box shown in Figure 5-15.

2. **Use the Swatch book drop-down list to select a color matching system as shown in Figure 5-16.**

3. **Type in a number that corresponds to a color in a swatch book or select a color using the color slider.**

   The color you selected appears in the new color window.

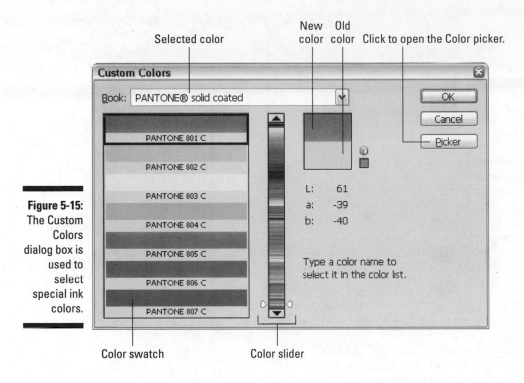

Selected color

New color   Old color   Click to open the Color picker.

Figure 5-15:
The Custom
Colors
dialog box is
used to
select
special ink
colors.

Color swatch   Color slider

4. If you want to return to the Color picker, click Picker; otherwise click OK.

Matching color from one document to another

Another interesting way to set color for your image is to use the new Match Color command. This command actually lets you apply the range of colors or a specific color from one image to another. For instance, suppose you had an image of a sunny landscape composed of bright blues and yellows and a rather gray landscape showing a river and mountains. You could transfer the range of colors from the sunny landscape to the gray river scene, completely changing the gray image to a brighter palette of colors.

To see this command in action, check out Color Plate 5-1. There you'll see three images: a "before" image that uses its original range of colors; the image whose colors will be to be transferred to the "before" image; and an "after" image that uses the new range of colors.

Swatch book drop-down list

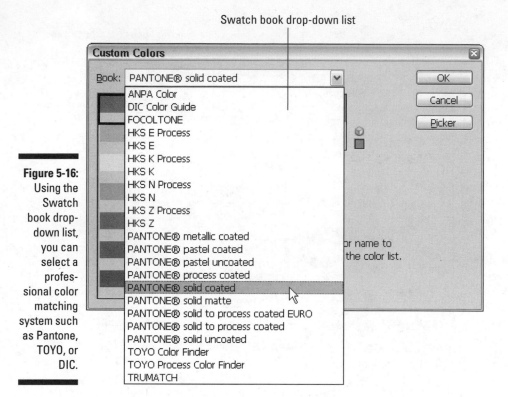

Figure 5-16:
Using the
Swatch
book drop-
down list,
you can
select a
profes-
sional color
matching
system such
as Pantone,
TOYO, or
DIC.

Here's how to transfer a colors from one image to another:

1. **Open two images in Photoshop.**

   Make sure that the image to which you want to transfer the new palette is in front (this means this is the active image and it is selected).

2. **Choose Image⇨Adjustments⇨Match Color.**

   The Match Color dialog box opens, as shown in Figure 5-17, listing the destination image and a displaying a source image. The destination image is the image you selected in step one. The source image is the other open image.

3. **Use the Source drop-down box in the Image Statistics area to select the source image, if necessary.**

4. **Adjust the brightness, color intensity, and how much the Color palette affects the destination image.**

   In the Image Options area, use the Luminance slider to adjust the brightness, the Color Intensity slider to adjust the saturation, and the Fade slider to adjust how much the Color palette changes the destination image.

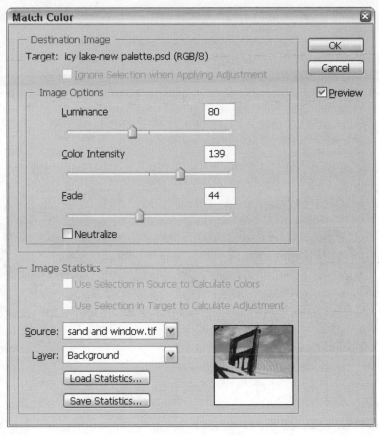

Figure 5-17:
Use the
Match Color
dialog box
to transfer a
range of
colors from
one image
to another.

If the Preview box is checked, you can watch how the color shifts in the destination image while moving the slider bars.

5. Click OK.

Going Grayscale

You can convert color images to grayscale in Photoshop in any of several interesting ways:

> ✔ **Convert an image to Grayscale mode by choosing Image➪Mode➪Grayscale.**
>
> If you use the Image➪Mode➪Grayscale conversion method and your color image contains more than one layer (as explained in Chapter 8), Photoshop asks whether you want to merge your layers. If you want to keep your layers, click on the Don't Merge button.

✔ **Select a grayscale channel.** Because channels are grayscale, you can select a grayscale channel that you like, and then discard the rest of the channels. (For more information about channels, see the "Channels" section earlier in this chapter.)

To select a grayscale channel and discard the rest of the channels, take a look at the Channels palette. Click each individual channel to view it in the image window. When you find the channel you want to use, drag the unwanted channels to the trash can. Figure 5-18 shows a grayscale image and a blue channel used as a grayscale image.

Figure 5-18: The difference between converting a color image to grayscale (left), and throwing away all but the blue channel (right).

✔ **Use a black-filled layer set to the Color blending mode, and then flatten the layers.** (To find out how to add layers to an image, change blending modes, and flatten layers turn to Chapter 8.)

To add a black-filled layer set to the Color blending mode, take a look at the Layers palette as shown in Figure 5-19. Click the Create a new layer button. Press X on the keyboard to restore the Foreground and Background colors to their defaults (black and white, respectively). Then select the Paint Bucket tool and click on the image window to fill it with black. In the Layers palette, use the blending mode drop-down list to select the Color blending mode. Your image changes to a very detailed grayscale. To flatten the layers, choose Layer⇨Flatten Image.

If you use the single channel conversion method and your image contains more than one layer, the layers are flattened when you convert to grayscale. So before you go ahead with the conversion, do all editing that involves layers and also make a backup copy of the layered image.

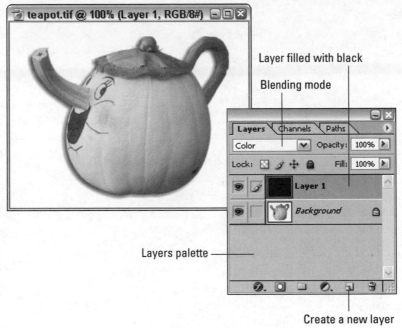

Layer filled with black

Blending mode

Figure 5-19:
Use the
Layers
palette to
create a
black layer
and select
the Color
blending
mode.

Layers palette

Create a new layer

Chapter 6

Going to Hard Copy

*I*n this chapter, I explain how to go from on-screen image to hard copy. Photoshop has a lot to offer in this department. You can just flat out print an image or do much more: preview the image before its printed, change its size and position on the printed page, create a contact sheet, make a photo picture package, and even save it as an Acrobat presentation.

I have to confess that there's a lot I don't know, so I'm going to be totally rash and assume that you have a printer that is plugged in, turned on, and it doesn't have a 16-ton weight sitting on top of it. In other words, your printer works.

If you've used your printer before, everything is probably ready to go. But if something goes wrong, check your printer's manual for troubleshooting advice. If you can't find a solution there and you're lucky enough to know a local printer magician, call and ask for advice.

This May Be All You Need to Know about Printing

When things are in working order, printing isn't a difficult process. Though it involves slightly more than picking up your mouse and saying "print" into it, printing doesn't require a whole lot of preparation. In fact, a quick perusal of the following steps may be all you need to get up to speed. If you need more details, read "Choosing a printer" and "Understanding your printing options," which follow this section and expand on some of the basics here:

1. **Turn on your printer.**

   And don't forget to remove that printer cozy your uncle knitted for you.

2. **Choose File⇨Save or press Ctrl+S (⌘+S on a Mac).**

   It's always a good idea to save your image immediately before you print it. Your computer derives a unique kind of satisfaction by delivering works of art from the printer and then locking up at the last minute, all the while knowing that the image saved on disk is several hours behind the times. If you weren't the butt of the joke, you'd probably think that it was amusing, too.

3. **Choose File⇨Print with Preview . . . Ctrl+Alt+P (⌘+Option+P on a Mac).**

   In the Print dialog box shown in Figure 6-1, you can adjust the position and size of the image on the page and preview the print job. You also can set the image's position on the printed page, adjust its size, set the printed color tone to match your computer screen, and select the printer you are going to use.

4. **Make sure that the image fits on the page.**

   In the upper-left side of the Print dialog box is a preview of your image. If the image is too large or small for the paper size you're using, drag one of the little square handles to resize the image or enter a scale percentage in the Scale text box. Or if you're feeling lazy, click in the Scale to Fit Media check box to have Photoshop do the work for you.

   If you're sure that your image should fit on the selected paper size, but Photoshop barks at you with a little dialog box like the one in Figure 6-2, telling you that some clipping will occur, click the Cancel button to close the warning box. (The portion of an image that can't fit on the printed page won't print or will be *clipped off.*) Then click the Page Setup button and double-check the page orientation. If the paper is big enough for the image in a portrait orientation but the file is oriented in a landscape, Photoshop will think it's too large.

   Changing the size of the image in the Print dialog box has no effect on the actual image; it only affects how the image will print. To change the size of the image itself, use the Image Size dialog box discussed in Chapter 4.

Set image's printed size   Set page orientation and printer.

Preview pane   Set where the image prints on the page.

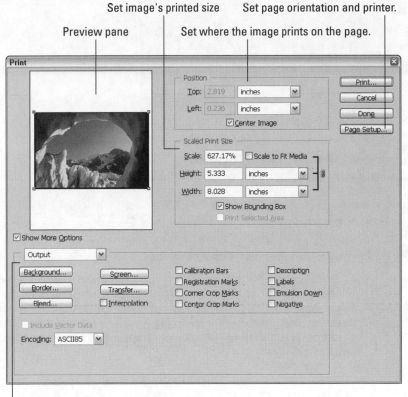

Figure 6-1:
A preview of
your image
appears on
the left side
of the Print
dialog box.

Professional printing options

5. Click Print.

Wait, nothing's printing! No, you're not quite there yet; another Print
dialog box like the one in Figure 6-3 appears to let you set how many
copies you would like. If you need to select a specific printer, you can do
that here, too.

Figure 6-2:
If you see
this
warning,
check the
image's
orientation
on the page.

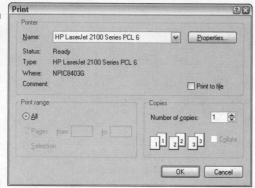

Figure 6-3:
You can use
this dialog
box to
select a
printer and
set how
many
copies
to print.

6. **Click OK or press Enter (Return on a Mac).**

Your printer will go to work and the printed image will appear in the printer's output tray. Congratulations!

If your image did not print correctly on the page, you might need to change the size of the paper you are printing on. Take a look at "Setting Paper Size and Page Orientation" for more details. Also, if your image looks smooth on the screen and jagged on the printed page, resolution could be your problem. Check out Chapter 4 for details about setting image resolution.

Setting Paper Size and Page Orientation

If you are using special paper to print invitations or want to add a colorful logo to an envelope, you need to select the right paper size for your printed document. Setting paper size doesn't affect the size of your image's canvas or the image size in Photoshop, but it does set the type of paper that the image will be printed on. (The canvas is the area around your image in the image window.)

To set paper size and page orientation:

1. **Open the Page Setup dialog box by choosing File⇨Page Setup or pressing Ctrl+Shift+P.**

Using the Page Setup dialog box as shown in Figure 6-4, you can set paper size and page orientation. You can select a printer here, too. (For more about selecting a printer, see "Choosing a Printer.")

2. **Use the Size drop-down list box in the Paper area to select a paper size.**

TIP

Printing on-the-fly

Photoshop, being the versatile program that it is, offers two simple ways to print images in addition to the one I describe earlier in this chapter in the section, "This May Be All You Need to Know about Printing." If you're in a hurry, here are your other options:

✔ Choose File➪Print (Ctrl+P or ⌘+P on a Mac) to skip the print preview and only use

the just-plain-vanilla Print dialog box (refer to Figure 6-3).

✔ Choose File➪Print One Copy (Ctrl+Alt+ Shift+P or ⌘+Option+Shift+P on a Mac) to bypass all the dialog boxes and print . . . well, one copy.

---

3. **In the Orientation area, click a radio button to set the page orientation.**

   Page orientation uses two terms — portrait or landscape — to describe the direction of the paper. Portrait orientation means that the paper is taller than it is wide; landscape orientation means that the paper is wider than it is tall — it looks like it is laying down on its side.

4. **Click OK to close the dialog box.**

   To see how the image fits on the paper size you selected, you can view the image using the Print with Preview menu item discussed in "This May Be All You Need to Know About Printing" or use the instructions in the tip below.

Figure 6-4:
Select a printer, paper size, and page orientation.

A quick way to find out whether an image will fit on the printed page is to click and hold the mouse down over the file information box located at the left side of the status bar. (If you don't remember where the status bar is located, check out Chapter 3 for a refresher.) A preview box appears. Inside the box is a rectangle with an X in it. The white box represents the current paper size and the rectangle with the X through it represents your image. If the X fits entirely inside the white area, your image fits on the page. If the X exceeds the boundary of the white area, the image is too big for the page and needs to be adjusted.

Choosing a Printer

If you have only one printer hooked up to your computer, you can skip this section entirely. But if you're part of a network or you have more than one printer attached to your computer, you need to tell Photoshop which printer you want to use.

For Windows users

To select a printer in Windows, follow these steps:

1. **Open the Page Setup dialog box by choosing File⇨Page Setup or pressing Ctrl+Shift+P.**

   A dialog box like the one shown in Figure 6-4 appears.

2. **Click the Printer button in the Page Setup dialog box.**

3. **Choose a printer name from the Name drop-down list and click OK.**

4. **Click OK or press Enter to exit the dialog box.**

You can also select your printer in the Print dialog box (refer to shown in Figure 6-3), but you don't have access to paper size or paper source options.

For Mac users

If you've been poking around the operating system, you may have discovered that Mac OS X automatically selects your printer if you're connected to a USB printer. If you're on a network, you can use the Print Center to select your printer from the Printer List. But to make it even easier on you, you can also just select your desired printer from the Print dialog box by choosing File⇨ Page Setup or pressing ⌘+Shift+P.

If, by chance, your printer doesn't show up in the Printer List, go to the Print Center. If you don't have a desktop icon for Print Center, you can find it in the Utilities folder in the Application folder.

To choose a printer in the Print Center, follow these steps:

1. **Click the Add Printer button.**

2. **Choose the type of connection and then, depending on that connection, either select a Printer Model from the pop-up menu or enter the printer's IP address or DNS name.**

    If you're unsure of this information, check the documentation that came with your printer.

    If any other message appears — one announcing that the printer is not available or has taken leave of its senses, for example — you very likely have a cabling problem or your printer is not turned on. Otherwise, you're in business.

Understanding Professional Printing Options

When you select the Print with Preview item on the File menu (as mentioned in the earlier section "This May Be All You Need to Know about Printing") the huge dialog box shown in Figure 6-1 appears. This dialog contains lots of interesting and cryptic looking options that enable you to make sure that the image prints exactly as you want it to:

✔ **Center Image:** Use this option to position your image. By default, images are centered. If you don't want to center the image, uncheck the Center Image option and enter new position values in the top and left alignment boxes at the top of the dialog box.

To quickly reposition your image, simply drag the image around the preview window.

✔ **Scaled Print Size:** Use this area to reduce or enlarge the image size for printing. Enter any percentage below 100% to reduce the dimensions of the printed image. Enter any percentage above 100% to enlarge the printed image. You can also enter a value in either the Height or Width boxes. The scale, width, and height settings are linked, meaning that changing any one setting affects the other two.

When you use this option, the printer still prints all the pixels in the image, but the pixels are just smaller or larger.

✔ **Scale to Fit Media:** Use this option to fit the image exactly to the printable edges of the paper. A white border will remain around the edges; this is the part of the paper on which your printer can't print.

✔ **Show Bounding Box:** Use this option to place a *bounding box* around your image in the preview pane. This feature is handy if you have a white border around your image and can't quite tell where the image boundaries are on the preview thumbnail. That way, you can see where the edges of your image are in relation to the paper and resize the image before printing, if necessary.

✔ **Print Selected Area:** Use this option to print only the selected area of your image (for more information about selecting portions of your image, check out Chapter 7).

If you just want to take a quick, close-up look at an isolated area of an image, you can use this option to save time.

✔ **Show More Options:** Put a check in this check box to display Color Management and Output options (a drop-down list box below Show More Options lets you toggle between the two). I discuss most of those options in the sections, "Taking a Look at Color Management Print Options," and "Printing Color Separations."

✔ **Orientation:** Click on the Page Setup button and choose Portrait or Landscape. If you choose Portrait, your image prints on a page that is taller than it is wide; if you choose Landscape, Photoshop prints the image on a page that is wider than it is tall.

Keep in mind that changes made inside the Print Options and Page Setup dialog box have absolutely no effect on anything except how your image prints. You can't do any permanent damage to your image in this dialog box, so feel free to experiment with the settings.

✔ **Color Management:** Every hardware device and software program handles color differently. Try opening an image using several different programs, and you may be surprised to discover that the image looks quite different every time. In fact, try scanning an image and opening the scan in all these different programs. I guarantee that none of the output will match the color of the original image. For more about color management, take a look at Chapter 5.

When printing, Photoshop helps you deal with these different *color spaces* by adjusting color so it appears the same no matter what kind of device or program (printer, Web browser, output bureau, and so on) is used for the output.

Color space is just a fancy term for how a device creates color. For instance, a computer monitor uses red, green, and blue light to create color, a color inkjet printer uses black, red, blue, and yellow inks to create color, and digital camera records the colors it sees using the daylight present (which has a yellowish cast) or a flash (which has a bluish cast). How can any of these devices create a color match without some type of color correction? They can't. That's what color management and color profile conversion are all about. See Chapter 5 for more about this topic.

To set the color space *profile* for your printer, select Color Management from the drop-down list box below Show More Options. Then use the Profile drop-down list box in the Print Space area to select the type of output device, for instance Apple RGB, ColorMatch RGB, or your monitor's specific brand and model number. This information tells Photoshop how to adjust the colors to match printed output to what you see on the screen. This is a one-time setting; Photoshop saves the information that you enter and use this data every time you print something. If you have more than one printer, you can change printers by using the Profile drop-down list box to select it. Photoshop automatically sets the color to match this new printer.

Creating and Printing a Contact Sheet

Photoshop can create a digital version of a traditional contact sheet. This feature takes a folder of images, creates thumbnails for each image, and arranges them on a single page. Contact sheets are good for record-keeping purposes because they enable you to catalog large quantities of files. They're also useful for checking out a big batch of images without wasting a sheet of paper for every image.

Here's what you need to do to set up a contact sheet:

1. **Choose File⇨Automate⇨Contact Sheet II.**

   The Contact Sheet II dialog box opens like the one shown in Figure 6-5.

2. **Click the Browse button.**

   The Browse for Folder dialog box opens, letting you find the images.

3. **Set the size and resolution of the contact sheet.**

   Make sure the Width and Height are set smaller than the paper you plan to print the contact sheet on. If you're not sure about setting the resolution, check out Chapter 4 for a crash course.

4. **Specify a color mode.**

   There are four modes to choose from — Grayscale, RGB Color, CMYK Color, or Lab Color. If you're not sure which color mode is right to use for your image, take a look at Chapter 5.

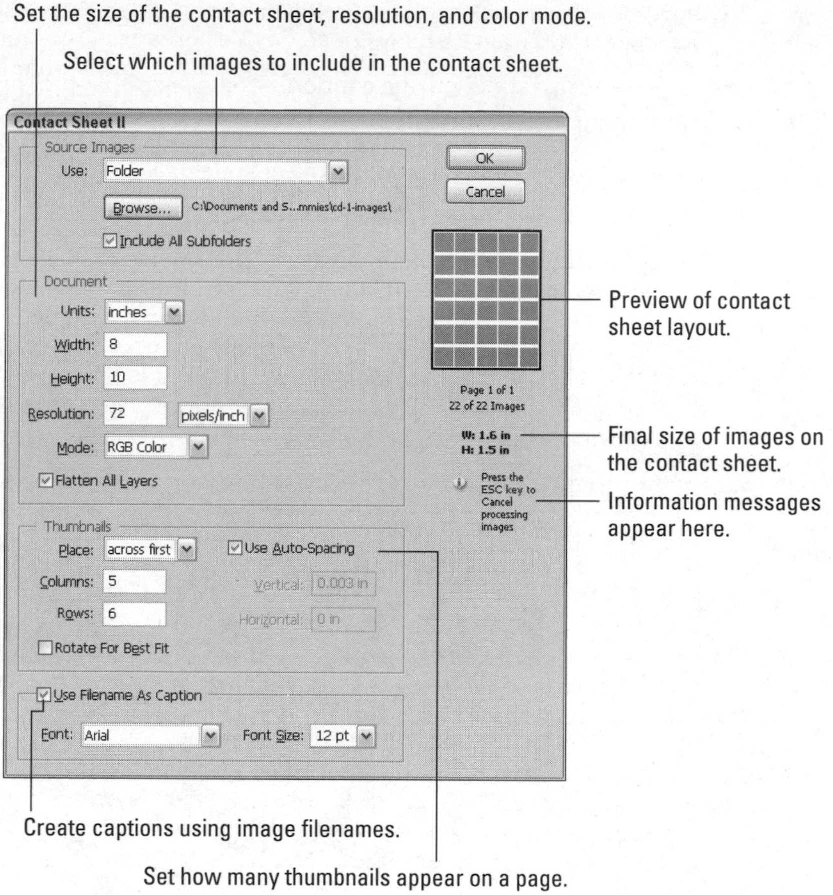

Set the size of the contact sheet, resolution, and color mode.

Select which images to include in the contact sheet.

Contact Sheet II

Source Images

Use: Folder

Browse... C:\Documents and S...mmies\cd-1-images\

☑ Include All Subfolders

OK

Cancel

Document

Units: inches

Width: 8

Height: 10

Resolution: 72 pixels/inch

Mode: RGB Color

☑ Flatten All Layers

Preview of contact sheet layout.

Page 1 of 1
22 of 22 Images

W: 1.6 in
H: 1.5 in

Press the ESC key to Cancel processing images

Final size of images on the contact sheet.

Information messages appear here.

Thumbnails

Place: across first ☑ Use Auto-Spacing

Columns: 5 Vertical: 0.003 in

Rows: 6 Horizontal: 0 in

☐ Rotate For Best Fit

☑ Use Filename As Caption

Font: Arial Font Size: 12 pt

Figure 6-5:
This dialog box lets you set image resolution and how many thumbnails you want to print on a page.

Create captions using image filenames.

Set how many thumbnails appear on a page.

5. **Check the Flatten All Layers option if you want to squash your image.**

   To flatten or not to flatten, that is the question. If you check this option, Photoshop will smoosh all the image layers into one layer. Leave this box unchecked if you want to tweak a caption or rearrange the order of some images after creating the contact sheet. Then, when you're satisfied, you can then choose Layer⇨Flatten Image, and then you're good to go. (For more about layers and flattening images, check out Chapter 8.)

6. **Use the Thumbnails area to specify the order and number of columns and rows for your layout.**

   Don't worry if there are more images in the folder than will fit on one page; Photoshop automatically creates as many pages of thumbnails as needed.

7. **To use filenames as captions on the contact sheet, click in the Use Filename as Caption checkbox.**

   If you decide to add filename captions, you can specify the font and size in which they are displayed. If you don't select this option, Photoshop will not include captions (this could be a bit confusing when you're looking at 52 images and you want to select specific files).

8. **Click OK or press Enter (Return on a Mac).**

   Photoshop goes to work madly opening, copying, and pasting each file into position in your contact sheet.

   When the process is complete — it might take a few minutes depending upon the speed of your computer — you have your very own contact sheet, similar to the one in Figure 6-6, ready for printing.

9. **Save the contact sheet, modify it if you want, and then print it.**

   You can also access the Contact Sheet II plug-in via the Automate menu in the File Browser. For more about the File Browser and how to use it, turn to Chapter 3.

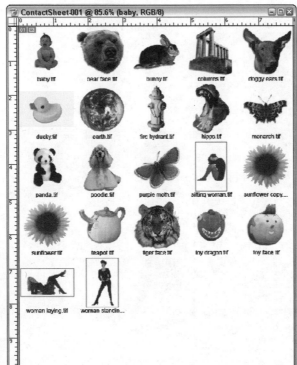

Figure 6-6:
Contact sheets are handy for quickly checking images or cataloguing them.

Printing Picture Package Prints

Ever go to a big store at the mall dressed in your best to get your portrait taken? Chances are when you ordered your photographs, you chose from different picture packages containing maybe one 5 x 7 for your mother, a 4 x 6 for your dog, and a million wallet-sized photos that you never know what to do with.

Well, with Photoshop you can create and print custom picture packages, and if you don't want 27 wallet-sized photos, you don't have to include them. Follow these steps to set up your own picture package:

1. **Choose File⇨Automate⇨Picture Package.**

   The Picture Package dialog box (shown in Figure 6-7) appears, ready for action.

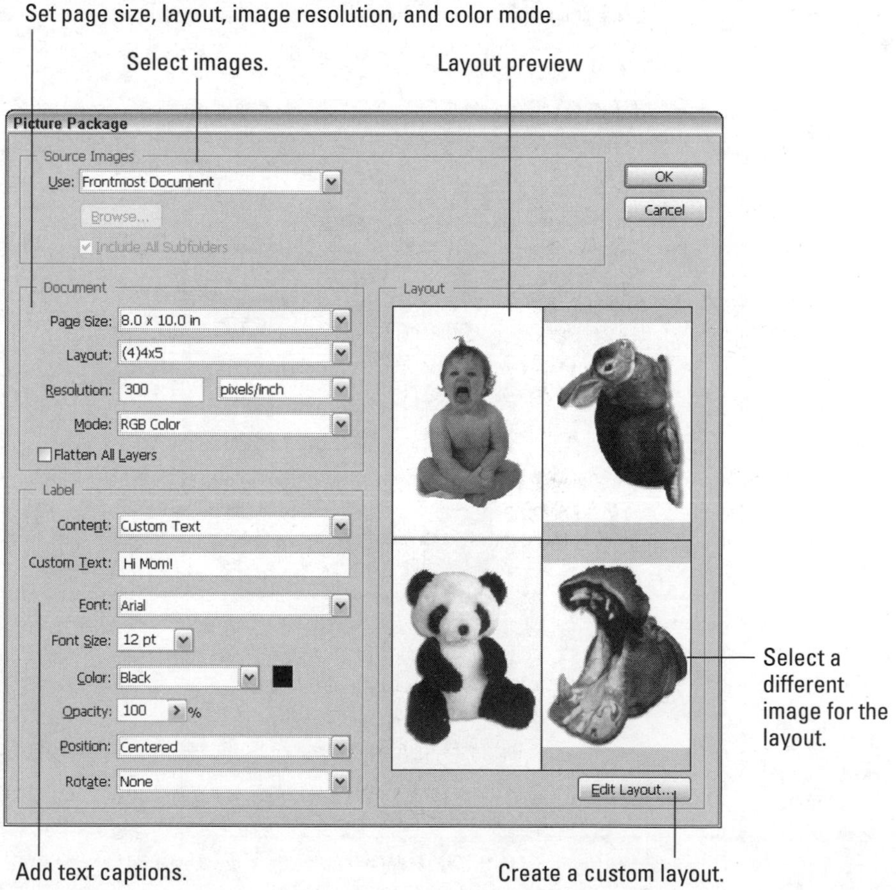

Set page size, layout, image resolution, and color mode.

Select images.

Layout preview

Figure 6-7: Creating enough pictures for your whole clan is easy. (Don't forget Mom!)

Select a different image for the layout.

Add text captions.

Create a custom layout.

2. Choose a Page Size and Layout.

In the Document area, you can select from three different page sizes and a whole slew of layout options — and there's even a layout option that will print a million tiny wallet-sized photos (nah, just kidding!).

If you have a hankering to create a personalized layout, you can use the Picture Package Edit Layout dialog box. To access it, click the Edit Layout button at the lower right corner of the Picture Package dialog box.

3. Find the images you want to use.

With the Use drop-down list in the Source Images area you can select File, Folder, Frontmost Document, or Selected Images from the File Browser. If you select a folder or file, click the Browse button to locate said folder or file. If you have several images open in Photoshop, the Frontmost Document choice refers to the image that is *active* (it is in front of the other images and its title bar is not grayed out).

4. To create a Picture Package with more than one image, click on one of the thumbnails in the preview area.

The Select an Image dialog box appears, letting you select a file for that position in the picture package.

5. Specify Resolution and Color Mode.

Depending on what you are preparing the picture package for — as a catalog page for the Web, printed as gifts for your family — you will need to set the proper resolution and color mode. If you need to refresh your knowledge about resolution, take a look at Chapter 4; for information about color modes look at Chapter 5.

6. Check the Flatten All Layers option to squash your image, if you want to.

When this option is checked, all the layers are flattened together onto one layer. If this option is not checked, Photoshop automatically puts each of your images and labels on a separate layer, that way you can edit the captions and move the images around before printing, if you want to.

7. Select the content for picture captions and format them, if you wish to add them.

If you want to add text or a description to the picture package, use the Content drop-down box in the Label area to select a descriptive item such as the image's filename, copyright information, a description, image credit, title or custom text. If you choose to add custom text, use the Custom Text box to type a personalized caption.

8. Click OK.

Photoshop roars into action with amazing speed and agility, creating your picture package in the blink of an eye (actually, it might take 5 or 10 blinks depending upon how many images you selected). When Photoshop is done, a picture package something like the one shown in Figure 6-8 appears in the image window.

Figure 6-8:
Making
presents for
friends and
family are
especially
easy!

9. **Save the picture package and then print it.**

You can also access the Printer Package plug-in via the Automate menu in the File Browser. For more about the File Browser and how to use it, turn to Chapter 3.

Creating PDF Presentations

Suppose you're creating a new line of baby food labels at your computer in New York City while your boss is sitting in a marketing meeting in Cleveland, discussing the baby food labels with marketing representatives. Suddenly, the folks in Cleveland decide that they have to see the labels right *now!*

The pressure is on; your job is on the line. You're beginning to sweat trying to remember what operating system they're running in Cleveland — was it Mac, Windows, Linux? When you remember a new Photoshop 8 feature, smile, snap your fingers, and do a quick tap dance on your desk.

The new PDF Presentation plug-in that comes with Photoshop cs enables you to combine multiple image files into a single, multi-page presentation that you can quickly e-mail to Cleveland. It doesn't matter what operating system they're running. Adobe Acrobat Reader is available for free to anybody on any operating system and any platform. Acrobat's real benefit is file compatibility. What you create in Photoshop is exactly what the recipient of your PDF Presentation will see.

The PDF files you create in Photoshop can be viewed on most versions of Acrobat Reader, including older versions of the program. To be on the safe side, however, I recommend that you visit the Adobe Web site and download the latest version of Acrobat Reader. After all, it's free! If an older version of Acrobat Reader cannot read the file, you'll get you a heads up that directs you to the Adobe site to download the latest version.

Here's all you need to do to create a PDF Presentation:

1. **Choose File➪Automate➪PDF Presentation.**

   A PDF Presentation dialog box like the one shown in Figure 6-9 appears.

2. **Add the files you want to include in the presentation.**

   In the Source Files area, check the box next to Add Open Files if you want to include files already open in Photoshop. To add files from various folders on your computer, click Browse.

3. **In the Output Options area select the Presentation radio button.**

   This option tells Photoshop to create the PDF file as a presentation.

4. **Make your presentation into a slide show, if you want.**

   If you want, you can create a slide show of your presentation by adding options from the Presentation Options area. Set your images to advance a specified increment, continue looping, and whether to add a transition (wipes, dissolves, splits) between images.

   Any notes you add to the images using the Notes tool in Photoshop are included in the presentation. The recipient of your presentation can open the notes when they look at the presentation using Acrobat Reader. For more about the Notes tool and adding notes, take a look at Chapter 3.

5. **When you're done, click Save.**

   The Save dialog box opens, prompting you to select a folder and enter a name for your presentation.

6. **Click Save again.**

   The Save dialog box closes and a PDF Options dialog box opens. Here you can set the file to compress to the smallest possible size. Also, you can set security options such as passwords, as well as the recipient's editing/printing options (whether they're allowed to make changes to the presentation or print it in low or high resolution).

7. **Click OK.**

   Photoshop goes to work, creating the presentation and storing it in the folder you selected. When it's finished a small dialog box opens and coolly announces that the `PDF Presentation was successful`.

   You also can access the PDF Presentation plug-in via the Automate menu in the File Browser. For more about the File Browser and how to use it, turn to Chapter 3.

Currently selected files

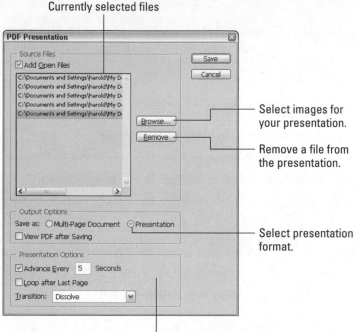

Select images for your presentation.

Remove a file from the presentation.

Select presentation format.

Figure 6-9:
You can make your own slide show using a PDF Presentation.

Set presentation loop and transition options.

Photoshop and Offset Printing

Photoshop contains many high-level features that enable users to produce professional-quality separations and other materials used for the highest quality offset printing. However, as is usual with anything that involves the words "professional" and "quality," creating these separations can be quite complicated.

You may be glad to know that until you become extremely proficient in Photoshop, there's no reason that you need to know the nuts and bolts of creating separations. For the most part, you can easily get quality results from a Photoshop image by following the simple directions that a third-party printer or service bureau provides. If you are going to be working with offset printing, you should have a basic idea of how the process works.

Understanding how offset printing works

When you prepare a project — a brochure, newsletter, poster, and so on — for commercial printing, you will probably deal with a print shop or a service bureau.

Talk to your service bureau or printer first

These days most service bureaus and printers use Photoshop, so they will most likely ask for regular Photoshop .PSD files. Once you become a fantastic Photoshop whiz, you may want to create your own RGB or CMYK separations for your output purposes using specialized output settings. To start with, you probably won't need to do anything so fancy. Just ask the service bureau or printer you use for directions. They will probably be very happy to accept your completed Photoshop file and perform any conversions needed for you.

Traditionally, a service bureau takes your prepared Photoshop files and either prints them using a high-resolution printer, giving you *camera-ready* output, or more likely images the files onto film. If you get camera-ready output, the print shop will use a camera to shoot pictures of the output to create film.

With the advent of computers and transportable large storage media such as writable CD-ROMs, Zip drives, and removable storage media, many graphic artists skip the service bureau, cutting out the intermediate step of film or camera-ready output, and go straight to the print shop with disks containing their project files. Many service bureaus and print shops work directly with Photoshop, but some may prefer to use encapsulated PostScript (.EPS) files.

The print shop takes any of these media — camera-ready output, film, or computer files — and uses them to make printing plates. The printing plates are usually made of acid-etched metal. The plates are then put on large rollers on a printing press by the *pressman*. If your project contains more than one color, the pressman uses *registration marks* to make sure all the plates are exactly aligned. He or she then runs the printing press. As the plates rotate on the rollers, they pick up a very thin coating of ink and an ink impression is transferred to the paper.

After the ink dries, the paper is trimmed and folded using *crop marks* as a guide. The *print job* may then be stapled or bound, depending upon the print job's number of pages. The completed print job is then packed in boxes and shipped to you.

Preparing an image for a service bureau or printer

When you prepare an image file for a service bureau or printer, you may need to add *registration marks, crop marks, calibration bars,* or a *bleed* to your image. Registration marks are special marks that a printer uses to align color separations. Crop marks are short little lines printed outside of your image to indicate where the printer should trim or fold the final printed page. Calibration bars are grayscale or color calibration strips printed outside your image that allow the printer to adjust the amount of ink used to get the color of the printed image just right. A bleed is a small amount at the edge of the image that is cut away when the printed page is finished, eliminating any paper-colored border. Figure 6-10 shows some of the various output options.

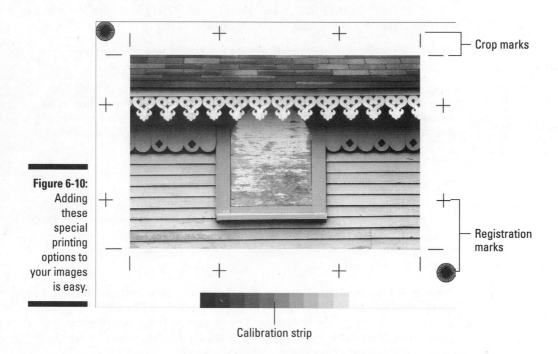

Figure 6-10: Adding these special printing options to your images is easy.

— Crop marks

— Registration marks

Calibration strip

Setting up these special items for the service bureau or printer is easy. Here's how:

1. **Choose File➪Print with Preview. . . or Ctrl+Alt+P (⌘+Option+P on a Mac).**

   The Print dialog box shown in Figure 6-1 opens. You can use this dialog box to quickly add printers' marks.

2. **Put a check mark in the Show More Options check box.**

   The bottom of the Print dialog box will expand to show color management and output options as shown in Figure 6-11.

3. **Select Output from the drop-down list.**

   Printing options such as bleed, crop marks, registration marks, and calibration bars will become available.

4. **Put check marks by the items you want to select.**

   As you select the items, the marks will appear in the preview pane around your image.

5. **To add a Bleed, click the Bleed button.**

   The bleed dialog box opens, letting you specify the width of the bleed you want to create in either inches, millimeters, or points. Click OK when you've set the bleed width to return to the Print dialog box.

6. **Click Done.**

   The Print dialog box will close and Photoshop will save the printing options that you selected. When you take the file to a service bureau or printer, these options will print with your image.

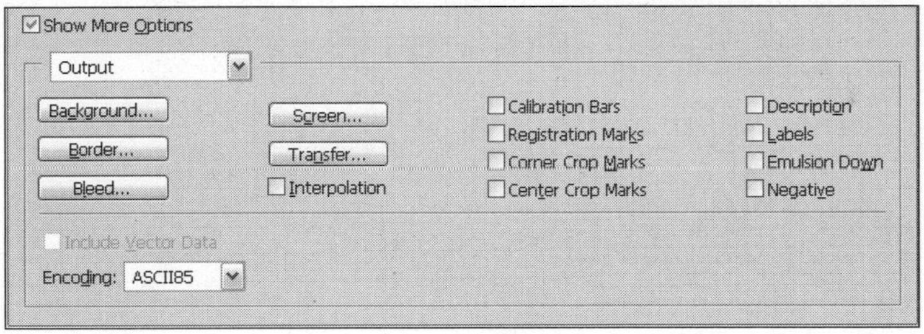

Figure 6-11:
The bottom
of the Print
dialog box
offers
special
printing
options.

Saving an image as a PostScript file

If you're service bureau or print shop requests a PostScript file of your image, Photoshop can help you quickly and easily create one.

First off, though, you should always talk to the service bureau or print shop to find out whether any special printing options such as crop marks or registration marks need to be added to your image (check out "Preparing an image for a service bureau or printer" for details on how to add these and other printing options).

To save an image as a PostScript file:

1. **Open the image in Photoshop.**

2. **Add any special printing options necessary.**

   Take a look at "Preparing an image for a service bureau or printer" for information about these options and how to add them to your image.

3. **Select File⇨Save As or enter Ctrl+Shift+S (⌘+Shift+S on a Mac).**

   You can use the Save As dialog box shown in Figure 6-12 to save images in PostScript file format.

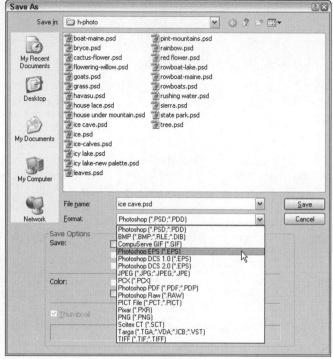

Figure 6-12:
Select
Photoshop
.EPS from
the Format
drop-down
list to save
your file
as a Post-
Script file.

4. **Select the folder where you want to save the file.**

5. **Type a name for your image in the File name text box.**

6. **Select Photoshop EPS from the Format drop-down list box.**

7. **Click Save.**

   An EPS Options dialog box will open letting you select preview and *encoding* options. Encoding means how the image data is saved.

8. **Select TIFF (8 bits/pixel) from the Preview drop-down list.**

   This item selection sets your image preview for grayscale or color (it will show in grayscale or color depending upon whether the image is set in grayscale or color).

9. **Set the Encoding drop-down list box to Binary.**

   Binary encoding is accepted by most printers and does not suffer from data loss.

10. **Click OK.**

    The PostScript file you just created will be saved in the folder you selected. Your file is now ready for the service bureau or print shop.

Part III
Selections and Layers

The 5th Wave — By Rich Tennant

NATIONAL ENQUIRER PHOTO IMAGING WORKSHOP

"Remember, your Elvis should appear bald and slightly hunched. Nice Big Foot, Brad. Keep your two—headed animals in the shadows and your alien spacecrafts crisp and defined."

In this part . . .

In this part you learn about the tools and techniques Photoshop provides for selecting portions of your images and adding layers for safe editing and creating cool effects.

Chapter 7 explains how to select portions of an image by using the Lasso tools, Marquee tools, and the Magic Wand tool. You also learn how to clone, feather, and transform selections. And after creating a complicated selection, you find out how to save it for later use.

Understanding the effective use of layers is vital to becoming proficient with Photoshop. Chapter 8 defines layers, shows you how to work with the Layers palette, and explains how to stack, rename, and hide layers. In addition, you find out how to turn a selection into a layer, link layers together, and create layer sets. Then, you'll discover a new Photoshop cs feature *layer comps*. Layer comps are snapshots you can make of current layer attributes such as position, visibility, and blending modes for later use.

Chapter 7

Making Selections

● ●

In This Chapter

▶ Picking the right selection tool

▶ Roping pixels with the Lasso tools

▶ Drawing straight-sided selections

▶ Selecting rectangular and oval areas

▶ Using the Magic Wand tool

▶ Using the Color Range command

▶ Deleting and moving selections

▶ Intersecting and feathering selections

▶ Smoothing and transforming selections

▶ Saving a selection

● ●

*I*f you're an old ranch hand, you may find it helpful to think of the pixels in your image as a bunch of cows. A pixel may not have any horns and it rarely moos, but it's a cow all the same. Consider these amazing similarities: Both pixels and cows travel in herds. (When's the last time you saw one pixel out on its own?) They're also dumb as dirt and obstinate, to boot. And — here's the absolute clincher — you round them both up by using a lasso.

The only difference between pixels and cows is in the vernacular. When you lasso a cow or two on the lone prairie, it's called ropin'. When you lasso a mess of pixels, it's called selectin'.

After you select the desired pixels, you can do things to them. You can move them, duplicate them, and apply all kinds of alterations that I describe in upcoming chapters. Selecting lets you grab hold of some detail or other and edit it independently of other portions of your image. It's a way of isolating pixels to manipulate them.

This chapter discusses methods for selecting portions of an image. With a little practice, you can rustle pixels better than most hands rope doggies, and that's no bull.

If you are working with an image that contains more than one layer, and you create a selection, the layer that is currently active is the only one that will be affected by the selection and any editing you do. So before you edit an area that's selected, make sure the correct layer is selected. (To learn more about layers, turn to Chapter 8.)

The Pen tool, Freeform Pen tool, and shape tools can be used to create complex paths and shapes. A *path* is a temporary outline that you can convert into a selection. So, if you need to make a complex, exact selection, keep these tools (and especially the Pen tool) in mind. To find out how to create paths and convert paths to selections, turn to Chapter 16.

Learning the Ropes

Photoshop provides several selection tools, all labeled in Figure 7-1. These tools include the Lasso, the Polygonal Lasso, the Magnetic Lasso, four so-called marquee tools, and an automatic color-selector known as the Magic Wand tool. Here's how they work:

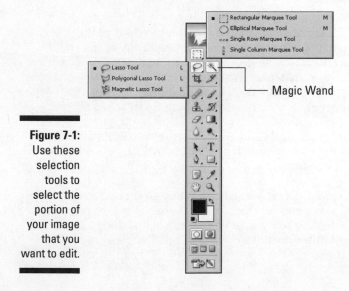

Figure 7-1:
Use these selection tools to select the portion of your image that you want to edit.

 ✔ Drag inside the image with the Lasso tool to select free-form areas. The shape of the selection conforms to the shape that you drag.

- Use the Polygonal Lasso tool, which shares a flyout menu with the regular Lasso, to draw polygonal selections — that is, selections made up of straight sides.

  Another way to create polygonal selections is to hold down the Alt (Option on a Mac) key and click with the regular Lasso.

- Click the Magnetic Lasso tool, which also shares a flyout menu with the other two lasso tools, on the edge of your object and then move the lasso around that edge. See the following section, "Selecting with the Magnetic Lasso tool," for more details.

- Select a rectangular area with the Rectangular Marquee tool. Just drag from one corner of the area you want to select to the other. The outline you draw with the tool looks like a border of moving dots — which is how "marquee" managed its way into the tool name.

- Select an elliptical area with the Elliptical Marquee tool.

- Select continuous areas of color with the Magic Wand tool. For example, if you want to select the sky without selecting the clouds, you just click in the sky. Turn to "Selecting using the Magic Wand tool" to find out how to use it.

Accessing the Marquee and Lasso tools

Now that you know how the tools work, look at how to get to the tools. The arrow in the lower-right corner of the Marquee and Lasso tool icons in the Toolbox indicates that a flyout menu of hidden tools lurks beneath each icon. (See Chapter 2 for more information.)

To switch between the tools on the flyout menus, Alt+click (Option+click on a Mac) the tool icon that happens to be visible in the Toolbox. You also can select tools using these keyboard shortcuts:

- **Press the M key to access the active marquee tool.** If the Rectangular Marquee is active, press Shift+M to toggle the Elliptical Marquee. You can't access the Single Row and Single Column Marquee tools with this keyboard shortcut.

- **Press L to get the lasso tools.** As with the marquee tools, the same shortcut switches you between the three lasso tools: If the regular Lasso tool is active, pressing Shift+L brings up the Polygonal and the Magnetic Lasso tools.

- **Press the W key to get the Magic Wand tool.** The tool is more unpredictable than magic, making W — for Wacky Wand — a logical keyboard equivalent.

Selecting everything

If you want to select an entire layer, then choose Select⇨All or press Ctrl+A (⌘+A on a Mac) on the keyboard.

If you're working with a layer that includes transparent pixels and you only want to select colored pixels (not the transparent ones), Ctrl+click (⌘+click on a Mac) that layer in the Layers palette. To find out more about layers, turn to Chapter 8.

Throwing Lassos

Both the regular Lasso tool and the Polygonal Lasso tool are pretty easy to use, relatively speaking. The Magnetic Lasso tool is trickier, but it's nothing you can't pick up with a little guidance.

Using the regular Lasso tool

I have only one instruction for using the Lasso tool: Trace around the portion of the image that you want to select with the tool. That's it. In Figure 7-2, for example, I dragged around the mushroom to select it independently of its surroundings.

The Lasso tool is great for quickly selecting irregularly shaped areas. It's a little hard to control at first, though. Part of the selection boundary you create will probably be a bit wobbly. To precisely select irregularly shaped areas you can try using the Magnetic Lasso tool described in "Selecting with the Magnetic Lasso" or use the Pen tool as described in Chapter 16 (though the Pen tool takes a bit of time to use).

As the figure shows, Photoshop displays a dotted outline around the selected area after you release the mouse button. This outline represents the exact path of your drag.

If you release before completing the shape — that is, before meeting up with the point at which you began dragging — Photoshop simply connects the beginning and ending points with a straight line. You don't hurt anything if you release too early.

Drawing straight-sided selections

Suppose that you want to select and remove a door or a window pane from an image. You can drag around it with the Lasso tool, but a better option is to use the Polygonal Lasso tool, which makes it easy to create selections with straight sides.

Selection outline

Lasso cursor

Figure 7-2: I selected the mush-room by dragging around it with the Lasso tool.

To select an object in this manner, click with the Polygonal Lasso tool to set the beginning of the first line in the selection. Then move the mouse cursor to the point where you want the line to end and click again. Keep clicking to create new line segments. To complete the selection, you have two options:

- ✔ Double-click to draw a segment between the spot you double-click and the first point in your selection.

- ✔ Move the cursor over the first point in your selection until you see a little circle next to the Polygonal Lasso cursor. Then click to close the selection.

You can use the Polygonal Lasso tool for images with both curved and straight segments. To create a curved segment, switch to the regular Lasso while selecting: just press and hold down the Alt (Option on a Mac) key and drag to draw your curved line. When you release the Alt (Option on a Mac) key, the tool reverts back to the Polygonal Lasso tool.

Selecting with the Magnetic Lasso tool

 The Magnetic Lasso tool takes a little getting used to and may not produce a great selection in all cases. But it's easy to use, and if you take some time to understand the method behind its madness, it can be a quick remedy to your selection needs.

The Magnetic Lasso tool works best with high-contrast images — that is, it works great if the element you want to select is a different color than the background. Using the settings on the Options bar, the Magnetic Lasso tool analyzes the difference in the color of the pixels between the element you want to select and the background, and snaps to your element's edge. Here's how to use this quirky tool:

1. **Select the Magnetic Lasso tool.**

   Press L and then Shift+L twice to use the keyboard shortcut.

2. **Click on the edge of the element you want to select.**

3. **Move the cursor around the edge of the element.**

   Don't click and drag — just move the mouse.

   The magnetic lasso creates an outline with square anchor points around the edge of the element. If the line is off the mark, back up your mouse and try again.

4. **If you need to delete an anchor point as you're moving around the edge, press the Backspace (Delete on a Mac) key.**

   Click to create your own anchor points. Adding your own anchor points can be helpful if the Magnetic Lasso tool seems reluctant to stick to the edge you select.

5. **Continue around the element and click on your starting anchor point to close the outline.**

   You see a small circle next to your cursor indicating closure of the outline.

6. **As soon as the outline is closed and you release the mouse, a selection marquee appears.**

7. **Press Esc or Ctrl+period (⌘+period on a Mac) to stop using the Magnetic Lasso tool.**

Exploring your Lasso options

Whether you use the regular Lasso, Polygonal Lasso, or Magnetic Lasso tools, you can modify the performance of the tool with the two options common to all three tools on the Options bar. (See the next section for options specific to the Magnetic Lasso tool.) Though small in number, the options for the lasso tools are some tough little hombres.

Both options — Feather and Anti-aliased — affect future selection outlines drawn with the lasso tools. In short, the Feather option makes the outline fuzzy, and the Anti-aliased option slightly softens the edge of the outline. If you want to modify an outline that you've already drawn, you have to choose a command from the Select menu. For more about Feathering a selection, turn to "Feathering a selection," later in this chapter.

✔ **Anti-aliased:** Selections drawn with the lasso tools usually have soft, natural-looking edges. This softening is called *anti-aliasing*. To turn off the softening, click the Anti-aliased check box on the Options bar to uncheck the option. From then on, outlines drawn with the tool have sharply defined and sometimes jagged edges.

Figure 7-3 shows two lassoed selections moved to reveal the white background in the image. In the left example, the Anti-aliased check box was turned off; in the right example, the option was turned on. The edges of the left example are jagged; the edges of the right example are soft.

Anti-aliasing off   Anti-aliasing on

Figure 7-3:
The
difference
between
dragging a
jagged (left)
and anti-
aliased
(right)
selection.

Jagged edges   Soft edges

Most of the time, you want to leave the Anti-aliased check box turned on. Just turn it off when you want to select precise, hard-edged areas. (Which may be never. Who knows?)

✔ **Feather:** Enter a value into the Feather text box to make the outline fuzzy. *Feathering* is used to create smoother blending between the selected area to the new background a copied and pasted selection will be placed on. The value determines the radius of the fuzziness in pixels. If you enter a value of 3, for example, Photoshop extends the fuzzy region 3 pixels up, 3 pixels to the left, 3 pixels down, and 3 pixels to the right. As shown in the left example of Figure 7-4, that's a lot of fuzz. A higher value results in a more fuzzy selection outline, as witnessed in the right example, which sports a Feather value of 10.

Feather 3 pixels   Feather 10 pixels

Figure 7-4:
A bigger
Feather
value
means
fuzzier
fungus.

Looking at the unique Magnetic Lasso options

The Magnetic Lasso tool has unique options on the Options bar that are related to the sensitivity of the tool's operation:

- **Width:** Determines how close to an edge you have to move the mouse for Photoshop to see the element. You can set it to a higher number for smooth, high-contrast elements, and it still hugs the edge of the element. Set it to a lower value if the image has a lot of nooks and crannies or the contrast isn't that high. The range of the width option is 1–256 pixels. To change it while you're actually using the tool, press the [key to lower the number and the] key to raise the number.

- **Edge Contrast:** Tells the Magnetic Lasso tool how much contrast is required between the element and the background before the lasso can be attracted to that edge. The range for the Edge Contrast option is 1–100%. If you find a good deal of contrast between the element and the background, put in a higher value in order to get a cleaner selection. If the image is low contrast, lower the value for this option.

- **Frequency:** Tells the Magnetic Lasso tool when to automatically insert anchor points. The range for Frequency is from 0–100%. If you want more points, insert a higher number; for fewer points, use a lower value. High values are better for rough, jagged edges, and low values are better for smooth edges. As you move around the edge of your element and create the outline, Photoshop pins it down with an anchor point.

Selecting Rectangles, Squares, Ellipses, and Circles

 If you want to create a selection that's rectangular or elliptical, you use — guess what — the Rectangular and Elliptical Marquee tools, respectively. The Rectangular and Elliptical Marquee tools are so easy to use that they make the lasso look complicated. You just drag from one corner to the opposite corner and release the mouse button. (Okay, ellipses don't have corners, so you have to use your imagination a little bit.) The dotted marquee follows the movements of your cursor on-screen, keeping you apprised of the selection outline in progress.

But Photoshop has never been one to provide you with only one way to use a tool — or, in this case, two tools. For example, you can also use these tools to select perfect squares or circles.

Grabbing a square or circle

Every so often, you may feel the urge to apply some puritanical constraints to your selection outlines. Enough of this random width and height business — you want perfect squares and circles. Lucky for you, Photoshop obliges these fussbudget impulses by letting you constrain shapes selected with the Marquee tool.

To select a perfect square, press the Shift key after you begin dragging with the Rectangular Marquee tool. To draw a perfect circle, press Shift after you begin dragging with the Elliptical Marquee tool. For the best results, you should first begin dragging, press and hold Shift, drag to the desired location and release the mouse button, and finally release Shift. In other words, press Shift after you start the drag and hold it until after you complete the drag.

 If you press Shift before dragging, you run the risk of adding to the previously selected area. Here's the deal: If a portion of your image was selected before you started Shift+dragging, Photoshop sees to it that the area remains selected and selects the marqueed area as well. Meanwhile, the shape of the marquee is not constrained to a square or a circle. Befuddling, huh? If this happens to you, press Ctrl+Z (⌘+Z on a Mac) to undo the selection; then try again, taking care to press Shift during — not before — your drag.

Getting even more control over selections

Are you crazed for control? Do your tyrannical desires know no bounds? If so, you probably aren't appeased by drawing a square or a circle. What you want is to apply even more stringent constraints.

Like the Lasso options discussed earlier in "Exploring your Lasso options," the Marquee options I discuss in the following sections sport Anti-aliased and Feather options, which respectively soften the selection outline and make it blurry. However, the Anti-aliased check box is dimmed when you use the Rectangular, Single Column, and Single Row Marquee tools. Perpendicular edges never need softening because perpendicular edges can't be jagged.

The Fixed Aspect Ratio option

Suppose that you're the sort of pixel-oppressor who wants to select a rectangular or oval area that's exactly twice as wide as it is tall. With your Marquee tool selected, choose the Fixed Aspect Ratio option from the Style pop-up menu on the Options bar. The Width and Height text boxes come to life, letting you specify an aspect ratio, which is a precise proportion between the width and height of a marquee. To make the marquee twice as wide as it is tall, enter **2** as the Width value. Then press Tab to highlight the Height value and enter **1**.

The Single Row and Single Column options

You can set up the marquee to select a row or column of pixels that is a single pixel tall or wide. To do this, select the Single Row or Single Column icon from the Marquee flyout menu in the Toolbox. Then click to create the marquee. If you select Single Row, the marquee is 1 pixel tall and extends across the entire width of your image; if you select Single Column, the marquee is 1 pixel wide and as tall as your image. After you click to create the marquee, you can drag it to reposition it if necessary.

The Fixed Size option

To constrain the marquee to an exact size, select the Fixed Size option from the Style pop-up menu. Then enter the exact dimensions of your desired marquee into the Width and Height text boxes.

Wielding the Wand

The Magic Wand tool is easier to use than even the Marquee tools. To use the tool, you just click inside an image. Photoshop then selects the area of continuous color that surrounds the cursor. Sounds great, right? Yeah, it is — with one flaw; it's difficult to predict exactly what the Magic Wand tool will select.

'Scuse me while I click the sky

Figure 7-5 shows how the Magic Wand tool works. In the first image, I clicked with the Magic Wand tool in the sky above the fake Tyrannosaurus

Rex. Photoshop automatically selected the entire continuous area of sky. In the second example, I made the selection more apparent by pressing Ctrl+Backspace (⌘+Delete on a Mac), which filled the selection with the white background color. I also got rid of the selection outline by deselecting the area. (Deselecting is explained in "Deselecting selections.")

Figure 7-5: Look what happens when I click on the sky above the T-Rex with the Magic Wand tool (top) and fill the selection with white (bottom).

Notice that the wand selects only uninterrupted areas of color. The patch of sky below the T-Rex's tail, for example, remains intact. Also, the selection bit slightly into the edges of the dinosaur. Very small pieces along the top of the plastic behemoth were removed when I pressed Ctrl+Backspace (⌘+Delete on a Mac).

Teaching the wand tolerance

You can modify the performance of the Magic Wand tool by accessing the Options bar's four options — Anti-aliased, Contiguous, Use All Layers, and Tolerance.

I discuss the Anti-aliased option earlier in this chapter, in the section "Exploring your Lasso options." The Use All Layers option comes into play only when your image contains more than one layer. (See Chapter 8 for more about layers.) When the Use All Layers option is turned off, the Magic Wand tool selects colors only on the active layer. If you want the wand to select colors from all visible layers, turn the option on.

When the Contiguous option is checked, the Magic Wand tool selects only pixels that are adjacent to each other. If it is deselected, the wand looks throughout the image for any pixels that fall within the Tolerance range.

The Tolerance option has the most sway over the performance of the Magic Wand tool. The Tolerance option tells Photoshop which colors to select and which not to select. A lower Tolerance value instructs the wand to select fewer colors; a higher value instructs it to select more colors.

Extending the Magic Wand

Two Select menu commands, Grow and Similar, are extensions of the Magic Wand tool. The Grow command expands the size of your selection to include still more continuous colors. For example, if clicking with the Magic Wand doesn't select all the colors you want it to, you can increase the Tolerance value on the Options bar and click again with the tool, or you can just choose Select⇨Grow to incorporate even more colors.

The Similar command selects all colors that are similar to the selected colors regardless of whether they're interrupted by other colors. In other words, Similar selects all the continuous colors that Grow selects, as well as all similarly colored pixels throughout the image.

Both Grow and Similar judge color similarity exactly like the Magic Wand tool does — that is, according to the Tolerance value in the Options bar. If you increase the Tolerance value, the commands select more colors; if you decrease the value, the commands select fewer colors. For example, if you want to select all colors throughout the image that are exactly identical to the ones you've selected so far, enter **0** into the Tolerance option box, and choose Select⇨Similar.

Working with Selections

After you create a selection, there are many things you can do to it to make the selection just right for your purposes, including adding to or subtracting from the selection, moving, cloning, feathering, smoothing, transforming, and the list goes on.

Deselecting selections

If you're finished using a selection or change your mind about the area you want selected, you can easily deselect a selection by:

- Clicking inside a selection with any of the selection tools.
- Right-clicking (Control+clicking on a Mac) inside a select with any of the selection tools and choosing Deselect from the context-sensitive menu.
- Press Ctrl+D (⌘+D on a Mac)

Reselecting the last selection

If you deselect a selection and decide you want to use that selection again, just right-click (Control+click on a Mac) on the image (with any tool selected) and choose Reselect. You can also press Ctrl+Shift+D (⌘+Shift+D on a Mac).

Moving a selection

When someone says "move a selection," he or she could mean two things: the person might want to move the selection marquee or the person could want to move the selected area inside the marquee. Here's how to do either of these:

- ✔ To move the selection marquee, choose any selection tool from the Toolbox, position the mouse pointer inside the selection, and then click and drag the selection marquee to its new position.

- ✔ To move the area of an image or layer that is selected, choose the Move tool from the Toolbox, position the mouse pointer inside the selected area, and then click and drag the selected area to its new position.

- ✔ You can move a selection marquee (with or without a selected area) from one image window into another image window.

If you want to move a copy of a selected area instead of the area itself, hold down the Alt key (Option key on a Mac) while dragging with the Move tool. A *clone* of the selected area will move to the new position. To find out more about tools that create clones, turn to Chapter 10.

Swapping the unselected and selected areas

Suppose you want to select a shape that is on a solid color background. Selecting the solid background is easy, all you need to do is to click with the Magic Wand tool, but selecting the shape can be trickier. The easy way to select the shape is to select the background, and then switch to the *inverse* selection which will automatically select the shape. Figure 7-6 shows the original selection and then the inverse selection.

Figure 7-6: Selecting a background with the Magic Wand tool is easy (left). After switching to the inverse selection, the duck is selected (right).

Background is selected.

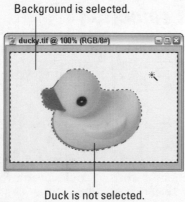

Duck is not selected.

Background is not selected.

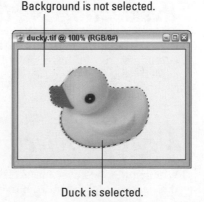

Duck is selected.

✔ Select any of the selection tools, and then right-click (Control+click on a Mac) in the image window and choose Select Inverse from the context-sensitive menu.

✔ Or you can choose Select⇨Inverse or press Ctrl+Shift+I (⌘+Shift+I on a Mac) on the keyboard.

Adding or subtracting from a selection

If you discover you need to add to a selection you already made or subtract from a selection, you can do so quickly using the Options bar or keystrokes.

✔ To add to a selection, choose any of the selection tools from the Toolbox. Click the Add to Selection button on the Options bar and use the selection tool to add to the selection. Alternatively, you can hold down the Shift key while using the selection tool to add to the selection.

✔ To subtract from a selection, choose any of the selection tools from the Toolbox. Click the Subtract from Selection button on the Options bar and use the selection tool to subtract from the selection. Or you can hold down the Alt key (Option key on a Mac) while using the selection tool to remove a portion of the selection.

Intersecting a selection

You also can create a selection from the overlapping areas of two selections. This is called an *intersection*. Here's how:

1. **Create the first selection using the selection tool of your choice.**

2. **Click the Intersect with selection button on the Options bar or hold down Alt+Shift (Option+Shift on a Mac) on the keyboard.**

3. **Using the selection tool of your choice, make a second selection that overlaps the first selection, covering the intersecting selection area that you want to create.**

   After finishing the second selection, if you're holding down the keyboard keys, release them.

   The area where the two selections overlapped becomes the active selection, as shown in Figure 7-7.

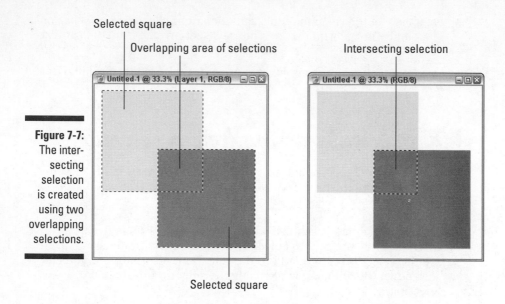

Selected square

Overlapping area of selections

Intersecting selection

Figure 7-7:
The inter-
secting
selection
is created
using two
overlapping
selections.

Selected square

Feathering a selection

Feathering makes the transition from the selection to the surrounding area smoother. With Photoshop, you can feather an existing selection using the Feather command.

To feather a selection, right-click (Control+click on a Mac) in the image window and choose Feather from the context-sensitive menu that appears. (Alternatively, you can choose Select➪Feather.)

In the Feather Selection dialog box, enter a Feather Radius value — the larger the number you enter, the wider the feathered edge will be. Click the OK button to close the dialog box and add the feathering to the selection.

Using the Border command

Adding a border selection can be very handy. For example, say you're creat-ing a vignette from a photograph, or adding an outline. Here's how:

1. **Create a selection using the selection tool of your choice.**

2. **Choose Select➪Modify➪Border.**

   Set the width of the border selection by entering the number of pixels in the Border Selection dialog box.

3. **Click OK.**

Figure 7-8 shows a selection boundary. The areas that are selected and are not selected are labeled.

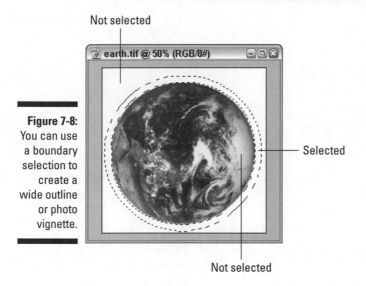

Not selected

earth.tif @ 50% (RGB/8#)

Figure 7-8: You can use a boundary selection to create a wide outline or photo vignette.

Selected

Not selected

Expanding or contracting a selection

Using the Expand command or Contract command, you can enlarge or shrink the entire selection by a set number of pixels.

✓ To enlarge a selection, choose Select➪Modify➪Expand, and then enter a value in pixels in the Expand Selection dialog box. Click OK and the selection will expand the specified number of pixels.

✓ To shrink a selection, choose Select➪Modify➪Contract, and then enter a value in pixels in the Contract Selection dialog box. Click OK and the selection will shrink the number of pixels you specified.

Transforming selections

To transform a selection marquee, choose Select➪Transform Selection. A box with handles and a *center point* (also referred to as an *origin point*) appears, framing your selection marquee, as shown in Figure 7-9.

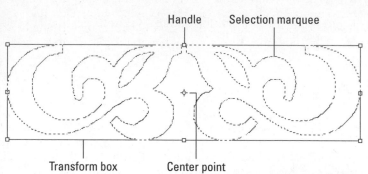

Figure 7-9: Apply transformations to selection marquees without affecting pixels.

Handle   Selection marquee

Transform box   Center point

Using this box you can apply the following transformations:

- **Scale:** Drag any handle to scale your selection. Press Shift+drag to maintain proportions. Press Alt+drag (Option+drag on a Mac) to scale from the center point outward.

  You can move the center point by dragging it.

- **Rotate:** Position the center point where you want the axis for the rotation to be. Drag outside the transform box to rotate the selection. Your cursor appears as a double-headed curved arrow.

- **Skew:** To skew a selection marquee, Ctrl+Alt+drag (⌘+Option+drag on a Mac) a side, top, or bottom handle. Skew permits distortion on a given axis.

- **Distort:** Ctrl+drag (⌘+drag on a Mac) a corner handle. Distort enables handles to move independently with no axis restrictions.

- **Perspective:** Ctrl+Shift+Alt+drag (⌘+Shift+Option+drag on a Mac) a corner handle. The opposite corner handle on the same side moves as well.

- **Flip Horizontal or Vertical:** Right-click (Control+click on a Mac) your image to access the shortcut menu (described and shown in Chapter 2) and choose Flip Horizontal or Flip Vertical.

- **Rotate 180 degrees, 90 degrees CW, and 90 degrees CCW:** To rotate in these predetermined amounts, right-click (Control+click on a Mac) your image to access the shortcut menu, and choose the Rotation value.

- **Numeric:** To make a transformation by entering a numeric value, use the settings in the Options bar. You can move, scale, rotate, or skew via the Options bar. Entering the values applies the transformation.

After you finish transforming, press Enter (Return on a Mac) or double-click inside the transform box or click on the Commit button (the check icon) in the Options bar. To cancel, press Esc or Ctrl+period (⌘+period on a Mac).

You can transform paths and individual layers. A *path* is a temporary outline that you can use to create shapes, selections, and masks. Take a look at Chapter 16 for details about creating paths and transforming them. Turn to Chapter 8 to find out how to select a layer and transform it.

Saving a selection

When you make a complicated selection, chances are that you will want to use it again. You can save any selection you create to a channel. You can use the saved selection again at any time by loading it. For details on loading a channel and using saved selections, turn to Chapter 15.

To save a selection follow these steps:

1. **Choose Select⇨Save Selection.**

   Or right-click in the image window (+click on a Mac).

2. **Choose Save Selection from the context-sensitive menu.**

   The Save Selection dialog box appears.

3. **Type a name that describes the selection in the Name text box, and then click OK.**

To view your saved selection, open the Channels palette and look down the list of channels. You'll find the saved selection at the bottom of the list. (To find out how the Channels palette works and what you can use saved selections for, turn to Chapter 15.)

Chapter 8

Working with Layers

*W*hen you create a new image in Photoshop, it consists of a *Background layer*. You can think of the Background layer as the canvas under a painting. One or more layers can be added on top of the Background layer.

Layers are like clear glass windows stacked one on top of the other. You can draw (or paste an image) on one of the glass windows, then see how the layer blends with those below it using *opacity* and *blending modes*. You can edit an area on one layer without affecting image elements on other layers.

In this chapter, you discover how to use the Layers palette to set the *active layer* and edit layer properties. Also, you find out how to create new and duplicate layers, move layers up and down the stacking order, delete layers, and create layer groups. From there, you learn about advanced layer techniques including setting blending modes, setting layer opacity, and adding adjustment layers.

To see an example of layers in action, turn to Color Plate 8-1 in the color insert. There you'll see an image made up of four layers. The Layers palette is displayed to show how the layers are stacked. In addition, there is a description of how each layer was modified.

Layer Basics

A large number of the manipulations you'll perform in Photoshop involve *layers*. One of the benefits of working with layers is that you can edit a part of an image that is on a layer while the other layers remain unchanged. This is good news because it means that you can protect portions of an image while radically changing parts of the same image.

Each Photoshop image must have at least one layer and can have an almost unlimited number of layers. You select and manipulate layers by using the tools provided in the Layers palette.

Figure 8-1 shows an image with four layers. Each image — the paint and brushes, colored pencils, and crayons — is on its own layer. The fourth layer is the Background. These four layers are shown in the Layers palette. The layers are shown from top to bottom with the Background layer (which is behind the three layers) at the bottom of the list. This is the *stacking order*.

The stacking order is very important because it determines the appearance of a final image. The layer that is at the top of the list in the Layers palette (at the top of the stacking order) appears in front of all the other layers.

To imagine how the stacking order works suppose you have a Photoshop image with two layers. One layer shows a pink rabbit and the other layer is solid black. If the rabbit layer is above (or on top of) the black layer, then you can see the rabbit. On the other hand, if the black layer is above (or on top of) the rabbit layer, then the rabbit will not be visible.

In order to preserve layers in an image, you must save the image file in either the Photoshop PSD or the special Photoshop TIF and PDF formats. Saving the image in any other format will automatically flatten the layers into a single layer. (For more about file formats, turn to Chapter 3.)

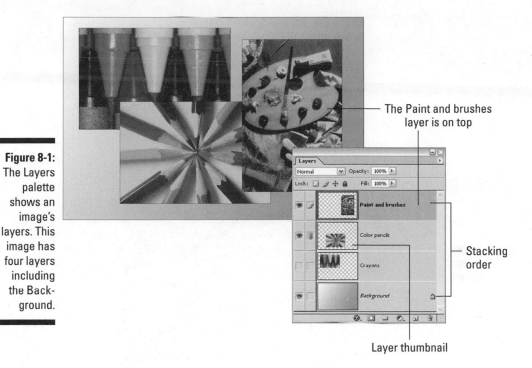

Figure 8-1: The Layers palette shows an image's layers. This image has four layers including the Background.

The Paint and brushes layer is on top

Stacking order

Layer thumbnail

Introducing the Layers Palette

When working with layers, you'll use the Layers palette (Figure 8-2). By default, the Layers palette is grouped with the Channels and Paths palette. You can remove the Layers palette from the group by dragging its tab out of the group window. If the Layers palette is not displayed, you can view it by choosing Window⇨Layers or pressing F7 on the keyboard.

Two of the most important layers in the Layers palette are the active layer and the Background layer. The *active layer* is the layer that is currently selected and being edited. You need to be very clear about which layer is active when you are working on an image. The *Background layer* is a special layer that does not have all the functionality of a regular layer, but has a great deal of impact on the way an image looks and behaves.

The Background layer

The Background layer listed on the layers palette is a special case. It is created automatically by Photoshop in many cases. The Background layer is important because it affects the overall look and behavior of an image. If the Background layer is deleted (or if an image doesn't have a Background layer), then any uncolored areas of the image are transparent.

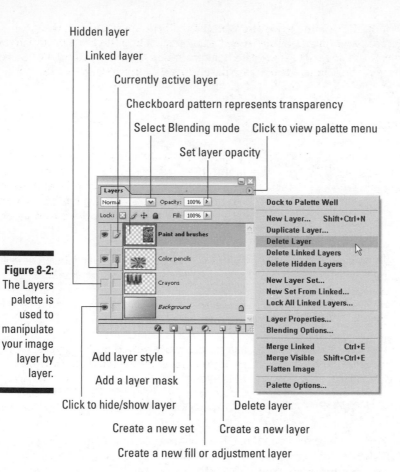

Hidden layer

Linked layer

Currently active layer

Checkboard pattern represents transparency

Select Blending mode   Click to view palette menu

Set layer opacity

Figure 8-2:
The Layers
palette is
used to
manipulate
your image
layer by
layer.

Add layer style

Add a layer mask

Click to hide/show layer   Delete layer

Create a new set   Create a new layer

Create a new fill or adjustment layer

You can paint on the Background, paste to it, fill it with color or a pattern, but that's about it. The things you can usually do to a layer — for instance, moving it up or down in the layer stack, adding opacity and blending modes, and creating a layer mask — cannot be done to the Background. You can, however, convert the Background into a true layer and then edit it as you please. You can also convert a layer into the Background. (To find out more about changing the stacking order see "Moving a layer up and down the stacking order," for setting opacity, see "Setting layer opacity," and for using blending modes, turn to "Using blending modes." Layer masks are discussed in Chapter 15.)

✔ **To convert the Background to a new layer:** either double-click on the Background in the Layers palette or choose Layer⇨New⇨Layer from Background. Type a name for the layer in the New Layer dialog box, and then click OK.

✔ **To convert a layer into the Background:** choose Layer⇨New⇨ Background from Layer. The layer is immediately moved to the bottom of the stack in the Layers palette and is renamed "Background."

If you are creating an image for the Web using Photoshop and you want to include transparent areas in the image, you must delete the Background layer or convert it to a layer (because the Background is always opaque). For more about creating Web images and transparent pixels, turn to Chapter 18.

The active layer

When the Layers palette is open, you'll notice that one of the layers is highlighted (see Figure 8-2). The highlighted layer is the *active layer*. In the image window, the title bar lists which layer is currently selected. Any changes you make using Photoshop tools and filters affect the active layer. Other layers aren't affected. To make a layer active, simply click that layer in the Layers palette.

Don't forget to select the layer you want to work on! If you use a filter or tool and another layer is selected, that layer is the one that will be modified. Always take a look at the Layers palette to make sure the layer you want to use is highlighted. (And, if you make a mistake, you can always undo it by pressing Ctrl+Z (⌘+Z on a Mac) on the keyboard.)

Transparent (uncolored) pixels in a layer are represented in the Layers palette with a checkerboard pattern. If you erase areas on a layer (a layer that isn't the Background layer, that is) you erase to transparency, not to a color. Take a look at Figure 8-1, and compare the image to the layer thumbnails in the Layers palette. The checkerboard pattern in the layer thumbnails shows where the transparent areas of the layer are.

Creating a New Layer

There are two ways to add a new layer to an image. You can create a layer using the default settings (a Normal blending mode and 100% opacity) or create a *custom layer*. (For more about blending modes, turn to "Using blending modes" later in this chapter.)

✔ **To create a new layer with the default settings:** click the Create new layer button at the bottom of the Layers palette (see Figure 8-2 for the button's exact location).

✔ **To create a custom layer:** choose New Layer from the Layers palette menu, press Ctrl+Shift+N (⌘+Shift+N on a Mac), or choose Layer⇨New⇨ Layer. The New Layer dialog box, shown in Figure 8-3, opens. Using this dialog box you can set the layer's name, color code the layer in the Layers palette for identification, set a blending mode, and change the layer's opacity settings. (For more about blending modes and opacity, take a look at "Using blending modes" and "Setting layer opacity" later in this chapter.)

Duplicating a layer

If you want to try out a technique or need a copy on an image element, creating a duplicate layer could help you out. There are three places you can put the duplicate layer: in the current image, in a new image, or in another open image.

- ✔ **To duplicate a layer in the same image window:** In the Layers palette, simply drag the name of the layer you want to copy to the Create new layer button at the bottom of the palette. The duplicate layer appears selected above the original layer in the Layers palette. You can also duplicate a layer by selecting the layer in the Layers palette, then choosing Layer➪New➪Layer via Copy or press Ctrl+J (⌘+J on the Mac).

- ✔ **To place the duplicate layer in a new image window:** In the Layers palette, select the layer you want to copy, and then choose Duplicate Layer from the Palette menu. In the Duplicate Layer dialog box that opens, use the Document drop-down list to select New, and then click OK.

- ✔ **To place the duplicate layer in another image window that's open:** Drag the layer from the Layers palette into the image window where you want to place the duplicate.

Turning a selection into a layer

When creating a layer using a selection, you can either copy the portion of the selected image and paste it to the new layer or cut the selected image area and paste it to the new layer.

- ✔ **To copy the selected area and paste it to the new layer:** Use any of the selection tools to create a selection. Right-click (Control+click on a Mac) in the image window and choose Layer via Copy from the context-sensitive menu.

✔ **To cut the portion of the image that is selected and paste it to a new layer:** Use any of the selection tools to create the selection. Then, right-click (Control+click on a Mac) in the image window and choose Layer via Cut from the context-sensitive menu.

Renaming and hiding layers

If you are working on a complex image with many layers, you might need to rename layers for clarity or hide layers to remove the visual distraction while working on other layers.

✔ **To rename a layer:** In the Layers palette, double-click the layer you want to rename, type a new name in the text box that appears, and then press Enter (Return on a Mac).

✔ **To hide a layer:** in the Layers palette click on the eye icon to the left of the layer you want to hide. When the eye icon disappears, so does the layer. To show the layer again, simply click the blank box where the eye was to make the eye (and, thus, the layer) visible again.

Moving a layer up or down the stacking order

You can change the way layers are stacked, moving them up or down the list in the Layers palette. To move a layer to another position in the stack, in the Layers palette select the layer you want to move, and then drag it up or down the layers list.

As you drag a horizontal line appears in the palette between the layers, as shown in Figure 8-4. This line indicates where the layer would appear in the stack if you released the mouse button. When the line is in the right place, release the mouse button.

The Background layer always remains at the bottom of the stack. If you want to move the Background up, you have to convert it into a layer first. For directions on how to do this, take a look at "The Background" earlier in this chapter.

Moving layers in the image window

In Photoshop, you can move an image in the image window one layer at a time or link several layers and move the linked layers at the same time. To find out how to link layers, turn to "Linking Layers" later in this chapter.

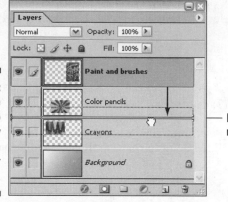

Figure 8-4:
Drag the
layer to
its new
position in
the Layer
palette.

Horizontal line shows
new layer position.

To move a single layer or multiple linked layers:

1. **In the Layers palette, select the layer you want to move.**

   If you want to move several layers at once, use the Layers palette to link
   them together.

 2. **Select the Move Tool from the Toolbox or if any other tool is selected,
   hold down the Ctrl key (⌘ key on a Mac).**

3. **Position the mouse in the image window, press the mouse button, and
   drag the layer(s) to the new position.**

Locking layers

You can quickly lock layers to make sure that they aren't moved or edited by
mistake. You can

- Lock a layer's image
- Lock a layer's position
- Lock transparent pixels on a layer to avoid editing

Figure 8-5 shows the layer locking buttons.

- **To lock a layer's position, but still allow it to be edited:** Select the layer
  in the Layers palette, and then click the Lock position button on the
  Layers palette. To unlock the layer, click the button again.

- **To lock a layer so it can't be edited, but it can be moved:** Select the
  layer in the Layers palette, and then click the Lock image pixels button
  on the Layers palette. To unlock the layer, click the button again.

✔ **To lock layer position and protect it from edits:** Select the layer in the Layers palette, and then click the Lock All button. To unlock the layer, click the button again.

✔ **To lock all transparent pixels on a layer:** Select the layer in the Layers palette, and then click the Lock transparent pixels button. When this lock is selected, you can't lock any of the transparent pixels on the layer. Only colored pixels can be edited or recolored. To unlock the layer, click the button again.

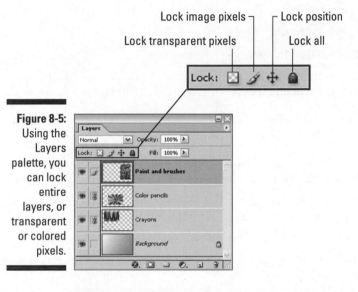

Figure 8-5: Using the Layers palette, you can lock entire layers, or transparent or colored pixels.

Merging and flattening layers

Most file formats don't support multiple layers. If you need to save an image in a format other than native Photoshop PSD, PDF, or TIF file formats, then you must *flatten* the image. When layers are flattened, all the layers in an image are merged together into one layer.

One advantage to a flattened image is that it makes for a smaller file, but once an image is flattened, all the layers are gone. (You can always undo the Flatten Image command or use the History palette to undo the command, but after you've saved a flattened file and closed it, the layers are really gone forever.)

If you decide to flatten an image, save a copy of it first. That way, you'll always have the original layered image on hand if you need it later. (To find out how to save a copy of a file, turn to Chapter 3.)

The Merge Down and Merge Visible commands let you choose specific layers you want to merge together rather than flattening the entire image. If you're finished editing several layers and you want to combine them, merging them together can be useful. Merging reduces the number of layers in an image (and if you have a lot of layers, figuring out which one is which can be difficult) and helps decrease file size.

To flatten all layers:

1. **In the Layers palette, make sure all the layers you want to flatten have eye icons next to them.**

   This icon signifies that all the layers are visible.

2. **Choose Layer⇨Flatten Image.**

   The image is flattened down to the bottommost visible layer. If the image contains any hidden layers, Photoshop deletes those layers when the visible layers are flattened.

To merge two layers into one layer:

1. **In the Layers palette, make sure the two layers you want to merge together are next to each other in the layer stack.**

   If the layers are not next to each other, move one of the layers up or down in the stacking order so the two layers are together.

2. **Select the top layer of the two layers you want to merge together.**

3. **Choose Layer⇨Merge Down or choose Merge Down from the Layer palette menu.**

   The active layer you selected in Step 2 merges down into the layer directly below it.

To merge several layers at once:

1. **In the Layers palette, make sure all the layers you want to merge have eye icons next to them (making them visible).**

2. **Select one of the layers you want to merge together.**

   If one of the layers you are merging is an editable type layer, after the layer is merged you won't be able to change type formatting such as font, style, or size. An *editable type layer* is created when you add text to an image using one of the type tools. For information about creating type and using editable type layers, turn to Chapter 17.

3. **Choose Layer⇨Merge Visible or choose Merge Visible from the Layer Palette menu.**

   The visible layers merge together, but the hidden layers won't be deleted; they are still available in the Layers palette.

Deleting layers

Photoshop, being Photoshop, never gives you just one way to do anything; consequently, there are several ways to delete layers:

✔ **To delete a single layer:** Select it in the Layers palette and drag it to the little trash can at the bottom right of the Layers palette, or choose Delete Layer from the Layers palette menu.

✔ **To delete all hidden layers at the same time:** Choose Delete Hidden Layers from the Layers palette menu or choose Layer⇨Delete⇨Hidden Layers.

✔ **To delete a group of linked layers at the same time:** Choose Delete Linked Layers from the Layers palette menu or choose Layer⇨Delete⇨Linked Layers.

Thankfully, deleting a layer is not a permanent thing in Photoshop CS. If you realize that you didn't mean to delete the layer, simply choose Edit⇨Undo, press Ctrl+Z (⌘+Z) on the keyboard, or select a previous state in the History palette. (Turn to Chapter 14 to find out about the powerful History palette.)

Linking Layers

Being able to link layers is really handy. Linking secures several layers' positions in relation to one another. When layers are linked together, you can move them as a single unit, duplicate them by dragging and dropping the layer unit into another image window, and *transform* them — rotate, skew, scale, and so on — as a unit. (For details on layer transformations, see "Transforming Layers" later in this chapter.)

To link layers, follow these steps:

1. **Open the Layers palette and select one of the layers you want to link.**

2. **Click in the column to the left of the layer you want to link to the selected layer.**

   See Figure 8-6. A tiny chain link appears in the column.

3. **If you want to link more layers, click in the column to the left of each layer you want to link.**

4. **To unlink a layer, just click the chain link to remove it.**

Linked layer

Selected layer is also linked

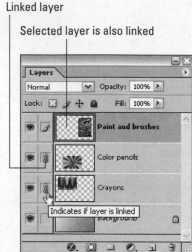

Figure 8-6:
The tiny
chain link
icon
indicates
that a layer
is linked.

Creating Layer Sets

If you create an image that contains many layers, keeping track of them all can be a bit of a headache. With Photoshop you can organize layers into *layer sets*. When layers are arranged into sets, you can display just the layer set name in the Layers palette, or click the arrow next to the layer set name to display all the layers contained within that layer set.

The layers in a layer set are not linked together; they are just organized visually in the Layers palette. To find out how to link layers together, turn to "Linking Layers" earlier in this chapter.

- ✔ **To create a layer set:** Click the Create a new set button at the bottom of the Layers palette, rename the layer set, and then drag the layers you want in the layer set to the set's folder icon. Figure 8-7 shows a layer set containing three layers.

- ✔ **To remove a layer from a layer set:** Simply drag the layer out of the layer set and move it to another position in the Layers palette.

Creating Layer Comps

A powerful new feature of Photoshop CS is the ability to create *layer comps*. A layer comp is like a snapshot of an image's layers that is saved for later. Using layer comps you can save the current settings of an image's layers. These settings allow you to specify the layers' positions in the image window, whether layers are hidden or displayed, opacity settings, and which blending modes are applied to each layer.

Layer set folder

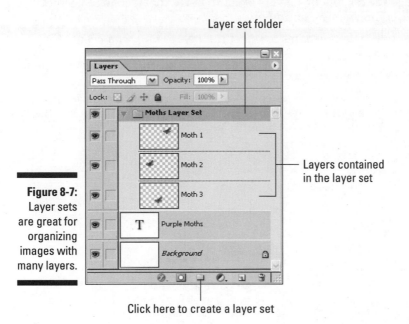

Layers contained in the layer set

Figure 8-7:
Layer sets are great for organizing images with many layers.

Click here to create a layer set

Say you create a layer comp, and then you decide to change something about a document's layers — for instance, you change a few blending modes, and move a few layers around. If you don't like what you've done, you can return to the layers' previous positions and settings by selecting the layer comp you created.

Seeing is believing. After you discover the awesome power of layer comps you'll never want to give them up. Here's how to use them:

1. **Open an image with several layers, position the layers as you will, change blending modes, set layer opacity, and set whether layers are hidden or displayed.**

2. **Choose Window⇨Layer Comps.**

   The New Layer Comps palette, shown in Figure 8-8, appears.

   You also can find the Layer Comps palette docked in the Palette Well on the Options bar (this is its default location).

3. **Click the Create New Layer Comp button on the Layer Comps palette or choose New Layer Comp from the palette menu.**

   The New Layer Comp dialog box opens.

4. **Enter a name for the layer comp and set whether to save the layers' visibility, position, and appearance. Then click OK.**

5. **Change the document's layers around, move them, change visibility and blending modes, and so on.**

6. **In the Layer Comps palette, select the layer comp you created in Steps 3 and 4.**

   Your image's layers return to their previous states.

   You can create several layer comps and cycle through them, viewing your image in various layer states by clicking the arrow buttons at the bottom of the Layer Comps palette.

Figure 8-8:
The new Layer Comps palette lets you take snapshots of layers' settings and positions in the image window.

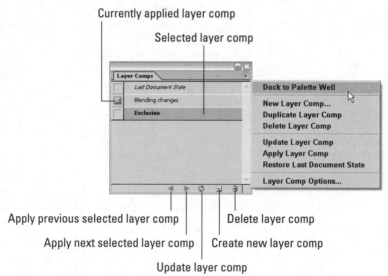

Currently applied layer comp

Selected layer comp

Apply previous selected layer comp

Apply next selected layer comp

Update layer comp

Delete layer comp

Create new layer comp

✔ **To cycle through layer comps:** In the Layer Comps palette, hold down the Shift key and select the layer comps you want to apply. Next, click either the Apply Previous Selected Layer Comp or the Apply Next Selected Layer Comp button. Keep clicking either button to apply the different layer comps you have created in your document.

✔ **To update a layer comp to the layers' current state:** Click the Update Layer Comp button on the Layer Comps palette.

Transforming Layers

Using commands or the mouse, you can flip layers horizontally or vertically and rotate layers around an axis. In addition, you can perform even wilder transformations such as skewing, distorting, and adding perspective to layers.

Transforming layers can come in handy. For instance, if you have a photo where two people are not facing each other, but you want them to look at each other, you could cut and paste each person to an individual layer and flip each layer horizontally. Or suppose you've created an image of a building and you want to make it look very, very tall. Just add perspective to the building and suddenly it looks like a skyscraper.

Using the Flip and Rotate commands

Using the Flip and Rotate commands quickly gets layers spinning and looking like mirror images of themselves. With these commands, you can flip a layer vertically or horizontally, or rotate layers 90 degrees clockwise or counterclockwise or 180 degrees.

To flip or rotate a layer, select the layer in the Layers palette; then choose Edit⇨Transform and choose the Flip or Rotate command you want to use from the Transform submenu.

You can flip and rotate several layers at the same time if you link them. Take a look at "Linking Layers" earlier in this chapter.

Creating transformations using the mouse

You can transform layers with a few drags of the mouse. For example, you can scale, rotate, skew, distort, and change a layer's perspective. Open an image and give it a try. It's really fun to pull and push a layer around, changing its shape.

To scale, rotate, skew, distort, or change a layer's perspective:

1. **Select the layer you want to transform using the Layers palette.**

2. **Choose Edit⇨Transform and choose either Scale, Rotate, Skew, Distort, or Perspective from the submenu.**

    A gray bounding box appears around the opaque part of the layer, as shown in Figure 8-9.

3. **Drag the bounding box lines or tiny square handles to transform the layer in the manner you selected in Step 2.**

    • **Scale:** To scale a layer horizontally and vertically, drag one of the corner handles. To scale a layer only horizontally or vertically, drag one of the side handles.

- **Rotate:** To rotate a layer, drag the bounding box in a circular direction. To hold the rotation to 15-degree increments, hold down the Shift key while you drag.

- **Skew:** To skew the layer, drag a handle vertically or horizontally.

- **Distort:** To distort a layer, drag any of the handles in any direction.

- **Perspective:** To change a layer's perspective, drag one of the corner handles vertically or horizontally, then drag one of the side handles to change the vertical or horizontal perspective.

Bounding box   Handles

Figure 8-9:
Drag the bounding box lines or tiny square handles to transform a layer.

 4. **When you're finished, click the Commit transform button on the Options bar or press Enter (Return on a Mac).**

 If you decide you don't like the transformation, click the Cancel button on the Options bar or press Esc on the keyboard.

 If you want to transform several layers at the same time, link the layers together as described in "Linking Layers" earlier in this chapter. You also can transform a selection by choosing Select⇨Transform Selection. To find out how to create a selection and transform it, turn to Chapter 7.

Figure 8-10 shows the various types of transformation.

Advanced Layer Techniques

This section takes you through some of Photoshop's advanced layer techniques such as setting layer opacity, using blending modes, adding adjustment and fill layers, and creating special layer style effects such as drop shadows, glows, bevels, and overlays.

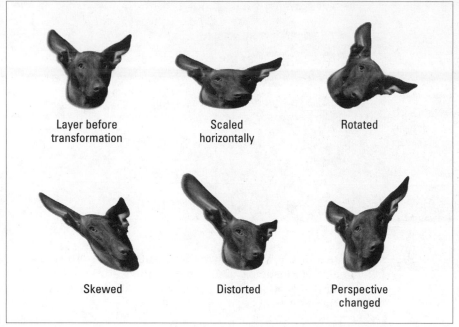

Layer before
transformation

Scaled
horizontally

Rotated

Skewed

Distorted

Perspective
changed

Figure 8-10:
Using the
mouse,
you can
transform a
layer in
many ways.

Setting layer opacity

When working with a layered image, you may want to create a special effect by making one or more layers semi-transparent. Creating transparent and semi-transparent layers lets the layers below show through. The lower the opacity setting in the Layers palette, the more transparent the layer is.

To set the opacity for a layer, select the layer in the Layers palette, and then use the Opacity or Fill slider bars to set a layer's transparency (see Figure 8-11). The Opacity slider sets transparency for the entire layer, affecting blending modes and any layer styles, whereas the Fill slider affects only painted pixels or shapes drawn on the layer.

Using blending modes

Blending modes work with layer transparency. A blending mode is used to specify the way a layer's pixels blend with the layer(s) below it. You also can use blending modes to modify the way the brush tools, the Bucket tool, Clone Stamp, Pattern Stamp, or Gradient tool apply color to a layer. Some of the blending modes are quite subtle, only changing a few colors or shifting hues, while others produce dramatic effects.

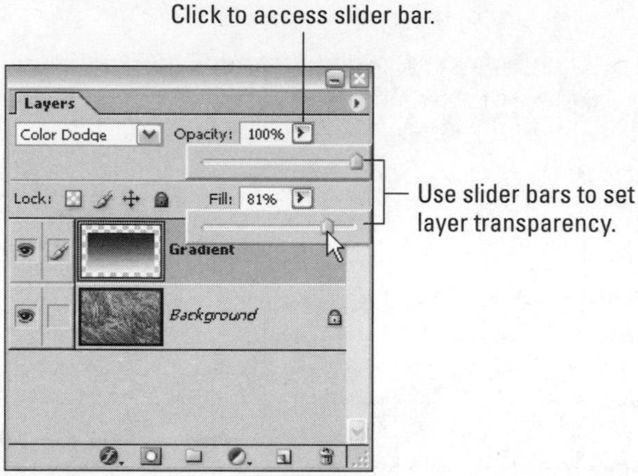

Click to access slider bar.

Figure 8-11:
Use the
Opacity or
Fill slider
bars to set
layer trans-
parency.

Use slider bars to set
layer transparency.

Most of the blending modes work by changing either the dark or light pixels
in an image. For instance, setting the blending mode to Multiply only affects
the darker pixels on the layer below, making the layer darker; the lighter
pixels remain unchanged.

These blending modes are available using the Blending Mode drop-down list
on the Layers palette or the Options bar with any of the brush tools, the
Bucket tool, Clone Stamp, Pattern Stamp, or Gradient tool selected. If you
take a look at the Blending Mode drop-down list on the Layers palette (see
Figure 8-12), you'll notice that the list is divided into groups. The blending
modes are grouped by how they change a layer's pixels — whether the
darken, lighten, both darken and lighten, invert dark and light pixels, or
enhance saturation and brightness.

Color Plates 8-4 and 8-5 give you a sampling of just a few of the effects you
can produce with blending modes.

Adding adjustment layers

An *adjustment layer* is a special kind of layer that lets you try different effects
on an image without permanently changing the image.

Adjustment layers use the same adjustment commands found on the Image➪
Adjustments submenu. Although the commands from the Adjustments submenu affect only the selected layer, an adjustment command applied using an
adjustment layer affects an entire image (not just one layer). This feature can
come in handy, for instance, if you need to color correct an entire image with
many layers. You can create the correction on an adjustment layer instead of
having to correct each layer separately.

Lightens pixels

Darkens pixels

Default blending mode (does not change pixels)

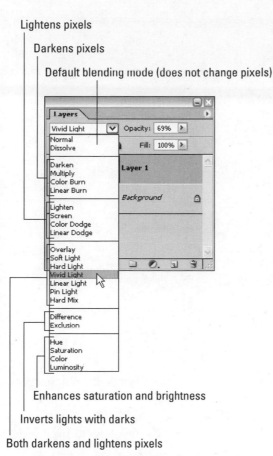

Figure 8-12:
Blending
modes are
grouped on
the drop-
down list
by how
they affect
a layer's
pixels.

Enhances saturation and brightness

Inverts lights with darks

Both darkens and lightens pixels

To see adjustment layers in action, take a look at Color Plate 8-2. There you'll see how an adjustment layer can change the saturation, curves, or hue of a layer containing sock monkeys.

 If you like an adjustment layer you create and want to add it to another image, simply drag the adjustment layer from the Layers palette into the new image window. The adjustment layer is automatically added to that image's layers.

To add an adjustment layer:

1. **In the Layers palette, select the layer that you want the adjustment layer to appear above.**

 2. **Click the Create new fill or adjustment layer button at the bottom of the Layers palette.**

   Choose one of the adjustment commands from the menu that appears, as shown in Figure 8-13. (I discuss the adjustment commands and what they do in detail in Chapter 9.)

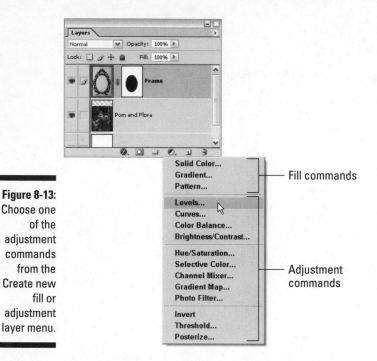

Fill commands

Adjustment commands

Figure 8-13:
Choose one of the adjustment commands from the Create new fill or adjustment layer menu.

3. In the dialog box that appears make the desired adjustments and then click OK.

For instance, if you chose the Levels command from the menu, the Levels dialog box appears. Adjust the levels as desired using the dialog box and click OK.

The new adjustment layer you created appears above the selected layer (Figure 8-14), and the image changes depending upon the type of adjustment you made.

If you don't like the effect that the adjustment layer makes on the image, you can either modify the adjustment layer or just throw it away.

✔ **To modify an adjustment layer:** Double-click the adjustment layer's thumbnail to open the adjustment dialog box. Make the changes you want and click OK.

✔ **To delete an adjustment layer:** In the Layers palette, click the adjustment layer to select it and then drag it to the trash can icon at the bottom of the palette.

You also can select a blending mode and opacity for an adjustment layer. To choose a blending mode, select the adjustment layer in the Layers palette, then use the Blending Mode drop-down list to select the blending mode. To change the opacity, select the adjustment layer and then use the Opacity slider bar.

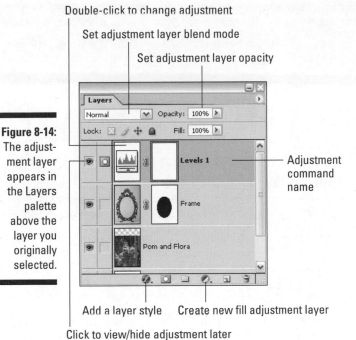

Double-click to change adjustment

Set adjustment layer blend mode

Set adjustment layer opacity

Figure 8-14:
The adjust-
ment layer
appears in
the Layers
palette
above the
layer you
originally
selected.

Adjustment
command
name

Add a layer style   Create new fill adjustment layer

Click to view/hide adjustment later

You can add as many adjustment layers to an image as you want. If you want
to compare different kinds of adjustments, create the adjustment layers, and
then hide each adjustment layer in the Layers palette by clicking the eye icon.
Make the adjustment layers visible one-by-one to check out their affects.

Creating Fill layers

A *fill layer* is similar to an adjustment layer in that it affects an entire image.
Instead of using an adjustment command, though, a fill layer contains a solid
color, pattern, or gradient. And, just like an adjustment layer, a fill layer can
be changed or removed without affecting any other layers.

You'll be surprised at the effects you can quickly create. Here's how to add a
fill layer:

1. **In the Layers palette, select the layer that you want the adjustment
   layer to appear above.**

2. **Click the Create new fill or adjustment layer button at the bottom of
   the Layers palette.**

   Choose one of the fill commands from the menu that appears, as shown
   in Figure 8-13. (The fill commands and what they do are discussed in
   detail in Chapter 12.)

3. **In the dialog box that appears, select the desired fill, gradient, or pattern (depending upon the fill command you chose), and then click OK.**

   For instance, if you chose the Pattern command from the menu, the Pattern fill dialog box appears. Select a pattern and then click OK.

   The new adjustment layer you created appears above the selected layer.

If you don't like the way the fill layer changes your image, you can adjust the fill layer by double-clicking the layer thumbnail in the Layers palette and making changes. Or, you can delete the fill layer entirely by dragging it to the trash can icon in the Layers palette.

You can select a blending mode and opacity for a fill layer. To do so, choose a blending mode, select the fill layer in the Layers palette, and use the Blending Mode drop-down list to select the blending mode. To change the opacity, select the fill layer and then use the Opacity slider bar.

Adding Layer Styles for Amazing Effects

Using layer styles you can quickly add stunning effects to your images. You can apply layer styles to regular layers and editable type layers, but not to the Background. (Editable type layers are discussed in Chapter 17. Take a look at "The Background layer" earlier in this chapter for more information about the special Background layer.)

To see some of the layer styles in color, turn to Color Plate 8-3. There you'll see how layer styles can create amazing effects from simple shadows to complete color changes.

Nine of the ten layer styles are shown in Figure 8-15. (The tenth layer style, Color Overlay, only shows up in color.) Table 8-1 offers a brief description of what each layer style does.

Table 8-1	Layer Styles and Effects
Layer Style	*Does*
Drop Shadow	Adds a soft shadow behind the elements on the layer.
Inner Shadow	Adds the shadow to the layer element itself. For instance, if you are adding an inner shadow to a type layer, the shadow appears inside the letters.
Outer Glow	Adds a glow or halo effect around a layer element.
Inner Glow	Adds a halo effect inside the layer element.

Layer Style	Does
Bevel and Emboss	Creates a 3D raised or lowered edge around the outside or inside edge of a layer element.
Satin	Adds a shiny finish to the layer elements by shading the shapes in the layers.
Color Overlay	Adds a color "film" to the layer elements, changing their hue. For instance, you could add a color overlay to a layer showing a blue car and quickly turn the car red.
Gradient Overlay	Creates a color and transparency gradient effect. Using this layer style you can make layer elements fade in or out.
Pattern Overlay	Adds patterns to layer elements. For instance, you could add a bubble pattern as an overlay to the word "bubble," making the type look like it has bubbles on it.
Stroke	Creates a stroke or line around layer elements.

All of the layer effects are applied and edited using the Layer Style dialog box shown in Figure 8-16. Each effect has uses different options such as angle, speed, and noise. The dialog box changes depending upon the layer style you select.

Here are basic directions for adding a layer style to a layer. Open an image, select a layer, and try these fantastic styles on for size. You'll be amazed at the quick results:

1. **In the Layers palette, select the layer to which you want to add the layer style.**

2. **Click the Add a layer style button at the bottom of the Layers palette and choose a layer style.**

   The Layer Style dialog box shown in Figure 8-16 opens with the layer style you chose selected. If you decide you want to use another layer effect or add a second layer effect, just put a check in that layer style's check box, and then click the name of the layer style to select it.

3. **Use the options in the Layer Style dialog box to select settings for the type of layer style you chose:**

   • **For Drop Shadow:** Select a blending mode and opacity, the angle of the shadow, its distance from the layer element, how far the shadow spreads, and its size.

   • **For Inner Shadow:** Select a blending mode and opacity, the angle of the shadow, its distance from the layer element, how far the shadow spreads, and its size.

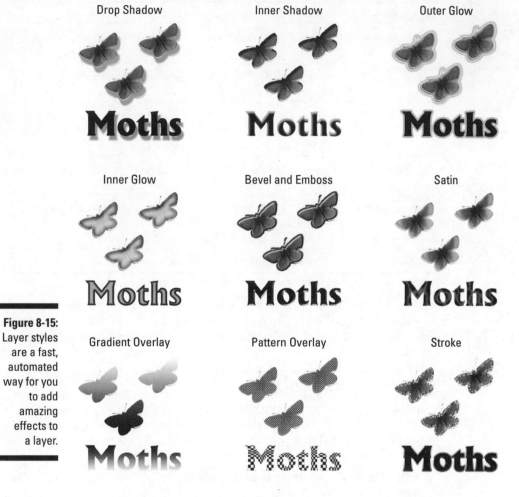

Figure 8-15: Layer styles are a fast, automated way for you to add amazing effects to a layer.

- **For Outer Glow:** Set the glow's color, spread from the edge of the layer element, and the glow's size.

- **For Inner Glow:** Set the glow's color, spread from the inner edge of the layer element, and the glow's size.

- **For Bevel and Emboss:** Set whether it is an outer bevel, inner bevel, emboss, pillow emboss, or stroke emboss. Then set whether the bevel or emboss has a hard or soft edge, whether it is going up or down, and its size. Next, set the bevel or emboss angle, its shading and highlights, and shade and highlight colors.

- **For Satin:** Select a blending mode and opacity, the angle, distance and size of the satin effect from the edge of the layer element.

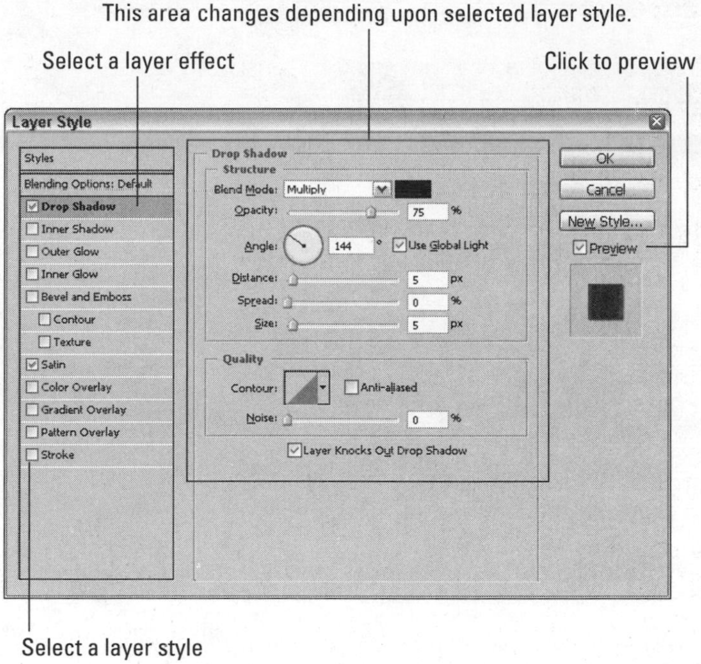

This area changes depending upon selected layer style.

Select a layer effect

Click to preview

Figure 8-16:
Use the
Layer Style
dialog box
to select a
layer effect
and choose
settings.

Select a layer style

- **For Color Overlay:** Choose the overlay color, opacity, and blending mode.

- **For Gradient Overlay:** Select a blending mode and opacity, the gradient style, gradient angle, and scale of the gradient blend.

- **For Pattern Overlay:** Select a blending mode and opacity, the pattern, and set the size of the pattern using the Scale slider bar.

- **For Stroke:** Set the width of the stroke using the Size slider bar, the stroke's position on the edge of the layer element, a blending mode, and an opacity. Next, select whether the stroke will be filled with a color, pattern, or gradient.

4. **When you are finished adding layer styles, click OK.**

The Layer Style dialog box closes and a layer effects list appears below the layer you selected in the Layers palette as shown in Figure 8-17.

You can add more than one layer style to a layer. Try out several effects and see what happens!

After a layer effect is applied to a layer you can modify it or even copy it to another layer. Also, if you decide that you don't like a layer effect, you can remove it entirely.

View the layer effects applied to that layer

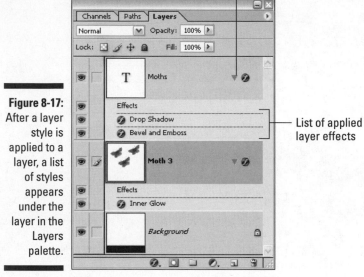

Figure 8-17:
After a layer
style is
applied to a
layer, a list
of styles
appears
under the
layer in the
Layers
palette.

List of applied
layer effects

✔ **To modify an existing layer effect:** Double-click the layer effect's name in the Layers palette. The Layer Style dialog box opens, letting you make changes to the current layer style settings.

✔ **To copy a layer effect to another layer:** Select the layer containing the layer style(s) you want to copy, right-click (Control+click on a Mac), and then choose Copy Layer Style from the context-sensitive menu. Next, select the layer where you want to paste the layer style, right-click (Control+click on a Mac), and then choose Paste Layer Style from the context-sensitive menu.

✔ **To delete a single layer effect:** In the Layers palette click the layer effect's name to select it and then drag the layer effect to the trash can icon.

✔ **To delete all layer effects from a layer:** Right-click (Control+click on a Mac) the layer and then choose Clear Layer Style from the context-sensitive menu.

Part IV
Basic Editing

The 5th Wave By Rich Tennant

"Mary Jo, come here quick! Look at this special effect I learned with Photoshop CS."

In this part . . .

*A*fter scanning a photograph and opening it in Photoshop, you may discover (to your shock) that the scanned image doesn't look anything like the original photo. That's where color correction comes in. Many images require color correction before they are perfect. In a photographic darkroom, color correction used to be a laborious and time consuming process, but Photoshop offers many simple, sublime ways to correct the color in your images. Chapter 9 explains how to use the color correction features that Photoshop has to offer.

Copying and cloning are among the most powerful image manipulation techniques available in Photoshop. Chapter 10 shows you how to effectively copy and paste image selections within the same image or into another image. You'll find out how to duplicate an image to keep the original safe if you want to try out a new technique. And, you'll discover the fun of creating clones, using the Clone Stamp tool, and covering everything with custom patterns using the Pattern Stamp tool. From there, you'll use the Patch tool to quickly fix larger flaws in an image and use the Healing Brush tool to clone areas while simultaneously blending color and texture.

One of the fastest ways to transform a mundane original into a spectacular Photoshop image is to use one of almost 100 Photoshop filters (you can even apply more than one filter if you wish). Chapter 11 explains the basics of how filters work and shows you how to use the new Photoshop cs Filter Gallery.

Chapter 9

Adjusting Color and Tone

• •

In This Chapter

▶ Using Auto Level, Auto Contrast, and Auto Color

▶ Setting Levels

▶ Adding color balance

▶ Correcting color using Variations

▶ Replacing color

▶ Adjusting brightness and contrast

▶ Inverting, saturating, and equalizing an image

▶ Using the new Shadow/Highlight command

▶ Using the Dodge and Burn tools

▶ Saturating and desaturating with the Sponge tool

• •

*E*ventually, you will come across an image — be it a photograph, scanned image, or image from another source such as a digital camera — that needs to be adjusted. Photoshop CS offers many color correction tools to enhance and adjust the color and tone of an image. All of these tools work in basically the same way — by determining the existing range of pixel values in an image and replacing them with a new range of values. The main difference between the color correction tools is the amount of control you have over the range of values.

This chapter takes you through using Photoshop's color correction tools, from the most sophisticated ones that give the greatest control (such as Levels) to those that give the least control (such as Threshold, Desaturate, and Posterize). The Levels tools let you make exact adjustments to a layer's highlights, midtones, and shadows using the lightest and darkest pixels in each individual channel. The simpler tools make adjustments using the combined values of all channels.

All of the commands in this chapter can be applied to a selected area of a layer, an entire layer, or as an adjustment layer (all of which I discuss in Chapter 8). The more complex tools let you see a preview of an adjustment so that you can decide whether the change is what you want before you make a commitment.

Automatic Color Enhancements

These three commands — Auto Levels, Auto Contrast, and Auto Color —
automatically enhance an image's color and contrast using light and dark
pixels. These commands work quite well with a minimum of fuss. If you find an
image needs a little help, these three commands may be all you'll ever need.

Auto Levels

Auto Levels automatically enhances highlights and shadows by replacing the
darkest pixels with black pixels and lightest pixels with white pixels. Auto
Levels then redistributes the other pixel values in the image proportionately,
making an image appear brighter and less murky.

To see an example of the difference Auto Levels can make, take a look at Color
Plate 9-5. The image at the bottom right shows Auto Levels applied to an image
that is rather dark and murky looking, making it brighter and more vibrant.

To apply Auto Levels to a layer or selected area:

1. **Use the Layers palette to select a layer or the Background.**

   Figure 9-1 shows an image before the Auto Levels command is applied.

Figure 9-1:
This
scanned
image has a
gray cast
that needs
correcting.

2. **If you want to apply Auto Levels to only part of a layer, use the selection tool of your choice to select an area of the image.**

   For directions on how to use the selection tools, turn to Chapter 7.

3. **Choose Image➪Adjustments➪Auto Levels.**

   Figure 9-2 shows the image from Figure 9-1 after Auto Levels have been applied.

Figure 9-2:
After applying Auto Levels, the high-lights and shadows really stand out.

Auto Contrast

Auto Contrast automatically adjusts the contrast by replacing the darkest pixels with black pixels and lightest pixels in the image with white ones. As a result, shadows appear darker and highlights are lighter. Unlike Auto Levels, Auto Contrast does not change the way other colors look, it only affects the overall contrast of an image.

To apply Auto Contrast to a layer or selected area:

1. **Use the Layers palette to select a layer or the Background.**

2. **If you want to use Auto Contrast on only part of the layer, use the selection tool of your choice to select an area of the image.**

3. **Choose Image⇨Adjustments⇨Auto Contrast.**

   Figure 9-3 shows the image from Figure 9-1 after Auto Contrast has been applied.

Figure 9-3: After applying Auto Contrast to the image, the lights and darks are much more pronounced.

Auto Color

Auto Color adjusts the shadows, *midtones* (the middle range of colors in an image), and highlights of an image. Auto Color *samples* the image and evens out the midtone colors while enhancing the light and dark areas.

Any bright image that appears overexposed (where the colors look washed out) would benefit from the Auto Color command. Darks are enhanced, the extra brightness is toned down, and colors become clearer and more saturated.

To apply Auto Color to a layer or selected area:

1. **Use the Layers palette to select a layer or the Background.**

2. **Use the selection tool of your choice to select part of the image or layer if you don't want to use Auto Color on the whole image.**

   For directions on how to use the selection tools, turn to Chapter 7.

3. **Choose Image⇨Adjustments⇨Auto Color.**

Figure 9-4 shows the image from Figure 9-1 after Auto Contrast has been applied.

Figure 9-4:
When Auto Color is applied, the entire image becomes brighter and colors are more saturated.

Levels

Levels are used to make exact adjustments to the tonal range of a layer or selection. Levels precisely adjust highlights, midtones, and shadows using a *histogram*. A histogram is a graph that shows the number of pixels at each level of brightness in a layer or selection.

Take a look at Color Plate 9-5 to see Levels in action. The figures in the color plate show histogram levels and how changing the tonal ranges affect the image. Compare how manually changing levels differs from the change made by the Auto Levels command.

To adjust color and tone using Levels:

1. **Use the Layers palette to select a layer or the Background.**

You also can set levels using an adjustment layer. To do this, click the Create new fill or adjustment layer button at the bottom of the Layers palette and choose Levels from the menu. If you create an adjustment layer, skip to Step 4. (To find out more about adjustment layers, turn to Chapter 8.)

2. **If you want to use Levels on only part of the layer or selection, use the selection tool of your choice.**

   For directions on how to use the selection tools, turn to Chapter 7.

3. **Choose Image⇨Adjustments⇨Levels.**

   Using the Levels dialog box shown in Figure 9-5, you can make exact adjustments to the shadows, midtones, and highlights.

Input midtones slider

Input shadows slider   Input highlights slider

Figure 9-5: The Levels dialog box lets you set highlights, midtones, and shadows using input and output sliders.

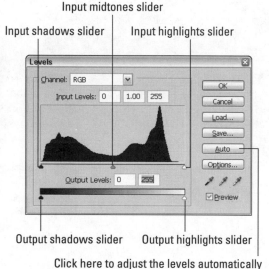

Output shadows slider   Output highlights slider

Click here to adjust the levels automatically

4. **Make sure the Preview check box is checked.**

5. **If you're a first-time user, leave RGB selected in the Channel drop-down list.**

   If you've never used the Levels dialog box before, leave the Channel drop-down list set to RGB so that you can experiment with setting the levels for all the channels at the same time. After you have used the Levels dialog box and understand how it works, then try experimenting with setting each channel individually.

6. **Use the various sliders shown in Figure 9-5 to adjust the shadows, midtones, and highlights.**

   To brighten highlights and increase contrast, move the Input highlights slider to the left.

   To adjust the midtones lighter or darker, move the Input midtones slider left or right, respectively.

   To darken shadows, move the Input shadows slider to the right.

To lighten the image and decrease contrast, move the Output shadows slider to the right.

To darken the image and decrease the contrast, move the Output highlights slider to the left.

As you move the sliders, watch the image to see the changes you are making.

7. **When you're finished adjusting the levels, click OK.**

If you don't like the levels changes you've made, click the Cancel button.

Color Balance

When adjusting individual color elements in an image, it's important to remember that each color adjustment affects the overall color balance of an image. The Color Balance command is used to change and enhance the way colors are mixed in an image. This tool uses a generalized color correction, creating subtle changes in color.

To adjust color balance:

1. **Use the Layers palette to select a layer or the Background.**

   You also can set color balance using an adjustment layer. To do this, click the Create New Fill or Adjustment Layer button at the bottom of the Layers palette and choose Color Balance from the menu. If you create an adjustment layer, skip to Step 4. (To find out more about adjustment layers, turn to Chapter 8.)

2. **You can use the selection tool of your choice to select an area of the image if you want to use Color Balance on only part of a layer.**

   For directions on how to use the selection tools, turn to Chapter 7.

3. **Choose Image⇨Adjustments⇨Color Balance.**

   Using the Color Balance dialog box shown in Figure 9-6, you can make adjustments to an image's color mixture.

4. **Make sure the Preview check box is checked.**

5. **Use the channel sliders to adjust the color balance.**

   In Figure 9-7, notice that there is a slider for each channel. The channel name — Red, Green, or Blue — is listed at the right side of the slider. Each channel's complementary color is listed at the left side of the slider.

6. **When you are finished adjusting the color balance, click OK.**

Complementary colors

Figure 9-6:
The Color
Balance
dialog box
lets you
make pre-
cise correc-
tions and
interesting
color
mixtures.

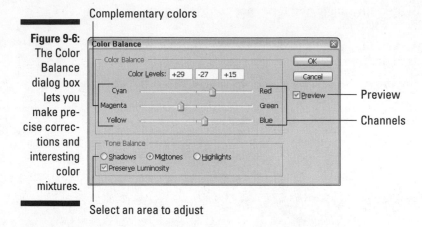

Preview

Channels

Select an area to adjust

Using Variations to Make Color Corrections

The Variations dialog box is an excellent tool for quickly correcting color in an image. Using thumbnails, the Variations dialog box shows how an image would look with various color corrections applied.

To open the Variations dialog box, choose Image⇨Adjustments⇨Variations. As shown in Figure 9-7, the dialog box shows the original image and current pick at the top, and various color corrections from more green, more yellow, and more magenta to lighter and darker.

✓ **To use Variations:** Select the tonal range to be adjusted — shadows, midtones, highlights, or saturation. Move the Fine/Coarse slider to set the amount of the adjustment. Click any of the More thumbnails (such as More Cyan) to increase the amount of a particular color in the layer. When you're finished, click OK.

✓ **To change the brightness of the image:** Click Lighter or Darker at the right side of the Variations dialog box.

After you adjust one tonal range, you can change another: Make all the adjustments you need.

Color Plate 9-6 shows how Variations can dramatically change the color and saturation in an image. The peacock was looking rather drab, so various colors were first used to find the right hue. Yellow looked best, so Cyan was added to brighten the peacock's feathers. Finally the Saturation radio button was selected and increased to make the peacock's body appear more vibrant.

Click a thumbnail to add more color   Use slider to set intensity of changes

Select an area to adjust   Click this thumbnail to lighten

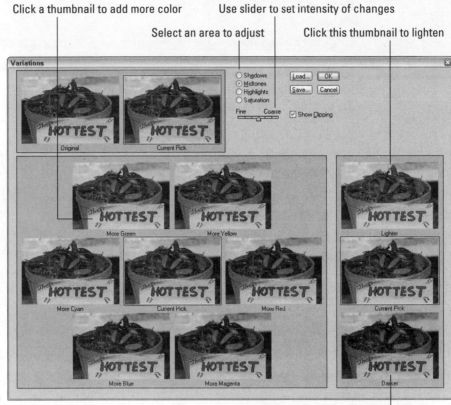

Figure 9-7:
The Variations dialog box thumbnails let you view several color corrections at the same time.

Click this thumbnail to darken

Replace Color

The Replace Color command replaces a sampled color from the image with another color. The Replace Color commands can be applied to selections or an entire layer.

Color Plate 9-3 shows how the Replace Color command can quickly change an image. First, the basket containing the red peppers and the sign were selected. Then, using the Replace Color dialog box, the red was sampled and replaced first with blue, then yellow.

To use the Replace Color command:

1. **Use the Layers palette to select a layer or the Background.**

2. **If you wish, use the selection tool of your choice to select an area of the image.**

   For directions on how to use the selection tools, turn to Chapter 7.

3. **Choose Image➪Adjustments➪Replace Color.**

   Using the Replace Color dialog box shown in Figure 9-8, you can quickly select a color from your image and change it using the Replacement slider bars.

4. **Make sure the Preview check box is checked.**

5. **In the Selection area click the Eyedropper button, then move the mouse to the image, and click to select a color from the image.**

   The color you sampled appears in the Color box at the top of the Replace Color dialog box.

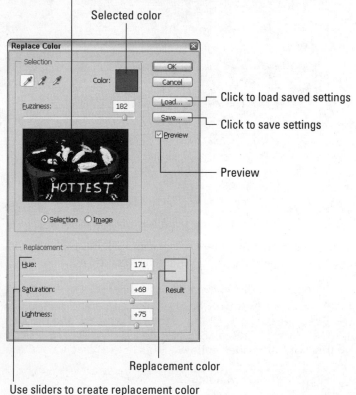

Preview pane (white indicates selected areas)

Selected color

Click to load saved settings

Click to save settings

Preview

Figure 9-8:
The Replace Color dialog box lets you quickly change a sampled color in an image.

Replacement color

Use sliders to create replacement color

The preview pane shows the selected areas in white and the unselected areas in black. To select more colors in the image, move the Fuzziness slider to the right. To select fewer colors, move the Fuzziness slider to the left.

6. **In the Replacement area, use the Hue slider to substitute another color, and then use the Saturation and Lightness sliders to set the tone of the color (bright or dark) and the overall brightness of the replacement color.**

   The resulting color appears in the Result color box and is previewed in the image window.

7. **Click OK.**

Brightness and Contrast

Like Levels, the Brightness/Contrast command adjusts the highlights, midtones, and shadows in an image, but in a simpler way. Instead of making adjustments channel by channel, Brightness/Contrast makes changes using all the pixel values in an image at the same time.

To adjust brightness and contrast:

1. **Use the Layers palette to select a layer or the Background.**

   You also can set brightness and contrast using an adjustment layer. To do this, click the Create new fill or adjustment layer button at the bottom of the Layers palette and choose Brightness/Contrast from the menu. If you create an adjustment layer, skip to Step 4. (To find out more about adjustment layers, turn to Chapter 8.)

2. **Use the selection tool of your choice to select an area of the image if you want to use this command on part (but not all) of a layer.**

   For directions on how to use the selection tools, turn to Chapter 7.

3. **Choose Image⇨Adjustments⇨Brightness/Contrast.**

   Using the Brightness/Contrast dialog box shown in Figure 9-9, you can quickly make adjustments.

4. **Make sure the Preview check box is checked.**

5. **Use the Brightness and Contrast sliders to adjust the image.**

6. **When you are finished adjusting the brightness and contrast, click OK.**

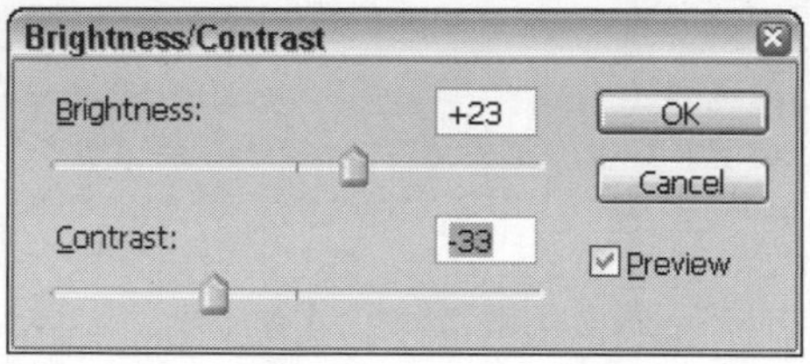

Figure 9-9:
The
Brightness/
Contrast
dialog box
lets you
quickly
adjust the
brightness
and
contrast.

Brightness/Contrast	✕
Brightness: +23	OK
	Cancel
Contrast: -33	☑ Preview

Making Specialized Adjustments

There are several other commands that also change the brightness values and colors in an image. These include Invert, Equalize, Desaturate, Posterize, Threshold, Gradient Map, and the new Shadow/Highlight command. In many cases, these specialized commands create dramatic effects that can be applied to entire layers or selected areas, or applied as adjustment layers.

By and large, these commands are used to create special effects and enhance the color in an image rather than correct it. Figure 9-10 shows several of these commands in action. Take a look at Color Plate 9-2 to see how the Photo Filter, Invert, and Posterize commands can change the color, tonal range, and brightness of an image.

Invert

The Invert command switches pixel color values with opposite color values, making a positive image appear as a negative and a negative image appear as a positive.

You can invert a layer or selection, or create an adjustment layer that uses the Invert command. To invert a layer or selection, choose Image⇨Adjustments⇨Invert. To create an adjustment layer, click the Create New Fill or Adjustment Layer button at the bottom of the Layers palette and choose Invert from the menu.

See Figure 9-10 for an example of an inverted image.

Original image

Equalize

Gradient Map

Invert

Figure 9-10:
These quick
adjustment
commands
can create
dramatic
results.

Posterize

Threshold

Equalize

The Equalize command finds the brightest and darkest values in an image
and averages them out so the darkest value becomes black and the brightest
value becomes white. This command can improve dark images or images that
don't have enough contrast.

To equalize a layer or selection, choose Image➪Adjustments➪Equalize. Refer to Figure 9-10 to see an example of an equalized image.

Desaturate

The Desaturate command removes color from the currently selected layer or selection. You can create an attention-getting effect by leaving one object colored while removing all other color from an image.

To desaturate a layer or selection, choose Image➪Adjustments➪Desaturate.

Posterize

The Posterize command reduces the number of color levels in each channel, and then converts pixel colors to the closest matching level.

You can posterize a layer or selection, or create an adjustment layer that uses the posterize command. To posterize a layer or selection, choose Image➪Adjustments➪Posterize. To create an adjustment layer, click the Create new fill or adjustment layer button at the bottom of the Layers palette and choose Posterize from the menu. In the Posterize dialog box (Figure 9-11), enter the number of levels, and then click OK.

Figure 9-11:
Set the number of levels in the Posterize dialog box, and then click OK.

Figure 9-10 shows an example of a posterized image.

Threshold

The Threshold command changes color or grayscale images to high-contrast, black-and-white images. With this command, you can specify a threshold range. Any pixels lighter than the specified threshold are converted to white. Any pixels darker than the specified threshold are converted to black.

You can apply the Threshold command to a layer or selection, or create an adjustment layer that uses the Threshold command. To apply Threshold to a layer or selection, choose Image⇨Adjustments⇨Threshold. To create an adjustment layer, click the Create new fill or adjustment layer button at the bottom of the Layers palette and choose Threshold from the menu. In the Threshold dialog box (see Figure 9-12), move the Threshold slider right or left to set where the cutoff point is for black and white values, and then click OK.

Figure 9-12:
Move the slider left to increase the white pixels; move the slider right to increase the black pixels.

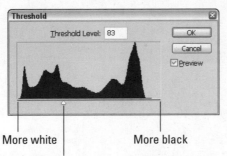

More white   More black

Slide to change amount of black and white

Shadow/Highlight

The new Shadow/Highlight command opens a dialog box that does more than simply adjust shadows and highlights (although you can use the tool to do just that — with a great deal of precision). Using the Shadow/Highlight dialog box shown in Figure 9-13 you also can correct color, add more contrast to the midtones, and increase or decrease the amount of white or black pixels in an image, layer, or selection.

Color Plate 9-1 shows the Shadow/Highlight command in action. Using an image that looked rather murky, shadows and highlights were first adjusted. Then, color and midtones contrast was corrected, creating an image that is more vibrant and has more contrast.

To use the Shadow/Highlight command:

1. **Use the Layers palette to select a layer or the Background.**

2. **If you want to use the command on just part of a layer, use the selection tool of your choice to select an area of a layer.**

   For directions on how to use the selection tools, turn to Chapter 7.

Use sliders to adjust highlights

Use sliders to adjust shadows

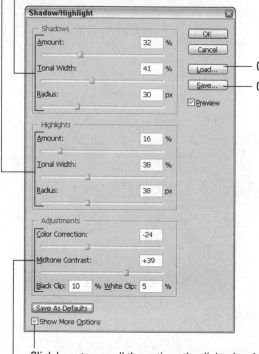

Figure 9-13: The Shadow/ Highlight dialog box lets you set highlights and shadows and perform a little color correction as well.

Click to load saved settings

Click to save settings

Click here to see all the options the dialog box has to offer

Use sliders to adjust image contrast and saturation

3. **Choose Image⇨Adjustments⇨Shadow/Highlight.**

    The Shadow/Highlights dialog box shown in Figure 9-13 is broken up into three areas — Shadows, Highlights, and Adjustments.

4. **Make sure the Preview and the Show More Options check boxes are checked.**

5. **In the Shadows and Highlights areas use the sliders to adjust shadow and highlight settings.**

    The Amount slider bars enable you to set the amount of shadows and highlights. The higher the percentage, the more these areas are changed.

    The Tonal Width slider bars set the contrast when shadows and highlights are adjusted. A higher percentage in the Shadows area creates less contrast. A higher percentage in the Highlights area adds more contrast.

    The Radius slider bars set how far the shadow or highlight spreads. A higher setting makes the shadow or highlight spread more.

6. **In the Adjustments areas use the sliders to correct color and add more midtone contrast.**

   To make shadows darker enter a percentage value between .001 and 50 in the Black Clip text box (the higher the value, the darker the shadows). To reduce shadows and make highlights brighter, enter a percentage value between .001 and 50 in the White Clip text box (the higher the value, the brighter the highlights).

7. **Click OK.**

   Figure 9-14 shows an image before and after adjusting shadows and highlights.

Before shadow and highlight adjustment

After adjustment

Figure 9-14: The Shadow/ Highlight command can add subtle shading and contrast correction to an image.

Gradient Map

The Gradient Map command allows you to substitute an image's original colors with the colors you select from a gradient. You can use this command to colorize a grayscale image or completely change the colors in a color image. The results are fast and can be dramatic, changing an image from an everyday palette to Day-Glo.

You can apply a gradient map to a layer, selected area of a layer, or an adjustment layer. To apply the Gradient Map command to a layer or selected area, choose Image➪Adjustments➪Gradient Map. To apply the command using an adjustment layer, click the Create new fill or adjustment layer button at the bottom of the Layers palette, and then choose Gradient Map from the menu. In the Gradient Map dialog box (Figure 9-15), select a gradient using the drop-down list box, then click OK.

Refer to Figure 9-10 to see an example of a gradient map applied to an image.

Color Plate 9-4 shows the amazing changes that the Gradient Map command can produce. The Gradient Map was applied separately to three duplicates of an image of a white peacock. One peacock was colored violet and orange, the second changed to copper, and the third peacock was colored with an entire rainbow.

Figure 9-15:
When you select a gradient, the new colors preview in the image window. Try out several gradients to see the effects they create.

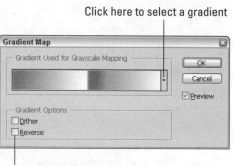

Click here to select a gradient

Put a check here to invert gradient coloring

Color Correction Tools

Three tools in the Toolbox also can be used to adjust image color and tone. The Dodge tool lightens pixels, and the Burn tool darkens pixels. The Sponge tool either "soaks up" pixel color, desaturating an area, or "drips" more color in, making the area more saturated.

Lighten or darken using the Dodge or Burn Tools

The Dodge and Burn tools are great for lightening or darkening small areas of an image by hand. With both of these tools, you can set brush size, whether shadows, midtones, or highlights are affected, and determine an *exposure* percentage. The exposure sets how quickly an area is dodged or burned. The higher the setting, the more quickly the pixels change.

1. **Use the Layers palette to select a layer.**

2. **Select the Dodge tool or the Burn tool from the Toolbox.**

3. **On the Options bar use the Brush Preset picker to select a brush width and set brush hardness.**

   The Options bar offers a range of settings for the Dodge and Burn tools, as shown in Figure 9-16. For more about the Brush Preset picker, turn to Chapter 12.

Figure 9-16: The Options bar lets you quickly select a brush size and hardness, the range of the dodge or burn, and the intensity (exposure) of the tool.

Select brush size and hardness

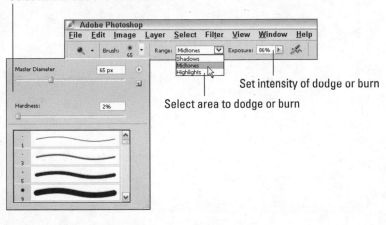

4. **Set the range of the dodge or burn and the amount of exposure.**

   On the Options bar, use the Range drop-down list to select Shadows, Midtones, or Highlights. Use Exposure slider bar to set a percentage value between 1 and 100. The higher the value, the higher the intensity of the tool.

5. **Click the Airbrush button if you want the dodge or burn to work more gradually.**

6. **Stroke with the Dodge or Burn tool on the image.**

   Figure 9-17 shows an image before being burned and dodged, and the results of burning and dodging.

REMEMBER

The Dodge and Burn tools can't be used on images set in Bitmap or Indexed Color mode.

Original image

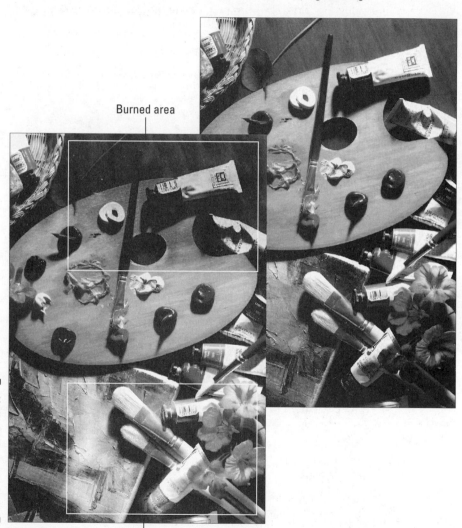

Burned area

Figure 9-17:
The burned areas are darkened while the dodged areas are lightened.

Dodged area

Using the Sponge tool to saturate and desaturate color

The Sponge tool is used to make colored areas more or less saturated. With just a few wipes of the sponge you can quickly add brighter colors to an image or tone areas down.

1. **Use the Layers palette to select a layer.**

 2. **Choose the Sponge tool from the Toolbox. It's on the flyout menu with the Dodge and Burn tools.**

3. **Select the brush width and hardness.**

   On the Options bar, click the Brush Preset picker to select width and set brush hardness as shown in Figure 9-18. For more about the Brush Preset picker, turn to Chapter 12.

Figure 9-18:
Select a brush width and hardness, whether to saturate or desaturate, and set a flow intensity.

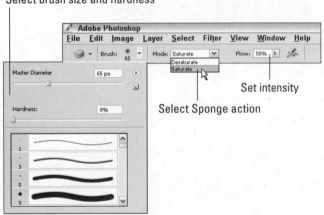

Select brush size and hardness

Set intensity

Select Sponge action

4. **Set the Sponge tool to saturate or desaturate using the Mode drop-down list.**

5. **Use the Flow slider bar to set the tool's intensity.**

6. **Stroke on an area of the selected layer.**

   To saturate or desaturate an area more, release the mouse button, and then stroke again. Figure 9-19 shows areas of an image that have been saturated.

Saturated area

Original image

Figure 9-19: Stroking the image with the Sponge tool set to Saturate can quickly add focal points to an image.

Chapter 10

Creating Composite Images

• •

In This Chapter

▶ Copying and cutting selections

▶ Pasting into a selection

▶ Creating clones

▶ Using the Pattern Stamp tool

▶ Repairing images using the Healing Brush

▶ Patching areas

▶ Sharpening and blurring edges

• •

Composite images are made by combining elements from different images or photographs into a single image file. Using the layer techniques I discuss in Chapters 8 and 9 (and throughout the book), you can place these different elements, one of top of the other, and manipulate them any way you want using opacity and blending modes.

By using familiar commands, such as copy, cut, and paste, you can create your own composite images and see your Photoshop aptitude increase substantially. In addition, you can *clone* portions of images, and then blur or sharpen the clones to create a uniform look.

In this chapter you find out how to copy and clone selections into selected areas, drag and drop selections between images, and paste into smaller images. Using the Healing Brush tool and the Patch tool, you can fix image imperfections and create patterns using the Pattern Stamp tool. Finally, this chapter shows you how to use the Blur tool to soften the edge of pasted areas and how to add focus to an area using the Sharpen tool.

Considerations when Cutting, Copying, and Pasting between Two Images

If you're going to copy (or cut) and paste a layer or selection from one image to another, there are a few things to keep in mind. First off, you need two images (of course): a source image and a destination image.

Look at the dimensions of the source image and take into consideration the following:

- ✔ If the selection you are pasting comes from a source image that has larger dimensions than the destination image, some of the pasted selection will extend beyond the image window. This area that extends beyond the image window is just hidden. Use the Move tool to bring it into view. (Take a look at Chapter 7 to learn more about the Move tool.)

- ✔ If there's a difference in resolution between the source image and the destination image, you may have undesirable results. For example, if the source image's resolution is lower than the destination image (say the source image is set at 96 ppi and the destination image is set at 300 ppi), the copied selection will appear smaller when it is pasted into the destination image. (To find out about image resolution, turn to Chapter 4.)

- ✔ To make the resolution of the source and destination images the same before copying and pasting, choose Image⇨Image Size, and change the resolution in the Image Size dialog box. (Complete directions for using the Image Size dialog box can be found in Chapter 4.)

Copying (or cutting) and pasting a selection

Copying and pasting is pretty basic. The copy and paste commands in Photoshop are the same as almost any other program — Ctrl+C (⌘+C on a Mac) to copy and Ctrl+P (⌘+P on a Mac) to paste.

Because Photoshop uses layers, there are a few extra wrinkles to the copying and pasting process. You'll need to use the Layers palette to select the layer you want to copy from. Also, the newly pasted area will appear on a new layer above the selected layer.

To copy and paste a selection, follow these steps:

1. **In the Layers palette, select the layer you want to copy from.**
2. **Use a selection tool of your choice to select an area of the layer.**

   To find out more about selection tools, turn to Chapter 7.
3. **Press Ctrl+C (⌘+C on a Mac) on the keyboard or choose Edit⇨Copy.**
4. **Use the Layers palette to select a layer to paste above.**
5. **Press Ctrl+P (⌘+P on a Mac) on the keyboard or choose Edit⇨Paste.**

   The pasted selection appears on a new layer above the selected layer, as shown in Figure 10-1.

You can also cut a selected area and paste it as well. To cut a selected area, choose Edit⇨Cut or press Ctrl+X (⌘+X on a Mac). When a selected area is cut from the Background layer, the area where the selection was cut from is automatically filled with the Background color currently selected in the Toolbox. If a selected area is cut from a layer, the area where the selection was cut from will be transparent.

You also can turn a selection into a layer by choosing Layer⇨New⇨ Layer via Copy or right-clicking the selection (Control+clicking on a Mac) and choosing Layer via Copy from the context-sensitive menu.

Copy

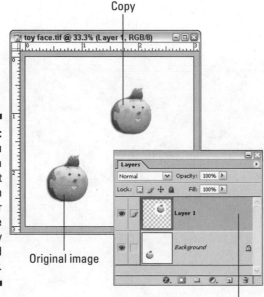

Figure 10-1:
When you paste a selection, it appears on a new layer above the currently selected layer.

Original image

Copy appears on a new layer

Using Paste Into

The Paste Into command pastes a copied selection onto a new layer and saves the selection marquee as a *layer mask*. Layer masks control access to a layer — much like a Halloween mask might reveal only someone's eyes — the holes in a layer mask let you edit only that exposed area of an image. To find out more about layer masks and how they work, turn to Chapter 15. To paste a selection into a layer mask, follow these steps:

1. **Select the area of a layer that you want to cut or copy, as shown in Figure 10-2.**

2. **Press Ctrl+C (⌘+C on a Mac) or choose Edit⇨Copy.**

   If you want to cut the area press Ctrl+X (⌘+X on a Mac) instead.

3. **Use the Layers palette to select another layer, if you wish.**

   You can leave the layer you originally selected in Step 1 as the active layer. If an editable text layer is selected the Paste Into command will not be available, so select another layer. When you add type to an image, an editable text layer is automatically created. This layer is different from a regular layer, so the Paste Into command won't work with it. To find out more about creating type and editable type layers, turn to Chapter 17.

4. **Select an area that you want to paste the copied area into as shown in Figure 10-3.**

Figure 10-2:
An area of
the berries
layer is
selected.

Selected area

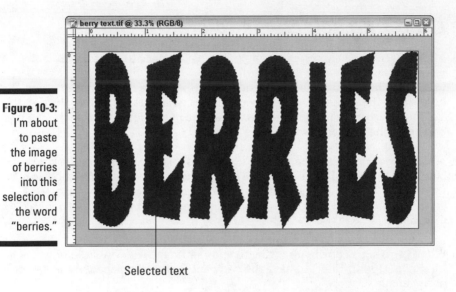

Figure 10-3:
I'm about to paste the image of berries into this selection of the word "berries."

Selected text

5. **Choose Edit➪Paste Into or press Ctrl+Shift+V (⌘+Shift+V on a Mac).**

The new layer (with its accompanying layer mask) appears, as shown in Figure 10-4.

Figure 10-4:
Pasting the original selection into the text creates a berry fill that complements the text.

Original selected area (berry photo)   Layer mask (berries text)

Dragging selections to create copies

Another technique for creating copies of selections is to drag them.

Create a selection using any selection tool. Change to the Move tool, then hold down the Alt key (Option key on a Mac) while dragging the selection to another area of the image or into another image window. The selected area is copied to the new position.

You can *move* the selection without holding down the Alt key (Option key on a Mac), but this action leaves behind a hole in the source image. This hole is filled with either the background color (on the Background) or transparency (on a layer). To find out more about moving selections with the Move tool, look at Chapter 7.

When creating a copy by dragging to another image window, hold down Alt+Shift (Option+Shift) to have the copy automatically placed in the center of the image window.

Duplicating an image

If you need to create a copy of an entire image (not just a selection or a layer), choose Image⇨Duplicate. Use the Duplicate Image dialog box that opens to name the duplicate, and then click OK. The duplicate image opens on-screen. Use a duplicate image to try out different techniques or variations without changing the original image file. Don't forget to save the duplicate if you like an effect you've created.

Creating Clones

A clone is a pixel-by-pixel copy of an image area that is applied to another area in the same image or a different image. With the cloning tools, you can doctor your photographs, for example, removing people you don't want in the photo, or giving that plump tummy a quick tuck. Cloning is great for fixing areas that have flaws and scratches, or for recreating a portion of an image that is lost. Also, you can clone areas for use as patterns.

Photoshop includes four amazing tools that use cloning for different purposes and with different results, but they are used for retouching images:

- **The Clone Stamp tool:** Copies pixels from one portion of an image and applies them somewhere else.
- **The Pattern Stamp tool:** Uses a selected area to create patterns.

🖊 **The Healing Brush:** Copies not only color but texture as well from one portion of an image and applies them elsewhere.

🖊 **The Patch tool:** Copies a selected area, but then matches brightness and color where the selected area is applied.

 All these cloning tools use brushes that you select using the Brush Preset picker on the Options bar. Think about what type of area you are retouching before you select a brush tip. A softer brush (with a lower hardness setting) enables you to blend areas better. A harder brush (with a higher hardness setting) lets you fix exact areas. Play around with brush hardness settings when using these tools. If you don't like the results you get, you can always undo the cloning by pressing Ctrl+Z (⌘+Z on a Mac) or using the History palette to select an earlier history state. (To find out more about brushes and selecting them, turn to Chapter 12. Turn to Chapter 14 for details about the History palette.)

The Clone Stamp tool

 The Clone Stamp tool copies pixels from one area of a layer to replace pixels on the same layer, a different layer, or a different image. Pixel colors are copied from a *source point* that you select on a layer. Then, as you use the Clone Stamp tool, the color from the source point is applied to the area you stroke. With the Clone Stamp tool, you can fill in missing areas of a photograph or scanned image, remove unwanted elements (think about that tummy tuck), and fix damaged areas.

1. **Select the Clone Stamp tool from the Toolbox.**

2. **Use the Options bar to select Clone Stamp Tool settings.**

   As shown in Figure 10-5, you can select a brush size and hardness, a blending mode, opacity, and flow to control the rate of application.

 Aligned mode: If the Aligned check box is checked on the Options bar, then it doesn't matter how many times you release and press the mouse. Every time you press the mouse to continue cloning, the cloning continues from where the mouse was released. For instance, if you're cloning a nose from one picture to another, even if you release the mouse button then press it again, the copy of the nose will continue seamlessly.

On the other hand, if the Aligned check box is unchecked, every time you release the mouse button the tool resets itself. The result is that cloned pixels are copied from the original source point. For instance, if you're cloning a nose from one picture to another and you release the mouse button, the tool resets to the original source point and starts to paint a second nose.

Although this information may seem confusing, if you try out the Clone tool with the Alignment mode on or off, you'll find out what it's doing very quickly. When the Alignment mode is on, the Clone Stamp tool is great for retouching. When the Alignment mode off, the Clone Stamp tool is great for duplicating.

If you want to clone pixels from only the currently selected layer, make sure Use All Layers is unchecked. To clone pixels from a combination of all the layers, put a check in the Use All Layers checkbox.

Airbrush Capabilities: To apply cloning using an airbrush style, click the Set to Enable Airbrush Capabilities button. The Airbrush options set the brush to work like a real airbrush. If you position the mouse pointer in one place and hold the mouse button down, the tool continues to pump out color until the mouse button is released. (To find out more about airbrushing, turn to Chapter 12.)

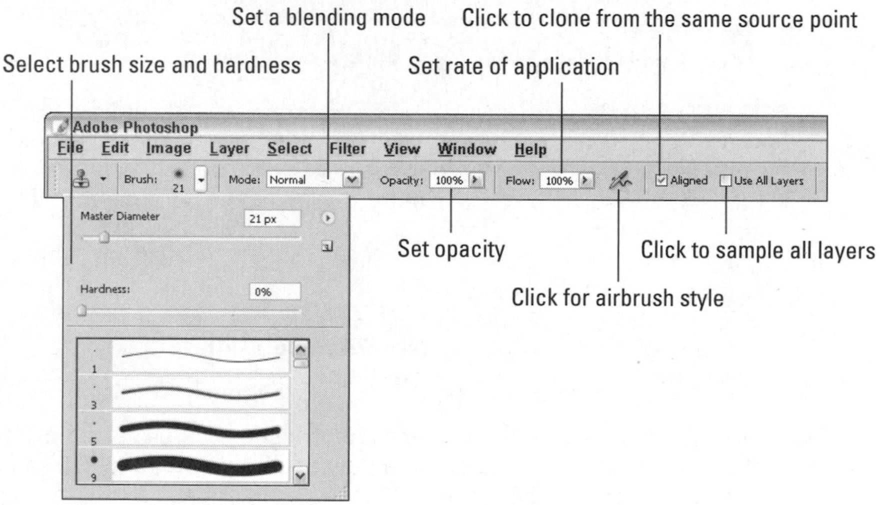

Set a blending mode   Click to clone from the same source point

Select brush size and hardness   Set rate of application

Figure 10-5:
Using the Options bar, you can set how the cloned areas will be applied.

Set opacity   Click to sample all layers

Click for airbrush style

3. **Use the Layers palette to select the layer from which you want to clone.**

4. **Position the mouse over the area you want to clone, hold down the Alt key (Option key on a Mac), and then click.**

    You have just created the source point — the area that the clone will be copied from. Notice that when you hold down the Alt key (Option key on a Mac), the mouse pointer turns into a target with crosshairs. This helps to accurately position the source point.

5. **On the same layer, a different layer in the same image, or in a different image window, click and hold the mouse button. Then stroke back and forth to create the clone.**

As you stroke, notice that there are two pointers on the screen, a crosshair over the source point that you selected in Step 4, and a stamp where you stroke the mouse and create the clone (see Figure 10-6).

You can always establish a new source point when cloning. Simply position the mouse pointer in the new source area and Alt+click (Option+click on a Mac).

Source point   Clone

Figure 10-6: As you create a clone, keep an eye on the source point crosshair so you know what area is being copied.

The Pattern Stamp tool

 The Pattern Stamp tool uses a rectangular selected area to copy pixels from one layer to another in the same image or in a different image. With this tool, you can create patterns for backgrounds or special effects, or create a pattern to seamlessly remove an area of an image. For instance, suppose you have a photograph of the ocean with a boat bobbing on the waves. You decide that you want to remove the boat from the picture. You could use the Pattern Stamp tool to copy a section of the waves, and then paint over the area where the boat is, hiding the boat and making the waves perfect. That way, it would look like the boat was never there in the first place.

1. **Select the Rectangular Marquee tool and use it to make a selection on the layer you want to copy.**

   This selected area becomes the pattern that you will stamp with the Pattern Stamp tool.

2. Choose Edit➪Define Pattern.

Use the Pattern Name dialog box shown in Figure 10-7 to name the area that you selected.

Selected area that will become pattern

Figure 10-7:
Enter a descriptive name for the selection that you're using as a pattern.

3. Use the Options bar to select Pattern Stamp tool settings.

As shown in Figure 10-8, you can select a brush size and hardness, a blending mode, opacity, and control the intensity of the flow when you apply the pattern.

Select brush size and hardness

Select a blending mode   Set rate of application

Check to align pattern tiles in a grid

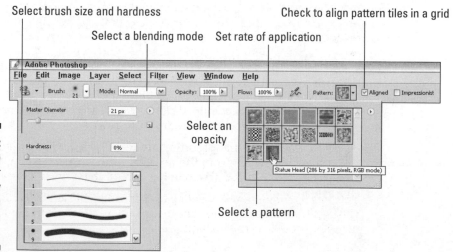

Figure 10-8:
Use the Options bar to set how your pattern will be applied.

Select an opacity

Select a pattern

Click to check in the Aligned check box if you want to create a tiled grid. With this setting the grid lines up no matter where you start painting or how many strokes you use. Uncheck the Aligned check box if you don't want the pattern tiles to line up.

To apply the pattern using an airbrush style, click the Set to enable airbrush capabilities button. (To find out more about airbrushing, turn to Chapter 12.)

Use the Pattern drop-down list to select a pattern. The custom pattern you created in Step 2 is the last pattern thumbnail in the list.

Put a check in the Impressionist check box if you want to create a blurred pattern.

4. **In the same image window or another image window, position the mouse pointer, click and hold the mouse button, and stroke back and forth to create the pattern.**

   As you can see in Figure 10-9, applying a pattern using different blending modes creates different effects.

The Healing Brush

 The Healing Brush tool uses pixels from a source point just like the Clone Stamp tool to replace pixels from one area to another. Unlike the Clone Stamp tool, however, this smart tool also simultaneously blends pixel color and tone to quickly create natural-looking, textured touch-ups. The Healing Brush tool is great for touching up areas in photographs (think crows feet and wrinkle removal).

To put this powerful tool's healing powers to work, follow these steps:

1. **Select the Healing Brush tool from the Toolbox.**

2. **Use the Options bar to select Healing Brush tool settings.**

   As shown in Figure 10-10, you can use the Brush picker to select brush size and hardness. Generally, a small brush with a lower hardness setting makes for good blending. If the brush is too hard, you'll create areas with edges in the places you are trying to retouch.

3. **Select Replace from the Blending Mode drop-down list to incorporate the grain and texture from the area on which you are using the Healing Brush into the pixels being copied from the source area.**

   This makes for smoother healing of blemishes on skin. You can also choose a different mode for another effect. (To find out more about blending modes, turn to Chapter 8.)

Darken, 60% opacity

Dissolve, 50% opacity

Hard Mix, 75% opacity

Figure 10-9:
Different
blending
modes and
opacities
create
different
effects.

Normal, 100% opacity

Linear Dodge, 50% opacity

Difference, 60% opacity

4. **Select Sampled as the Source and check Aligned to create a copy from the same source point no matter how many times you stop and resume painting.**

5. **Position the mouse over the area you want to use as the source, hold down the Alt key (Option key on a Mac), and then click.**

   You've just created the area that will become the source for the clone.

6. **Position the mouse over the area you want to repair, press the mouse button, and drag.**

   As you stroke, lines and wrinkles disappear, replaced by textured tones that smoothly blend in as shown in Figure 10-11.

Set brush size, hardness, and shape

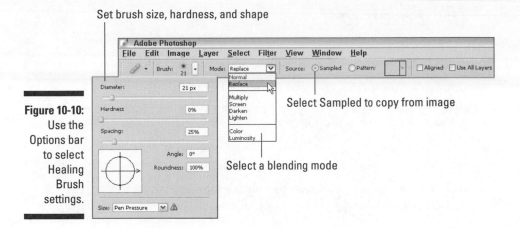

Select Sampled to copy from image

Select a blending mode

Figure 10-10: Use the Options bar to select Healing Brush settings.

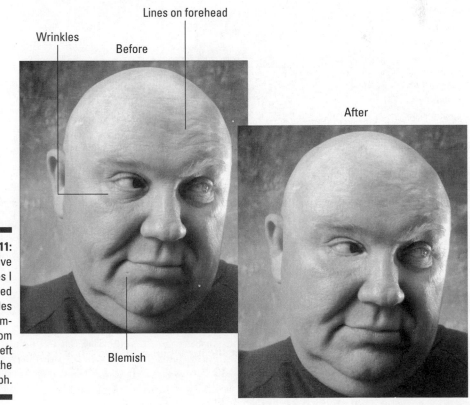

Wrinkles

Lines on forehead

Before

After

Figure 10-11: In about five minutes I removed wrinkles and blemishes from the left side of the photograph.

Blemish

The Patch tool

The Patch tool copies pixels from one area to another by using selections. First you select the source pixels that you want to copy, and then you select the area where you want to paste those pixels.

Instead of sampling a specific pixel like you do to use the Healing Brush tool, this tool samples an entire selected area. Use this tool to repair dust, scratches, and tears in scanned images and photographs.

1. **Select the Patch tool from the Toolbox.**

2. **Make sure Source is selected on the Options bar as shown in Figure 10-12.**

Figure 10-12:
The Options bar includes selection buttons to help with selecting the area you want to repair.

3. **Position the Patch tool over the area you want to repair, and drag a selection marquee around the area.**

   Just like creating any other selection, you can add or subtract from the selection using the Shift or Alt key (Option key on a Mac), respectively, and use the selection buttons on the Options bar. For more about selecting, turn to Chapter 7.

4. **Position the mouse inside the selection you created and drag it to the area you want to use to repair the selected area.**

   When you release the mouse button, the selection snaps back to its original position, and the sampled repair area is applied to the area you originally selected. Figure 10-13 shows a repair to a girl's nose.

Blurring and Sharpening

The Blur and Sharpen tools come in handy when blending cloned or pasted areas into an image. Sometimes cloned or pasted areas create hard edges that don't transition smoothly into the image. That's when it's time to use the Blur tool to soften the edge, easing the transition. Other times, a cloned or pasted area can lack focus and need clarity. The Sharpen tool increases pixel contrast and helps delineate a blurry shape.

Here are the details:

- ✔ **To blur a sharp edge:** Select the Blur tool from the Toolbox. Use the Options bar shown in Figure 10-14 to set brush size and hardness, blending mode, and strength (strength sets the rate of application). Position the mouse where you want to blur the image and drag the mouse across the area. To make the area blurrier, drag over the area again.

- ✔ **To sharpen edges:** Select the Sharpen tool from the Toolbox. Use the Options bar shown in Figure 10-14 to set brush size and hardness, blending mode, and strength (strength sets the rate of application). Position the mouse where you want to sharpen the image and drag the mouse across the area. To make the area sharper, drag over the area again.

Before

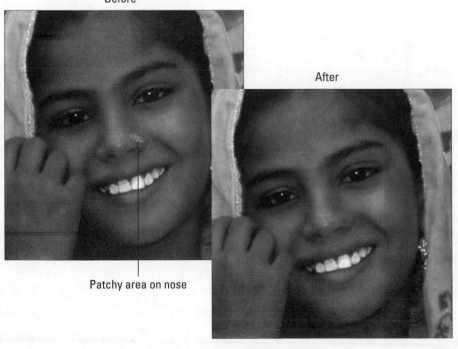

Figure 10-13: In the picture on the left, notice the patchy area on the girl's nose. After using the Patch tool, the image on the right is repaired.

Patchy area on nose

After

Select a brush size and hardness

Select a blending mode

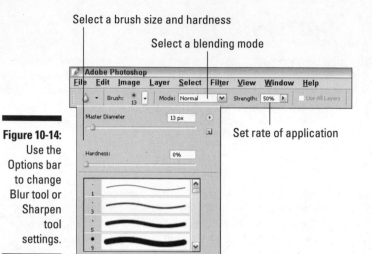

Set rate of application

Figure 10-14:
Use the
Options bar
to change
Blur tool or
Sharpen
tool
settings.

Chapter 11

Using Filters

*1*f you're a photographer, or if you've taken a photography course or two, you know how photographic filters work. Filters refine or refract light to modify the image as it comes into the camera. A *daylight filter* strains some of the blue out of the image; a *polarization lens* eliminates reflected light; a *fish-eye lens* refracts peripheral imagery into the photo.

So what do these photographic filters have to do with Photoshop? Glad you asked. Among the many tools and features that Photoshop has to offer, filters are (in my mind) possibly the coolest of all. Photoshop's filters can quickly add subtle effects or amazing distortions. For instance, you can apply artistic effects that make an image look like it's been painted with oils or created with mosaic tiles. You can use the Blur or Sharpen filters to subtly retouch an image. Apply distortion filters to make an image look like it's been engraved or embossed. And you can combine any number of filter effects using selections, layers, and layer masks.

Filters open up a whole new range of opportunities that no other Photoshop function quite matches. Filters can make poor images look better and good images look fantastic. And you can use them to introduce special effects, such as camera movement and relief textures. You have nearly 100 filters to play with in Photoshop. This chapter can't cover all of them in detail. Color Plate 11-1 shows you several filters in color.

A Few Fast Filter Facts

Before launching into explanations of Photoshop filters, check these facts:

- ✔ The filters are all found on the Filter menu (see Figure 11-1).

- ✔ To affect only a portion of your image with a filter, select that portion before applying the filter. The filter then affects only the selection and leaves the rest of the image unmodified. If no portion of the image is selected, the filter affects the entire image.

- ✔ To create smooth transitions between filtered and unfiltered areas in an image, blur the selection outline by choosing Select➪Feather. (Take a look at Chapter 7 for a more complete description of feathering.)

- ✔ You can get unique results by applying the same filter more than once; simply reapply the filter by choosing the first command on the Filter menu or by pressing Ctrl+F (⌘+F on a Mac).

- ✔ To control how the effects of the filter are applied, some filters display a dialog box when selected. If the last filter you chose was one of these, press Ctrl+Alt+F (⌘+Option+F on a Mac) to redisplay the dialog box and apply the filter again using different settings.

- ✔ Some filters take a few seconds or even minutes to apply. To cancel a filter in progress, press Esc.

- ✔ To undo the last filter, press Ctrl+Z (⌘+Z on a Mac). Unlike a *canceled* filter, the *undone* filter remains at the top of the Filter menu, so you can later apply it by pressing Ctrl+F (⌘+F on a Mac).

- ✔ To undo a filter if you don't like the results and you can't undo by pressing Ctrl+Z (⌘+Z on a Mac), use the History palette to return to a *source state* — Photoshop's term for a previous saved step — that you're happy with (see Chapter 14 for details on the History palette).

The Filter Gallery

New in Photoshop CS, the Filter Gallery is your place for filter one-stop shopping. As shown in Figure 11-2, the Filter Gallery displays the image in a Preview pane, gives access to many filter types, and lets you create filter effect layers so you can try out more than one filter at a time. You should know, however, that not all filters are available in the Filter Gallery. To use the filters not available in the Filter Gallery, you'll need to use the Filter menu.

New Filter Gallery

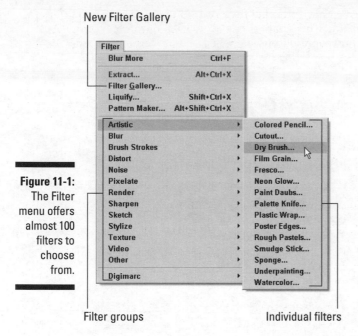

Figure 11-1:
The Filter
menu offers
almost 100
filters to
choose
from.

Filter groups   Individual filters

Here are some Filter Gallery basics:

✔ **To open the Filter Gallery:** Choose Filter➪Filter Gallery, or choose any
filter from the Filter➪Artistic, Brush Strokes, Distort, Sketch, Stylize, or
Texture submenus shown in Figure 11-1.

✔ **To use a filter:** Click one of the arrows next to a filter type, and then
click the filter's thumbnail. For instance, in Figure 11-2, the Brush
Strokes filter type has been opened to display those filters, and Spatter
is selected. Or, you can select a filter from the alphabetical Filter drop-
down list. When you select a filter, its setting options appear on the right
side of the dialog box. Use the sliders, drop-down list boxes, and radio
buttons to create the filter effects that you want.

✔ **To enlarge the Preview pane:** Click the Toggle Expanded View button.

✔ **To create an effect layer:** Click the New Effect Layer button at the
bottom right of the dialog box. The new effect layer appears in the Effect
Layer pane. Choose a new filter to apply to the image. The effect layer
saves those settings for you.

✔ **To view effect layers one-by-one:** Click the eye icon next to the effect
layer you want to hide or view. You can hide all the effect layers, then
view them one at a time or view two or more effects at once.

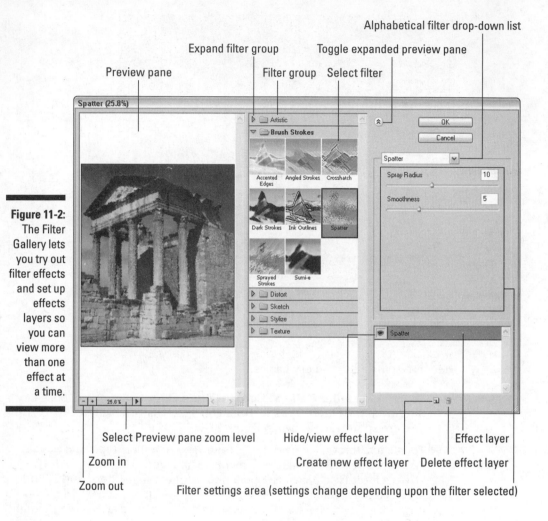

Alphabetical filter drop-down list

Expand filter group   Toggle expanded preview pane

Preview pane   Filter group   Select filter

Figure 11-2:
The Filter
Gallery lets
you try out
filter effects
and set up
effects
layers so
you can
view more
than one
effect at
a time.

Select Preview pane zoom level   Hide/view effect layer   Effect layer

Zoom in   Create new effect layer   Delete effect layer

Zoom out

Filter settings area (settings change depending upon the filter selected)

Sharpening the Details with the Unsharp Mask Filter

No matter how good an image looked before you scanned it, chances are that it appears a little out of focus on-screen. The image in Figure 11-3 is a good example of a typical photo snapped at the beach. It was probably taken pretty quickly and the camera was a little out of focus.

You can eradicate this kind of blurriness using the Unsharp Mask filter.

To use the Unsharp Mask command, choose Filter⇨Sharpen⇨Unsharp Mask. The Unsharp Mask dialog box appears, as shown in Figure 11-4.

Figure 11-3:
A typical
snapshot
taken at the
beach can
be improved
with the
Unsharp
Mask filter.

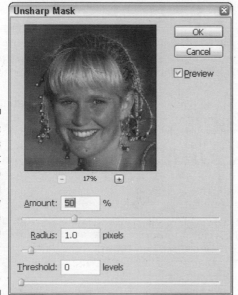

Figure 11-4:
Experts
agree that
the Unsharp
Mask dialog
box really
should be
called the
*Super-
sharpen*
dialog box.

Inside the Unsharp Mask dialog box

The Unsharp Mask dialog box enables you to preview what happens when you change the values in three important text boxes. You can preview the filter inside the dialog box and in the main image window. To sharpen an image, use the three slider bars like so:

- **Amount:** To control the amount of sharpening, adjust the Amount value from 1% to 500%. Higher Amount values produce more sharpening.

- **Radius:** To control the width of the edges you want to sharpen, adjust the Radius value. If the image is in pretty good shape, use a Radius of 0.5. If the edges are soft, like the ones in Figure 11-1, use a Radius of 1.0. And if the edges are almost nonexistent, go with 2.0.

  Generally, you don't want to set the Radius any lower than 0.5 or any higher than 2.0 (although 250.0 is the maximum). Another method you can use to determine the Radius value is to divide the resolution of your image by 200. So for example, if your image is 150 dpi, the radius would be .75 pixels.

- **Threshold:** To control the amount of contrast an area should have before it is modified, adjust the Threshold option. The default value of 0 tells Photoshop to sharpen the entire image. By raising the value, you tell Photoshop not to sharpen low-contrast pixels. A Threshold setting between 8 and 20 usually works very well for skin tones.

Some sharpening scenarios

Figure 11-5 demonstrates the effects of several different Amount value (shown as a percentage) and Radius value (shown as a number) on the same image from Figure 11-3. Throughout Figure 11-5, the Threshold value is 0.

To create the images in the top row of Figure 11-6, I started with an Amount value of 200% and a Radius value of 0.5. Then I halved the Amount value and doubled the Radius value in each of the next two images. Although the effect is similar from one image to the next, you can see that the top-right image has thicker edges than the top-left image. (The differences are subtle; you may have to look closely.)

The bottom row of the figure features more pronounced sharpening effects. I started with one set of Amount and Radius values — 500% and 0.5 — and progressively halved the Amount value and doubled the Radius value.

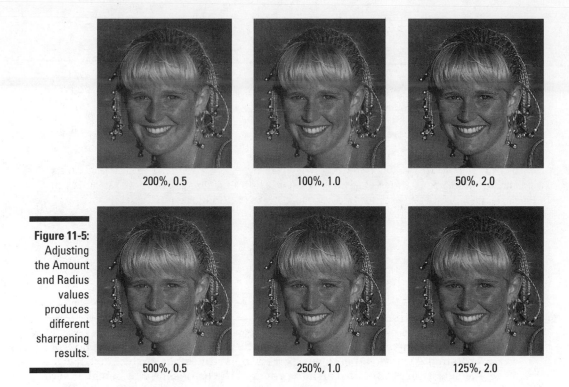

200%, 0.5   100%, 1.0   50%, 2.0

Figure 11-5: Adjusting the Amount and Radius values produces different sharpening results.

500%, 0.5   250%, 1.0   125%, 2.0

Having Fun with Filters

In this section, I show you how to apply several filters and techniques that you can use to create interesting filter effects. Even though I don't show you how to use all the filters that are available, you can apply these techniques to any of the filters that Photoshop provides — they all work in basically the same way.

Embossing an image

Embossing gives an image the look of pressed metal. The edges of the image appear in relief, and the other areas turn silvery gray.

When you choose Filter⇨Stylize⇨Emboss, Photoshop displays the dialog box, shown in Figure 11-6.

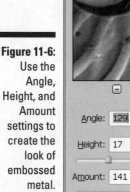

Figure 11-6:
Use the Angle, Height, and Amount settings to create the look of embossed metal.

Enter the angle of the light shining on the metal into the Angle text box, or rotate the spoke in the Angle circle to adjust the light's angle. Then, use the Height slider to set how high the edges of the emboss will be; a higher setting makes edges that appear to be raised higher. Finally, use the Amount slider to set the contrast. A higher setting adds more contrast, making the embossed image appear brighter.

In Figure 11-7, I applied the Emboss filter to the image on the left and ended up with the image on the right, which almost looks like real metal.

Giving an image the appearance of motion

Using the Motion Blur and Radial Blur filters, you can give an image the appearance of motion. The key to making these filters do your bidding is to select the part of the image that you want to stay "still" while the rest of the image is blurred. This simple trick gives the impression of motion.

Take a look at Color Plate 11-2. There I took an image of a kayaker and blurred the background to give the impression of motion. Then, I applied different filters to the blurred background to show the different effects you can create.

Figure 11-7:
The original
image on
the left was
embossed
using the
following
settings:
Angle was
set to 129
degrees,
Height was
set to 17
pixels, and
Amount was
set to 141%.

Original image

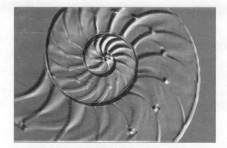

Emboss filter applied

Open an image of a car or another object that moves and give the following steps a try:

1. **Use the selection tool of your choice to select the area of an image that will remain still.**

   For example, in Figure 11-8, the entire car is selected. I'm going to add a Motion Blur to the background and later a radial blur to the tires.

Figure 11-8:
This car
isn't moving
yet, but it
will be.

2. **Feather the selection.**

   Choose Select⇨Feather or right-click (Control+click on a Mac) and select Feather from the context-sensitive menu. In the Feather dialog box that opens, enter a value of 10 pixels, and then click OK to close the dialog box.

3. **Choose Layer⇨New⇨Layer via Copy.**

   The pasted selection appears on a new layer exactly on top of the original selection. (Turn to Chapter 10 for details on copying and pasting a selection.)

4. **Click on the original layer in the Layers palette to make it active.**

5. **Choose Filter⇨Blur⇨Motion Blur.**

   In the Motion Blur dialog box shown in Figure 11-9, set the blur's angle to correspond with the direction the object is moving in. Use the distance slider to set the amount of the blur.

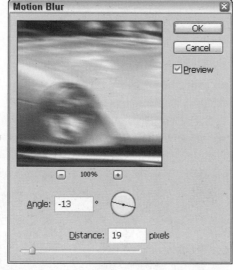

Figure 11-9: The Motion Blur filter has two settings, Angle and Distance.

Figure 11-10 shows the Motion Blur effect applied to the car picture from Figure 11-8. Notice that while the background is moving, something still looks wrong. When a car moves, its tires rotate. The next step is to add a radial blur to the tires.

6. **Make sure the copied layer is selected, then select the tires (if you're making a vehicle move), and choose Filter⇨Blur⇨Radial Blur.**

   In the Radial Blur dialog box, set the Amount of the Blur, the Blur Method (which in this case is Spin), and the Quality. Click OK to close the dialog box.

Figure 11-10:
The car
appears to
be moving,
but the tires
look wrong
because
they appear
stationary.

This dialog box doesn't have a preview window, so you may need to experiment a few times before you get the right setting. Before you try a new radial blur, just undo the previous one by pressing Ctrl+Z (⌘+Z on a Mac).

Figure 11-11 shows the car moving right along with both a motion blur and a radial blur.

Figure 11-11:
With a
Radial Blur
applied to
the tires,
the car
appears to
be moving
very fast.

Creating a lens blur

The new Lens Blur filter was created to mimic camera optics. The filter uses an *Iris* setting to create the effect. The iris is the window inside the camera lens. Depending upon the type of opening or *aperture* selected for the camera lens, the iris forms a different shape (such as a polygon or octagon). The effects you create using this filter mimics those created by the lens aperture.

An image with some bright light source, such as a sunset or bright sunbeam, works best with this filter. For instance, if you apply this filter to an image with a sunbeam and apply an Octagon Iris setting, the sunbeam takes on an octagonal shape.

To use the Lens Blur filter, choose Filter⇨Blur⇨Lens Blur. The Lens Blur dialog box shown in Figure 11-12 opens offering iris, highlight, noise, and focal distance settings.

Here's some information on using this powerful filter:

✔ Use the Blur Focal Distance slider to set where the image goes out of focus, nearer or farther away.

✔ In the Iris area, use the Shape drop-down list to select the shape of the iris, the Radius (amount of blur), the Blade Curvature (how wide the camera lens opening is), and the Rotation (the amount of light entering the lens). The shape of the Iris setting changes the way the light source in the image is reshaped. The Blade Curvature and Rotation settings affect the brightness of the light in the image.

✔ Use the Specular Highlights area to set image brightness, and the threshold (contrast).

✔ In the Noise area, set the amount of speckles added to the image to imitate film grain.

This new filter creates some interesting effects. Take a look at Figure 11-13. On the left is the original sunset photograph and on the right is the image after the Lens Blur filter has been applied. Notice that the sun's circular shape has been changed to a more octagonal shape. Also, the light reflecting off the clouds has been brightened. The filter Iris settings I used for the photo on the right are Shape: Octagon, Radius: 51, Blade Curvature: 77, Rotation: 144.

When you take pictures with a camera, you can dramatically change the color and tone of an image by attaching colored filters to the lens. You can use simple colors such as red, yellow, or blue, or you can use more complex filters that create specific effects, such as a warming filter that is an orange-brown shade, a cooling filter that is an intense blue, or a brownish sepia filter that creates the effect of a sepia-toned photograph.

Photo Filter adjustment layers

Using Photoshop CS, you can now create interesting photographic effects using a Photo Filter adjustment layer. An *adjustment layer* is a special kind of layer that you can use to try effects without permanently changing the image. (For more about adjustment layers and how to use them, turn to Chapter 8.)

Set shape of opening, blur, and amount of light entering lens

Preview pane

Set focus and where blur starts

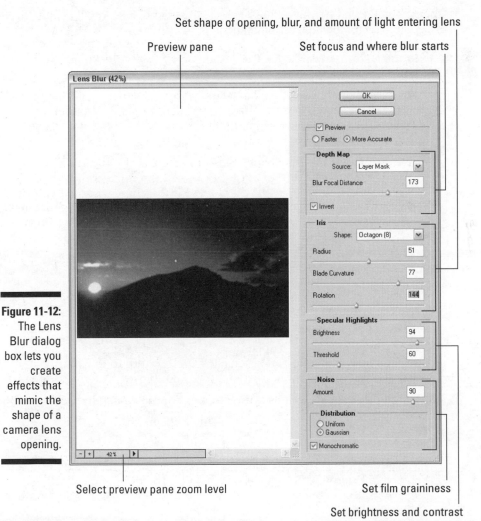

Figure 11-12: The Lens Blur dialog box lets you create effects that mimic the shape of a camera lens opening.

Select preview pane zoom level

Set film graininess

Set brightness and contrast

Figure 11-13:
The Lens Blur filter adds an interesting photographic effect.

Original image

Lens Blur filter applied

Open an image and try out a Photo Filter adjustment layer. You'll be surprised at some of the interesting results.

 1. **In the Layers palette, click the Create new fill or adjustment layer button, and then choose Photo Filter from the menu.**

   The Photo Filter dialog box shown in Figure 11-14 opens, offering preset color filters. Or you can use the Color picker to create a custom filter.

Figure 11-14:
The Photo Filter dialog box offers preset color filters.

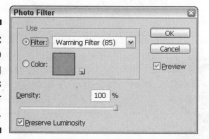

2. **Use the Filter drop-down list to select a preset color filter or click the color square to select a custom filter color.**

   Click the color square to open the Color picker. Use the Color picker to select a new filter color, and then click OK to return to the Photo Filter dialog box. (To find out more about the Color picker, turn to Chapter 4.)

3. **Use the Density slider to set the intensity of the color filter.**

   The higher the setting, the more the filter affects the image.

4. **Click OK.**

   The new Photo Filter adjustment layer appears in the Layers palette, as shown in Figure 11-15. If you want to change the Photo Filter settings, just double-click the adjustment layer's thumbnail to access the Photo Filter dialog box.

You also can set a blending mode and opacity for the adjustment layer. These settings can dramatically change the effect of the Photo Filter. Turn to Chapter 8 for details about blending modes and opacity settings.

Double-click thumbnail to access Photo filter dialog box

Adjustment layer

Figure 11-15: The new Photo Filter adjustment layer appears in the Layers palette.

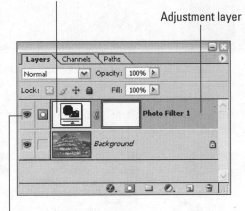

Click to view/hide adjustment layer

Fading Filter Effects

Using the Fade command, you can dramatically change the results of a filter. The Fade command lets you change the effect the filter has on the image by setting opacity and a blending mode.

To blend a filtered image, choose Edit➪Fade or press Ctrl+Shift+F (⌘+Shift+F on a Mac) immediately after applying a filter. The Fade dialog box appears, as shown in Figure 11-16, enabling you to play with the opacity and blend mode of the filtered image.

This command enables you to create all sorts of variations on a filter, as shown in Figure 11-17. In this example, I applied the Colored Pencil filter once, then used the Fade command with a 60% Opacity setting, and finally applied the Vivid Light blend mode.

You also can apply the Fade command after you've painted, focused, or toned an image. In other words, you can fade the effect created with any of the following tools: Brush, Pencil, Rubber Stamp, Pattern Stamp, Healing Brush, Patch, History Brush, Art History Brush, Gradient, Blur, Sharpen, Smudge, Dodge, Burn, Sponge, and all the Eraser tools. And if that isn't enough, you also can apply the Fade command to an area you have filled, stroked, liquefied, or applied a pattern to with the Pattern Maker command.

Figure 11-16:
Using the
Fade dialog
box, you can
set how a
filter is
applied to
an image by
changing
opacity and
blending
modes.

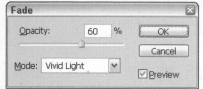

Original image

Colored Pencil filter

Figure 11-17:
Adjusting
opacity and
blending
modes
changes
filter results.

Fade: 60% Opacity

Fade: 60% Opacity,
Vivid Light blending mode

You must apply the Fade command *immediately* after you apply the filter. If you choose another command or apply a painting or editing tool to the image, you can't use the Fade command. The only alternative is to use the History palette and revert to the source state prior to applying the filter. You can reapply the filter and then choose the Fade command. (For more about the History palette, see Chapter 14.)

Making Taffy with the Liquify Command

I bet you thought Photoshop couldn't possibly give you any more ways to take your image out of the realm of reality, right? Well, hold on to your mouse.

The Liquify command lets you warp, twirl, pucker, and bloat an image. It's downright amazing!

Photoshop CS enhances the Liquify feature even further with additional tools and a couple of other goodies I describe in a minute. So take a deep breath and prepare to become *liquefied.*

Pick out an image that you want to distort and follow these steps:

1. **Open an image and decide whether you want to distort the whole image or just a portion.**

   You can use an area selected with one of the tools described in Chapter 7. Or you can select a single layer. When you select an area, the unselected areas aren't affected by the distortion. Save any selections as channels by choosing Selection➪Save Selection. (For more about saving selections turn to Chapter 8.)

   In these steps, I've saved three selections — the shoulders of the man shown in Figure 11-18, a selection of the textured background behind his head, and a selection of his eyes.

   If you want to warp text you've added to an image, you must *rasterize* the type before it can be warped with the Liquify command. Type in Photoshop is drawn using mathematical formulas called *vectors.* In order to warp, text it must be rasterized or turned into pixels first. After you rasterize your type, you lose the ability to edit that text. If editing is critical, then try the Warp option from the Type tool Options bar. For more about editable text and warping text, turn to Chapter 17.

2. **Choose Filter➪Liquify.**

   The huge Liquify dialog box appears, as shown in Figure 11-18.

Push Left tool

Bloat tool

Pucker tool

Twirl Clockwise tool

Reconstruct tool

Forward Warp tool

Brush settings

Load saved mesh   Save mesh

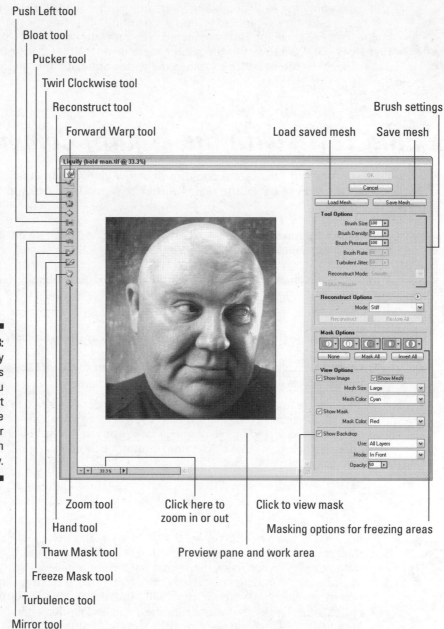

Figure 11-18:
The Liquify dialog box is where you can distort your image into another dimension of reality.

Zoom tool

Hand tool

Thaw Mask tool

Freeze Mask tool

Turbulence tool

Mirror tool

Click here to zoom in or out

Click to view mask

Masking options for freezing areas

Preview pane and work area

3. Select your desired brush size and pressure in the Tool Options portion in the top right of the dialog box.

Enter a numeric value or access the slider via the right-pointing arrow. A lower pressure allows for less intense distortions.

4. Define any areas you want frozen.

If you saved selections as described in Step 1, you can use the new Mask Options portion of the Liquify dialog box (see Figure 11-19) to freeze selected areas from distortion. You can use these options to mask some of the image, all of the image, or even remove the mask altogether.

You also can freeze an area anytime during the Liquify process even if you didn't save a selection. Use the Freeze Mask tool, (refer to Figure 11-18) and select a brush size and pressure setting. Drag over the desired area.

The Freeze Mask tool covers the area with a reddish tint, referred to as a *mask*. The amount of freezing depends on the pressure of the brush. If the brush pressure is 100%, the area is fully frozen. The varying pressure enables you to partially freeze an area so that the effect of the distortion isn't as intense. If you make an error, press Ctrl+Z (⌘+Z on a Mac) to undo.

After you have a frozen area, you can invert it by clicking Invert All, which then freezes the other portion of the image instead. Or you can choose None, which deletes all the frozen areas. You also can use the Thaw Mask tool (refer to Figure 11-18) to drag over any areas you want to unfreeze. Again, brush size and pressure settings affect the amount of thawing.

Take the time to preview all the different effects you can create. Check out "Previewing your liquefactions" to find out how to change your View options and prepare to make your proposed effects a (sur)reality. When you're ready to make your changes permanent, skip to "Applying your liquefactions."

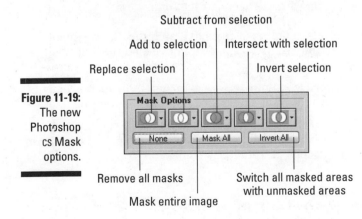

Figure 11-19: The new Photoshop cs Mask options.

Extending distortions into frozen areas

In addition to refining the effects you applied to your image, you also can extend your distortions from frozen areas into unfrozen areas. This option is great, for example, if you want some transition between your distorted and undistorted areas. Mask all or part of the areas you've already distorted, or you can click on the Invert button in the Mask Options area to flip-flop your masked and unmasked areas.

Select the Reconstruct Tool, and then choose one of the following from the Reconstruct Mode drop-down list. Drag the mouse over the unfrozen area that you want to unfreeze:

- **Rigid:** Keeps the right angles in the pixel grid at the edge between frozen and unfrozen areas. (Check the Mesh option from the View area of the Liquify dialog box to see this effect in action.) Unfrozen areas begin to appear more like the original distorted areas.

- **Stiff:** At the edge between frozen and unfrozen areas, the unfrozen areas continue the distortions in the frozen areas. The closer a distortion comes to the frozen areas, the greater the distortions.

- **Smooth:** Continues the distortions from frozen areas into unfrozen areas. The impact is smooth and continuous.

- **Loose:** Similar to Smooth, but offers even more continuity and seamlessness.

You can perform reconstruction to match your distorted areas at certain points in the image. Think of this option as using a kind of warped Clone Stamp tool. (See Chapter 10 for the lowdown on using the Clone Stamp.) Choose one of these remaining options in the Mode menu in the Reconstruct Options area in conjunction with the Reconstruct Tool:

- **Displace:** Moves pixels in unfrozen areas to match the displacement at the reference point. You can use Displace to move all or part of the image to a different location.

- **Amplitwist:** Moves pixels in unfrozen areas to match the displacement, rotation, and scaling applied at a reference point. Use it to duplicate areas in an image.

- **Affine:** Moves pixels in unfrozen areas to match all distortions at the reference point — displacement, rotation, scaling, and skew.

Previewing your liquefactions

Check out the View Options area in the Liquify dialog box. You can select to only show the image, show the mesh, or both. You can also assign a color to the mesh so the mesh stands out when you view it superimposed on the image. The *mesh* is a grid of horizontal and vertical lines that hovers over your image. As you distort the image, you can see how the pixels distort based on the twisting and turning of the mesh grid. You can choose the size and color of the mesh as well.

After you take the time and get your liquefied effect just so, you can save your mesh for later use. Simply click the Save Mesh button at the top right of the Liquify dialog box. Click the Load Mesh button to apply it to another image.

If you only want to view the active layer in the Preview pane, keep the Backdrop option in the View Options area deselected. To show one or all layers, check the Backdrop option. Choose All Layers or a particular layer from the drop-down list and choose an Opacity setting.

In the Tool Options area, the Turbulent Jitter option controls how tightly the Turbulence tool mixes pixels. Select the Stylus Pressure option to enable Photoshop to utilize input from a pressure-sensitive tablet.

Check out "A potpourri of Liquify tools" to see the crazy things you can do to your images. When you're ready to put make your effects final, skip to "Applying your liquefactions."

A potpourri of Liquify tools

And now for the fun stuff. Use any one of the following tools to wreak havoc on your image. Check out the effects of each in Figure 11-20.

- ✔ **Forward Warp Tool (previously called the Warp Tool):** Pushes the pixels forward under your brush as you drag, creating a stretched effect. This tool gives the most taffy-like effect.

- ✔ **Reconstruct Tool:** Returns areas to their initial state. Used in conjunction with the Reconstruct Mode drop-down list box.

- ✔ **Twirl Clockwise Tool:** Rotates the pixels clockwise under your brush as you either drag with the mouse or hold the mouse in one place while pressing the mouse button. Hold down the Alt key (Option key on a Mac) to twirl counterclockwise.

- ✔ **Pucker Tool:** Moves the pixels toward the center of your brush as you drag or hold the mouse in one place while pressing the mouse button, giving a kind of pinched look.

- ✔ **Bloat Tool:** The opposite of Pucker — moves pixels away from the center, creating a kind of spherical effect as you drag or hold the mouse in one place while pressing the mouse button.

Warp

Twirl Clockwise

Pucker

Bloat

Figure 11-20:
The various
effects of
the Liquify
command
can be
downright
amusing.

Push Left

Mirror

✔ **Push Left Tool:** Shifts pixels to the left of the mouse cursor. Hold down the Alt key (Option key on a Mac) to shift pixels to the right.

✔ **Mirror Tool (previously called the Reflection Tool):** Stretches and pulls pixels like a funhouse mirror. Copies pixels from the area perpendicular to the direction you drag. This tool is good for making reflections on shiny surfaces such as water, an automobile hood, or patent leather shoes.

✔ **Turbulence tool:** Mixes pixels in a wavelike manner. It can be used to make flames, waves, and other elements of nature.

There are Zoom and Hand Tools to help you view and navigate around your preview image. These tools work exactly like they do within the Photoshop window.

When you're ready to finalize the effects you've created with the Liquify tools, move on to the following section, "Applying your liquefactions."

Restoring liquefied areas in your image

If you got totally carried away, which is easy to do with these tools, you can tone down the effects on all or part of your image by using the Reconstruct tool and Reconstruction command.

Here are some of the finer points of regaining what you just messed up:

- **To get your entire image (all unfrozen areas, that is) back to its pre-liquefied, original state:** Click the Restore All button in the Reconstruct Options area of the Liquify dialog box.

- **To change a portion of your image (any unfrozen areas) back to its original state:** Choose Revert from the Mode drop-down list box in the Reconstruct Options area. Select the Reconstruct tool and drag or hold down over an area.

- **To slowly reverse the distortion you applied to the image:** Click the Reconstruct button. Each time you click the Reconstruct button, the image will step back one distortion.

Applying your liquefactions

After you use the various tools to pucker, twirl, warp, and generally render your image into something resembling a Salvador Dali painting, you're ready to apply the distortion:

1. **In the Liquify dialog box, click OK if you like your crazed masterpiece and want to apply the distortion to the image.**

   Up till now, Photoshop has been displaying a temporary preview. Clicking OK closes the Liquify dialog box and applies the Liquify filter to the image.

2. **If you're not ready for this kind of commitment, click the Cancel button to get the heck outta there.**

   Because the preview image in the Liquify dialog box was only temporary, if you click Cancel the real image isn't changed in any way. Any changes you made in the Liquify dialog box disappear.

The best advice that I can give you for understanding the inner workings of the Liquify command is to play, play, play. If you have a few spare moments, open an image and do some reality altering of your own.

Part V
Using Your Virtual Paintbrush

The 5th Wave   By Rich Tennant

"Why don't you try blurring the brimstone and then putting a nice glow effect around the hellfire."

In this part . . .

In real life, a paintbrush is a fairly static tool. Dip it in paint and drag it across the canvas and you see a line. The line may vary in width and length depending on how much paint you dab onto the brush and how hard you press, but your options are limited. In Photoshop, on the other hand, a single tool is capable of literally hundreds of variations. In Chapter 12, you find out how to change the size of the brush tip, the angle of the brush, the translucency of the paint, and the way colors mix. Also, you find out how to combine two brushes, a new Photoshop cs feature, to create a dual brush tip that paints with the shape of the combined brushes.

If you have large areas to fill or want to create a special effect, a brush may not be the tool of choice. Chapter 13 moves on to filling areas with colors, patterns, and color blends called *gradients*. Find out how to use the Bucket tool to fill with a single color and then for more color, how to use the Gradient tool to create broad color blends. Next, you find out how to stroke a line of color using a selection as the guide.

Chapter 14 takes you back to the future. The History palette records every action you perform as a *history state*. Although the Undo command removes only one action, you can use the History palette to remove up to 100 previous actions. Just click a previous history state to remove all the actions after that state. And what's more, you can paint using history states. If you want to return to a previous history state in a portion of your image, just use the handy History Brush tool to paint your image back to the past.

Chapter 12

Painting 101

*1*n Chapter 5, you learn how to choose colors using the Color picker, the Color palette, and the Swatch palette. In this chapter, you discover how to apply those colors using the Brush tool and the Pencil tool.

You won't find many of these brushes available from the Brushes palette in a traditional painter's box. In this chapter you find out how to change preset brushes, create custom brushes, save your brushes, and load brush libraries into the Brushes palette. In addition, you use the new Color Replacement tool to paint with one color while removing another (a great tool for removing red eye). Finally, you learn how to create a panorama or photo montage with several images using the new Photomerge command.

The Brushes Palette and Brush Preset Picker

You can modify both the Pencil tool and the Brush tool to a degree that no mechanical pencil or conventional paintbrush can match. For starters, you can change the size and shape of the tip of the tool. You can draw thick strokes one moment and then turn around and draw thin strokes the next, all with the same tool. But the fun doesn't stop there. Photoshop cs supplies a toy box full of options to play with.

Photoshop cs includes a bevy of brush *presets,* or libraries, of different brushes. The program offers so many presets, in fact, that you may find that you never have to explore the other brush options.

To select a brush, just click on a brush shape from the Brush Presets list in either the Brushes palette or the Brush Presets picker; both are shown in Figure 12-1.

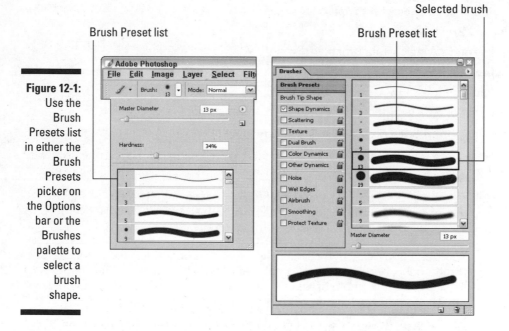

Figure 12-1: Use the Brush Presets list in either the Brush Presets picker on the Options bar or the Brushes palette to select a brush shape.

Setting basic Brush tool options

As you might expect, using the Brush tool is easy. But, before you use it to paint lines and shapes, you need to select the color you want to use, the brush diameter, and a few other things. Here's how:

1. **Select the layer you are going to paint on using the Layers palette.**

   You also can use one of the selection tools to select an area that contains brush strokes just in that selected area.

2. **Select the Brush tool from the Toolbox.**

3. **Choose a Foreground color.**

   The current foreground color is displayed in the Foreground color square in the Toolbox. To find out how to pick a Foreground color, turn to Chapter 5.

4. **Use the Options bar to select Brush tool options.**

   Open the Brush Preset picker on the Options bar, double-click a brush from the Brush presets list to select it, and close the Brush Preset picker.

   Use the Mode drop-down list to select a blending mode. (Turn to Chapter 8 for more about blending modes.)

   Set the opacity of the brush. An opacity setting of 100% completely obscures the underlying pixels.

   Use the Flow slider bar to set a flow percentage. This sets how intensely (and quickly) the paint is applied.

   If you want to paint using airbrush capabilities, click the Airbrush button. The brush continues to pump out paint as long as you keep the mouse button held down.

5. **Stroke across the image in any area you like.**

   If you selected the Airbrush button and press the mouse button down and hold it in one spot, the painted area widens and becomes more opaque.

 If you want to keep the transparent portions of a layer transparent, click the Lock transparent pixels button on the Layers palette. That way, only non-transparent pixels will be painted on.

The Pencil tool

The Pencil tool is pretty straightforward. Unlike the Brush tool that you can use to paint soft strokes, the Pencil tool always draws hard-edged lines.

1. **Select the layer you are going to draw on using the Layers palette.**

   You can also use one of the selection tools to select an area that contains the pencil strokes just in that selected area.

 2. **Select the Pencil tool from the Toolbox.**

3. **Choose a foreground color.**

   The current foreground color is displayed in the Foreground color square in the Toolbox. To find out how to pick a Foreground color, turn to Chapter 5.

4. **Use the Options bar to select Pencil tool options.**

   Open the Brush Preset picker on the Options bar, and double-click a brush on the Brush presets list to select it and close the Brush Preset picker.

   Use the Mode drop-down list to select a blending mode. (Turn to Chapter 8 for more about blending modes.)

   Set the opacity of the brush. An opacity setting of 100% completely obscures the underlying pixels.

5. **Stroke across the image in any area you like.**

You can use the Pencil tool to erase areas using the Auto Erase option on the Options bar. To find out how to do this, turn to Chapter 14.

The Pen tool, by the way, doesn't draw lines as you would expect it to. In Photoshop, the Pen tool is used to create *paths*. Paths enable you to finely select a portion of an image by creating a sort of connect-the-dots outline. The Pen tool and paths are covered in detail in Chapter 16.

Temporarily changing brush diameter

In the Brush Presets picker and the Brushes palette, the diameter of the brush appears with the brush thumbnail or name, and also in the Master Diameter text box (refer to Figure 12-1).

You can temporarily change the diameter of the preset brush by dragging the Diameter slider or typing a value in the Master Diameter text box. The brush Preview pane displays the changed brush.

The new diameter remains the same until you select another brush or change the diameter again.

Pencil and Brush tool tips

Here are some tips about using the Pencil and Brush tools:

✔ **Use the crosshair cursor for precision:** By default, Photoshop displays a little brush or pencil cursor when you select the painting tools. If you press the Caps Lock key, however, the cursor changes to a crosshair cursor that makes it easier to see what you're doing. Use the crosshair when the standard cursor gets in your way. Press Caps Lock again to return to the standard cursor.

✔ **Make the cursor reflect the actual brush size:** To make the cursor reflect the brush size, press Ctrl+K (⌘+K on a Mac) to display the Preferences dialog box. Then choose Display & Cursors from the top drop-down list or press Ctrl+3 (⌘+3 on Mac) to get to the cursor options. Select Brush Size from the Painting Cursors radio buttons and press Enter (Return on a Mac).

✔ **Use keyboard shortcuts to select various painting tools:** You can select either of the painting tools from the keyboard. Press B or Shift+B to select the Brush or the Pencil, which share the same flyout menu in the Toolbox.

✔ **Use keyboard shortcuts to select various brush sizes:** To change the brush size from the keyboard, even when the Brushes palette is hidden, press the right bracket key] to select a larger brush in varying increments. Increments are as follows: 1 pixel in brushes from 1 to 10 pixels in size; 10 pixels in brushes from 10 to 100 pixels in size; 25 pixels in brushes from 100 to 200 in size; 50 pixels in brushes from 200 to 300 in size; 100 pixels in brushes from 300 to 2500 in size (2500 is the max). Press the left bracket key [to select a smaller brush by the same increments.

✔ **Use keyboard shortcuts to change the hardness of the brush:** To raise the hardness of a brush in 25% increments, press Shift+]. To lower the hardness, press Shift+[.

✔ **Create two points and connect them to create a straight line:** To create a straight line, click at one point in the image with either of the painting tools, and Shift+click at another. Photoshop automatically creates a straight line between the two points.

✔ **Create a perfectly straight horizontal or vertical line:** To create a straight line that's exactly vertical or horizontal, click and hold with one of the painting tools, press and hold the Shift key, and then drag with the tool while the Shift key remains down. In other words, press Shift immediately after you begin to drag, and hold Shift throughout the length of the drag. If you release the Shift key while dragging, the line returns to its naturally free-form and wiggly ways.

✔ **Suck up a color and lay it down again:** To lift a color from the image, Alt+click (Option+click on a Mac). Then drag to start painting with that color. Pressing Alt (Option on a Mac) when you're using the Brush or Pencil tools accesses the Eyedropper tool.

✔ **Undo errors with no fuss or muss:** When using the Pencil or Brush tools, you can eliminate the last stroke by choosing Edit➪Undo or pressing Ctrl+Z (⌘+Z on a Mac). Everyone makes mistakes, and the Undo command is there for you to correct those errors. If you need to undo back a few steps, you can use the History palette. (See Chapter 11 for details.)

Using the Brushes Palette

The Brushes palette, which by default is docked in the Palette Well on the Options bar, offers many options for customizing the brush tips for many Photoshop tools. The Brush and Pencil tools aren't the only ones that use brush tips. The Art History Brush, Background Eraser, Blur, Burn, Clone Stamp, Color Replacement, Dodge, History Brush, Pattern Stamp, Sharpen, Smudge, and Sponge tools do, too. (Phew!)

The options in the Brushes palette, which is shown in Figure 12-2, are organized into categories such as Dual Brush, Color Dynamics, Shape Dynamics, Texture, and Wet Edges. Two views of the Brushes palette are shown in Figure 12-2. The view on the left shows the palette with the Brush Presets category selected and the view on the right shows the palette with the Brush Tip Shape category selected.

If you're using a graphics pad with some kind of pen or stylus, you can also use the Brushes palette to select airbrush and input options for this kind of input device.

Brush setting categories

Selected category

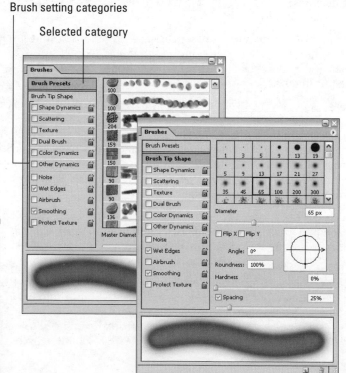

Figure 12-2:
There are literally hundreds of brush combinations to choose from.

Creating custom brushes

If you want to create your own custom brushes, the best way to get started is to modify an existing brush preset that comes with Photoshop. After you find out what you like in a brush — size, shape, texture, and other options — you can create one of your own and save it.

To open the Brushes palette, click the Brushes palette tab in the Palette Well on the Options bar, choose Window➪Brushes, or press F5 on the keyboard. If the palette is docked in the Palette Well, you can use the palette tab to drag it out into the Photoshop window.

Here's a list of the brush options you can select when creating a custom brush. Figure 12-3 shows many of these options to help you get started.

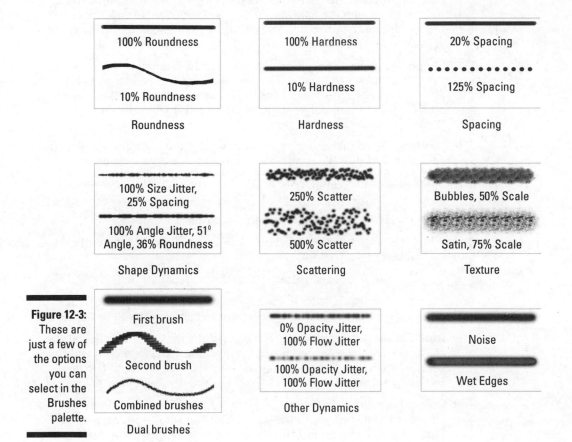

Figure 12-3:
These are just a few of the options you can select in the Brushes palette.

✔ **Brush Presets:** Click this category to choose from the collection of preset brushes in the Brush presets list as shown in Figure 12-3.

✔ **Brush Tip Shape:** Use this category to select a basic brush shape and size as shown in Figure 12-3.

- Use the Tip Shape grid to select a new brush shape and the Diameter slider bar to change its size (from 1 to 2500 pixels).

- Enter a degree value the Angle text box or drag the arrowhead on the circle to change the slant of the brush tip.

- Use the Roundness text box to set the tip shape (from fully round to elliptical) or drag the tiny dots on the circle.

- Change the Hardness value to set the fuzziness of a round brush tip. The higher the setting, the smoother the tip.

- Set the distance between the paint daubs that make up a brush stroke using the Spacing slider. The lower the setting, the closer together the paint daubs, creating a solid line. A higher setting creates a dotted stroke.

✔ **Shape Dynamics:** Use this category to set the amount of variation the brush tip shape can have when painting. Use the Size Jitter, Angle Jitter, and Roundness Jitter slider bars to set the amount of random variation allowed for the Size, Angle, and Roundness that you selected in the Brush Tip Shape category.

✔ **Scattering:** Use this category to set how far paint spatters off the brush stroke. The higher the Scatter setting is, the more splattering of paint.

✔ **Texture:** Use this category to add texture from a pattern to your brush strokes:

- Use the Pattern Picker to select a pattern.

- Put a check in the Invert check box to switch the light and dark areas of the pattern.

- Set the size of the pattern using the Scale slider bar.

- Use the Depth slider to set how much paint sinks into the pattern. The lower the setting, the less pattern texture you will be able to see.

✔ **Dual Brush:** Believe it or not, you can paint with two brush tips at the same time! Select a second brush tip from the Tip Shape grid, and then set the brush tip's diameter, spacing, scatter, and tip count (tip count sets the width of the stroke).

✔ **Color Dynamics:** Use this category to set how much the color can change as you stroke with the brush. You can set the percentage of Foreground/Background Jitter to set the amount of variation between the Foreground and Background colors. Then, you can set the Hue Jitter, Saturation Jitter, and Brightness Jitter to control how much the hue, saturation, and brightness of the Foreground and Background colors can vary. Use the Purity slider to set how much of the Foreground color appears in a brush stroke. The lower the setting, the grayer the stroke.

- ✔ **Other Dynamics:** Use these options to set how much the opacity can change as you paint. The higher the Opacity Jitter setting, the more opacity variation occurs. Flow Jitter sets how much color is applied during the stroke. A lower setting makes for a smoother stroke, and a higher setting makes for a splotchy stroke.

- ✔ **Noise:** Use this option to add graininess to the brush tip, making brush strokes look rougher.

- ✔ **Wet Edges:** Use this option to simulate the wet edges of watercolors.

- ✔ **Airbrush:** Use this option to pump out paint as long as the mouse button is held down.

- ✔ **Smoothing:** Use this option to smooth out wiggly looking curved brush strokes.

- ✔ **Protect Texture:** Use this option to set a uniform texture for an entire image. If you want to apply the same texture pattern already used by other brushes, put a check in this box.

You may have noticed the little padlock icons next to the brush options categories (refer to Figure 12-2). This is a new Photoshop CS feature that lets you lock the category options when you have them set to your liking. With a category locked, any brush you select will use those locked settings even if the brush's preset settings are different.

Creating a custom brush based on an existing Brush Preset

After you get a basic understanding of the brush options available to you as described above in "Creating custom brushes," creating your own brush from a preset brush is easy.

Just use the Brushes palette to select a Brush Preset that is as close as possible to the type of brush you are trying to create. Then, use any of the options described above in "Creating custom brushes" to alter the appearance of the brush. That's it! Take your new brush for a spin and find out what you created.

Saving a custom brush as a tool preset

After creating a custom brush, you can save it as a Brush Preset using the Brush Preset picker. Open the Brush Preset picker on the Options bar and click the Create a New Preset from This Brush button. In the Brush Name dialog box, type a name for the brush, and then click the OK button. The custom brush appears at the bottom of the Brush Preset picker on the Options bar.

Loading a brush library

In addition to the standard brush set that is installed with Photoshop, several extra brush libraries ship as well. These brush libraries contain brushes that create special effects, such as calligraphy tips, drop shadow brushes, and textures. If you find you have the need for a special brush or just want to have some fun, try loading a new brush library. Here's how:

1. **Open the Brushes palette and select the Brush Presets category.**

2. **Click the tiny arrowhead at the upper right of the Brushes palette to access the palette menu.**

   As shown in Figure 12-4, the brush libraries are available at the bottom of the menu.

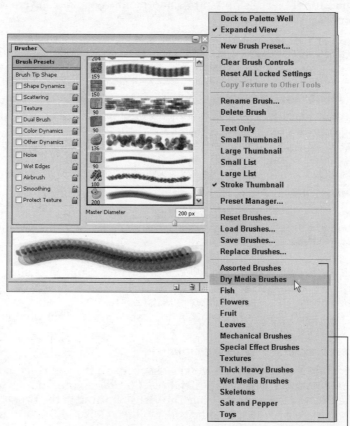

Figure 12-4: The menu in the Brushes palette offers many brush libraries.

Brush libraries

3. **Select a new brush library from the menu.**

   Photoshop opens a dialog box asking whether you want to replace the brushes that are currently loaded with the selected library or append the new library to the ones that are already loaded.

4. **Click OK to replace the current brushes with the new brush library or Append to add the brushes to the currently loaded brushes.**

Removing unwanted brushes

If you find that you've got too many extra brushes cluttering up your Brush Presets list in Brush Preset picker on the Options bar or in the Brushes palette, you can delete the ones you don't need or remove all those extra brushes entirely and return to the default set that comes with Photoshop.

✔ **To reset the brush list:** Open the Brush Preset picker or the Brushes palette, and then choose Reset Brushes from the picker or palette menu (Figure 12-5 shows the Brushes palette menu). A Photoshop dialog box opens, asking whether you want to replace the current brushes with the default brushes. Click OK to do so.

✔ **To delete a brush:** Use the Brush Preset picker to select the brush that you want to delete. Choose Delete Brush from the Brush Preset picker menu as shown in Figure 12-5.

Click to open menu

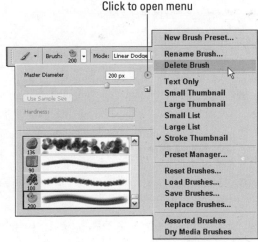

Figure 12-5:
Use the menu in the Brush Preset picker to delete a brush.

The Smudge Tool

 The Smudge tool pushes color from one portion of an image into another. When you drag with this tool, Photoshop grabs the color that's underneath your cursor at the start of your drag and smears it in the direction of your drag.

The Smudge tool is great for smearing away scars, wrinkles, and other imperfections in an image. Figure 12-6 shows a magnified view of the Smudge tool working on a butterfly wing. The various outlines and shapes on the left wing have been smeared and smudged on the right wing.

Figure 12-6: The butterfly wing on the right has been smeared using the Smudge tool.

 Notice that in Figure 12-6, I swirled and smeared the colors in the butterfly wing beyond recognition. You'll get more natural-looking results if you carefully trace along the details of your subject and don't simply drag haphazardly all over the place like I did.

Using Smudge-specific controls

You can modify the performance of the Smudge tool by using the Smudge options found on the Options bar as shown in Figure 12-7.

- ✔ **Change brush size:** Select another brush size using the Brush Presets picker. (For more about changing brushes diameters, see "Temporarily changing brush diameter" at the beginning of this chapter.)

- ✔ **Smudge straight:** Click and Shift+click to smudge in a straight line, or Shift+drag to smudge horizontally or vertically.

Figure 12-7:
The Options
bar lets you
select brush
tip size,
blending
modes, and
stroke
strength.

- ✔ **Change smudge attributes:** Access the various smudge options on the Options bar. For example, you can adjust the Strength slider by clicking on the black arrow to the right of the default setting of 50 percent to create more subtle retouching effects. Increase the Strength setting to make the smudging effect more pronounced.

- ✔ **Use blending modes:** Use the Darken and Lighten blending modes in the Mode drop-down list to smear only those colors that are darker or lighter than the original colors in the image.

- ✔ **Smudge without losing detail:** Use the Color brush mode to smear the colors in an RGB image without harming the detail. Pretty nifty.

- ✔ **Access the Brush Presets menu:** The context-sensitive menu appears when you right-click (Control+click on a Mac) your canvas.

- ✔ **Get your hands dirty:** Select the Finger Painting check box to dip your brush into the Foreground color before smudging. Photoshop applies a little dab of Foreground color at the beginning of your drag and then begins to smear into the existing colors in the image as usual.

  To temporarily turn on Finger Painting when the check box is dese-lected, press Alt (Option on a Mac) as you drag with the Smudge tool. If the Finger Painting check box is selected, Alt+drag (Option+drag on a Mac) to smudge in the normal fashion.

- ✔ **Smudge on all layers:** Check the Use All Layers check box if you're edit-ing an image with layers. This setting enables you to pick up the colors from all of your layers.

Using the Color Replacement Tool

The new Color Replacement tool lives in the Toolbox flyout menu with the Healing Brush tool and the Patch tool. To access the Color Replacement tool from the keyboard, press Shift+J until it appears on the Toolbox button.

This tool is really fabulous. With just a few strokes of the brush you can quickly replace one color with another. Removing red eye in photos is quick and easy.

Here's how it works. First you the use the Eyedropper tool to sample the color that will be replaced to the Background color square. Next, you choose the color that you want to use as the replacement — this color goes in the Toolbox's Foreground color square. Then, after setting a few options on the Options bar, you stroke on the new color while the old sampled color is automatically replaced.

Color Plate 12-1 shows a bad case of red eye that is quickly fixed. All I did was sample the red area in the pupil, select black as the Foreground color, and brush away the red eye with the Color Replacement tool.

Open an image and give this tool a try to remove dreaded red eye from a photograph or replace one color for another in an image:

1. **In the Toolbox, click the Background color square if it isn't already active.**

 2. **Select the Eyedropper tool from the Toolbox and sample the color you want to replace from the image.**

    You can set the size of the color sample that the Eyedropper tool takes using the Sample Size drop-down list on the Options bar. Unless you're trying to replace a single, specific color, the 3 by 3 Average or 5 by 5 Average settings work best for this tool.

3. **Click the Foreground color square in the Toolbox to select it.**

4. **Use the Color Picker, Color palette, or Swatches palette to specify the replacement color. Or use the Eyedropper to sample the replacement color from another area of the image.**

 5. **Select the Color Replacement tool from the Toolbox.**

6. **Use the Options bar to select Color Replacement tool settings.**

   As shown in Figure 12-8, the Options bar offers many settings.

Figure 12-8:
The Options
bar offers
sampling,
color re-
placement,
blending
mode, and
tolerance
settings.

7. **Open the Brush Preset picker to set the size of the brush tip.**

   A small, slightly fuzzy tip works best for removing red eye (for this example, I'm using a brush set at a 5 pixel diameter and 90% Hardness).

8. **Select a blending mode using the Blend drop-down list.**

   The selections you can make are Hue, Saturation, Color, or Luminosity. Color mode works well for fixing red eye. (Blending modes are discussed in Chapter 8.)

9. **Set the way the tool will replace the color using the Sampling drop-down list.**

   • Choose the Once setting to sample the color you want to replace from the pixel where you start to use the tool (no need to sample a Background color using the Eyedropper tool). Besides sampling the color, the tool also samples the color's saturation and lightness. The tool only replaces that color.

   • Choose the Continuous setting to continuously sample colors as you use the tool (no need to sample a Background color using the Eyedropper tool). The replacement color's saturation and lightness adjusts as you paint over areas that are lighter or darker and more or less saturated.

   • Choose the Background Swatch to use the Background color selected by the Eyedropper tool as the color that will be replaced.

10. **Use the Limits drop-down list to set how far the replacement color will spread.**

   • Choose the Discontiguous setting to spread paint to similarly colored pixels that are in the "neighborhood" you're painting in (but which aren't necessarily right next to the pixels you are recoloring).

   • Choose the Contiguous setting to paint the replacement color only to neighboring pixels.

   • Choose the Find Edges setting to let painting occur until the tool senses that there is an edge — an area of pixels that contrast sharply with the surrounding pixels.

11. **Use the Tolerance slider to set the range of colors that the tool will replace.**

   A lower setting paints colors that are very similar to the color being replaced. A higher setting selects a broader range of colors.

12. **Put a check in the Anti-aliased check box to set the tool to blend the edges of a newly painted area.**

For sharp edges, uncheck this option.

13. **Stroke with the Color Replacement tool on the color you want to replace.**

If you are painting small areas such as eyes, it helps to zoom in so you can see what you're doing. In Figure 12-9, the child's eyes in the photo on the right have been repainted to eliminate red eye. You can see another photograph with the red eye removed in Color Plate 12-1.

Figure 12-9: The child in the original image on the left has a red gleam in his eye. On the right, his eyes have been retouched.

Creating a Panorama or Photo Montage

The first time I tried the new Photomerge command out, I said to myself "Dang! This thing is smart!"

This Photoshop feature takes all the trouble out of combining photographs to create panoramas. It compares the pixels from one image with the pixels in another image, and it finds the areas with the same pixel values. *Then,* it plops the two images on top of each other, creating a new seamless image. *And,* you're not stuck with just creating a panorama with two photos. You can use as many photos as you like.

Another great use for the Photomerge option is creating photo mosaics of related pictures. For instance, you could create a great montage of family portraits.

I just ran outside with my digital camera and took five pictures of a tree. The first photo I shot was the bottom of the tree and the successive photos moved up the tree to its top as shown in Figure 12-10. Let's see what Photomerge does with the pictures.

Figure 12-10: Five photos of the tree across the street. If I can put them together, they will create a view of the entire tree.

1. **Choose File➪Automate➪Photomerge.**

   An initial Photomerge dialog box opens as shown in Figure 12-11. You'll use this dialog box to select the images that will be combined. If you have a previous Photomerge composition saved, you can also open it here.

2. **With the Use drop-down list, select where the images will come from.**

   Your options include Files, which lets you select individual files; Folder, which lets you select all the images in a folder; or Open files.

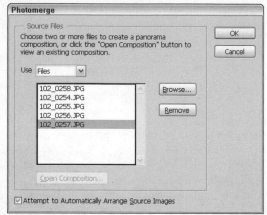

Figure 12-11: The initial Photomerge dialog box lets you select the images that will be combined.

3. **If you selected Files in step 2, click the Browse button to locate the images you want to merge and load them into the Photomerge dialog box.**

4. **Click OK to continue.**

   Photoshop goes to work comparing the images and trying to place them together. If some (or all) of the image can't be placed together, a dialog box appears telling you so. Click OK to continue. (You can fit the images in that couldn't be placed later.)

   Figure 12-12 shows the large Photomerge dialog box that opens. This is where you can create your photo composition, be it a panorama or montage.

5. **Move the images around in the Composition area to match areas within the photos or create a photo mosaic.**

   If you're creating a panorama, drag photos that have areas that are the same toward each other, get them lined up as best you can (it doesn't have to be perfect), then release the mouse button. The photos snap together as Photomerge automatically lines the photos up exactly.

   When creating a panorama from photographs taken while moving the camera for each shot, the panorama can appear stretched or slightly warped. To remove this distortion, click the Perspective button. Photoshop automatically angles and skews the photographs to remove the distortion and make the panorama look normal.

6. **When you're happy with the way the photos have been combined, click the Save Composition As. . . button.**

   This step is optional, but if you save the composition in Photomerge, you can come back and edit it later in the Photomerge dialog box.

Move View tool

Zoom tool

Set Vanishing Point tool

Rotate Image tool

Select Image tool

Drag photos from Preview area to Composition area

Save composition for later editing

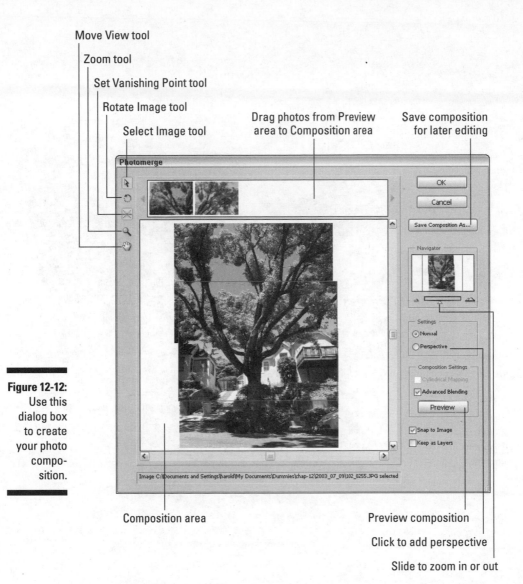

Figure 12-12:
Use this dialog box to create your photo composition.

Composition area

Preview composition

Click to add perspective

Slide to zoom in or out

7. Click OK.

Photoshop copies and layers the photos, finally opening the merged composition in a Photoshop image window. You can now edit the merged photo as you would any other image in Photoshop.

Figure 12-13 shows the five tree photos merged together into one tree image. Figure 12-14 shows a montage of family photos.

Figure 12-13:
This single
image is a
combination
of the five
photos
shown in
Figure 12-12.

Figure 12-14:
This photo montage was creating using various family photos.

Chapter 13

Coloring inside the Lines

● ●

In This Chapter

▶ Painting and editing inside a selection outline

▶ Using the Paint Bucket tool

▶ Filling from the keyboard

▶ Using the Fill command

▶ Creating gradients

▶ Applying different types of gradients

▶ Stroking a selection

● ●

*I*n Photoshop, making a selection outline works the same way as spray painting a stencil. Just as a stencil isolates the area affected by the spray paint, a selection outline isolates the area affected by a paint or edit tool. You can also fill a selection outline with color or trace around the selection outline.

Sounds easy, doesn't it? Chapter 7 explains how to create and manipulate selection outlines. This chapter shows you what to do with the selection outlines — for instance, fill them with solid color, gradients, and outline them.

Putting Down Newspaper before You Paint

If some portion of an image is selected, Photoshop treats all unselected areas as protected. You can use any paint or edit tool inside the selection without worrying about harming areas outside the selection. Photoshop calls the protected area of an image a *selection mask*.

In this chapter, I took a jar-in-a-nook — it's just the sort of prop that would feel right at home in a hoity-toity kitchen of the idle rich — and I mucked it up. Specifically, I painted inside the jar without harming the background. And you can, too. To this end, do the following:

1. **Select part of an image.**

   In my example, I selected the body of the jar with the Elliptical Marquee tool.

   If you have problems getting the marquee exactly on the object you're selecting — it's hard to know where to start dragging so that it comes out right — just make sure that the marquee is approximately the right size, select one of the Marquee or Lasso tools, and then use the arrow keys to nudge the outline into position.

2. **Make any modifications you deem necessary.**

   In this case, you may want to blur the selection outline a tad using Select⇨Feather, as I explain in Chapter 7. If your selection outline isn't exactly perfect, the Feather command helps to fudge the difference a little.

3. **Choose View⇨Extras or press Ctrl+H (⌘+H on the Mac).**

   This step is extremely important. By hiding the selection outline, you can see how your edits affect the image without those distracting *marching ants* getting in your way.

4. **Paint and edit away.**

   Feel free to use any tool you want. You can paint with the Pencil tool; the Brush tool and its many varieties; edit with the Smudge, Dodge, or Burn tools; clone with the Rubber Stamp tool; use the Eraser tool and erase to a previous version of the image — all with the assurance that the area outside the selection will remain as safeguarded from your changes as the driven snow (or whatever the saying is).

While editing away, try not to press Ctrl+D (⌘+D on a Mac) or click with one of the selection tools. Because the selection outline is hidden, you can't see any difference when you deselect the image. If you do inadvertently deselect, press Ctrl+Z (⌘+Z on a Mac) right away. If you wait until after you apply a brush stroke, Ctrl+Z (⌘+Z on a Mac) undoes the stroke but not the selection outline.

But don't fret. Even after performing several actions, you can retrieve your last selection by choosing Select⇨Reselect or pressing Ctrl+Shift+D (⌘+Shift+D on a Mac).

In Figure 13-1, I painted inside my selected jar using a single tool — the Brush tool with the Airbrush option — with a single brush size and only two colors, black and white. As a result, I was able to transform the jar into a kind of marble. Looks mighty keen, and there's not so much as a drop of paint outside the lines.

Figure 13-1:
Using the Brush tool with the Airbrush option, I painted inside the selected jar. (The selection outline is hidden.)

Dribbling Paint from a Bucket

The Paint Bucket tool is part selection tool and part fill tool. The Paint Bucket tool (which looks like a tilted bucket of paint) shares a flyout menu with the Gradient tool and lets you fill an area of continuous color by clicking on the area.

In Figure 13-2, for example, I set the Foreground to white and clicked with the Paint Bucket tool on the row of broccoli in the jar. Photoshop filled the broccoli with white, turning it into the rough facsimile of cauliflower.

To adjust the performance of the Paint Bucket tool, access the Options bar, shown in Figure 13-3. If you've used the Magic Wand tool, you'll know that the Tolerance value determines how many pixels are affected. With the Paint Bucket tool, the Tolerance setting works the same way. The only difference is that the Paint Bucket applies color instead of selecting pixels like the Magic Wand. You also can select the Anti-aliased check box to soften the edges of the filled area. (In Figure 13-3, the Tolerance value is 32, and Anti-aliased is selected, as it is by default.)

Figure 13-2:
The Paint Bucket fills a continuous area of color with a different color.

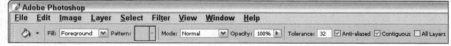

Figure 13-3:
The Options bar lets you set fill, blending mode, opacity, and tolerance.

Applying Color to Selection Innards

It's time to move on to the other ways you can fill a selection outline in Photoshop:

- ✔ **To fill a selection with the Foreground color:** Press Alt+Backspace (Option+Delete on a Mac).

- ✔ **To fill a selection with the Background color:** Press Ctrl+Backspace (⌘+Delete on a Mac).

- ✔ **To fill the opaque part of a selection on a layer with the Foreground color while leaving the rest of the selection transparent:** Press Shift+Alt+Backspace (Shift+Option+Delete on a Mac).

- ✔ **To fill the opaque area with the Background color:** Press Ctrl+Shift+Backspace (⌘+Shift+Delete on a Mac).

For more about layers, turn to Chapter 7, where I explain layers and transparency.

✔ **To display the Fill dialog box:** Choose Edit⇨Fill. This menu option lets you fill the selection with color, a pattern, or history. (See Chapter 14 for more on history.)

✔ **To create a gradient (a gradual blend) between two or more colors:** Drag with the Gradient tool.

Using the Fill Command

Choose Edit⇨Fill to display the Fill dialog box, shown in Figure 13-4. The Use drop-down list lets you specify the color or stored image with which you want to fill the selection; the Blending options let you mix the filled colors with the colors already inside the selection. I discuss all these options in more detail in the following sections.

Figure 13-4: Specify how you want to fill a selection by using the options in the Fill dialog box.

You also can display the Fill dialog box by pressing Shift+Backspace (Shift+Delete on a Mac).

Selecting your fill color

The most important part of the Fill dialog box is the Use drop-down list. Here you select the stuff you want to use to fill the selection. The options are as follows:

✔ **The Foreground Color option:** Fills the selection with the Foreground color, and the Background Color option fills the selection with the Background color.

✔ **The Pattern option:** Fills a selection with a repeating pattern. You can define a pattern by selecting a rectangular area and choosing Edit⇨Define Pattern. You can access the patterns with the Custom Pattern pop-up palette. For more about patterns, turn to Chapter 10.

✔ **The History option:** Fills the selection with a previously saved step of that portion of the image. In short, the History palette remembers all your previous steps, which are called *source states*. You select a previous source state in the palette, and the selection fills with the image as it appeared at that point in time. Check out Chapter 14 for more about the History palette.

✔ **The Black, 50% Gray, and White options:** Fill the selection with black, medium gray, and white, respectively.

How not to mix colors

You can enter a value into the Opacity text box of the Fill dialog box to mix the fill color or history source state with the present colors in the selection. You also can mix the fill and the selected color using the options in the Mode drop-down list box, which include Multiply, Screen, Difference, and other blending modes. (See Chapter 8 for more about blending modes.)

Notice that I said you can do these things, not that you *should* do these things. The truth is, you don't want to use the Fill dialog box's Blending options to mix fills with selections. Why? Because the Fill dialog box doesn't let you preview the effects of the Blending options. Even seasoned professionals have trouble predicting the exact results of Opacity setting and Mode option, and it's likely that you will, too. And, if you don't like what you get, you have to undo the operation and choose Edit⇨Fill all over again.

Creating Gradients

 The Gradient tool lets you fill a selection with a fountain of colors that starts with one color and ends with another. By default, the two colors are the Foreground color and Background color.

But Photoshop can do more than create simple two-color blends. You can create custom gradients that blend a multitude of colors and vary from opaque to transparent throughout the blend. Photoshop has five gradient types: Linear, Radial, Angle, Reflected, and Diamond. And the Options bar offers settings that enable you to play with blend modes, opacity, and reversing colors.

 Right-click (Control+click on a Mac) anywhere in the image window to bring up the Gradient picker.

Checking out the Gradient tool

Gradients can add interesting effects to an image. Open an image and try this out:

1. **Select some portion of your image.**

   If you don't select a portion of your image before using the Gradient tool, Photoshop fills the entire image with the gradient. (Or, if you're working on a layer, as discussed in Chapter 8, the gradient fills the entire layer.)

2. **Select the Gradient tool.**

   To do it quickly, just type **G**.

3. **From the Options bar, select your desired gradient type.**

   Figure 13-5 shows the Gradient picker open and the other settings available on the Options bar.

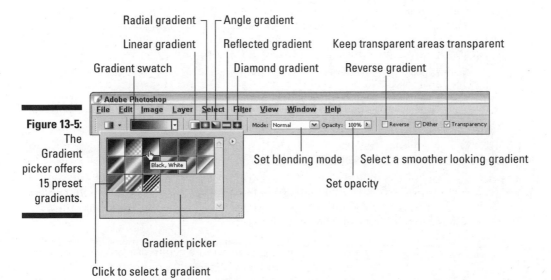

Figure 13-5: The Gradient picker offers 15 preset gradients.

4. **Select the Foreground to Background option, the first gradient, from the Gradient picker on the Options bar.**

   It creates a gradient that begins with the Foreground color and ends with the Background color.

5. **Set the Foreground and Background colors the way you want them.**

   This step is up to you. You can stick with black and white or select new colors with the Eyedropper tool or Color palette.

6. **Begin dragging at the point where you want to set the Foreground color.**

7. **Release where you want to position the Background color.**

If you Shift+drag with the Gradient tool, Photoshop constrains the direction of your drag to a horizontal, vertical, or 45 degree angle.

You also can apply a gradient to a layer using the Gradient Map command. This command applies the colors from a gradient to an image based on the light and dark pixels in an image. To find out how to apply the Gradient Map command to an image, turn to Chapter 9.

Changing gradient types

You can alter the performance of the Gradient tool by accessing the settings on the Options bar (refer to Figure 13-5).

Choosing between the five gradient types

Photoshop gives you five gradient tools, which are described below and illustrated in Figure 13-6.

- ✔ **Linear:** Creates a gradient in which colors blend in a straight line.

- ✔ **Radial:** The colors blend in concentric circles; by default, the blend begins from the center of the selection and moves outward, but you can move focal point.

For consistency, every example in Figure 13-6 uses a black Foreground color and a white Background color. However, you almost always want to set the lighter color to the Foreground color when using the Radial option because doing so creates a glowing effect. If the Foreground color is darker than its Background color, then the gradation looks like a bottomless pit.

- ✔ **Angle:** Creates a conical gradation with the colors appearing counter-clockwise.

- ✔ **Reflected:** If dragged from edge to edge of your selection, a reflected gradient acts like a standard linear gradient. However, if dragged from the interior to an edge of the selection, the gradient creates symmetrical linear gradients on both sides of the origin point.

- ✔ **Diamond:** Like the radial gradient, this tool creates concentric shapes — in this case, diamonds or squares, depending on the angle you drag.

Choosing gradient options

You find three check boxes on the Options bar: Reverse, Dither, and Transparency. Here's what they do:

Linear  Radial

Figure 13-6:
Jar filled
with five
different
gradient
types —
Linear,
Radial,
Angle,
Reflected,
and
Diamond.

Angle   Reflected   Diamond

✔ **Reverse check box:** When selected, the gradient starts with the Background color and ends with the Foreground color. This option is useful for creating radial gradients while keeping the default colors intact.

✔ **Dither check box:** When selected, this option helps eliminate banding. *Banding* occurs when you see distinct bands of color in a gradient.

✔ **Transparency check box:** When selected, this option retains transparency information. Here's how it works. Gradients can include areas that are partially or fully transparent. In other words, they fade from a solid color to a more transparent color. When the Transparency check box is deselected, Photoshop creates the gradient by using all opaque colors, ignoring the transparency information.

The best way to get a grip on what the Transparency check box does is to try a little experiment. First, select the check box and press D to get the default Foreground and Background colors. Then, choose the Transparent Rainbow option (the next to last swatch) from the Gradient picker pop-up palette and draw a gradient. You get a fill pattern that consists of a multicolored rainbow with your background peeking out at the beginning and end of the gradient. Next, draw the gradient with the Transparency check box deselected. You now get a fill of a multicolored rainbow with no background peeking out because Photoshop ignores the transparency at either end of the gradient. In most cases, you don't need to bother with the check box — just leave it selected.

Selecting your colors

The Gradient picker on the Options bar (refer to Figure 13-5) lets you change the way colors blend across the gradient. The preset gradients that come with Photoshop use different colors to create different effects. Here's a brief description of the colors that some of the preset gradients blend:

- ✔ **Foreground to Background gradient:** Shown in the upper-left corner of the Gradient picker, this is the default selection. This gradient does just what it sounds like it does: It blends between the Foreground and Background colors, as in the examples in Figure 13-6.

- ✔ **Foreground to Transparent, Transparent Rainbow, and Transparent Stripes:** If you select one of these gradients, which include transparency, the gradient tool blends the Foreground color into the original colors in the selection. The examples in Figure 13-7 were created with the Foreground to Transparent option selected.

Linear   Radial

Figure 13-7:
Here's the
jar filled
with a linear
and radial
gradient and
with the
Foreground
to Trans-
parent
option
selected.

Foreground to Transparent

- ✔ **Other preset gradients:** The remaining options in the Gradient picker create a variety of preset gradients, some involving just a few colors and others blending a whole rainbow of colors.

- ✔ **Gradient libraries:** Photoshop offers a vast array of gradient libraries that contain preset gradients that you can easily load for your painting pleasure. Open the Gradient picker menu by clicking the tiny arrow at the upper right of the picker, and scroll down to the bottom where you find the various gradient libraries. Select one and either replace or append your current gradient set.

Creating custom gradients

It's pretty easy to design your own custom gradient if you just spend a few minutes looking at Gradient Editor dialog box.

To open the Gradient Editor dialog box, click the gradient swatch on the Gradient picker on the Options bar, as shown in Figure 13-8.

Click here to open Gradient Editor

Figure 13-8:
Click the
gradient
swatch.

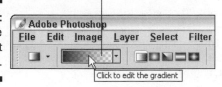

The Gradient Editor dialog box, shown in Figure 13-9, contains everything you need to create nifty gradients.

The following list gives you a brief introduction to the dialog box and starts you on the path of creating your own gradient:

- ✔ **Presets:** The palette at the top of the dialog box lists all the preset gradients — the same ones in the Gradient picker on the Options bar. Select the gradient you want to use as a starting point for your custom gradient from this palette.

- ✔ **Gradient Type:** You can choose between gradients made with Solid colors or those created with Noise. *Noise* gradients add a grainy quality that randomizes the colors of selected pixels.

- ✔ **Smoothness:** Drag the slider or enter a value to determine how smoothly you blend one color into another color. The Smoothness slider changes to a Roughness slider when a Noise gradient type is selected.

- ✔ **Roughness:** This option is only available if you choose a Noise gradient. Roughness affects how smooth or sharp one color transitions into another.

The following options are available only when the Noise gradient type is selected:

- ✔ **Color Model and Color sliders:** Change the color model and/or limit the color range by moving the sliders.

- ✔ **Restrict Colors:** Limits the colors to printable CMYK colors. (See more about CMYK in Chapter 4.)

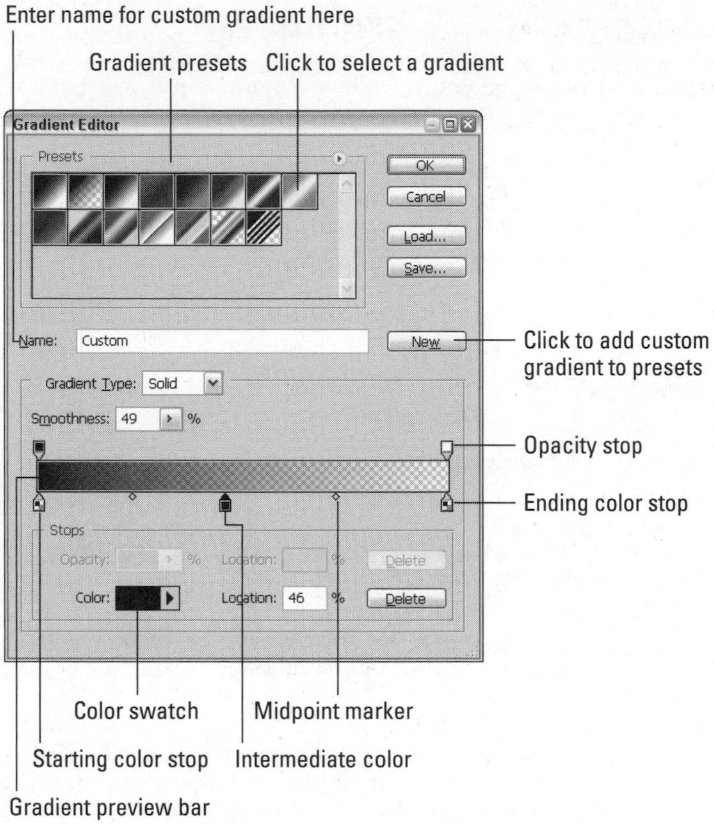

Enter name for custom gradient here

Gradient presets   Click to select a gradient

Figure 13-9:
The
Gradient
Editor gives
you
complete
control over
your
gradients.

Click to add custom
gradient to presets

Opacity stop

Ending color stop

Color swatch   Midpoint marker

Starting color stop   Intermediate color

Gradient preview bar

- ✔ **Add Transparency:** Enables you to incorporate transparency in your noise gradient.

- ✔ **Randomize:** Changes the colors in a Noise gradient. Remember, this option is *random* and every time you click you get a new set of colors.

- ✔ **Gradient Preview bar:** Displays both the colors and transparent areas of your gradient. Transparent areas are represented by a gray-and-white checkerboard pattern.

- ✔ **Stops:** The little house-shaped boxes beneath the Gradient Preview bar are called *stops*. Color stops are on the bottom, and opacity stops are on the top of the Gradient Preview bar. You use these stops to change the colors, opacity, and location of the gradient, as explained in the upcoming two sections.

- ✔ **The Save button:** Saves your gradient to a different location on disk. You don't need to save the gradient using this button unless you want to store your gradient in some spot other than where the rest of the gradients are located. After you edit and name a gradient, click the New button, and then click OK; the gradient is automatically added to the Gradient picker palette on the Options bar for the gradient tools.

To remove a gradient from the list, press Alt+Shift (Option+Shift on a Mac) and click the gradient. Note that the scissors icon signifies the Delete option.

Choosing colors

To change one of the colors in the gradient, first check to see whether the roof on that color's color stop is black. The black *roof* indicates the active color stop — the color that is affected by your changes. If the roof isn't black, click the color stop to make it active.

After you activate the color stop, you have one of three choices for picking a color:

✔ You can click the colored square next to Color. The Color picker appears.

✔ You can select the Foreground or Background color by clicking the arrow to the right of Color. Then select either Foreground or Background from the drop-down list.

✔ You can click a color in your image, a color in the color bar of the Color palette, or a color in the Swatches palette.

Adding, removing, and deleting colors

Here's some more stuff you need to know about playing with the colors in your gradient:

✔ **To add a color to the gradient:** Click just below the Gradient Preview bar at the point where you want the color to appear. You get a new color stop icon representing the color.

✔ **To remove a color from the gradient:** Drag its color stop down and away from the Gradient Preview bar.

✔ **To change the position of a color in the gradient:** Drag the color stop to the right or left. Suppose you have a gradient that fades from black to white. If you want more black and less white, drag the black color stop toward the white stop.

✔ **To change the midpoint between two colors in the gradient:** Drag the little diamond below the Gradient Preview bar. Using the example of a black-to-white gradient again, the *midpoint* marks the spot at which the gradient contains equal amounts of black and white.

Changing the transparency

Photoshop lets you adjust the amount of opacity in a gradient. You can make a portion of the gradient fully opaque, completely transparent, or somewhere in between the two.

Suppose you want to create a gradient that starts out white, gradually fades to completely transparent, and then becomes completely white again. In other words, you want to create a variation of the effect shown back in Figure 13-7. Here's how to create such a gradient:

1. **Make the Foreground color white.**

2. **Click the gradient swatch on the Options bar to open the Gradient Editor dialog box (refer to Figure 13-8).**

3. **Inside the Gradient Editor dialog box, choose the Foreground to Transparent (the second swatch) gradient from the Gradient palette.**

4. **Take the opacity stop on the right and move it to the center of the Gradient Preview bar. Leave the Opacity setting at 0% (completely transparent).**

5. **Add another opacity stop at the far right. Change the Opacity setting to 100% (completely opaque).**

   The Gradient Preview bar now shows your gradient in terms of transparent and opaque areas (see Figure 13-10).

   Black stops represent opaque areas; white stops represent transparent areas.

   The Gradient Preview bar also shows you the opaque areas in their actual colors and transparent areas in a gray and white checkerboard pattern.

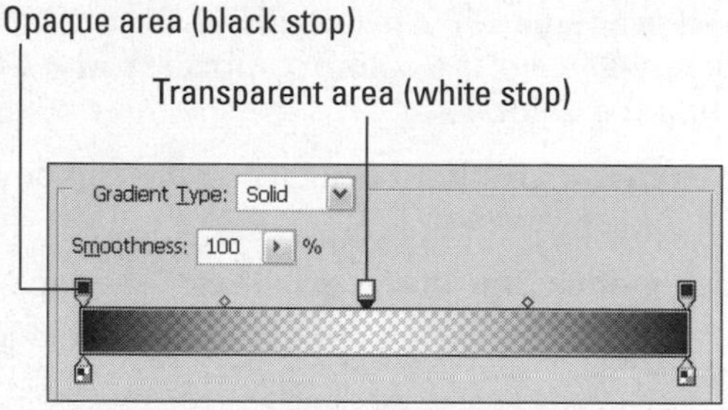

Opaque area (black stop)

Transparent area (white stop)

Figure 13-10: The Gradient Preview bar shows you where the opaque and transparent areas of a gradient are.

Gradient Type: Solid

Smoothness: 100 ▸ %

6. **Type a name for your gradient in the Name text box.**

7. **Click the New button.**

   Your gradient, with its new name, is added to the gradient palette in both the Gradient Editor and the Gradient picker on the Options bar, as shown in Figure 13-11. You now have a gradient that fades from fully opaque white to transparent and then to fully opaque white again. Apply the gradient to an image to get a better idea of what you just created.

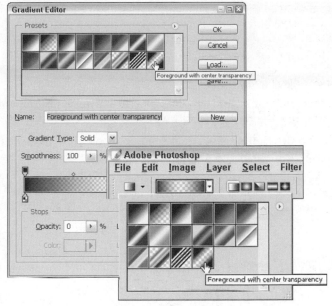

Figure 13-11:
Your custom gradient is added to the gradient palette in the Gradient Editor and in the Gradient picker on the Options bar.

You can add as many opacity stops as you want and set different Opacity values for each stop. To move an opacity stop, just drag it right or left; to delete a stop, drag it off the bar. To move a midpoint, drag it right or left.

Don't forget that the Transparency check box on the Options bar determines whether transparency settings are ignored when you apply a gradient. If the check box is deselected, your gradient is completely opaque. For example, if you deselect the check box when applying the gradient created by the preceding steps, you get a completely white gradient instead of one that fades from white to transparent and back again.

Using the Stroke Command

The Stroke command traces borders around a selection. When you choose Edit⇨Stroke, Photoshop displays the Stroke dialog box, shown in Figure 13-12. Enter the thickness of the border you want into the Width text box. This value is measured in pixels and the range is 1 to 250 pixels.

You can enter units other than pixels. For example, if you type **2 inches** into the Width text box, Photoshop converts the value to an equivalent number of pixels.

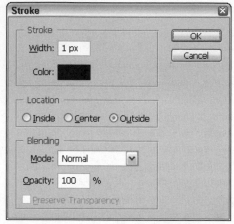

Figure 13-12:
Use the
Stroke
dialog box
to draw a
border
around a
selection.

Creating a border with the Stroke command

You can use the Stroke command to add artistic border effects to images. For example, In Figure 13-13 I traced a 16-pixel wide black border around the jar. Then I swapped the Foreground and Background colors, chose Edit➪Stroke again, and entered 8 into the Width text box. The result is a white border inside a black border.

By default, the stroke color is based on the current Foreground color, but you can pick a different color from within the Stroke dialog box itself. Simply click the color swatch, and you're transported to the Color picker.

Making the border ride the track

The Location options in the Stroke dialog box determine how the border rides the selection outline. The border can cruise around fully inside or fully outside the selection, or it can sit astride (centered on) the selection.

Why might you want to change this setting? Well, take another look at Figure 13-13. If, instead of having the white border flanked on either side by black (just choose the Center option to create this effect), you want the borders to sit beside each other, simply select the Inside option. As a result, the white border appears inside the selection, and the black border appears inside the white border. If you select the Outside option, the white border traces the outside of the jar, and the black border extends even farther.

Figure 13-13:
The classic double-border effect, so in demand at today's finer jar emporiums.

Mixing your stroke after you press Enter (Return)

Like the Blending and Opacity options in other dialog boxes, the ones in the Stroke dialog box don't provide you with a preview of how the effect will look when applied to your image. So, if you want to play with the blend modes or opacity of your stroke, ignore the options in the dialog box. Instead, create a new layer (as explained in Chapter 7) and do your selecting and stroking on that layer. You can then adjust the blend mode and opacity using the Layers palette (also discussed in Chapter 7).

On the off chance that you're curious about the Preserve Transparency check box, it affects only images with layers. It ensures that the transparent portions of layers remain transparent.

Chapter 14

Changing History and Erasing Pixels

• •

• •

*T*he Undo command is standard equipment with just about every Windows and Macintosh program out there. With one press of Ctrl+Z (⌘+Z on a Mac) — the Undo command's keyboard equivalent — your previous operation disappears for good, leaving you one step backward in time.

But Photoshop doesn't stop there. You're also lucky enough to have access to *multiple undos* by way of the amazing History palette. Not only can you undo as many as 100 actions, but also you can actually *skip* previous steps. In other words, if you have performed five actions and want to return to the way your image looked after your second action, you aren't required to first undo steps five, four, and three. You merely select step two in the History palette.

In this chapter, I explain all the Photoshop methods for regaining the past so that you can edit worry-free, safe in the knowledge that almost everything you do can be undone. But before you explore the wide and wonderful world of the History palette, look at the Photoshop old-and-trusty ways of undoing what's been done.

Undoing the Last Operation

The Undo command, Edit⇨Undo, puts you back one step, removing the last modification.

After you choose the Undo command from the Edit menu, the command changes to the Redo command on the Edit menu. In other words, you can undo an action, and then redo it, and then undo it, and then redo it, and so on, until you make up your mind or collapse from exhaustion, whichever comes first.

The Undo command works even after you choose File➪Print or File➪Print One Copy. This means that you can adjust an image, print it to see how it looks, and undo the adjustment if you don't like it.

Choosing File➪Page Setup — or any other command except Print — wipes out your chance to undo an adjustment. The Undo command also doesn't work after you print with the File➪Print with Preview command. So, if you need to undo an adjustment after using Print with Preview, you'll need to use the History palette to move back a few steps.

The Revert Command

Sometimes you make small mistakes, and sometimes you make big ones. If, after several minutes of painting and editing, you decide that you want to return the entire image to its last saved appearance so that you can start over again, you can do one of two things:

✔ **Select the top step, technically referred to as a *state*, in the History palette.** (Turn to "The History Palette" later in this chapter for more details.) Selecting the top step restores the image back to the way it appeared when you first opened it.

✔ **Choose File➪Revert.** Photoshop displays an Alert box to make sure that you didn't choose the wrong command. If you click the Revert button or press Enter (Return on a Mac), the program reloads the image from disk and throws away all changes.

You have an advantage in using the History palette rather than the File➪Revert command. The History palette restores the *original* image regardless of whether you saved along the way, whereas File➪Revert reloads the last saved version, which may include some undesired changes.

Just in case you change your mind or your fingers slipped, you can undo File➪Revert, so breathe easy. And if you've executed another command, don't despair. The Revert command is recorded in the History palette as a state and can be deleted.

The Powers of the Eraser

What artist's toolbox would be complete without an eraser? None that I know of. But Photoshop provides not just one eraser, but three — the Eraser tool, the Background Eraser tool, and the Magic Eraser tool.

Working with the Eraser tool

 The Eraser tool is the sixth tool from the top on the left side in the Toolbox, and it lets you erase in a couple of ways:

- **Erasing in an image with only one layer:** If you drag with the Eraser tool in an image that contains only one layer, the tool paints in the currently selected Background color, which is by default white.

- **Erasing in an image with more than one layer:** Drag the eraser on the background layer, and the eraser paints in the Background color, as usual. But on any other layer, the pixels you scrub with the Eraser tool become transparent, revealing pixels on underlying layers. This assumes that the Lock Transparent Pixels option is unselected in the Layers palette. If you select Lock Transparent Pixels on the Layers palette, the Eraser tool paints using the Background color. For more about layers, check out Chapter 7.

- **Erasing back to a selected step in the History palette:** Hold down the Alt key (Option key on a Mac) and drag the Eraser tool to erase back to a selected step in the History palette. I explain this feature further in the section "Erasing away the present" later in this chapter.

- **Changing the size of the eraser:** Change the brush size specified in the Brushes palette or the Brush Preset picker. Use the bracket keys [and] to make the brush size larger or smaller.

Adjusting Your Eraser

The Eraser tool comes in three eraser modes. To switch modes, select an option from the Mode drop-down list on the Options bar shown in Figure 14-1.

Two eraser modes Brush and Pencil, work with brushes. You change the eraser's size by changing the brush size in the Brush Preset picker. In addition, you can adjust the Opacity setting to partially reveal the image or, in a layered image, make pixels only partially transparent. (For a refresher on changing brush size and opacity, review Chapter 12.)

The third option, Block, changes the eraser to the square, hard-edged, fixed-size eraser. The options in the Brushes palette aren't available for the block eraser, nor are the Opacity slider bar or any of the other settings on the Options bar, except Erase to History. The Block Eraser can be useful when you want to completely erase general areas, but you probably won't take it up very often.

Figure 14-2 shows the Eraser tool in action. The image consists of two layers. The upper layer shows a checkered flag. The lower layer shows crayons. In my example, I made sure the Lock transparent pixels button in the Layers palette wasn't selected. Then, on the left side of the image I erased the upper layer's pixels to transparency, revealing the crayon layer beneath. Next, I selected the Lock transparent pixels button on the Layers palette and erased again, this time on the right side of the image. With the Lock transparent pixels button selected, the Eraser tool erased to the default Background color (white) leaving a white area.

The Magic Eraser tool

 If you're familiar with the Magic Wand tool (see Chapter 7), then the Magic Eraser tool is a cinch. The Magic Wand tool and the Magic Eraser tool operate virtually identically, except that the wand selects and the eraser erases.

When you click a pixel with the Magic Eraser tool, Photoshop identifies a range of similarly colored pixels, just as it does with the Magic Wand tool. But instead of selecting the pixels, the Magic Eraser tool makes them transparent, as shown in Figure 14-3.

 In Photoshop transparency requires a separate layer. So if the image is flat, consisting of only the Background layer, Photoshop automatically moves the image to a new layer. Any erased areas become transparent. Hence the checkerboard pattern denoting transparency as shown in Figure 14-3.

Figure 14-2:
I erased the flag layer on the left side to transparency, revealing the crayons layer. On the right side, I erased the upper layer to reveal the white Background color.

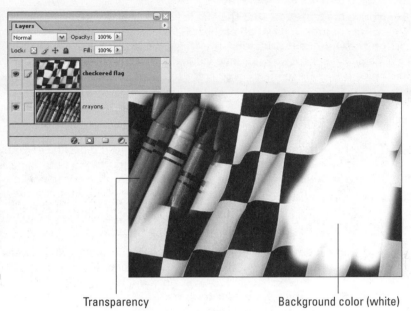

Transparency   Background color (white)

Figure 14-3:
Clicking several white areas of the checkered flag with the Magic Eraser tool leaves transparency (shown in Photoshop with the checkerboard pattern).

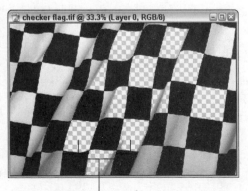

Transparent areas

Notice in Figure 14-3 that the Magic Eraser tool deleted some portions of the white squares, but not all of them. This is a function of the Tolerance value on the Options bar. Just like the Magic Wand tool's Tolerance value, the Magic Eraser tool's Tolerance value determines how similar a neighboring color has to be to the clicked color to be made transparent. A higher value affects more colors; a lower value affects fewer colors.

The other options work as follows:

- **Anti-aliased:** To create a soft fringe around the outline of your transparent area, leave this option selected. If you prefer a hard edge — as when using a very low Tolerance value, for example — deselect this option.

- **Contiguous:** To delete contiguous colors only — that is, similar colors that touch each other — select this option. If you prefer to delete all pixels of a certain color, deselect the Contiguous option.

- **Use All Layers:** To tell Photoshop to factor in all visible layers when erasing pixels, select this option. The Magic Eraser tool continues to erase pixels on the active layer only, but it erases them according to colors found across all layers.

- **Opacity:** To make the erased pixels translucent instead of transparent, lower the Opacity value. Low values result in more subtle effects than high ones.

The Background Eraser tool

 The Background Eraser tool deletes background pixels as you drag over them, as shown in Figure 14-4. If the image is flat, consisting of only the background layer, Photoshop floats the image to a new layer to accommodate the transparency.

The tool is intelligent enough to erase background pixels and retain foreground pixels provided — and here's the clincher — that you keep the cross in the center of the eraser cursor squarely centered on a background color pixel. Move the cross over a foreground pixel, and the background eraser deletes foreground pixels as well. As Figure 14-5 demonstrates, it's the position of the cross that counts.

 To change your mouse cursor from a picture of the selected tool to a precise crosshair, choose Edit➪Preferences➪Display & Cursors (Photoshop➪ Preferences➪Display & Cursors on a Mac) to open the Preferences dialog box. Select the Precise radio button in the Other Cursors area, and then click OK to close the dialog box.

Figure 14-4:
Drag around the edge of an image with the Background Eraser tool to erase the background but leave the foreground intact.

Figure 14-5:
Keep the cross of the background eraser cursor over the background you want to erase (top). If you inadvertently move the cross over the foreground, the foreground gets erased (bottom).

Like the standard Eraser tool, the Background Eraser tool responds to the brush size specified in the Brushes palette or the Brush Preset picker. Use the bracket keys [and] to make the brush size larger or smaller.

You can also modify the performance of the Background Eraser tool by using the options on the Options bar.

- **Brush Presets picker:** Use the picker to access various settings to customize the size and appearance of your eraser tip. If you're using a pressure-sensitive drawing tablet, the last two options allow you to determine the size and tolerance by the pressure you apply with the stylus pen or thumbwheel. These settings are covered in detail in Chapter 12.

- **Limits:** To erase similarly colored pixels as long as they are contiguous with the color immediately under the cross, select this option. To erase all similarly colored pixels, whether contiguous or not, select the Discontiguous option. The Find Edges options searches for high-contrast areas — edges — as you brush and emphasizes them.

- **Tolerance:** Raise the Tolerance value to erase more colors at a time; lower the value to erase fewer colors. Low Tolerance values are useful for erasing around tight and delicate details, such as hair.

- **Protect Foreground Color:** Select this check box to prevent the current Foreground color (by default, black) from ever being erased.

- **Sampling:** Determine how the Background Eraser tool decides what it should and should not erase with the options in the Sampling drop-down list box. The Continuous setting tells the eraser to continuously sample which colors should be erased as you drag. If the background is pretty homogenous, you may prefer to use the Once option, which samples the Background color when you first click and erases only that color throughout the drag. Select the Background Swatch option to erase only the current Background color (by default, white).

Erasing Using the Pencil Tool

The Pencil tool also can be used as an eraser. If you select the Auto Erase option on the Options bar, the Pencil tool applies the Background color if the mouse cursor passes over pixels colored with the Foreground color. If the mouse cursor passes over any other color, the Pencil tool paints with the Foreground color. (For more information about the Foreground and Background colors and how to select them, turn to Chapter 5.)

Introducing the History Palette

Now it's time to explore the powerful History palette. With the History palette you can undo up to 99 previous actions (called *states*). Using the palette you can selectively restore areas to a prior state using the History Brush or the Art History Brush. You can also fill a selection with a history state, and erase to a history state.

Photoshop is set to undo up to 20 history states by default. To raise the number of states that you can undo, choose Edit⇨Preferences⇨General or press Ctrl+K (⌘+K on a Mac). In the Preferences dialog box, enter the number of states you want to be able to undo in the History States text box. You should know, however, that if you set increase the number of states, you may see a negative impact on the performance of your computer because these history states are held in temporary memory. If you find your computer slowing down, lower the number of history states.

By default the History palette is located with the Actions palette in a palette group at the right side of the Photoshop window. If you don't see it, choose Window⇨History to display the palette, as shown in Figure 14-6.

The History palette records all your operations and creates a running list of the states, kind of like those timelines you studied in history classes. (Maybe that's why they named it the History palette.) As you perform each operation, Photoshop names each state and displays a corresponding icon according to the tool or command used. It ignores recording operations, such as palette and tool settings and color and preferences changes.

After you close your image, its history disappears forever. The states in the History palette are not saved with the file.

Clearing the palette

You can completely clear the History palette for all open images or the currently selected document. Clearing the palette can help free up memory. Make sure that you want to clear the History palette before you do so because once the states are cleared, they're gone. There's no way to undo it.

To clear the History palette for the active document (the one that's in front in the Photoshop window), choose Clear History from the History palette menu. To clear history states from all open documents, choose Edit⇨Purge⇨ Histories.

If you find computer performance slowing down, clearing the History palette can speed it back up because history states are saved in temporary memory. To find out how to lower the number of history states, turn to "Introducing the History Palette" earlier in this chapter.

Source state

Opened state

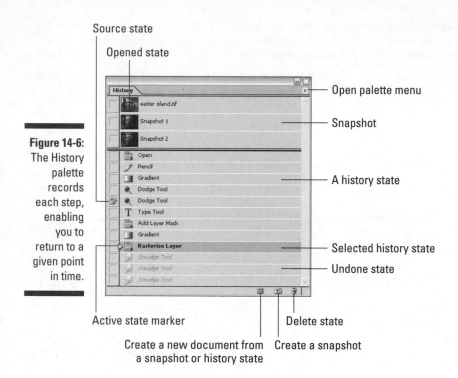

Open palette menu

Snapshot

A history state

Figure 14-6:
The History
palette
records
each step,
enabling
you to
return to a
given point
in time.

Selected history state

Undone state

Active state marker

Delete state

Create a new document from
a snapshot or history state

Create a snapshot

Deciding between linear and non-linear states

The History palette can be set to work in two ways: *linear mode* and *non-linear* mode.

If the History palette is set to work in linear mode and you click an earlier state in the History palette, then resume editing your image or delete that earlier state entirely, all subsequent states (the ones that are grayed out) will be deleted.

If the palette is working in non-linear mode and you click an earlier state or delete it, any subsequent states *won't* be deleted. And, if you resume editing your image, the new edits show up at the bottom of the History palette as the latest states and the earlier states are available still.

So, when would you want to work in linear mode and when would you want to work in non-linear mode? Here's quick information to help you decide:

✔ **Go linear if you want to make a clean break:** If you want the History palette to revert back to an earlier mode, automatically deleting any subsequent states, creating a clean break, then linear mode is for you.

✔ **Go non-linear if you're not sure what you want:** If you want to be flexible, trying out things, going back and forth to different history states, then non-linear mode would work for you.

Changing from linear to non-linear (and vice versa)

To set whether the History palette is working in linear or non-linear mode, follow these steps:

1. **Choose History Options from the History palette menu.**

   See Figure 14-7.

   The History Options dialog box opens.

   The default setting is Linear History mode.

2. **To switch from linear to Non-Linear History mode, add a check in the Allow Non-Linear History check box.**

3. **To set the History palette to work in linear history mode, uncheck the Allow Non-Linear History check box.**

4. **Click OK to close the History Options dialog box.**

   To cancel your changes, click Cancel.

Figure 14-7:
You can set the History palette to work in two modes: linear and non-linear.

Working with history states

The History palette is incredibly flexible. You can revert to previous states, redo states, step backward through states, duplicate states, and much more. Here's the lowdown:

- ✔ **Revert to a previous state:** Click the desired state. Notice that Photoshop temporarily undoes all steps after that state, and that they appear grayed out. Press Ctrl+Z (⌘+Z on a Mac) or choose Edit⇨Undo to return to your last state; you also can simply click your last state.

- ✔ **Redo an undone state:** Undone states are the ones that appear grayed out. Simply click the grayed out state to reactivate it

  If you perform a new operation, the undone states disappear. Choose Edit⇨Undo or Ctrl+Z (⌘+Z on a Mac) *immediately* to get the undone states back. After you move on to other commands, they're gone for good.

- ✔ **Step backward through the History palette one state at a time:** Press Ctrl+Alt+Z (⌘+Option+Z on a Mac). To move forward, press Ctrl+Shift+Z (⌘+Shift+Z on a Mac). These commands also are accessible via the History palette pop-up menu.

- ✔ **Duplicate a state:** Alt+click (Option+click on a Mac) a state. The duplicate state is listed at the bottom of the History palette as the latest state.

- ✔ **Work on multiple images simultaneously and independently of each other:** Because every file has its own history, you don't have to worry about managing history states in multiple files. Photoshop does all that for you.

- ✔ **Establish the number of maximum history states:** You can choose any number (from 1 to 99) of states to retain by choosing Edit⇨Preferences⇨General (Photoshop⇨Preferences⇨General on a Mac).

  If your computer is low on RAM, you may want to set this value to a lower number.

  After you exceed your maximum, the oldest step disappears, then the next oldest, and so on.

- ✔ **Delete a single state:** Select the state and choose Delete from the History palette menu. You also can simply select the state and drag it to the trash can icon at the bottom of the palette. (Refer to Figure 11-1.)

Introducing Snapshots

Snapshots are like pictures of an image that save layer settings, blending modes used, and everything about the way an image looks.

You can use snapshots to try out different effects and then choose between them. For instance, suppose you had an image that you wanted to apply a filter to. You can take a snapshot of the original image, apply a filter, and then take another snapshot. Then, you can switch back and forth between the snapshots to compare the way the image looks.

After you close an image, all snapshots are automatically deleted.

Creating a snapshot

Saving the way an image looks with a snapshot is easy. In the History palette, make sure that the last change you made to the image is the selected history state. Click the Create New Snapshot button at the bottom of the History palette. If the Show New Snapshot Dialog by Default option is checked in the History Options dialog box, then the New Snapshot dialog box opens. Enter a name for the snapshot, and then click OK.

If the option is not checked in the History Options dialog box, then Photoshop bypasses the New Snapshot dialog box, and creates the new snapshot with a default name. (You can always rename a snapshot by double-clicking the snapshot's name in the History palette, and then typing in a new name.)

Working with snapshots

As you work on an image and create snapshots of various history states, you can set a snapshot to become the latest history state and create a new document from a history state. When you finish with a snapshot, you can delete it.

- **To make a snapshot the latest state:** Click a snapshot thumbnail to select it. That's all you have to do. If the History palette is set to work in Non-Linear mode, any subsequent history states will remain in the palette. If the History palette is set to work in Linear Mode, any subsequent states appear grayed-out. Then, when you resume editing, any grayed-out states are automatically deleted.

- **Create a new document from a history state or snapshot:** Drag the snapshot or history state to the Create New Document from Current State button at the bottom of the History palette (the button is shown in Figure 14-6). The new image window appears, named for the history state it was made from. Save this image! It's only a duplicate and it's unsaved until you save it.

- **Delete a snapshot:** Drag the snapshot to the trash can icon at the bottom of the History palette.

Some snapshot tips

Here are some tips for using snapshots effectively:

- ✔ **Make sure the Automatically Create First Snapshot option in the History Options dialog box is checked (it is checked by default).** This way, you can always get back to your original image. To open the History Options dialog box, choose History Options from the bottom of the History palette menu (refer to Figure 14-8).

- ✔ **Another good option to check in the History Options dialog box is Automatically Create New Snapshot When Saving.** If this option is selected, Photoshop creates a snapshot every time you save the image and names it based on the time you save the file. (If you do a ton of saving, though, you will end up with a zillion snapshots, so this may not work for you.)

- ✔ **Check the Show New Snapshot Dialog by Default option in the History Options dialog box.** Photoshop displays the New Snapshot dialog box every time you click the New Snapshot icon.

Erasing and Restoring History

You can select any state or snapshot in the History palette and use it as a "painting" source for the History Brush tool, the Art History Brush tool, and the Eraser tool. When working with one of these tools and with an earlier state selected, you can paint away (or erase) any subsequent states in an area of an image, creating interesting effects.

Erasing history

The Eraser tool is pretty straightforward. To use it to erase a portion of a layer to a previous history state, follow these steps:

1. **Select the Eraser tool from the Toolbox.**

2. **Select the layer in the Layers palette that you want to erase from.**

   This layer must be an image layer, not an editable type layer or shape layer. (To find out more about type layers, turn to Chapter 17; for more about shape layers, turn to Chapter 16.)

3. **Set Eraser tool options.**

   As shown in Figure 14-8, use the Options bar to choose Eraser settings. Use the Brush Preset picker to select the eraser tip diameter and hardness, choose an eraser mode — Brush, Pencil, or Block, select an opacity setting, and choose the amount of flow.

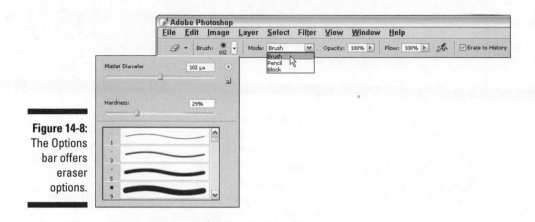

Figure 14-8:
The Options bar offers eraser options.

4. **On the Options bar, select Erase to History.**

5. **In the History palette, click in the column to the left of the history state or snapshot that you want to erase to.**

   A tiny History Brush icon appears in the column, as shown in Figure 14-9.

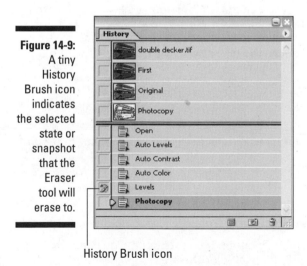

Figure 14-9:
A tiny History Brush icon indicates the selected state or snapshot that the Eraser tool will erase to.

History Brush icon

6. **Drag the Eraser tool to restore portions of the image to the selected history state or snapshot.**

   Figure 14-10 shows the Eraser tool in action. A snapshot of the double-decker bus image on the left was taken to save its original state. Then, the Photocopy filter was applied as shown in the middle image. Next, the tiny History Brush icon was positioned next to the snapshot in the

History Palette. Finally, using the Eraser tool with its Erase to History option checked and the original source state selected, the upper deck of the bus was restored with a few swipes of the Eraser tool.

Figure 14-10:
A double-
decker bus
gets its
upper deck
restored
using the
Eraser tool.

Original image

Photocopy filter applied

Upper deck restored

Filling a layer or selection with a history state

Using the Edit➪Fill command, you can erase a portion of a layer or selected area to a previous history state or snapshot. Here's how:

1. **In the Layers palette, choose the layer that you want to fill with a history state or a snapshot.**

   If you want to only fill a portion of the layer, use any of the selection tools to select those areas. (To find out how to use the selection tools, turn to Chapter 7.)

2. **Click in the left column next to the history state or snapshot that you want to use as the fill.**

   A tiny History Brush icon appears in the column as shown in Figure 14-9.

3. **Choose Edit➪Fill to open the Fill dialog box.**

4. **In the Contents area, select History from the Use drop-down list box.**

   Figure 14-11 shows the History option being selected. You can also choose a blending mode and opacity for the fill in this dialog box. If the layer you selected has transparent pixels, put a check in the Preserve Transparency check box to replace only colored pixels.

5. **Click OK.**

   The Fill dialog box closes and the layer (or selections) are filled with the previous history state or snapshot. In Figure 14-12, the windows of the double-decker bus shown in Figure 14-10 with the Photocopy filter applied, were selected then filled with the original history state.

Figure 14-11:
In the Fill dialog box, select History from the Use drop-down list in the Contents area.

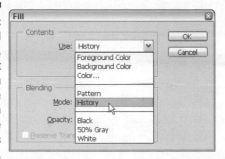

Figure 14-12:
You can select a layer or image and fill it with a previous history state.

The History Brush tool

The History Brush tool works like Eraser tool and Fill command, but with more painterly results because a previous history state or snapshot is stroked onto the image. And, the History Brush tool has all the power and flexibility of the Brush tool — you can select brush tips using the Brushes palette, including the incredible brush options such as Shape Dynamics,

Scattering, Dual Brush settings (as discussed in Chapter 12), set blending modes, opacity, flow, and airbrush capabilities.

To use the History Brush tool, follow these steps:

1. **Select the History Brush tool from the Toolbox.**

2. **Use the Options bar to select History Brush tool options.**

   As shown in Figure 14-13, you can select a brush tip size and hardness from the Brush Preset picker, select a blending mode, set the opacity, select flow percentage, and airbrush capabilities.

   If you want to create a custom brush shape, you can use the Brushes palette as discussed in Chapter 12.

Figure 14-13:
When the History Brush tool is selected, the Options bar offers the same settings as the Brush tool.

3. **In the History palette, click in the left column next to the history state or snapshot that you want to use as the pixel source for the History Brush tool.**

   A tiny History Brush icon appears in the column as shown in Figure 14-10.

4. **In the Layers palette, select the layer you want to restore.**

5. **Use the History Brush tool to paint strokes on the layer.**

   The pixel data from the state or snapshot you selected in Step 3 is used to restore the stroked areas to that earlier state.

   Figure 14-14 shows three versions of the same image. On the left is the original photograph of a ballet dancer. Using the History palette, I took a snapshot of this history state. Next, I applied the Watercolor filter to the photograph (middle image). Then, I positioned the tiny History Brush icon next to the snapshot in the History Palette. Finally, I stroked the head, arms, and upper torso of the ballet dancer with the History Brush tool, restoring the dancer's original skin tones and facial features (right image).

Figure 14-14:
These three images show the History Brush tool at work.

Original image   Watercolor filter applied   Skin tones and facial features restored

The Art History Brush tool

The Art History Brush tool is great for adding painterly watercolor-like effects to an image by blending adjacent colors with special brush tips only available to tool.

 The Art History Brush tool spreads paint like a watercolor brush. As you stroke with the brush, paint flows more into darker areas and less into lighter areas. Painting on a high-contrast image works best.

 1. **Select the Art History Brush tool from the Toolbox.**

2. **Use the Options bar to select Art History Brush tool options.**

   As shown in Figure 14-15, you can select a brush tip size and hardness from the Brush Preset picker, select a blending mode, and set the opacity. In addition, you can select a brush style, the area the painting will spread to, and the tolerance setting. A higher tolerance will restore more of the image at one time.

 This tool works best with a small, hard tip selected. Also, area and tolerance settings should be set quite low; otherwise the brush covers a lot of area *very* fast. If you have a stylus, by all means use it. The Art History Brush tool works well when stroked with a stylus.

3. **In the History palette, click the left column next to the history state or snapshot that you want to use as the pixel source for the History Brush tool.**

   A tiny History Brush icon will appear in the column as shown in Figure 14-10.

4. **In the Layers palette, select the layer you want to restore.**

5. **Use the Art History Brush tool to paint strokes on the layer.**

   Figure 14-16 shows three versions of the same image. On the left is the original photograph of flowers and leaves. Using the History palette, I took a snapshot of this history state. Next, I applied the Find Edges filter to the photograph (middle image). Then, I positioned the tiny History

Brush icon next to the snapshot in the History Palette. Finally, I stroked the leaf edges and veins with the Art History Brush tool, restoring the original state with a watercolor touch as shown in the right image.

Preset Brush picker   Special brush types

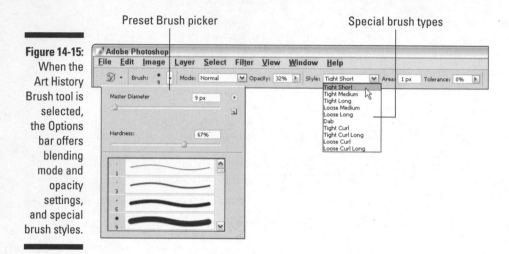

Figure 14-15:
When the Art History Brush tool is selected, the Options bar offers blending mode and opacity settings, and special brush styles.

Figure 14-16:
Using the Art History Brush tool set to a 3 pixel Tight Short Style brush, 32% Opacity, an Area of 1 pixel, and 0% Tolerance, the leaf edges and veins were restored to the original history state with a dappled watercolor appearance.

Original image

Find Edges filter applied

Leaf edges and veins stroked with the Art History Brush

Part VI
Heavy-Duty Photoshop

The 5th Wave   By Rich Tennant

"I'm going to assume that most of you—but not all of you—understand that this session on 'masking' has to do with Photoshop CS.

In this part . . .

Chapters 15 through 17 delve into more advanced Photoshop topics. Now that you have the basics under your belt it's time to move on to the great effects you can create using layer masks, channel masks, and vector masks. Chapter 15 gives full details about all these mask types, and explains how to use them to add texture, hide a portion of a layer, and use a layer as a cutout.

In Chapter 16, I introduce you to the world of *vector graphics.* Besides being a painting program (and not just any painting program!), Photoshop includes the ability to create vector-based shapes and paths for use in your images. What does this mean for you? Crisp, clean-edged shapes that can add definition to an image, be filled with gradients, and even filled with a history state. Also, you discover how versatile paths are. Paths aren't just shapes on an image; paths can be transformed into selections, masks, and even filled with type.

A picture may be better than a thousand words, but words — and type — often tell the story. Chapter 17 explains how to work with the world-class typography tools that Photoshop provides. Find out how to use the Character and Paragraph palettes to format type, add color, and even warp type into fantastic shapes. Use a new Photoshop cs feature that allows you to place text on a path. You can draw any path you want, and the type will follow the path's curves, bumps, and even travel upside down. Cool!

Chapter 15

Using Masks and Channels

*E*very image you create in Photoshop contains *channels*. These channels store an image's color information. The number of channels in an image depends upon the color mode in which the image is set. For instance, an image set in RGB mode has three default channels — a Red channel that stores red information, a Green channel that stores green information, and a Blue channel that stores blue information. If an image has more than one layer, each layer has its own set of channels.

Alpha channels are grayscale channels that you can add to an image. They are used to store selections. Alpha channel selections are used to protect specific areas of an image from editing while changes, such as recoloring, filters, and other effects, are applied to the rest of the *unmasked* (unselected) image.

Layer masks in Photoshop are like Halloween masks: A Halloween mask covers the face, concealing it; but any cutouts — for eyes or mouth, for instance — leave those areas visible. You put layer masks on top of an image and make "cutouts" to make some areas visible and editable.

Layer masks control how different areas of a layer are revealed. You can use layer masks as test areas for applying special effects without permanently changing an image. If you like the effects and want to make them permanent, you can then apply a mask to an image.

Layer masks and channels can be saved in the Photoshop's native PSD file format and Photoshop's enhanced TIF and PDF formats.

Introducing Channels

Each channel is a grayscale image that stores specific color information. Each channel can contain up to 256 shades of gray. Channels are available on the Channels palette, as shown in Figure 15-1.

The individual color channels — Red, Green, and Blue — are listed first (depending upon the color mode you are working in, a CMYK image contains Cyan, Magenta, Yellow, and Black channels). The color channels store the color information for an image. Then come any *alpha channels* that have been added. An alpha channel can contain a saved selection or layer mask. A thumbnail showing a channel's contents appears to the left of the channel name.

To see the separate color channels and how combine to create a color image, turn to Color Plates 5-2 and 5-3. Color Plate 5-2 shows an RGB image broken down into its Red, Green, and Blue channels. In addition, the color plate shows how the image looks when two channels are combined. Color Plate 5-3 shows the same image from 5-2 converted to CMYK mode and broken down into the Cyan, Magenta, Yellow, and Black channels. Color Plate 5-3 also shows how the color in a CMYK image is created as the channels are put together.

Color Plate 15-2 shows how you can modify channels to change the look of an image. In Color Plate 15-1, I first adjusted the highlights and midtones of the red channel in an RGB image. Next, I applied the Sponge filter to the Blue channel, and then I applied the Watercolor filter to the Green channel.

Figure 15-2 shows the three color channels that make up an RGB image.

Getting to know alpha channels

Just like regular channels that store color information, alpha channels are represented as grayscale images that store layer masks or selections. What sets alpha channels apart from other channels is the fact that they store selections that can be activated at anytime. (Regular channels store color information only.) This means that you can always load a saved selection into an image, reactivating the selection.

Alpha channels also can be used to contain layer mask transparency and opacity information because layer masks hide or reveal areas of a layer.

You can paint on an alpha channel to change the selected areas or alter the visible areas of a layer mask. (I cover working with and editing layer masks later in this chapter in "Layer Masks.")

When working with an alpha channel that is a saved selection, its thumbnail in the Channels palette appears as black and white as shown in Figure 15-3. By default, the white area represents the selected area of the image that can be edited. The black area represents the protected part of the image that cannot be edited. Alpha channels appear at the bottom of the Channels palette.

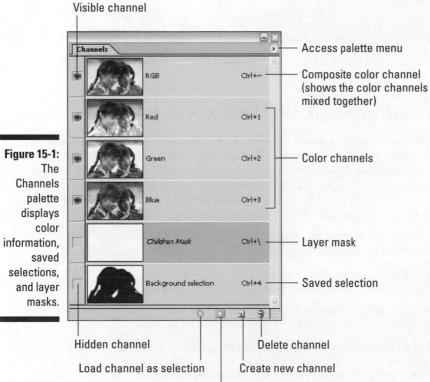

Visible channel

Access palette menu

Composite color channel
(shows the color channels
mixed together)

Color channels

Layer mask

Saved selection

Figure 15-1:
The
Channels
palette
displays
color
information,
saved
selections,
and layer
masks.

Hidden channel

Load channel as selection

Save selection as channel

Delete channel

Create new channel

Red channel

Green channel

Figure 15-2:
This image
of two girls
is made up
of red,
green,
and blue
channels.

Blue channel

Composite RGB image

Working with the Channels palette

Using the Channels palette, you can select, show, hide, and delete channels.

- ✔ **To select a channel:** Click the channel's name to make it active. The channel becomes highlighted. You can now make changes to the active channel. For instance, you could adjust the levels or curves of the channel, or add special effects such as applying a filter.

- ✔ **To select more than one channel at a time:** Hold down the shift key and click the channels you want to select.

- ✔ **To hide a channel:** Click the eye icon in the column to the left of the channel. To view the channel, click the eye icon again.

- ✔ **To rename a channel:** Double-click the channel's name, type in a new name, and then press Enter (Return on a Mac).

- ✔ **To view the color channels showing their colors** (red, green, and blue, for instance), choose Edit⇨Preferences⇨Display & Cursors. In the Preferences dialog box, select Color Channels in Color.

- ✔ **To create a new alpha channel:** Click the Create New Channel button at the bottom of the Channels palette. The channel is automatically named Alpha 1 (or Alpha 2 if you already have an Alpha 1).

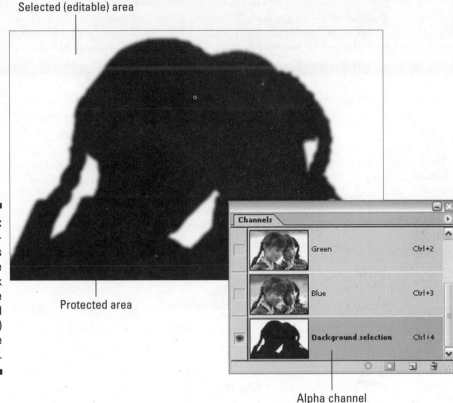

Selected (editable) area

Figure 15-3: The protected areas of the image are black and the selected (editable) areas are white.

Protected area

Alpha channel

✔ **To duplicate a channel:** Select the channel you want to duplicate in the Channels palette. Then choose Duplicate Channel from the Channels palette menu. In the Duplicate Channel dialog box, enter a name and select whether the new channel appears in the current document or a new document, and then click OK. If you want to create a grayscale image using a channel, duplicating a channel and saving it as in a new document is a good way to go. For more about creating grayscale images by selecting a color channel, turn to Chapter 5.

✔ **To move an alpha channel up or down in the stacking order:** Drag the channel up or down the stack to its new location. Alpha channels have a stacking order just like layers do in the Layers palette. (Notice that you cannot reposition an alpha channel up with the color channels because the color channels always appear at the top of the stacking order.)

✔ **To set the color display for masked and unmasked areas in an alpha channel:** Double-click the channel you want to change. In the Channel Options dialog box, you can select how the masked (protected) and selected areas are colored. By default, the setting for coloring the masked and selected areas is Color Indicates: Masked Areas (Figure 15-4). As this chapter has discussed, this sets the selected areas to white and the protected areas to black. If you select Color Indicates: Selected Areas, you make the selected areas black and the white areas protected. Don't get confused! This chapter is written using the default setting.

✔ **To delete a channel:** Drag it to the trash icon at the bottom of the channels palette. If you delete a color channel, the image is automatically converted to Multichannel mode (for details about color modes, turn to Chapter 5).

If you're working with a large image, keep in mind that channels add to image file size. It's always good to do some housekeeping when working on a big project. If you find that you don't need a saved selection anymore, just delete the alpha channel that's storing the selection.

Figure 15-4:
The Color Indicates: Masked Areas selection is the default. It sets an alpha channel to show the selected (editable) areas as white and the protected (unselected) areas as black.

Using Alpha Channels

By default, in a selection that's been saved as an alpha channel, the black area represents the isolated area of the image that cannot be edited and the white area represents the part of the image that can be changed. You can edit and reshape the black and white areas with the Brush and Pencil tools, thereby, changing the shape of the selection. A selection that's been saved as an alpha channel can be loaded onto any image whenever you need it.

Saving a selection as an alpha channel

To save a selection as an alpha channel choose Select↔Save Selection or right-click in the image window (Control+click a Mac) and choose Save Selection from the context-sensitive menu. In the Save Selection dialog box, type a name that describes the selection in the Name text box, and then click OK. To view your saved selection, open the Channels palette and look down the list of channels. You'll find the alpha channel that is your saved selection at the bottom of the list.

Loading an alpha channel as a selection

You can reload a saved selection that has been saved as an alpha channel at any time into an image. This is really handy if you've saved a complex selection and need to use it again while working on a project. Here's how to load an alpha channel as a selection:

1. **Select the alpha channel that you want to load as a selection in the Channels palette.**

   In Figure 15-5, the Block Tops channel is selected and appears in the Image window.

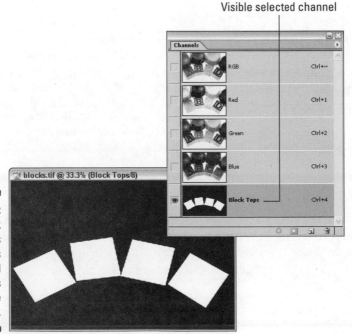

Visible selected channel

Figure 15-5: The Block Tops channel is selected and appears in the image window.

2. **Click the Load Channel as Selection button at the bottom of the Channels dialog box.**

   The selection appears in the image window.

3. **In the Channels palette, click the combined color channel at the top of the channel list to view the image with the selection.**

   If you're working with an RGB image, the combined or *composite* channel is named RGB. This composite channel is special. It doesn't contain any color information like the Red, Green, or Blue color channels; it's made up of the color channels mixed together. In a way, it's a shortcut that you can use to make all the color channels visible and active for editing.

   Figure 15-6 shows the Block Tops selection with the image.

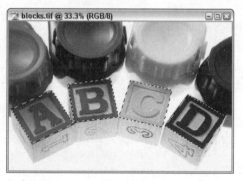

Figure 15-6:
The Block Tops channel selection is loaded into the image.

Reshaping an alpha channel

An alpha channel can be superimposed on an image as a colored overlay or mask. You can reshape the mask using the Brush tool or Pencil tool. When you change the shape of the mask, you are changing the protected and editable areas of the alpha channel. This reshaped alpha channel could be a selection you've saved or a completely new channel that you want to use to protect an area.

1. **In the Channels palette, select the alpha channel that you want to edit.**

   The eye icon appears next to the alpha channel.

2. **At the top of the Channels palette, click the left column next to the color composite channel to make the image visible.**

   Make sure the alpha channel stays highlighted and that it is the only one highlighted. The protected areas of the image are masked with a color overlay.

   In Figure 15-7, the Block Tops alpha channel is selected and the column next to the composite RGB channel has been clicked, but not selected (you can tell because the eye icon is visible). The mask overlay appears over the entire image except for the selected block tops. Notice the alpha channel's name appears in the image window's title bar.

3. **Select the Brush tool or the Pencil tool from the Toolbox and select the tool's settings.**

   On the Options bar, select a brush tip using the Brush Preset picker. Set the blending mode to Normal. To create a full mask (completely transparent or completely opaque), set Opacity to 100%. To create a translucent mask, choose a lower opacity percentage. (To find out more about selecting brushes and setting other Brush tool and Pencil tool options, turn to Chapter 12.)

4. **Reshape the masked (protected) and unmasked (editable) areas by painting with black and white.**

   You can quickly select black and white in the Toolbox by clicking the Default Foreground and Background Colors button, and then switch between black and white by clicking the Switch Foreground and Background Colors button (Figure 15-8).

5. **To make the editable (white) areas larger, paint with white. To make the masked (protected) area larger, paint with black.**

   Figure 15-9 shows the reshaped Block Tops alpha channel and how its mask now appears in the image window when superimposed on the blocks image. (Compare the alpha channel in Figure 15-9 with the one shown in Figure 15-5.)

Composite channel is visible

Figure 15-7: The Block Tops alpha channel is selected and the RGB channel has been made visible (but not selected). The mask overlay covers the entire image except for the block tops.

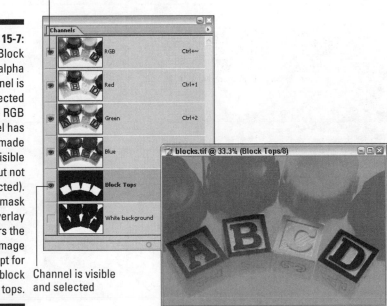

Channel is visible and selected

Foreground color square

Figure 15-8:
Use the
Toolbox to
quickly
select black
and white,
and switch
between the
two colors.

— Switch Foreground and
Background colors (X)

— Background color square

Default Foreground and
Background colors (D)

6. **When you're finished reshaping the mask, click the eye icon next to the channel to hide the channel again.**

   Or, you can select a layer in the Layers palette.

   If you have a large area that you want to reshape, you can use any selection tool to select the area; fill the selection with white or black using the Paint Bucket tool.

White painted here makes editable area larger (adding to selection)

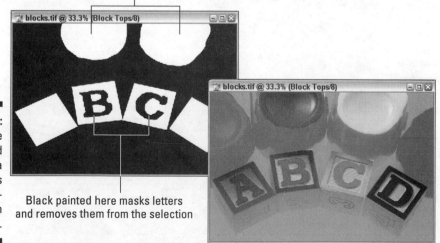

Figure 15-9:
The
reshaped
alpha
channel's
mask super-
imposed on
the blocks.

Black painted here masks letters
and removes them from the selection

Introducing Layer Masks

A *layer mask,* like a saved selection, is a saved as a grayscale alpha channel. But, that's where the similarity ends. Although selections are used to protect areas of an image from editing, layer masks control where a layer is visible or hidden. When you add a layer mask to a layer, the layer mask appears in the Layers palette next to the layer thumbnail as shown in Figure 15-10. (Because the layer mask is a channel, you can also see it at the bottom of the Channels palette.)

Notice the tiny link icon between the layer and the layer mask in Figure 15-1. This indicates that the layer and layer mask are linked (by default). If you use the Move tool to move a layer or a layer mask, both the layer and the layer mask move together. If you want to move a layer or layer mask independently, click the link icon to unlink them.

You can use layer masks to create fade in effects and hide portions of a layer from view. What's great about layer masks is that areas of a layer aren't permanently deleted; they're just hidden.

To see some layer masks in action, take a look at Color Plate 8-1 and Color Plate 15-1. The composition in Color Plate 8-1 is made up of four layers (this is also called a *composite image*). Look at the layer masks attached to each layer in the Layers palette. If you look carefully at the layer mask thumbnails, you'll notice that areas of the layer mask are black and other areas are white. These black and white areas correspond to the area of each layer that is visible (white) or hidden (black).

Link icon

Layer mask thumbnail

Figure 15-10:
A layer mask can hide or reveal portions of a layer.

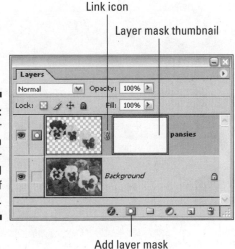

Add layer mask

Color Plate 15-1 uses the same layer mask techniques to show and hide parts of layers. Notice how the layer mask on the Morning Glory layer shows the center of the layer but hides the edges. Then, look at the Leaves layer and see how the layer mask hides the center of the layer and shows the edges.

Because a layer mask is a grayscale channel, you can only paint on it with black, white, and gray. If you paint on a layer mask with black, the layer attached to the layer mask is hidden, revealing the layer beneath. If you paint on a layer mask with white, the layer is revealed, obscuring the layer beneath. And, if you paint on a layer mask with gray, the layer becomes translucent revealing some of the layer beneath (using gray is great for creating fade-outs).

Figure 15-11 shows an image with several layers and their attached layer masks. Notice how the white and black in the upper layer mask reveals and hides the layer. Also, take a look at the gradient that's been applied to the other two layers, creating fade-out effects.

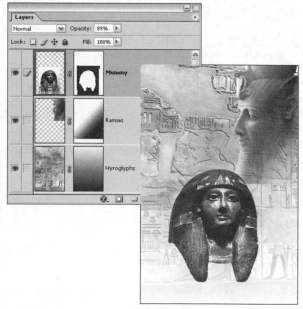

Figure 15-11:
The white and black areas of a layer mask reveal and hide the layer. Gradients create fade-out effects.

Adding a layer mask to a layer

When you create a layer mask there are four basic types to choose from:

- A white mask reveals the entire layer
- A black mask that hides the layer

✔ A combination black-and-white mask *reveals* the selected areas of the layer

✔ A combination black-and-white mask that *hides* the selected areas of the layer

To add a layer mask to a layer, open an image with multiple layers and follow these steps:

1. **In the Layers palette, select the layer you want to add the mask to.**

   To create a black-and-white mask that reveals or hides selected areas of the layer, use any of the selection tools to create the selections.

2. **Create the layer mask you need.**

   • Choose Layer⇨Add Layer Mask⇨Reveal All to create a white layer mask that is transparent and reveals the entire layer. Or, you can click the Add layer mask button on the Layers palette.

   • Choose Layer⇨Add Layer Mask⇨Hide All to create a black layer mask that is opaque and hides the entire layer. Or, you can Alt+click (Option+click on the Mac) the Add layer mask button on the Layers palette.

   • Choose Layer⇨Add Layer Mask⇨Reveal Selection to create a black-and-white layer mask that reveals selected areas of the layer.

   • Choose Layer⇨Add Layer Mask⇨Hide Selection to create a black-and-white layer mask that hides selected areas of the layer.

You can't add a layer mask to the Background layer. If you want to add a layer mask to the Background, you'll have to convert it to a regular layer first, by selecting it, and then choosing Layer⇨New Layer from Background.

Reshaping a layer mask

After you add a layer mask to a layer, you can reshape it to hide or reveal various areas of the layer.

Painting with white makes the layer visible, painting with black hides the layer, and painting with gray partially hides the layer, creating a translucent effect.

To reshape a layer mask to hide or show areas of the layer that it's linked to, follow these steps:

1. **Select the Brush tool or Pencil tool from the Toolbox and select the tool's settings using the Options bar.**

   To find out how to select Brush tool of Pencil tool options, turn to Chapter 12.

2. **Set how you want to view the layer mask while reshaping it.**

   • **To reshape the layer mask while viewing only the layer (not the layer mask itself):** Click the layer mask thumbnail in the Layers palette (don't click the layer's name). A thick border appears around the layer mask and the layer mask icon appears in the column to the left of the layer' thumbnail as shown in Figure 15-12.

   • **To view only the layer mask while reshaping it:** Alt+click (Option+ click on a Mac) the layer mask thumbnail in the Layers palette.

   • **To view the layer mask as a colored overlay on the layer:** Alt+Shift+click (Option+Shift+click on a Mac) the layer mask thumbnail in the Layers palette.

Figure 15-12:
When you select a layer mask, a dark border appears around the layer mask thumbnail and a layer mask icon appears to the left of the layer's thumbnail.

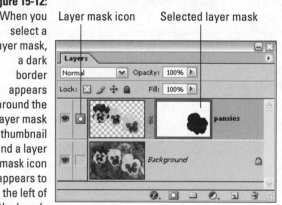

Layer mask icon   Selected layer mask

3. **Reshape the layer mask by painting with black, white, or gray.**

   To hide the layer, paint with black. To reveal the layer, paint with white. To partially reveal the layer, paint with gray. Figure 15-13 shows a layer mask being reshaped with these three colors.

   You can quickly select black and white in the Toolbox by clicking the Default Foreground and Background Colors button, and then switch between black and white by clicking the Switch Foreground and Background Colors button (refer to Figure 15-8).

4. **When you're finished reshaping the layer mask, click the layer thumbnail to return to normal display mode.**

Layer with layer maks above
white Background layer

Layer mask

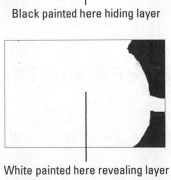

Background (white)   Layer

Hidden area   Visible area

Newly hidden areas

Black painted here hiding layer

Newly revealed area

White painted here revealing layer

Figure 15-13:
Use black,
white, and
gray to
reshape a
layer mask
to hide
or reveal
a layer.

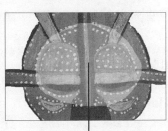

Area partially visible
(translucent)

Gray painted here partially
revealing layer

More about layer masks

There are a few more things you can do to layer masks to help with the image editing and creation process, disabling a layer mask in order to hide the effects of the layer mask, duplicating a layer mask, applying a layer mask to a layer, and discarding a layer mask altogether.

- ✔ **To deactivate a layer mask:** Shift+click the layer mask thumbnail in the Layers palette. A large red X appears over the thumbnail and the entire layer becomes visible. To reactivate the layer mask, Shift+click the layer mask thumbnail again.

- ✔ **To duplicate a layer mask and add it to a new layer:** In the Layers palette choose the layer you want the duplicate layer to appear in. Drag the thumbnail of the layer mask you want to duplicate over the Add layer mask button at the bottom of the Layers palette.

- ✔ **To apply a layer mask to a layer:** Right-click (Control+click on a Mac) the layer mask thumbnail and choose Apply Layer Mask from the context-sensitive menu.

- ✔ **To discard a layer mask:** Right-click (Control+click on a Mac) the layer mask thumbnail and choose Discard Layer Mask from the context-sensitive menu.

Creating an Interesting Layer Mask

There are as many ways to use layer masks as there are ideas in your head. You're limited only by your imagination. One interesting idea is to create a layer mask using a text cutout. Give this a try to get an idea of what a layer mask can do.

1. **Open an image with layers in it.**

2. **Use the Layers palette to select that layer that you want to add a text cutout layer mask to.**

   Make sure you select a layer that contains colored pixels; transparent pixels will just create invisible letters. Also, this technique won't work with the Background layer. In Figure 15-14, the zebra layer is selected.

3. **Select the Horizontal Type Mask tool from the Toolbox.**

4. **Select the font, font size, and other text settings using the Options bar or Character palette.**

   To find out more about the Horizontal Type Mask tool, how to select type settings, and the Character palette, turn to Chapter 17.

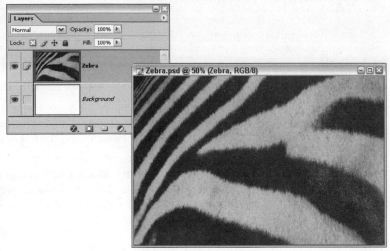

Figure 15-14:
I'm using the zebra layer as the fill for the cutout text. The layer mask hides the rest of the layer, creating the illusion of text filled with the zebra pattern.

5. **Click in the image window and type some text.**

   As you type, you'll notice that the image automatically switches to Quick Mask mode as shown in Figure 15-15.

 6. **When you're finished typing, click the Commit button on the Options bar to turn the type into a selection.**

Figure 15-15:
When typing text with the Horizontal Type Mask tool, the image display automatically changes to Quick Mask mode.

7. **Reposition the type selection if you need to.**

   To move the selection, use one of the selection tools, not the Move tool. (Position the selection tool within the type selection boundary, press the mouse, and drag the type selection to its new location.) If you use the Move tool, colored pixels under the selection type move as well.

8. **Choose Layer⇨Add Layer Mask⇨Reveal Selection to "fill" the text selection with the layer contents.**

   In actuality, you are creating a layer mask that obscures the rest of the layer, only leaving transparency where the type selection is.

   Figure 15-16 shows the zebra layer mask and the text created in the image window by the mask. Notice that the black areas of the mask hide the Zebra layer and that the white areas of the text (which used to be the selection) allow the Zebra layer to show through.

Take a look at the upper left letter in Color Plate 17-1. I used the Horizontal Type Mask tool to create the letter B, and then applied it as a layer mask to create filled type, performing the steps outlined above. Notice all the different effects that can be added to type created in this fashion. The sky's the limit!

Figure 15-16:
A layer mask can create cutout type using a layer.

Chapter 16

Using Paths and Shapes

*B*esides being an extraordinary painting program, Photoshop also uses *vector* graphics to create paths and shapes such as rectangles, circles, hearts, and stars.

As you found out at the beginning of Chapter 5, bitmap images are made up of tiny pixels that are arranged and colored to form a pattern. These bitmap images are the ones you usually create in a bitmap-based program such as Photoshop.

Vector graphics create shapes and objects, such as squares and stars, using mathematical formulas. Photoshop stepped over the bitmap-based program line in Version 6 when it included the ability to add vector graphics to Photoshop images.

Photoshop's shape tools and pen tools are used to create exact vector shapes. These vector shapes are called *paths*. Paths are classified in two ways:

✔ **Work paths:** Temporary paths that define the outline of a shape. They appear in the Paths palette, as shown in Figure 16-1.

✔ **Shape layers:** Paths that are created when a shape is drawn and automatically filled with the current Foreground color. The shape appears in the Layers palette as an outline that is stored in a *vector mask,* which also shows up in the Paths palette.

A vector mask works just like a *layer mask,* hiding some areas of the layer and revealing other areas. The vector mask is linked to a layer. This combination vector mask and layer makes up the shape layer.

You also can use the shape tools to create shapes, such as ellipses and triangles, directly on a layer. This type of shape is pixel based and they cannot be modified — transformed, reshaped, or used as selections — like the shapes saved in vector masks. Both are shown in Figure 16-2.

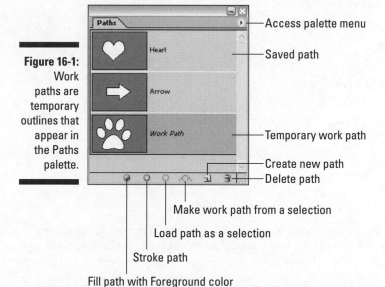

Figure 16-1: Work paths are temporary outlines that appear in the Paths palette.

Making Shapes

There are three kinds of shapes: those that are drawn on a layer, those that are saved in a vector mask as a shape layer, and those that are drawn as paths.

Shapes saved in a vector mask can be reshaped and transformed; you can change their fills at any time to include layer effects such as gradients, textures, and patterns. All the usual layer attributes, such as opacity and blending modes, can be applied to a shape saved in a vector mask.

Shapes that are drawn as paths appear as temporary outlines on the Paths palette. You can fill these shape paths with the Foreground color, load them into images as selections, and stroked with a brush to create outlines.

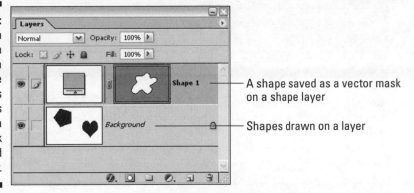

Figure 16-2: Shapes can be drawn directly on a layer. Shape layer saves the shape's outline in a vector mask that is linked to the layer.

A shape saved as a vector mask on a shape layer

Shapes drawn on a layer

Both the shapes saved in a vector mask and the shapes drawn as paths are created using mathematical formulas. These shapes are *vector objects*.

Shapes that are drawn on a layer are not as versatile. Although you can refill them with other colors, when you apply any layer effects to them you modify the *entire* layer (not just the shapes). Shapes that are drawn on a layer are called *rasterized* shapes — shapes that are created using pixels, not mathematical formulas.

Using the Shape tools

All of the shape tools are located on one flyout menu in the Toolbox, as shown in Figure 16-3. The shape tools work in conjunction with the Options bar, where you can select whether the shape will become a shape layer, a path, or a regular filled shape on a layer. The Options bar changes depending upon the type of shape you decide to draw: a shape layer, a path, or a filled shape. Figure 16-4 shows the Options bar with each of these types selected.

Creating a filled shape on a layer

Filled, rasterized shapes that are created on a layer are the least versatile shapes. After you create such a shape, it becomes part of the layer and is a rasterized, pixel-based shape, not the more versatile vector shapes. You might want to use a filled shape to quickly add a heart or star to an image.

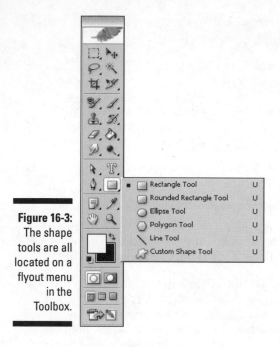

Figure 16-3:
The shape
tools are all
located on a
flyout menu
in the
Toolbox.

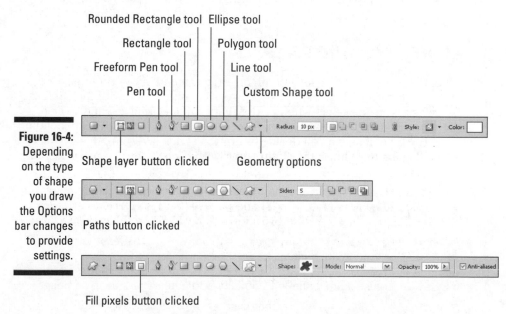

Figure 16-4:
Depending
on the type
of shape
you draw
the Options
bar changes
to provide
settings.

To create a rasterized shape on a layer, follow these steps:

   1. **Open an image with layers, and in the Layers palette, select the layer
      on which you want to draw the shape or create a new layer.**

To find out how to select layers or create new ones, turn to Chapter 8.

2. **Select a Foreground color.**

   For details on how to do this turn to Chapter 5.

3. **Select a shape tool from the Toolbox.**

   After you select a shape tool, you can change tools using the shape tool buttons on the Options bar.

4. **Click the Fill Pixels button on the Options bar.**

   The available settings on the Options bar change to those shown in the third Options bar (refer to Figure 16-4).

5. **Select settings for the shape tool you selected.**

   - **If you are using the Rounded Rectangle tool:** Set the Radius value to change how much the corners of the rectangle are rounded. The higher the value, the rounder the corners.

   - **If you are using the Polygon tool:** Set how many sides the shape will have, 3 for a triangle, 5 for a pentagon, and so on.

   - **If you are using the Line tool:** Set the width of the line by typing an amount into the Weight text box. By default, the Weight setting is in pixels. If you want to enter a width in a different measurement scale, such as inches or centimeters, just type in **1 lnch** or **1 cm**.

   - **If you are using the Custom shape tool:** Select a shape using the Custom Shape picker.

   - **For any shape tool:** Click the Geometry Options button to access shape options for the shape tool you selected. For instance, if you want to create a star and you selected the Polygon tool, click the Geometry Options button, and then check Star in the Polygon Options box that appears.

6. **Drag across the image window to draw a shape.**

   When you release the mouse button, the shape is filled with the Foreground color. You can now edit it with any of the brushes, editing tools, filters, and more to modify the shape's pixels (because it is a *rasterized* or pixel-based shape). Figure 16-5 shows some filled pixel shapes on a layer.

Creating a shape layer

A *shape layer* is a shape outline that is saved in a vector mask and linked to a layer. You can modify the contour of the shape, fill the layer with a color or pattern, and use layer effects on the shape without affecting the rest of the layer the shape is linked. You can quickly add cool effects, such as drop shadows, contours, and bevels to shape layers using shape layers.

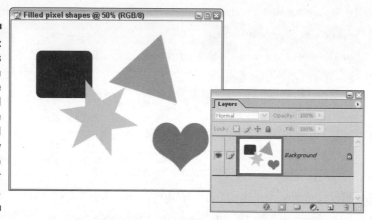

Figure 16-5: Shapes drawn on a layer are pixel-based and can be modified with any Photoshop tool or command.

To create a shape layer, follow these steps:

1. **Open an image with layers, and in the Layers palette, select a layer.**

   The new shape layer is created above this layer. (To find out how to select layers, turn to Chapter 8.)

2. **Select a Foreground color.**

   You can fill a shape layer with a pattern or gradient, as well. For details on how to do this, turn to "Working with Shape Layers" later in this chapter.

3. **Select a shape tool from the Toolbox.**

   After you select a shape tool, you can change tools using the shape tool buttons on the Options bar.

4. **Click the Shape Layers button on the Options bar.**

   The available settings on the Options bar will change to those shown in the first Options bar in Figure 16-4.

5. **Select settings for the shape tool you selected.**

   If you're not sure which settings to apply, see Step 5 in the previous section "Creating a filled shape on a layer" for details.

6. **Drag the mouse across the image window to draw a shape.**

   When you release the mouse button, the shape is filled with the Foreground color. A new shape layer appears in the Layers palette with a vector mask linked to it. Figure 16-6 shows some shape layers.

Creating a path using a shape tool

Shapes that are drawn as paths appear as temporary outlines on the Paths palette. These shape paths can be filled with the Foreground color, loaded into the image as a selection, and stroked with a brush to create an outline. To find out how to work with paths, turn to the "Paths" section later in this chapter. To create a path using a shape tool, follow these steps:

1. **Open an image with layers, and in the Layers palette, select a layer.**

   The new shape layer is created above this layer. (To find out how to select layers, turn to Chapter 8.)

2. **Select a shape tool from the Toolbox.**

   After you select a shape tool, you can change tools using the shape tool buttons on the Options bar.

3. **Click the Paths button on the Options bar.**

   The available settings on the Options bar change to those shown in the middle Options bar (refer to Figure 16-4).

4. **Select settings for the shape tool you selected.**

   If you're not sure which settings to apply, see Step 5 in the previous section "Creating a filled shape on a layer" for details.

5. **Drag the mouse across the image window to draw a shape.**

   When you release the mouse button, the work path appears in the image window and in the Paths palette. Figure 16-7 shows a rectangular work path.

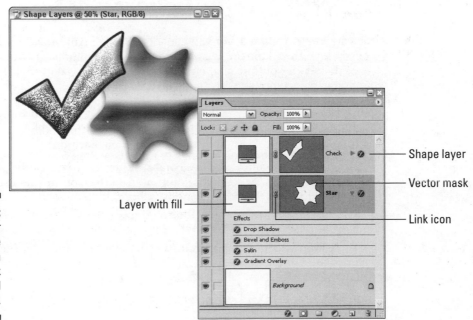

Figure 16-6:
These layer shapes are saved in a vector mask and linked to a layer.

A work path is a temporary path and is not saved. If you use a shape tool with the Paths button selected again, the path is automatically replaced. To save the work path so it cannot be replaced, double-click on Work Path in the Paths palette. Enter a descriptive name for the path in the Save Path dialog box, and then click OK.

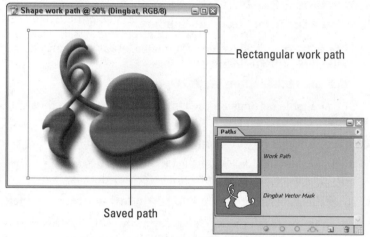

Rectangular work path

Figure 16-7:
A rectan-
gular work
path drawn
around
a shape
saved as a
shape layer.

Saved path

Working with Shape Layers

After you create a shape layer you can modify it in many ways. For instance, you can move the shape in the image window, rotate and skew the shape, change the shapes outline, and change its fill. Here's a smattering of ideas of what you can accomplish with shape layers:

 ✔ **To move a shape that's saved on a vector mask:** Select the shape layer in the Layers palette, select the Move tool from the Toolbox, and then drag the shape to its new position in the image window.

 ✔ **To transform a shape (scale, rotate, skew, distort, or add perspective):** Select the Direct Selection tool from the Toolbox, and then click on the shape in the image window. Choose any of the transformation commands from the Edit➪Transform Path menu. Perform the transformation. (I discuss transformations in detail in Chapter 7.)

✔ **To reshape a shape (shape shifting!):** Select the Direct Selection tool from the Toolbox and select the shape layer you want to modify in the Layers palette. Next, click on the edge of the shape in the image window. The edge displays its *anchor points*. Anchor points are the tiny squares along the path that control how the path is shaped. Drag an anchor point to change the contour of the shape. To find out more about anchor points and reshaping paths, turn to "Resshaping and Transforming Paths," later in this chapter.

✔ **To change the shape layer's fill:** Double-click the layer's thumbnail to open the Color picker and select a solid fill, or double-click the vector mask to open the Layer Style dialog box. Using the Layer Style dialog box, you can add drop shadows, gradients, glows, bevels, and much more to the shape layer. For complete details on using the Layer Style dialog box, turn to Chapter 8.

Rasterizing a shape layer

In order to edit a shape layer with Photoshop's pixel-based commands and tools (for instance, applying a filter or painting with the Brush tool), the shape layer must be rasterized (converted from a vector object into a pixel-based image).

1. **Open an image and select the shape layer in the Layers palette that you want to rasterize.**

2. **Choose a rasterize command from the Layer⇨Rasterize menu.**

   There are four options to choose from (their results are shown in Figure 16-8):

   - The **Shape** or **Layer** options both create the same results. If you select one of these options, the shape layer is converted into a pixel shape on a transparent layer.

   - The **Fill Content** option converts the shape layer's fill to cover the entire layer. The vector mask retains the exact outline of the shape layer's vector mask and acts as a mask cutout (like a layer mask), revealing only that portion of the layer. If there is no layer underneath, the masked (protected) areas reveal transparency.

   - The **Vector Mask** option converts the vector mask into a layer mask with the same shape as the vector mask. This option also converts the shape layer's fill to cover the entire layer. If there is no layer underneath, the masked (protected) areas reveal transparency.

   The shape layer is rasterized in the manner that you select. That's all there is to it.

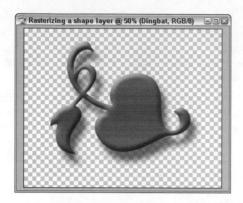

Image on transparent layer after rasterizing

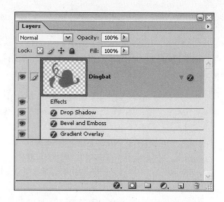

The layer after the Shape or Layer menu items are chosen

Figure 16-8:
When you rasterize a shape layer, there are four options to choose from.

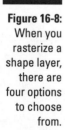

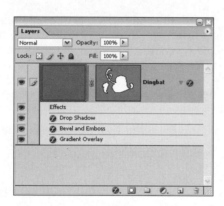

The layer after the Fill Content menu item is chosen

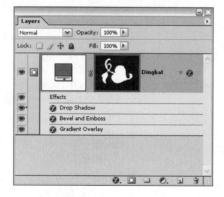

The layer after the Vector Mask menu item is chosen

A Path Primer

Paths can be *open* (like a line) or *closed* (like a triangle). Paths are made up of line *segments*. Segments can be curved or straight. *Anchor points* are located at the ends of path segments. The anchor points and their associated *direction lines* and *direction points* control how line segments are shaped and sized.

Anchor points come in two flavors. Anchor points on smooth curves are called smooth points. Anchor points on sharp curves (corners) are called *corner points*.

Look at Figure 16-9 as you read this section about the anatomy of a path and the functions of its various parts.

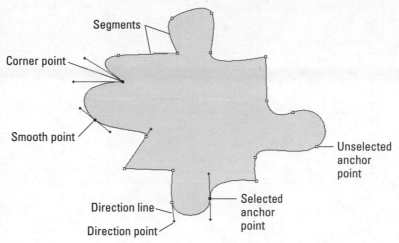

Segments

Corner point

Smooth point

Direction line

Direction point

Unselected anchor point

Selected anchor point

Figure 16-9:
Paths are
made up
of line
segments.
Anchor
points can
be found at
the ends
of path
segments.

You can move anchor points and direction points to reshape paths. When you move a direction line on a smooth point, the curved line segments on either side of the smooth point move at the same time. When you move a direction line on a corner point, only the line segment on the same side as the direction line moves; the line segment on the other side of the corner point remains stationary.

You can draw paths using the Pen tool, the Freeform Pen tool, and any of the shape tools (with the Paths setting on the Options bar selected) (see Figure 16-10). You modify the path shape using the Direct Selection tool and the Path Selection tool. You can add anchor points to a curve using the Add Anchor Point tool and delete anchor points from a curve using the Delete Anchor Point tool. Using the Convert Anchor Point tool, you can change an anchor point from a smooth point to a corner point and vice-versa.

Paths are amazingly versatile. You can create a complex path then convert it to a selection or layer mask. In addition, you can fill them with color to create a shape or stroke a path to create an outline. Because paths are not part of an image, they can be reshaped and modified without messing up the image.

Creating paths with the Pen tool

With the Pen tool, you click to create anchor points attached to straight line segments and drag to create curved line segments. If you make a mistake while using the Pen tool, you can press the Esc key once to delete the last anchor point or press Esc twice to delete the entire path. Here are more pointed directions for creating paths with the Pen tool:

1. Select the Pen tool from the Toolbox.

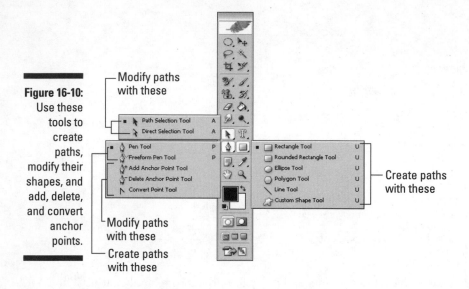

Figure 16-10:
Use these tools to create paths, modify their shapes, and add, delete, and convert anchor points.

Modify paths with these

Create paths with these

Modify paths with these

Create paths with these

2. **In the Paths palette, make sure all paths are deselected.**

3. **Select the Paths button on the Options bar.**

   Also, click the Geometry Options button and select the Rubber Band option, as shown in Figure 16-11. The Rubber Band option enables you to see the line segments as you draw them.

4. **Drag to create the path (see Figure 16-12).**

   • **To create a straight line segment:** Click once in the image window, move the mouse, and then click again.

   • **To create a curved line segment:** Position the mouse in the image window, press the mouse button, and drag. Direction lines appear after you release the mouse button.

Figure 16-11:
Click the Paths button on the Options bar and select the Rubber Band setting.

Click the Paths button

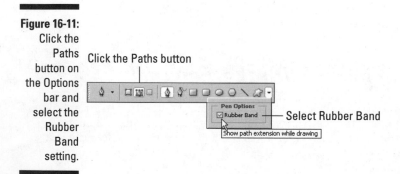

Select Rubber Band

Click to create straight segments

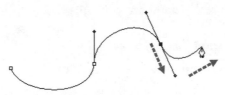

Drag to create curved segments

Figure 16-12:
Click to
create
straight line
segments
and drag to
create
curved line
segments.

Drag in the directions you want
the curve to go

5. **Continue adding line segments until the path is complete.**

   • **To end the path and leave open, creating an open path:** Ctrl+click
     (⌘+click on a Mac) away from the path in the image window or
     select another tool.

   • **To end the path and close it, creating a closed path:** Click the
     first anchor point you created. A tiny circle appears next to the
     mouse pointer.

The work path you just created is a temporary path. If you create another
path, this path will disappear forever. In order to save the path, click the
Work Path in the Paths palette, type a name in the Save Path dialog box,
and then click OK. The saved path appears in the Paths palette.

Creating paths with the Freeform Pen tool

The Freeform Pen tool works just like a pen or pencil. You drag to create a
path. When you release the mouse button, anchor points appear along the
path. At first, your paths may appear rough, but you can always refine them
using their anchor points. As you continue to practice with the Freehand
tool, drawing will come quite naturally.

Here are some general instructions for creating paths with the Freeform Pen tool:

1. **Select the Freeform Pen tool from the Toolbox.**

2. **In the Paths palette, make sure all paths are deselected.**

3. **Select the Paths button on the Options bar and make sure the Magnetic option is not selected.**

   Take a look at Figure 16-11 for the location of the Paths button.

4. **Position the mouse in the image window and drag to create a path.**

   If you want to create straight line segments, Alt+click (Option+click on a Mac). When you are finished creating straight line segments and want to return to freehand drawing, Alt+click (Option+click on a Mac) again.

5. **Continue drawing until your path is complete.**

   • **To create an open path:** Release the mouse button.

   • **To create a closed path:** Drag the path back over the place where you started drawing the path.

   Figure 16-13 shows a path created with the Freeform Pen tool.

   To save the path, click the Work Path in the Paths palette, type a name in the Save Path dialog box, and then click OK.

Figure 16-13:
Close a
freeform
path by
dragging the
mouse over
the place
where you
started
(left).
Anchor
points
appear
automati-
cally on the
new path
(right).

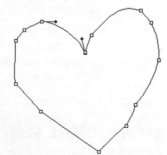

Using the Magnetic option with the Freeform Pen tool

If you use the Freeform Pen tool with the Magnetic option selected, the tool creates a path automatically as you drag next to high contrast areas. The Freeform Pen tool's Magnetic option works in a similar fashion to the Magnetic Lasso tool, but instead of creating a selection, you create a path. Remember that this tool works best tracing the edge of an object that is very distinct.

1. **Select the Freeform Pen tool from the Toolbox.**

2. **Click the Paths button on the Options bar and select the Magnetic option as shown in Figure 16-14.**

Figure 16-14:
Click the
Paths
button on
the Options
bar and put
a check
in the
Magnetic
check box.

Click the Paths button   Put a check here

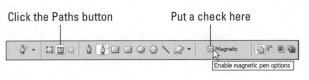

3. **In the Paths palette, make sure all paths are deselected.**

4. **Use the Layers palette to hide any layers that you don't want to trace.**

5. **Click the mouse where you want to begin the path, then move the mouse slowly around the object you want to trace.**

   You don't need to hold down the mouse button while you move the mouse to create the path. If the path snaps to an area you don't want to trace, manually create an anchor point by clicking the edge of the shape you *do* want to trace.

6. **Continue moving the mouse until your path is complete.**

   - **To create an open path:** Press Enter (Return on a Mac).

   - **To create a closed path:** Move the mouse back over the place where you started drawing the path.

   Figure 16-15 shows a magnetic path being created with the Freeform Pen tool.

Figure 16-15:
Click where
you want
to start
drawing a
path and
move the
mouse
to trace
around the
object (left).
To close the
path when
you're
finished,
simply move
the mouse
over the
place where
you started
drawing
(right).

You just created a temporary work path. If you create another path, this path will disappear forever. To save the path, click the Work Path in the Paths palette, type a name in the Save Path dialog box, and then click OK.

Converting a selection into a path

After creating a selection, you can turn it into a path using the Paths palette. Just click the Make Work Path from Selection button at the bottom of the Paths palette. The selection instantly changes into a path that can be reshaped like any other path.

To save the path, double-click the Work Path in the Paths palette, type a name for the path in the Save Path dialog box, and then click OK.

Path Manipulation Basics

After you create a path, you can move it in the image window, copy it and paste it into the same image window or drag a copy to another image window, display and hide the path, save it, and, of course, delete it. Here's the lowdown:

✔ **To move a path in the image window:** Select the path you want to move in the Paths palette, and then select the Path Selection tool from the Toolbox. Next, click in the path to select it, and then drag it to a new location.

✔ **To copy a path in the same image window:** Select the path you want to copy in the Paths palette. Then, drag the path over the Create New Path button at the bottom of the palette.

✔ **To copy a path into another image window:** Select the path you want to copy in the Paths palette. Then, drag the path from the Paths palette into the new image window.

✔ **To save a work path:** Double-click the Work Path in the Paths palette. Enter a name for the path in the Save Path dialog box, and then click OK.

✔ **To display a path in the image window:** Select the path in the Paths palette.

✔ **To hide a path and not show it in the image window:** Shift+click the path's name in the Paths palette.

 ✔ **To deselect a path in the image window:** Select the Path Selection tool from the Toolbox. Click outside the path in the image window. The path will still be displayed, but its anchor points will be hidden.

✔ **To delete a path:** Select the path you want to delete in the Paths palette, and then drag it over the trash icon at the bottom of the palette.

Reshaping and Transforming Paths

When you reshape a path you can drag anchor points to move segments and drag direction points to change the curve of a segment. You also can add and delete anchor points and convert anchor points from smooth points to corner points and vice versa.

With the entire path selected you can use the transformation commands found on the Edit menu to scale, rotate, skew, distort, and add perspective to an entire path. If you select a few anchor points along a path, you also can use the transformation commands on those selected points, transforming only a portion of the path.

After you are pleased with the shape of a path, you can fill it, add an outline to the path by applying a stroke, and convert it to a selection.

Reshaping a path

As you reshape a path, you'll use the Direct Selection tool to drag anchor points and direction points, the Add Anchor Point tool and Delete Anchor Point tool to add anchor points to and remove anchor points from the path, and the Convert Point tool to change corner points into smooth points and vice versa.

1. **Select the path you want to reshape in the Paths palette.**

   The path will appear in the image window.

2. **Select the Direct Selection tool from the Toolbox.**

3. **Click on the path in the image window to view its anchor points.**

4. **Start reshaping the path.**

   Figure 16-16 shows a path being reshaped, anchor points being added and removed, and anchor points being converted from one type to another.

   - **To move a segment of the path:** Drag an anchor point or drag the segment.

   - **To change the shape of a segment:** Select an anchor point by clicking it (the tiny anchor point changes from a hollow square to a filled one), and then drag the direction point. If you move a selection point connected to a smooth point, the two segments on either side of the smooth point also move. If you move a selection point connected to a corner point, only the segment near the selection point moves.

   - **To add an anchor point to a path:** Select the Add Anchor Point tool from the Toolbox, position the mouse over the line segment where you want to add the anchor point, and then click.

   - **To delete an anchor point from a path:** Select the Delete Anchor Point tool from the Toolbox, position the mouse over the anchor point you want to delete, and then click.

   - **To convert a smooth point into a corner point:** Select the Convert Point tool from the Toolbox, position the mouse over the smooth point you want to change and click.

   - **To convert a corner point into a smooth point:** Select the Convert Point tool from the Toolbox, position the mouse over the corner point you want to change, press the mouse button, and drag.

5. **When you are finished reshaping the path, click outside the path to deselect it.**

Transforming paths and points

Using the Direct Selection tool, you can select an entire path for transformation or you can select just a few anchor points.

1. **Select the path you want to transform in the Paths palette.**

   The path appears in the image window. If you are transforming the entire path, skip to Step 3.

2. **Select the Direct Selection tool from the Toolbox and use it to select the anchor points you want to transform.**

To select an anchor point, position the mouse pointer over the anchor point and click. To select multiple anchor points, hold down the Shift key while clicking.

Drag an anchor point with the
Direct Selection tool

Drag a direction with the
Direct Selection tool

Click to add a path with the
Add Anchor Point tool

Click an anchor point to delete
with the Delete Anchor Point tool

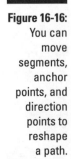

Figure 16-16:
You can
move
segments,
anchor
points, and
direction
points to
reshape
a path.

Click to convert a smooth point
to a corner point

Drag to convert a corner point to
as smooth point

3. Choose a transformation command from the Edit⇨Transform menu.

Depending upon whether you are transforming an entire path or are transforming selected anchor points, choose either the Transform Path option or Transform Points option.

As shown in Figure 16-17, a box with handles appears around either the entire path or the selected points.

Figure 16-17:
Drag the handles to perform a transformation on an entire path (left) or on selected anchor points (right).

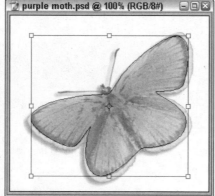 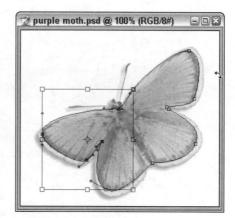

4. Drag the handles to perform the transformation.

Transformations are discussed in detail in Chapter 7.

 5. When the transformation is complete, click the Commit button on the Options bar to accept the transformation.

 Click the Cancel button on the Options bar to cancel the entire transformation.

Filling a path

Paths can be filled with solid color, a pattern, or imagery from a history state using the History palette. (History states and the history palette are discussed in detail in Chapter 14.) Here's how to fill a path:

1. Select the path you want to fill in the Paths palette.

You can fill either a closed path or an open path.

 2. Select the Direct Selection tool from the Toolbox.

3. **Use the Layers palette to select the layer on which you want the fill to appear.**

   Only a fill appears — not an outline of the path. To create an outline of a path, turn to "Adding a stroke to a path" later in this chapter.

4. **Select the color, pattern, or history state that will fill the path.**

   - **To fill the path with a solid color:** Choose a Foreground color using the Color picker, the Color or Swatches palette, or the Eyedropper tool.

   - **To fill a path with imagery from a history state:** In the History palette click in the column to the left of the state you want to use. The tiny History Brush icon appears next to the history state.

   - **To fill a path with a pattern:** Select a pattern using the Fill Path dialog box discussed in Step 5.

5. **Right-click (Control+click on a Mac) inside the path and choose Fill Path from the context-sensitive menu.**

   In the Fill Path dialog box shown in Figure16-18, you can select a fill, blending mode, and opacity.

Click here to select the fill

Figure 16-18:
Use the Fill Path dialog box to fill the path with the Foreground color, a pattern, or imagery from a history state.

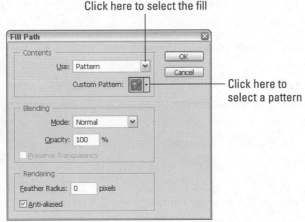

Click here to select a pattern

6. **In the Contents area, select a fill type from the Use drop-down list.**

   Select Foreground Color, History, or Pattern. If you choose Pattern, select a pattern using the Pattern picker in the dialog box.

7. **Click OK to close the dialog box and fill the path.**

   As shown in Figure 16-19, the pattern fills the entire path area but does-n't add an outline to the path. (See the next section "Adding a stroke to path" for directions on how to do this.)

To quickly fill a path with the current Foreground color, click the Fill path button at the bottom of the Paths palette.

Figure 16-19:
The original path is shown on the left and the filled area is shown on the right.

Adding a stroke to a path

You can use the attributes — brush size and hardness, opacity, blending mode, flow, and so on — from many of the painting tools to add a line around a path (a *stroke*).

1. **Use the Paths palette to select the path you want to stroke.**

   You can select either an open path or a closed path. Figure 16-20 shows the selected path in the Paths palette and the image window.

2. **In the Layers palette, select the layer where you want the stroke to appear.**

3. **Choose a tool from the Toolbox.**

   There are 15 tools you can choose from to create the stroke. They are shown in Figure 16-21.

4. **Use the Options bar to select settings for the tool you selected in step 3.**

   Using the Options bar, you can use the Brush Preset picker to select a brush and hardness, a blending mode, opacity, airbrush capabilities, flow, and any other options associated with the tool.

5. **Select a Foreground color.**

6. **Click the Stroke path button at the bottom of the Paths palette (shown in Figure 16-20).**

   Figure 16-22 shows the path from Figure 16-20 with a stroke.

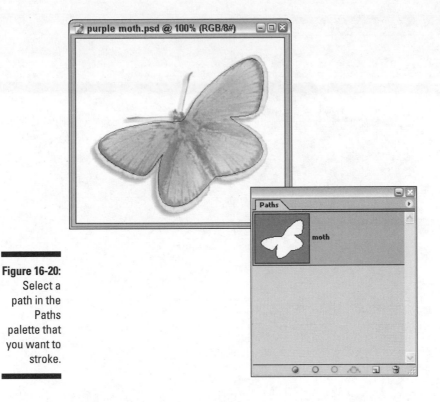

Figure 16-20:
Select a
path in the
Paths
palette that
you want to
stroke.

Converting paths to selections

After creating a path, you can quickly turn it into a selection by selecting the
path in the Paths palette, and then clicking the Load path as selection button
at the bottom of the Paths palette.

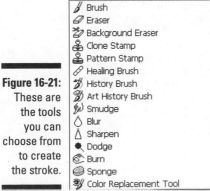

Figure 16-21:
These are
the tools
you can
choose from
to create
the stroke.

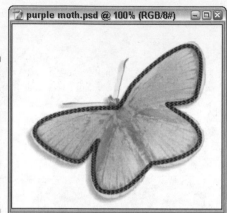

Figure 16-22:
The path stroked with a custom brush stroke selected using the Brushes palette.

Chapter 17

Adding and Manipulating Type

In This Chapter

▶ Using the type tools

▶ Setting character and paragraph formatting

▶ Working with type layer in the Layers palette

▶ Warping type

▶ Placing type on a path

▶ Converting type into shapes and paths

▶ Creating type-shaped selections

▶ Adding strokes and layer styles to text-shaped selections

▶ Creating translucent text

Type is created in Photoshop using four tools: Horizontal Type tool, Vertical Type tool, Horizontal Type Mask tool, and Vertical Type Mask tool.

The first two tools, the Horizontal Type and Vertical Type tools, create editable type. Besides being able to set the type's attributes — such as font, style, point size, alignment, color, kerning, tracking, and leading — you also can transform editable type, enhance it with layer effects and blending modes, and change its opacity.

When you create editable type it appears on its own layer, that way it can be edited, moved, and otherwise customized without affecting another layer. Type created in Bitmap, Indexed Color, or Multichannel images will be placed on the Background, not on a layer, so it won't be editable.

Just like the paths and vector shapes I discuss in Chapter 16, editable type is *vector type.* That means that it has a crisp, clear look because it is created using mathematical formulas, not pixels.

Because vector type is not pixel based, you won't be able to paint on the type or apply filters until it is *rasterized* or turned into pixels. And after you rasterize your type layer, you can't change the type's attributes.

The other two type tools, the Horizontal Type Mask tool and Vertical Type Mask tool, create selections in the shape of type characters. After you create a type-shaped selection, you can save the selection as an alpha channel, convert it into a layer mask, or turn it into a shape layer. (For more about alpha channels, turn to Chapter 15; for information on layer masks, see Chapter 8; for shape layers, look at Chapter 16.)

In this chapter, I show you how to create, transform, and modify editable type in your Photoshop projects.

Introducing the Type Tools

The four type tools are located in their own flyout menu in the Toolbox as shown in Figure 17-1. When you select a type tool, the Options bar displays type attribute settings such as font, style, size, alignment, and colors.

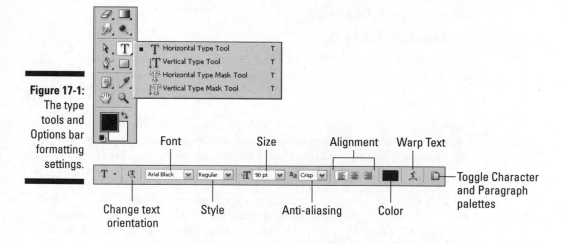

Figure 17-1:
The type tools and Options bar formatting settings.

Here's a brief description of the four type tools:

✔ **The Horizontal Type tool:** Creates text on an editable type layer, which enables you to work with the text without worrying about touching the underlying image. You can edit the text contents and attributes by simply highlighting the text with the Horizontal Type tool. Although you cannot use painting or editing tools on a type layer, you can make the text more or less translucent by adjusting the opacity percentage in the Layers palette; you can blend the text with the underlying layers using the Blend Modes drop-down list, as well.

When you click with the Horizontal Type tool, the type you create is automatically created placed on a separate type layer.

✔ **The Vertical Type tool:** Also creates type on an editable type layer, but enters the type vertically. You can edit vertical type by selecting it with the Vertical Type tool. This tool comes in handy for Asian fonts.

✔ **The Horizontal Type Mask and Vertical Type Mask tools:** Enable you to create selections shaped like type. You can manipulate, edit, paint, and otherwise play with a type-shaped selection outline as you would any other selection outline. Because these two tools create type-shaped selections, you can't edit the selections the way you would with the vector type created with the other two type tools.

Choosing the Right Type Tool for the Job

So which tool do you use when? If you want to create editable text, use the Horizontal Type tool or Vertical Type tool. Otherwise, it depends on what sort of effect you're trying to create. Here's the lowdown:

✔ **To create opaque type:** Use the Horizontal Type tool or Vertical Type tool.

✔ **To create filled letters:** Use the Horizontal Type Mask or Vertical Type Mask tool to create a type-shaped selection. Then convert the selection into a layer mask and apply any effect you would like. To see this technique in action, check out Color Plate 17-1.

✔ **To soften the edges of your letters:** Use the Horizontal Type tool or Vertical Type tool to create the type, and then add cool effects using layer styles. For example, you can create a fuzzy shadow behind your letters, add a beveled edge, or fill the text with a pattern or gradient. Check out Color Plate 17-2 to see layer styles in action.

Putting Your Words On-Screen

To type a few letters in Photoshop, select either the Horizontal Type tool or the Vertical Type tool and click inside the image window. It doesn't really matter where you click, by the way. Photoshop positions your text at the spot where you click, but you can always move the text after you create it.

After you click with a type tool, a little blinking cursor appears (called an *insertion marker*) that you be familiar with from working in other programs. After the insertion marker appears, you're free to enter your text. This click-and-type method results in *point type*. Photoshop gives you the option of creating either point type or *paragraph type*.

Creating point type

Point type is free-floating and independent; all the type lines are separate from each other. It's great for short bursts of text — a word or short line.

To create point type:

1. **Select either the Horizontal Type tool or Vertical Type tool from the Toolbox.**

2. **Click the image window to set an insertion marker.**

3. **Type your text.**

4. **Click on the Commit button on the Options bar when you're finished typing text.**

Creating paragraph type

Paragraph type is created in a *bounding box*. Paragraph type flows according to the dimensions of the bounding box. It's useful for larger quantities of type. Paragraph text is also useful if you want your text to automatically word wrap within the bounding box, or you want text that is justified — aligned to the left, center, or right.

To create paragraph type:

1. **Select either the Horizontal Type tool or Vertical Type tool from the Toolbox.**

2. **Drag the tool diagonally on the canvas to create a bounding box.**

   A dotted box with handles and an insertion maker within the box appear.

3. **Type your text.**

   As you type, the text automatically wraps within the boundaries of the box.

4. **Adjust the bounding box if necessary.**

   • **To scale the bounding box:** Drag a handle to change the horizontal or vertical size of the box.

   • **To rotate the bounding box:** Move the cursor outside one of the corner handles until a curved arrow appears. Drag the curved arrow in a circular direction to rotate the box.

   • **To skew the bounding box:** Press Ctrl (⌘ on a Mac) and drag a side handle.

   • **To scale both the bounding box and the type:** Press Ctrl (⌘ on a Mac) and drag a corner handle.

5. **Click on the Commit button on the Options bar.**

To convert between point type and paragraph type, select the type layer in the Layers palette and choose Layer⇨Type⇨Convert to Point Text or Convert to Paragraph Text.

Working with Type

When you create type, it appears on its own type layer. In the Layers palette, a type layer is indicated with a capital letter T icon, as shown in Figure 17-2. The name of the type layer corresponds to the text you typed.

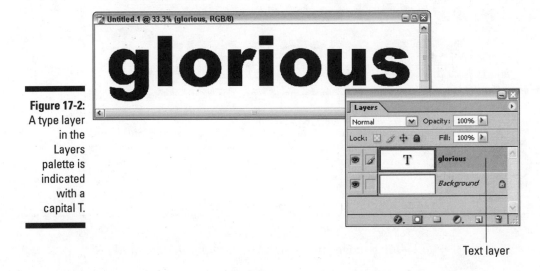

Figure 17-2: A type layer in the Layers palette is indicated with a capital T.

Text layer

Here are a few things you should know about working with text:

✔ If you make a mistake while typing, delete a letter by clicking after it and pressing the Backspace key (Delete key on a Mac). To add text, click at the point where you want to insert it and enter the new text from the keyboard.

✔ If you want to replace text, drag over it with the cursor to highlight it, and then enter the new text. To delete more than one letter, highlight the letters and press the Backspace key (Delete key on a Mac).

✔ If you're creating point type, Photoshop places all words on a single line unless you insert a line break by pressing the Enter key (Return key on a

Mac). In Figure 17-3, for example, I typed **Shiver**, pressed Enter (Return on a Mac), and then typed **me timbers!**

✔ To spell-check your Photoshop text, select the type layer in the Layers palette. Choose Edit➪Check Spelling. If you have multiple text layers and want to spell check all of them, select the Check All Layers option in the Check Spelling dialog box. And, if you happen to be typing in Portuguese, Dutch, or any other language, choose the desired dictionary using the Set Language drop-down list at the bottom of the Character palette (see Figure 17-4).

Figure 17-3:
Press Enter (Return on a Mac) to insert a line break.

While typing your text, you can use the Cut, Copy, Paste, and Undo commands on the Edit menu. These commands enable you to move text around and undo mistakes. For example, to move some letters from one place to another, follow these steps:

1. **Drag to highlight the text you want to move.**

2. **Press Ctrl+X (⌘+X on a Mac).**

   Photoshop removes the text and holds it in the Clipboard.

3. **Click where you want to place the text.**

   Your click repositions the insertion marker.

4. **Press Ctrl+V (⌘+V on a Mac).**

   Photoshop retrieves the text from the Clipboard and inserts it at the desired spot.

If you want to duplicate text, you can highlight it, press Ctrl+C (⌘+C on a Mac), reposition the insertion marker, and then choose Ctrl+V (⌘+V on a Mac). You can also undo the last edit by choosing Edit➪Undo or by pressing Ctrl+Z (⌘+Z on a Mac). If you need to undo more than one edit, use the History palette to move back a few history states. (Turn to Chapter 14 for more about history states and the History palette.)

Using the Character palette

The Character palette lets you set the formatting attributes of the type characters (see Figure 17-4). Some of these attributes include font type, style, size, and scale.

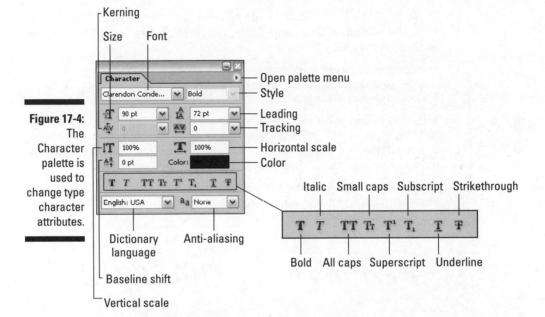

Figure 17-4:
The Character palette is used to change type character attributes.

In order to change type character formatting, you must first tell Photoshop what text you want to edit. If you only want to change a portion of the text, highlight it using either the Horizontal Type tool or Vertical Type tool. If you want to select all the text, you can either highlight it all or select the type layer in the Layers palette. Figure 17-5 shows many of these formatting attributes.

✔ **To change the font:** Select a typeface from the Font drop-down list. Select a style, such as bold or italic, from the Font style drop-down list.

✔ **To change the font's size:** Enter the new text size in the Set Font Size text box. Font size, by default, is measured in points. If you want to enter a different measurement system, just type it in. For instance, you could type in **.25 in** or **22 mm**. Photoshop automatically converts the entry to points. (If you want to change the default setting from points to another measurement system, choose Edit⇨Preferences⇨Units & Rulers, and then use the Units: Type drop-down list to select another system.)

✔ **To change the leading:** Enter a value in the Set the leading text box. *Leading* is the amount of space between lines.

✔ **To adjust kerning:** Enter a value in the Set the kerning text box. *Kerning* is the amount of space between two letters; positive values move letters apart, negative values move letters closer together.

✔ **To adjust the tracking:** Enter a value in the Set the tracking text box or select a value from the drop-down list. *Tracking* is the spacing between a series of characters; positive values spread characters apart; negative values move them closer together.

✔ **To vertically or horizontally scale type:** Enter a percentage in either the Vertically Scale or Horizontally Scale text boxes. These settings are great for distorting type.

✔ **To convert text from horizontal to vertical or vice versa:** Choose Change Text Orientation from the Character palette menu. You can find this command as a button on the Options bar (refer to Figure 17-1).

✔ **To quickly change formatting attributes:** Click the formatting buttons in the Character palette, such as Small Caps, Superscript, Underline, and others. Highlight the character(s) to be formatted and click the attribute button or select that attribute from the palette pop-up menu.

✔ **To smooth out the jagged edges of your type:** Use the Anti-aliasing drop-down list to choose an anti-aliasing setting. Figure 17-6 shows type that is anti-aliased and type that is not.

Figure 17-5:
You can quickly set type character attributes using the Character palette.

Kerning
Kerning

Kerning affects the space between the individual letters. Original text (top), kerned text (bottom)

TRACKING
TRACKING

Tracking affects spacing between a series of letters. Original text (top), tracked text (bottom)

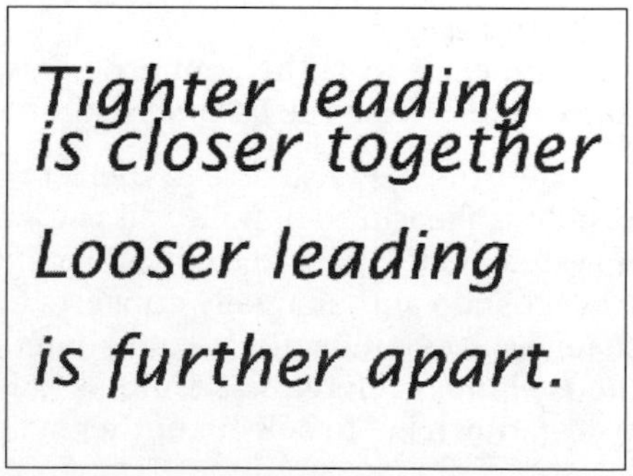

Tighter leading is closer together

Looser leading

is further apart.

Leading affects the spacing between lines of text. Tight leading (top) Loose leading (bottom)

SCALE
SCALE
SCALE

Scaling affects the shape of the text. Original text (top), 200% Horizontal Scale (middle), 200% Vertical Scale (bottom)

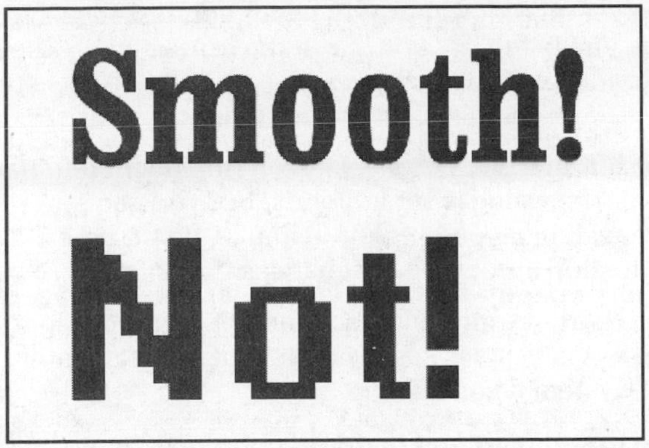

Smooth! Not!

Figure 17-6:
Anti-aliasing
type
smoothes
away the
jaggies.

Using the Paragraph palette

The Character palette's formatting partner is the Paragraph palette (see Figure 17-7). The Paragraph palette sets formatting attributes such as alignment, justification (whether the right edge of the text is straight or ragged), and hyphenation.

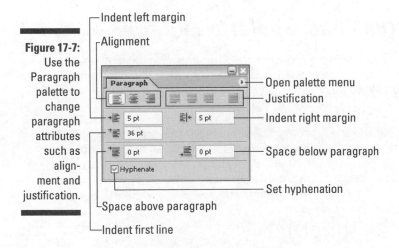

Figure 17-7:
Use the
Paragraph
palette to
change
paragraph
attributes
such as
align-
ment and
justification.

Indent left margin

Alignment

Open palette menu

Justification

Indent right margin

Space below paragraph

Set hyphenation

Space above paragraph

Indent first line

Here are the paragraph attributes you can set using the Paragraph palette:

- ✔ **To set paragraph alignment:** Click one of the alignment buttons at the top of the palette to set whether multiple lines of text are aligned by their left edges, right edges, or centers.

- ✔ **To justify paragraph text:** Click one of the justification buttons at the top of the Paragraph palette. This makes the right side of the paragraph text smooth instead of ragged. You can set paragraph text to justify the last text line on the left, justify the last text line in the center, justify the last text line on the right, or full justify all text (meaning the last line gets spread out to completely fill the bounding box from left to right).

- **To indent the left margin:** Enter a value in the Indent left margin text box. By default, this value is set in points, but you can enter another measurement system if you like. For instance, if you type **1 inch** in the text box, Photoshop automatically changes the entry to 72 points.

- **To indent the right margin:** Enter a value in the Indent right margin text box. By default, this value is set in points, but you can enter another measurement system if you like.

- **To indent the first line in a paragraph:** Enter a value in the Indent first line text box. The value in this text box is also set in points by default.

- **To add space above a paragraph:** Enter a value in the Add space before paragraph text box.

- **To add space after a paragraph:** Enter a value in the Add space after paragraph text box.

- **To allow hyphenation in a paragraph:** Put a check in the Hyphenate check box. If you don't want words hyphenated, uncheck the option.

Using the Layers palette and type layers

If you notice a misspelled word or some other typographical mistake, select the type layer in the Layers palette. Next, select either the Horizontal Type tool or Vertical Type tool and select the text by dragging. Then you can edit the type or any of its character or paragraph attributes.

The great thing about editable type layers is that they are saved with the image. That way, you can revise the text at any time, so long as you don't rasterize the text, outline the text, or flatten the layers. (See "Rasterizing a type layer," later in this chapter for more information about rasterizing, and check out Chapter 8 to find out more about layers.)

Here are some things you can do to a type layer without changing the ability to edit it:

- **Reorder or duplicate the type layer, just as you would with a regular layer.** To move a type layer up or down the stacking order in the Layers palette, drag it up or down the list of layers. To duplicate the type layer, drag the layer onto the Create a new layer button at the bottom of the Layers palette.

- **Move or clone the text.** After selecting the type layer in the Layers palette, drag with the Move tool to reposition the text in the image window. Use Alt+drag (Option+drag on a Mac) to clone the text.

When text is cloned it automatically creates a new type layer.

✔ **Change the orientation of a layer.** Choose Layer⇨Type⇨Horizontal or Vertical to change the orientation.

✔ **Apply any of the blending modes and adjust the opacity of the type layer.** I introduce blending modes and opacity in Chapter 8.

✔ **Perform transformation commands, such as Rotate, Skew, and Scale.** The Perspective and Distort transformation commands are not available for type layers.

✔ **Apply Layer Style effects to a type layer.** Even after you apply the effect, if the type changes in any way (such as a different font or even a different word), the effect magically updates to the changes! (For details on using layer styles, turn to Chapter 8.)

✔ **Delete the type layer.** If you decide that you don't want the type layer any longer, delete it by dragging the layer to the trash can icon at the bottom of the Layers palette.

Warping Type for Cool Effects

Photoshop comes with a large set of transformation functions that lets you twist, push, and pull editable type to create a variety of cool and crazy effects. Take a look at Figure 17-8 to see a small sampling of these effects. Check Color Plate 17-2. The type on the fish at the bottom of the page was warped using the Fish warp.

Follow these easy steps to warp your very own text:

1. **Select the type layer you want to warp in the Layers palette.**

2. **Select the Horizontal Type tool in the Toolbox and click Create warped text button on the Options bar.**

   The Warp Text dialog box appears.

3. **Select a warp type using the Style drop-down list.**

   See Figure 17-9.

4. **Play with the options.**

   Choose either Horizontal or Vertical orientation. Adjust the Bend value to apply more or less warping. Use the Distortion sliders to apply perspective to the warp.

5. **When you're happy with the warp, click OK.**

If you decide later that you want to change the text warp, just follow steps 1–5 again. You can change the warping as much and as often as you want before you rasterize the type.

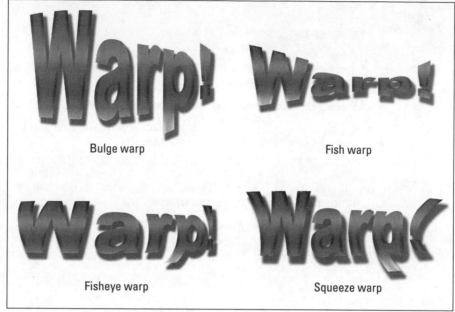

Bulge warp

Fish warp

Figure 17-8:
Warp type
into a
variety of
interesting
shapes.

Fisheye warp

Squeeze warp

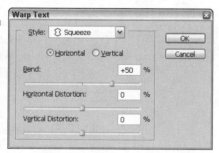

Figure 17-9:
Warping
text is easy
and fun
using the
Warp Text
dialog box.

Putting Editable Text on a Path

A great new feature of Photoshop CS is the ability to place text on a path. It doesn't matter how twisty or curvy the path is; the text zooms around curves and corners, rolls over bumpy hills, and even flows upside down. Here's how to put editable text on a path:

1. **In the Layers palette, select the layer you want to use to place text on a path or create a new layer.**

2. **Create a path using the Pen tool, Freeform Pen tool, or any of the shape tools.**

   If you already have a path saved in the Paths palette, select it to view it in the image window. To find out how to create paths, turn to Chapter 16. Figure 17-10 shows a circular path around an image of the Earth.

3. **Select the Horizontal Type tool from the Toolbox.**

4. **Set character attributes such as font, style, and size using either the Options bar or the Character palette.**

   Because you're creating editable type, you can always change the character formatting later.

5. **Position the mouse over the path where you want the text to start.**

   The mouse cursor changes to an I-beam with a little curved line passing through it.

6. **Click the mouse and then type.**

   The text follows the shape of the path. Figure 17-11 shows type moving around the circular path.

7. **When you're finished typing, click the Commit button on the Options bar.**

   The text is saved on a text layer and the path becomes a temporary type path. If you select another tool or a command, the path disappears. To save the type path, double-click it in the Paths palette, type a name for the type path in the Save Path dialog box, and then click OK.

Figure 17-10: For this example, text will be placed on the circular path around the Earth.

Figure 17-11:
As you type,
the letters
are placed
on the path.

After you've placed type on a path, you can edit it just like you would any editable type. You also can change where the text starts on the path by selecting the Path Selection tool from the Toolbox, clicking at the beginning of the text, and then dragging the text around the path to the place where you want it to start.

In addition to placing text on a path, you can use a path as a bounding box for text. As you type inside a path, the type fills the path area. To create text that fills a path, follow steps 1-4 above, and then place the mouse cursor inside the path. Click and type. The type fills the area inside the path.

Converting Editable Type to Pixels

In order to apply a filter or paint on a type layer, you must rasterize the type. *Rasterizing* means that type on a type layer is converted from vector type into pixels on a regular layer.

To rasterize type, select the type layer you want to convert in the Layers palette, and then choose Layer➪Rasterize➪Type.

After rasterizing, the type looks the same as it did before; however, you can no longer edit the type or change its character or paragraph attributes.

If you decide you would rather have editable text on a text layer after converting it, just choose Edit➪Undo or select a history state on the History palette prior to the conversion. (To find out more about the History palette, turn to Chapter 14.)

Converting Editable Type into Shapes and Paths

Two commands, Convert to Shape and Create Work Path, will convert editable type into a shape or a path.

If type is converted into a shape, the type layer automatically changes to a shape layer, as shown in Figure 17-12.

A shape layer consists of a vector mask linked to a layer. For a refresher on shape layers, turn to Chapter 16.

After you convert the type to a shape (the type layer also converts to a shape layer), you can modify the shape's contours with the Direct Selection, Add Anchor Point, Delete Anchor Point, or Convert Point tools. To find out about reshaping shapes, turn to Chapter 16.

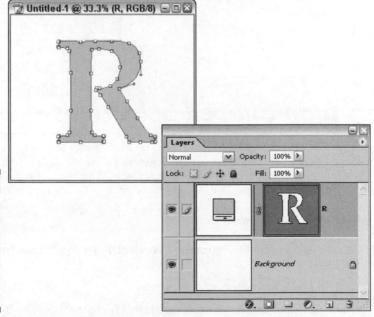

Figure 17-12: When type is converted into a shape, the shape is placed on a shape layer.

If a path is created using type, a temporary type-shaped work path appears in the Paths palette, and the type remains editable on its type layer, as shown in Figure 17-13. To save the path, double-click Work Path in the Paths palette, type a name in the Save Path dialog box, and then click OK.

After you create a path using type, you can reshape the path with the Direct Selection, Add Anchor Point, Delete Anchor Point, or Convert Point tools. You can convert the path to a selection using the Paths palette, as well. To find out about reshaping paths and turning them into selections, turn to Chapter 16.

Figure 17-13:
When a work path is created using type, the path appears in the Paths window and the editable type remains on its type layer in the Layers palette.

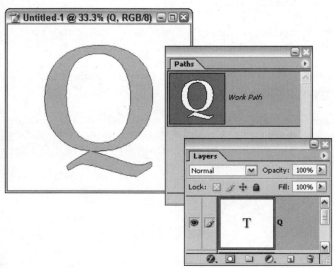

Creating Type-Shaped Selections

The Horizontal Type Mask and Vertical Type Mask tools are used to create type-shaped selections. You can set character and paragraph formatting for these tools just like you do for regular type using the Character and Paragraph palettes and the Options bar.

To create a type-shaped selection:

1. **Choose either the Horizontal or Vertical Type Mask tool from the Toolbox.**

2. **Click in the image window.**

   When you click, the image automatically changes to Quick Mask mode: a pink overlay covers the image. Any characters you type will appear white.

   There are two view settings for Quick Mask mode. If the Color Indicates: Masked Areas setting is selected, then the mask covers the entire image, except for the type. (This is the default setting.) If the Color Indicates: Selected Areas setting is selected, then the mask covers only the letters. For this example the default, Color Indicates: Masked Areas is used. To find out how to change these settings and to learn more about Quick Mask mode, turn to Chapter 16.

3. **Type the text that will become the selection.**

   Figure 17-14 shows the pink Quick Mask overlay and white type that will become a selection.

Figure 17-14:
When you use of the Horizontal or Vertical Type Mask tool to create a selection, Photoshop automatically changes to Quick Mask mode.

4. **Click the Commit button on the Options bar to turn the type into a selection.**

   Figure 17-15 shows the type-shaped selection created by the Horizontal Type Mask tool in Figure 17-14.

Figure 17-15:
A type-shaped selection can be used like any other selection.

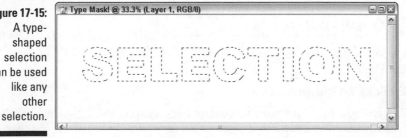

After you create the type-shaped selection, you can use it like any other selection. You can move it, save it to an alpha channel, use it to create a layer mask, stroke it, or fill it with a solid color or gradient.

Creating Great Text Effects

The following sections show you how to create some interesting text with type. You may have seen some of these effects on posters or in brochures. Following these directions, you can create these special effects and add them to your own projects.

Tracing outlines around your letters

Using the Horizontal Type Mask or Vertical Type Mask tool, you'll create a type-shaped selection and then choose the Stroke command to create outlined type. Figure 17-16 shows an example of outlined type created using the steps below.

Figure 17-16:
Creating outlined type is easy using a selection made with the Horizontal Type Mask tool or Vertical Type Mask tool.

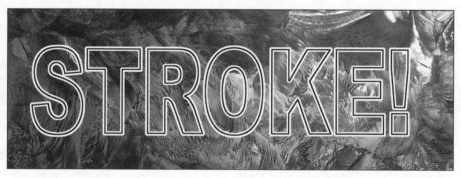

The area inside the letters is transparent and the letter contours are stroked with various colors. Using these directions you can make the borders as thick as you please.

1. **Create a new layer.**

   You don't have to put your text on its own layer, but doing so makes the text simpler to edit later on. To create a new layer, click the Create New Layer button at the bottom of the Layers palette. (Turn to Chapter 8 for more about layers.)

2. **Select the Horizontal Type Mask tool or Vertical Type Mask tool from the Toolbox.**

3. **Use the Character and Paragraph palettes to set formatting for the type-shaped selection you are going to create.**

   To find out more about formatting type, take a look at "Working with Type" earlier in this chapter.

4. **Click in the image window.**

   Photoshop automatically goes into Quick Mask mode. A pink overlay appears over the image window. When you type text, the text will appear white.

5. **Type your text.**

6. **Click the Commit button on the Options bar to turn the text into a selection.**

7. **If you need to move the type-shaped selection, use one of the selection tools or nudge the selection using the arrow keys.**

8. **Set the Foreground color to white.**

   You can quickly switch the Foreground color to white by pressing D and then pressing X.

9. **Make sure that the Lock transparent pixels check box in the Layers palette is not selected.**

   In the next step, a stroke is applied to the center of the selection outline (half the stroke appears on the inside of the outline and half appears on the outside). If you don't deselect the Lock Transparent Pixels check box, Photoshop won't let you paint on the transparent layer.

10. **Choose Edit⇨Stroke, select the Center radio button, enter 12 as the Width value, and click OK.**

    You now have a 12-pixel thick, white outline around your type-shaped selection.

11. **Select black or another dark color as the Foreground color.**

12. **Choose Edit⇨Stroke and enter 4 as the Width value, leave the Location at Center, and Click OK.**

    Congratulations! You get the effect shown in Figure 17-16. If you created the text on a new layer, as recommended back in Step 1, you can use the Move tool to reposition the text. You can also play with the blend modes and Opacity slider in the Layers palette to change how the text blends with the underlying image.

Adding drop shadows to letters

In these steps, you create letters with shadows, as shown in Figure 17-17. These kinds of shadows are commonly called *drop shadows* because they don't extend away from the letters; instead, they rest behind the letters. The automated layer styles feature makes applying shadows quick and easy. Take a look at Chapter 8 for complete directions on using layer styles.

1. **Select a Foreground color.**

   The Foreground color will be the color of the type that you create. You can use the Color picker, Color palette, or Swatches palette to select a color. (To find out how to select a Foreground color, turn to Chapter 4.)

2. **Use the Character and Paragraph palettes to set formatting for the type-shaped selection you are going to create.**

   To find out more about formatting type, take a look at "Working with Type" earlier in this chapter.

3. **Select the Horizontal Type tool or Vertical Type tool from the Toolbox.**

4. **Click in the image window and type your text.**

5. **Click the Commit button on the Options bar.**

   The type appears on its own type layer in the Layers palette.

6. **Use the Move tool to reposition the text, if you need to.**

7. **Click the Add Layer Style button at the bottom of the Layers palette, and then choose Drop Shadow from the menu.**

   The Layer Style dialog box opens with the Drop Shadow style checked and highlighted, as shown in Figure 17-18.

Figure 17-17: Drop shadows help to set off text from the background and make it look way cool.

Figure 17-18:
Use the Drop Shadow settings in the Layer Style dialog box to set the opacity, size, spread, distance, and angle of the drop shadow.

Make sure that the Preview check box is selected. That way, you can view the drop shadow in the image window as you create it.

I recommend leaving the Blend Mode setting at the default of Multiply. If you want your drop shadow to be a different color than gray (the default), click the color box next to the Blending Mode drop-down list to select a new color using the Color picker.

Use the Opacity slider to set how dark or light the shadow will be. The higher the setting, the darker the shadow.

8. **Rotate the line on the Angle dial or type a value to set the desired angle.**

   The Angle setting lets you determine where your light source is coming from to create the shadow.

The Distance setting determines how far the shadow offsets from the type. Keeping the shadow fairly close to the type usually results in a better effect. The Spread and Size settings affect the softness, intensity, and size of the shadow.

9. **Click OK when you're satisfied with the shadow's appearance.**

Try out some of the other styles in the Layer Styles dialog box. Use the Gradient Overlay or Pattern Overlay style to fill the type with a nifty gradient or pattern. Quickly add a stroke around the type using the Stroke style. Or add a beveled edge to the type using the Bevel and Emboss style. Play with the Layer Styles dialog box and see what kind of effects you can come up with. There's so much that you can do with just a few clicks of the mouse!

Creating transparent letters

You can create transparent letters using the Horizontal Type tool or Vertical Type tool. Transparent letters are great for creating tinted text, as shown in Figure 17-19. These effects look like they require a lot of effort, but you can achieve fantastic results by performing these simple steps:

1. **Open an image that will become the background behind the translucent type.**

   Or create a new image and fill the Background layer with a color of your choice using the Paint Bucket tool. If you use a dark background, you'll want to use light colored type for this effect. If you use a light background, you'll want to use dark colored type. The contrast between the type and the background is really important. If the background and type colors are very similar, you won't be able to see the type.

2. **Select a Foreground color.**

   The Foreground color will be used to color the type.

3. **Select the Horizontal Type or Vertical Type tool from the Toolbox.**

4. **Click in the image window, and type your text.**

Figure 17-19:
Transparent text lets the background image partially show through the letters.

5. Click the Commit button on the Options bar.

Photoshop creates type in the Foreground color and places it on a new type layer.

 6. Use the Move tool to reposition the text, if you need to.

7. In the Layers palette, use the Opacity slider to lower the opacity setting.

As you lower the opacity, notice that the type becomes more translucent. If you move the slider low enough, the type disappears altogether (it's still there, but the pixels are so translucent that you can't see the type). Move the slider until you're happy with the way the translucent text looks.

Part VII
Photoshop for Webbies

The 5th Wave · By Rich Tennant

"Ooo – look! Sgt. Rodriguez has the felon's head floating in a teacup!"

In this part . . .

The chapters in Part VII help you get started creating great Web graphics. If you are creating web pages, these chapters move you on down the road that takes your graphics from blah to fabulous. Photoshop and its sister program ImageReady provide world-class tools for preparing graphics for the Web.

Chapter 18 takes you through the basics of creating graphics for the Web using Photoshop and ImageReady, Photoshop's sister program. You find out about many of the new features in ImageReady, including the enhanced performance between the two programs, making it easier to jump back and forth between the programs. You'll discover which formats work best for the Web, which color palettes to use, and how to *optimize* images — keeping the file size down while preserving the display quality. After optimizing images, you find out how to save them. The end of the chapter discusses how to create type for the Web with ImageReady.

Slices are the fundamental building block for most of the graphic effects that you can create using Photoshop and ImageReady. Chapter 19 explains why and how to slice an image for the Web. Find out about the different types of slices you can create and how to duplicate, copy, and convert one type of slice to another. In addition, you can find out how to optimize individual slices within the same image using different file formats. After all the slicing, you can use the image map tools to create hotspots on your Web graphic and assign hyperlinks and alternate text to them.

Discover how to create rollovers and GIF animations in the bonus chapter. Visit www.dummies.com/go/photoshop_cs_fd. Using the Web Content and Animation palettes you'll have your graphics jumping around the Web page in no time.

Chapter 18

Spinning Graphics for the Web

• •

In This Chapter

▶ Taking a look at the ImageReady CS window

▶ Viewing image size and download times

▶ Finding out what tools are in the ImageReady Toolbox

▶ Jumping back and forth from ImageReady to Photoshop

▶ Learning about Web image basics

▶ Checking out color and color depth

▶ Finding out about dithering and anti-aliasing

▶ Selecting the Web Safe Color palette

▶ Checking out compression and Web file formats

▶ Optimizing and saving images for the Web

▶ Exporting an image in Flash SWF format

▶ Creating type for the Web

• •

*I*mageReady CS is a companion program that ships with Photoshop CS and is installed by default when Photoshop is installed. ImageReady is used to prepare images for display on the Web.

The fact of the matter is that if you are creating great images for use on the Web, you probably want to manipulate the images in Photoshop as well as prepare them for the Web in ImageReady. That's why Photoshop and ImageReady are so tightly integrated; it's really easy to move back and forth between the two programs by either clicking a button in the Toolbox or selecting a File menu command.

ImageReady provides many great tools that enable you to easily create stunning Web graphics. For example, you can use ImageReady to create image maps, rollovers, animations, and to break up large image files into pieces so they load more quickly into Web pages. In the process of creating these super effects, much of the time ImageReady produces HTML pages and JavaScript code for you (which means that you don't need to be a Web designer!), and saves graphic files in the formats that are specifically intended for optimal results on the Web.

What's New in ImageReady CS

There are so many improvements and enhancements to this version of ImageReady that it is hard to list them all! Here's a brief list of the many new features:

- ✔ **You can't open a document in Photoshop and ImageReady at the same time.** This tighter integration between the two programs means that you can easily work in one program then quickly switch to the other program for a specific feature. There are two ways to move back and forth between the two programs. Turn to "Moving back and forth between ImageReady and Photoshop" to find out the details.

- ✔ **Many layer commands, including duplicate, delete, link, and merge now work over multiple layers.**

- ✔ **You can group selected objects.** This feature lets you group related objects and move or transform them at the same time. In addition, grouping objects preserves their positioning in relationship to each other. Press Ctrl+G (⌘+G on a Mac) to group selected objects. Press Shift+Ctrl+G (Shift+⌘+G on a Mac) to ungroup objects. Groups of objects can be nested five deep.

- ✔ **You can select more than one object at a time.** Drag the mouse to marquee select multiple objects in the image window. This lets you move and manipulate multiple objects at the same time without having to select and manipulate each object individually.

- ✔ **You can drag multiple layers to the buttons at the bottom of the Layers palette.** This enhanced functionality enables you to instantly copy and delete multiple layers, and to create new layer sets quickly.

- ✔ **You can change formatting of objects *en masse*.** You can Shift+click to select several type objects at once, and then change their formatting settings at the same time.

- ✔ **You can use smart guides to align objects.** When dragging objects to line them up, new *smart guides* appear at the edges of objects to help with alignment.

- ✔ **You can directly export images to the Flash SWF file format.** Editable text and vectors created in ImageReady are preserved when exported to Flash. This is an extremely important feature for Flash creators who need to tweak and manipulate the images they use for Flash animations. Turn to "Exporting Images as Flash Files" for more information.

- ✔ **You can save individual layers, layer sets, and animation frames as individual files.** If you are exporting layers, you can choose the same format for the entire document or a different format for each layer.

- ✔ **You can use the newly designed Table palette to quickly access to new ImageReady table formatting options.** You can easily format border thickness, cell padding, cell spacing, and table dimensions.

✔ **You can create layer comps (just like in Photoshop) to save multiple configurations of a document including object position, layer blending options, and visibility.** (To find out more about layer comps, turn to Chapter 8.)

✔ **You can create multiple slice sets, hide slices, and cut, copy, or paste slices using the standard commands.**

Introducing the ImageReady cs Window

The ImageReady cs window is organized just like the main Photoshop window. The Menu bar and Options bar are at the top of the screen, the Toolbox is on the left side, and various palettes line the right side, as shown in Figure 18-1.

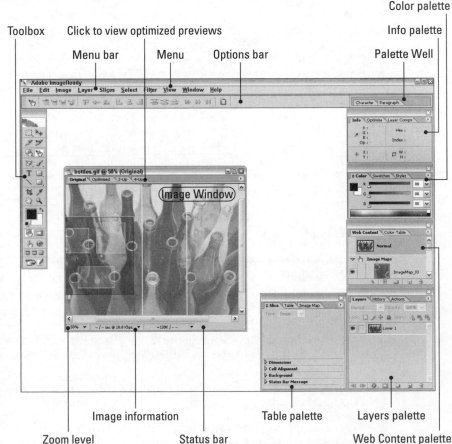

Figure 18-1: The ImageReady window with palettes and Toolbox in their default locations.

Viewing image size and download times

If you've ever accessed a Web site with a dial-up modem and found yourself going nuts waiting for images to *build* on-screen, then you have an inkling as to how important it is to manage file size and figure out just how long your images will take to load. You can test your images with a variety of connection speeds to get a good idea of what the range of online visitors will experience when they view your pictures.

To know how long an image will take to load on a Web page, you need to know the file size of a compressed image. Use the ImageReady Image Information menu at the bottom of the image window on the Status Bar to get this information (see Figure 18-2).

You can use the Image Information menu to select various connection speeds and to find out approximately how long an image will take to load. For instance a 240K image would take 44 seconds to load with a 56.6 Kbps modem connection, whereas that same 240K image would take 3 seconds to load with a broadband or DSL connection. As a general rule, you should try to keep image load times below 5 or 10 seconds. Remember, that this loading time is just for one image. If you have several images on a page, each one takes time to load. So, if you have four images that take five seconds to load, anyone viewing your Web page is going to have to wait for 20 seconds. Twenty seconds may not sound like a long time, but waiting even a minute for a Web page to load can be really frustrating.

As you can see in Figure 18-2, there are two slots on the status bar, where you can view image size and download times, compare two possible download scenarios, and see how long it would take for your image to load depending upon the connection speed.

Using ImageReady previews

You may have noticed that there are four tabs in the ImageReady image window that show different views of an open image (see Figure 18-3).

Here's a quick look at what the tabs mean:

- ✔ The Original tab shows the image without any *optimization*. (Optimization is the process that saves a file with a specific file size, file format, and color palette.)
- ✔ The Optimized tab shows the image using the current settings on the Optimize palette. This Optimized preview updates every time a setting or value on the Optimize palette changes. (I discuss the Optimize palette later in the Chapter in the "Optimization" section.)

An optimized file is one that has been saved with the smallest possible file size and the fewest colors, but whose image quality has not been degraded.

✔ The 2-Up tab shows two versions of the image. On the left is the original image that you would view if you selected the Original tab. On the right is the optimized image that you would view if you selected the Optimized tab.

✔ The 4-Up tabs show the original image, the optimized image based on the settings in the Optimize palette, and two other optimized previews based on variations of the settings in the Optimize palette.

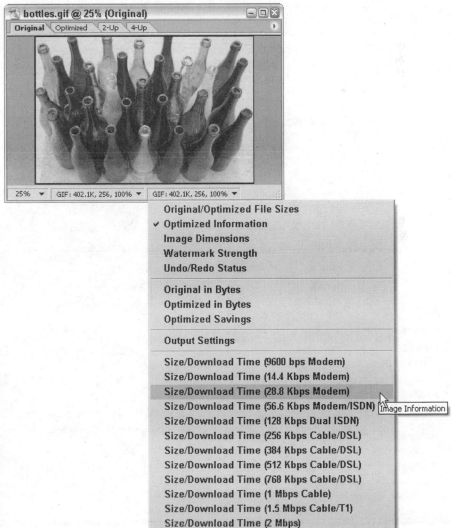

Figure 18-2:
Use the Image Information menu on the status bar to find out how long it will take an image to load on the Web.

You can use these different views of an image to compare the original image to optimized versions, checking for image quality. There's a real balance when an image is optimized. You can radically reduce file size by reducing an image's color palette, but you end up with a low-quality image. If you let the image have a larger color palette and better view quality, the file size is bigger. There's a breaking point where reducing colors for the sake of file size starts to impinge on image quality. Using these different view tabs in the image window can help you watch for that breaking point.

Using the ImageReady Toolbox

If you've used Photoshop, most of the tools in the ImageReady Toolbox are already familiar, though some tools are grouped differently. Also, there are a few extra Web related tools that are used for creating and viewing image maps, viewing and hiding slices, previewing rollovers and animations, and viewing documents in a Web browser. Figure 18-4 shows the ImageReady Toolbox and its fly-out tool menus.

Figure 18-3: The four views of an image, one with each tab selected: Original, Optimized, 2-Up, and 4-Up.

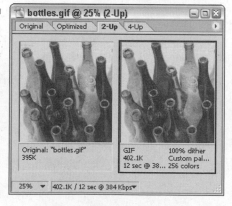

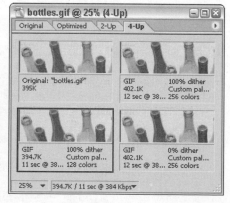

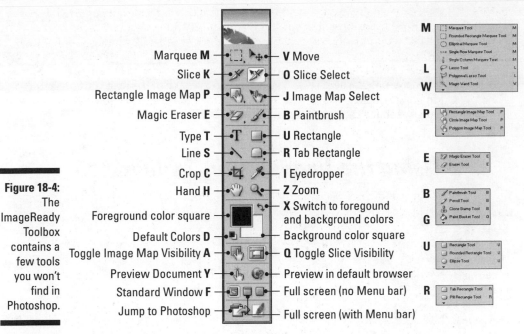

Figure 18-4:
The
ImageReady
Toolbox
contains a
few tools
you won't
find in
Photoshop.

Marquee **M** — **V** Move
Slice **K** — **O** Slice Select
Rectangle Image Map **P** — **J** Image Map Select
Magic Eraser **E** — **B** Paintbrush
Type **T** — **U** Rectangle
Line **S** — **R** Tab Rectangle
Crop **C** — **I** Eyedropper
Hand **H** — **Z** Zoom
Foreground color square — **X** Switch to foreground and background colors
Default Colors **D** — Background color square
Toggle Image Map Visibility **A** — **Q** Toggle Slice Visibility
Preview Document **Y** — Preview in default browser
Standard Window **F** — Full screen (no Menu bar)
Jump to Photoshop — Full screen (with Menu bar)

Anytime a tool is selected in ImageReady, the Options bar changes to display that tool's settings.

A great feature (which, in my humble opinion, the folks at Adobe should include in Photoshop!) is the ability to create mini toolbars containing the tools on a flyout menu. If you open one of the flyout menus on the ImageReady Toolbox, you may notice the tiny downward pointing arrow (look at Figure 18-5). If you drag the mouse down over that arrow, and then release the mouse button, a mini toolbar containing the tools on that flyout menu appears. You can drag the toolbar anywhere in the window and when you're finished with it, just click the Close button to make it disappear.

Palettes

Being the sister program of Photoshop, ImageReady contains many palettes that are probably familiar to you, including the Color, Swatches, Layers, History, Character, and Paragraph palettes (just to name a few). You can use the palettes just like the ones in Photoshop. To find out how to use these palettes turn to the relevant chapters earlier in this book.

There are several Web-related palettes that are used for creating animations, tables, managing image maps and slices, and for optimizing image size and quality when you save them. Figure 18-6 shows some of these Web-specific palettes.

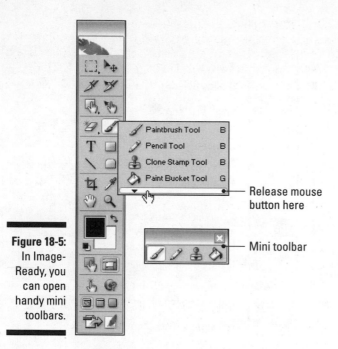

Release mouse
button here

Mini toolbar

Figure 18-5:
In Image-
Ready, you
can open
handy mini
toolbars.

Two palettes that deserve special mention are the Color and Swatches palettes, as shown in Figure 18-7. They are set up with all the Web-safe colors. Any color you pick using these palettes for your Web graphics looks good on the Web.

Moving back and forth between ImageReady and Photoshop

While working on Web graphics, leave both Photoshop and ImageReady open so that you can quickly jump from one to the other, making changes to the same open file.

 To jump back and forth between the programs, just click the Jump To button at the bottom of the Toolbox in either program or select File➪Edit in Photoshop or File➪Edit in ImageReady (depending upon which program you're in).

Previous versions of ImageReady and Photoshop kept an image open in both programs at the same time. When working on the image in one program, the image was grayed out in the other program.

With this version of Photoshop and ImageReady, the image is open in only one program at a time. Jumping back and forth between the programs is now faster, because the two programs only exchange layers that have changed (instead of opening and closing the entire image).

If you jump to Photoshop, perform some edits, then jump back to ImageReady, the Photoshop edits are identified in the History palette in ImageReady as a history state named Update from Photoshop. Any changes made in ImageReady are listed in Photoshop's History palette as Update from ImageReady. And, you can undo any edits made in the other program by selecting an earlier history state at any time. (To find out more about the History palette, turn to Chapter 14.)

Web Image Basics

There is a basic formula for creating an image for the Web — create an RGB image in Photoshop, adding all the bells and whistles that Photoshop has to offer, save it, jump to ImageReady, create any special animations or Web effects that you need in ImageReady, then save the image for Web output using the options the Optimize palette has to offer.

Figure 18-6:
Several ImageReady palettes are made just for creating specific Web content such as tables, animations, and slices.

Figure 18-7:
The Color
palette and
Swatches
palette are
loaded with
Web-safe
colors.

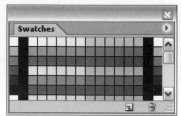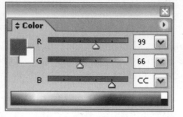

When you choose optimization settings, there are four key issues you'll have to keep in mind: the dimensions of the image (its height and width), the number of colors used in the image's color palette, the *bit depth* or *color depth* of the image (this is the amount of color information available for each pixel), and the file format the image is saved in (GIF, JPEG, or PNG).

Image size

The first thing you need to do when creating images for the Web is to consider the size of the viewing area and image resolution. There's a little formula you can use to figure out how large the image area is that you'll be designing for:

> Viewing area width / image resolution = max pixel width

> Viewing area height / image resolution = max pixel width

When selecting screen area settings for a computer monitor, three possible settings are available: 640 pixels x 480 pixels, 800 pixels x 600 pixels, and 1024 pixels x 768 pixels.

The most common setting for most computers that folks use is 800 pixels x 600 pixels, so Web images should typically be created for this screen size. Also, remember that the browser window takes up some of the screen real estate, so you'll need to decrease the width and height of your image by about an inch, making the viewing area about 720 pixels wide x 530 pixels high.

Images created for the Web should be set a 96 ppi (pixels per inch). A higher image resolution just makes the file size bigger and does not increase image quality.

Mac monitors view images at 72 ppi, whereas Windows monitors view images at 96 ppi. Setting Web images at 96 ppi lets both types of monitors view Web graphics equally well.

So, to plug the numbers in to the formula from above:

720 pixels wide / 96 ppi = 7.5 inches wide

530 pixels high/ 96 ppi = 5.5 inches high

How does this formula affect you as a Web graphics creator? The most important thing is to remember that the combined widths and heights of the design elements on the Web page must be smaller than these dimensions. For instance, suppose you want to create a horizontal navigation bar that runs along the top of the Web page. From the formula above, you'll know that it should be less than 720 pixels wide (and even smaller if you want to center the navigation bar and have a bit of space on either end).

Colors and color depth

Color depth (or bit-depth) determines how much color information is available for each pixel in an image. The lower the color depth in an image, the fewer colors the image can contain. Fewer colors and smaller color depth in a Web graphic reduces file size, making the graphic load faster in a Web page.

Reducing the number of colors and the color depth in an image can result in grainy looking edges and colors that are less vibrant, so you have to find out where the balance is between file size and image display quality. Table 18-1 shows the relationship between the number of colors an image has in its palette and the color depth of the image.

Table 18-1: Number of Image Colors versus Color Depth

If an Image Has This Many Colors. . .	Then Its Color Depth Is. . . .
256	8
128	7
64	6
32	5
16	4
8	3
4	2
2	1

You can reduce the number of colors and the color depth in an image using Photoshop's File⇨Save for Web command or ImageReady's Optimize palette. Both features let you preview how an image looks with fewer colors before you save it that way. (Both the Save for Web command and the Optimize palette are discussed in "Saving Web Files" later in this chapter.)

Dithering

Dithering is the term used to describe the mixing of two colors that are available in an image's color palette to create an approximation of a color that is not available in the color palette. Dithering is used to make images that have a fewer colors look like they have more colors and shades.

Alas, dithering is not a sure fix. Although it can create the impression of more colors, it can give an image a grainy look, as shown in Figure18-8.

Dithering tends to work best with photographic images that contain gradual changes in color and tone.

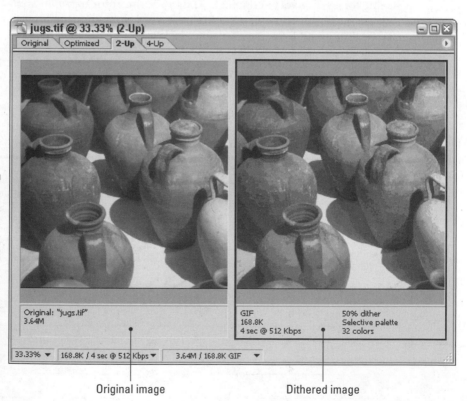

Figure 18-8: When an image is dithered, it does appear to have more colors, but it can become grainy looking.

Original image   Dithered image

Anti-aliasing

Anti-aliasing is the term used to describe the blending created between an object's edges and the background. When an object is anti-aliased, increasingly transparent pixels are added to the object's edges to help smooth the transition. If an object is not anti-aliased, its edges appear sharper because there is no blending transition. Figure 18-9 shows an anti-aliased image (left) with an area magnified (right) to make the anti-aliasing more apparent.

Figure 18-9: The transparent pixels in this anti-aliased image make a smooth transition to the background (left). When a portion of the image is magnified, the anti-aliasing becomes more apparent (right).

Anti-aliased area

When saving an image for the Web, you can control how much anti-aliasing is used in the image by using the Matte setting. This setting is available when you use the Save for Web command in Photoshop or the Optimize palette in ImageReady. (Both the Save for Web command and the Optimize palette are discussed in "Saving Web Files" later in this chapter.)

Selecting Web-safe colors

ImageReady and Photoshop both offer a Web Safe Color palette. The Web Safe Color palette is made up of the 216 colors that the Windows and Mac browsers have in common. To load the Web Safe Color palette in either program choose Window⇨Swatches to open the Swatches palette. Choose Web Safe Colors from the palette menu, as shown in Figure 18-10. A dialog box appears, asking whether you want to replace the current swatches with Web Safe Colors. Click Replace. From here on out, only Web Safe Colors are available in the Swatches palette.

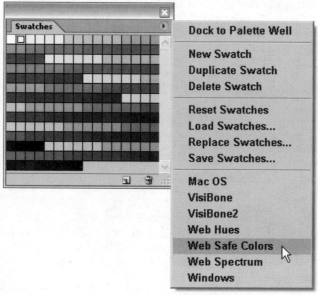

Figure 18-10:
Use the Swatches palette menu to select Web Safe Colors.

Compression and Web file formats

You can choose one of three Web graphic file formats: GIF, JPEG, and PNG. Each format has its strengths and weaknesses. And each file format uses a mathematical compression formula to reduce the file size of an image and make it load faster on the Web.

GIF file format

The GIF file format can contain 8-bits (8 color levels) and up to 256 colors. This file format is best for high-contrast images with sharp edges, including type. The GIF file format is used to retain transparency and create animations.

JPEG file format

The JPEG file format can contain 24-bit images with millions of colors. This file format works best for photographs and images that display subtle color changes, such as lighting effects.

But there's a trade-off with this file type (actually, there are two):

✔ That large 24-bit JPEG image can be compressed down to the size of an 8-bit GIF, but when the JPEG is loaded into a Web browser, the file has to be decompressed, which takes time.

✔ JPEG uses *lossy* compression, meaning that some file information is lost each time a JPEG is opened, edited, saved, and closed in either Photoshop or ImageReady. So, when creating an image for JPEG format, finish all editing before saving it as a JPEG.

PNG file format

The PNG file format was originally created to replace the GIF format (because of patent disputes) and is actually an improvement upon the old GIF standard.

The PNG file format saves transparent pixels using a process called *alpha transparency*. Alpha transparency is divided up into 256 levels of opacity, from totally transparent to totally opaque. In a PNG image, each pixel is assigned an alpha transparency setting.

There are two PNG formats, PNG-8 and PNG-24. PNG-8 can contain up to a maximum of 256 colors (8-bits, hence the -8 after PNG). PNG-24 can contain millions of colors and is similar to the JPEG file format. Because both PNG formats use *lossless* compression, no data is lost when images are saved and resaved.

The PNG format is great but there are a few drawbacks.

✔ You can't save animations as PNG files.

✔ PNG-24 files don't compress as much as JPEG files, so file size is bigger.

✔ The PNG format is only supported by the later file browsers: Microsoft Internet Explorer 4.0 and later, and Netscape Navigator 6 and later, and Safari, the new standard browser on the Mac.

Optimization

When creating images for the Web, you'll need to keep in mind the four key issues that are discussed in this section: image dimensions, the number of colors an image has, the image's color depth, and file format the image is saved in.

Each issue has its plusses and minuses.

As you discover in the "Color and color depth" section, there's a balance between reducing the number of colors (thereby reducing the file size) and maintaining image quality. Dithering and anti-aliasing can help when the color palette is reduced, but both options can add a grainy quality to an image. In addition, dithering adds extra information in a file, thereby increasing file size.

In the "Compression and Web file formats" section, I explain that not all file types are created equal. One is great for saving animations (GIF), another is great for saving photographs, but loses image data each time it's saved (JPEG), and another handles transparency like a GIF file and can save photographs, but doesn't compress as much (PNG).

What to do? Photoshop and ImageReady are there to help you make the choices when saving graphics for the Web. Both the Optimize palette in ImageReady and the File⇨Save for Web command in Photoshop help you select the correct file type for your image and all the options such as dithering, anti-aliasing, and transparency while letting you preview the image before saving. Turn to the next section, "Saving Web files," for a discussion of both these features.

Saving Web Files

Photoshop and ImageReady share many of the same features so your Web graphics files are small, yet retain great display quality. Photoshop's File⇨Save for Web command and ImageReady's Optimize palette let you select from an array of Web file formats and settings to suit the needs of your Web project. Using either feature, the Save for Web command or the Optimize palette, you can compare different optimized versions of an image side-by-side to maximize display quality while minimizing file size.

The Save for Web command and the Optimize palette

If you compare Photoshop's Save for Web dialog box with ImageReady's image window and Optimize palette, you'll discover that they perform the same functions with virtually the same interface. Figure 18-11 shows Photoshop's Save for Web dialog box on top and ImageReady's image window with its Optimize, 2-Up, and 4-Up tabs and the Optimize palette on the bottom.

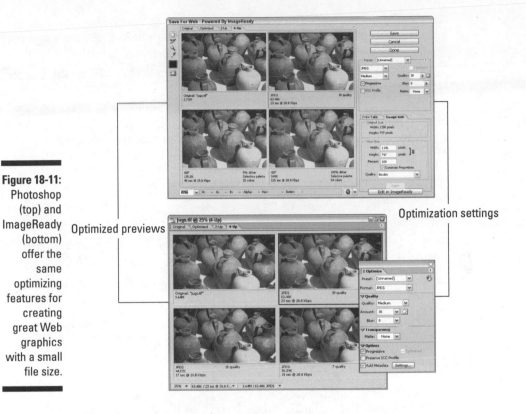

Figure 18-11:
Photoshop
(top) and
ImageReady
(bottom)
offer the
same
optimizing
features for
creating
great Web
graphics
with a small
file size.

Optimized previews

Optimization settings

Optimizing and saving an image in the GIF file format

This section takes you through optimizing an image in the GIF file format using either ImageReady's Optimize palette or Photoshop's Save for Web command. The area in the Save for Web dialog box that contains the same settings as the Optimize palette is on the right side of the dialog box. This area and the Optimize palette are shown in Figure 18-12.

To optimize an image in the GIF file format using either ImageReady's Optimize palette or Photoshop's Save for Web command, follow these steps:

1. **Open the image you want to optimize in either Photoshop or ImageReady.**

2. **If you are working in Photoshop, choose File⇨Save for Web. If you are working in ImageReady, open the Optimize palette by choosing Window⇨Optimize.**

As shown in Figure 18-12, Photoshop's Save for Web dialog box and ImageReady's image window and Optimize palette contain the same optimizing features and settings.

3. **Click the 2-Up tab in either the Save for Web dialog box or the Image Ready image window.**

This view displays the original image on the left and a preview of the optimized image on the right. As you select optimizing settings, the optimized preview changes to reflect the settings you've selected.

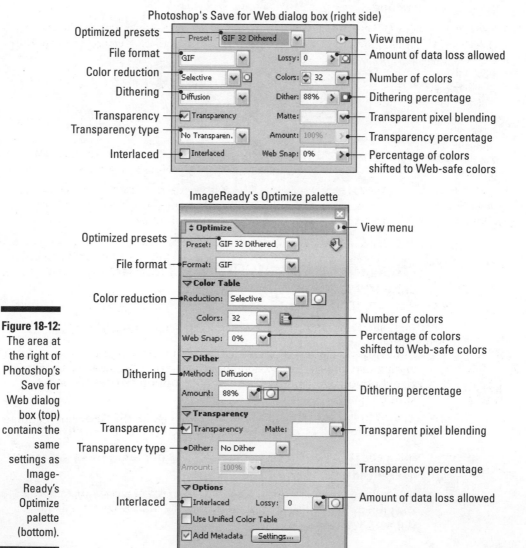

Figure 18-12: The area at the right of Photoshop's Save for Web dialog box (top) contains the same settings as Image-Ready's Optimize palette (bottom).

4. **Use the Preset drop-down list to select an optimized GIF preset combination.**

In Photoshop, the Preset drop-down list is at the right of the Save for Web dialog box. In ImageReady, the Preset drop-down list is at the top of the Optimize palette.

Even if you want to choose custom settings, selecting a preset combination is a good place to start. If you like the preset as it is, skip to Step 10. To choose custom settings continue with Step 5.

5. **Use the Reduction drop-down list to select a color reduction method.**

The GIF file format uses specific mathematical formulas *(algorithms)* to reduce the number of colors and thereby reduce file size. Here are the settings you can choose from:

- **Perceptual:** Creates a color table based on the colors in the image and how people see colors.

- **Selective:** Creates a color table using the flat colors and Web-safe colors in the image.

- **Adaptive:** Creates a color table based on the part of the color spectrum that contains most of the colors in the image.

- **Restrictive (Web):** Creates a color table by shifting the colors in the image to the 216 standard Web-safe colors that the Windows and Mac Web browsers have in common.

You also can use the Web Snap slider to set how wide a range of colors is automatically set to their Web-safe equivalents. The higher the percentage, the more Web-safe colors are used. Higher settings can create more dithering and graininess, though.

6. **Select a dithering method using the Dither method drop-down list.**

The dithering options are: No Dither, Diffusion, Pattern, or Noise.

Dithering simulates colors not available in the image's color palette by mixing two colors that are available. Dithering does add to the file size, but not significantly. The Diffusion option creates the most subtle results.

Also, you can set the amount of dithering using the Dither percentage slider.

7. **Put a check in the Transparency check box to preserve any transparent pixels in the image.**

If Transparency is unchecked, any transparent pixels will be colored with the currently selected Matte color. The Matte color is selected in the next step.

8. **Select a Matte setting to control how partially transparent pixels along the edge of an image blend with the background of the Web page.**

    If you know what the color of the Web page background is, use the Matte drop-down list to select the color. You can also select None, Foreground Color, or Background Color.

9. **Select the Interlaced option if you want to display the image in successively greater detail as it downloads on the Web page.**

10. **Save the image.**

    If you are using Photoshop's Save for Web dialog box, click Save; or if you are using ImageReady's Optimize palette, choose File➪Save Optimized As. Then, use the Save Optimized As dialog box to enter a name for the file and select a location where you want to save the file.

When you save image files in ImageReady using the File➪Save Optimized As, ImageReady also generates HTML files associated with the image files. These HTML files are necessary for making Web graphics such as rollovers and image maps work. To find out more about the HTML files check out the sidebar "ImageReady saves HTML, too!"

Optimizing and saving an image in the JPEG file format

This section takes you through optimizing an image in the JPEG file format using either ImageReady's Optimize palette or Photoshop's Save for Web command. The area in the Save for Web dialog box that contains the same settings as the Optimize palette is at the right of the dialog box. This area and the Optimize palette are shown in Figure 18-13.

To optimize an image in the JPEG file format using either ImageReady's Optimize palette or Photoshop's Save for Web command, follow these steps:

1. **Open the image you want to optimize in either Photoshop or ImageReady.**

2. **If you are working in Photoshop, choose File➪Save for Web. If you are working in ImageReady, open the Optimize palette by choosing Window➪Optimize.**

    As shown in Figure 18-13, Photoshop's Save for Web dialog box and ImageReady's image window and Optimize palette contain the same optimizing features and settings.

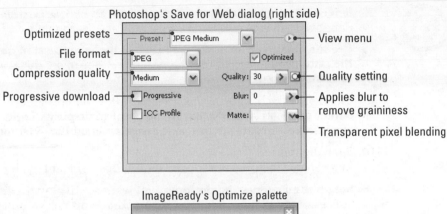

Photoshop's Save for Web dialog (right side)

Optimized presets — Preset: JPEG Medium — View menu
File format — JPEG — Optimized
Compression quality — Medium — Quality: 30 — Quality setting
Progressive download — Progressive — Blur: 0 — Applies blur to remove graininess
ICC Profile — Matte: — Transparent pixel blending

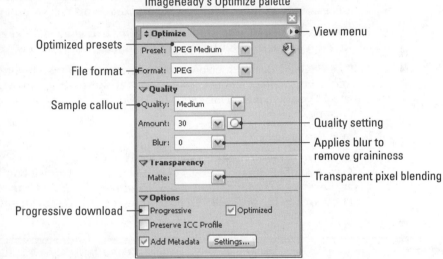

ImageReady's Optimize palette

Figure 18-13: The area at the right of Photoshop's Save for Web dialog box (top) contains the same settings as Image-Ready's Optimize palette (bottom).

Optimize — View menu
Optimized presets — Preset: JPEG Medium
File format — Format: JPEG
Quality
Sample callout — Quality: Medium
Amount: 30 — Quality setting
Blur: 0 — Applies blur to remove graininess
Transparency
Matte: — Transparent pixel blending
Options
Progressive download — Progressive — Optimized
Preserve ICC Profile
Add Metadata — Settings...

3. **Click the 2-Up tab in either the Save for Web dialog box or the Image Ready image window.**

   This view displays the original image on the left and a preview of the optimized image on the right. As you select optimizing settings, the optimized preview changes to reflect the settings you've selected.

4. **Use the Preset drop-down list to select an optimized JPEG preset combination.**

   In Photoshop, the Preset drop-down list is at the right of the Save for Web dialog box. In ImageReady, the Preset drop-down list is at the top of the Optimize palette.

   Even if you want to choose custom settings, selecting a preset combination is a good place to start.

If you like the preset as it is, skip to Step 8. To choose custom settings continue with Step 5.

5. Use the Quality drop-down list to select the compression quality for the optimized image or use the Amount slider to set the exact amount of compression.

The higher the quality setting, the lower the compression you end up with. The result is an image with higher display quality and a larger file size. Figure 18-14 shows the same image saved at Low, Medium, and High quality. Notice how dotty the low quality image is.

You can use the Quality slider to set the exact amount of compression.

6. Select the Progressive option if you want to display the image in successively greater detail as it downloads on the Web page.

7. Select a Matte color to set how partially transparent pixels along the edge of an image blend with the background of the Web page.

The JPEG file format does not support transparency, so if you know the color of the Web page background, use the Matte drop-down list to select the color. If the None setting is selected, transparent pixels are automatically colored white.

8. Save the image.

If you are using Photoshop's Save for Web dialog box, click Save; or if you are using ImageReady's Optimize palette, choose File⇨Save Optimized As. Then, use the Save Optimized As dialog box to enter a name for the file and select a location where you want to save the file.

ImageReady saves HTML, too!

ImageReady, by default, saves HTML files along with graphic files for the Web. These files contain the HTML and JavaScript code necessary to make features such as image maps and rollovers work.

When you use the File⇨Save Optimized command in ImageReady, the program also creates a folder structure in which to place the image files referenced by the HTML. By default, the folder for image files is named images.

You'll need to understand the structure that ImageReady creates when you publish these files on your Web site or if you want to combine the HTML created by ImageReady with your own HTML code. When you publish rollovers and image map graphics to your Web site, you must upload the accompanying HTML files also. Otherwise, the image maps and rollovers won't work.

Using the Save as type drop-down list in the Save Optimized As dialog box, you can tell ImageReady to only save image files (as opposed to HTML and image files which is the default). Or you can use the various dialog boxes accessed by choosing File⇨Output Settings to change the way in which HTML files are saved and named. In addition, you can use these same dialog boxes to set the folder names in which graphics and HTML files are saved.

Figure 18-14:
The same image saved as a JPEG with High quality (top), Medium quality (middle), and Low quality (bottom).

TIP

When you save image files in ImageReady using the File⇨Save Optimized As, ImageReady also generates HTML files associated with the image files. These HTML files are necessary for making Web graphics such as *rollovers* and *image maps* work. Rollovers are areas of a Web page that change when the mouse passes over them or perform some other action such as clicking. Image maps are hotspots on a Web page that have attached URLs. When a hotspot is clicked, the user is transported to that Web page. To find out more about the HTML files check out the sidebar "ImageReady saves HTML, too!"

Exporting an Image in Flash SWF Format

The ability to export images directly to Flash SWF format is a great new feature of ImageReady CS and Photoshop CS. Flash animators who want to quickly tweak their images can now do so in Photoshop, and then export them as Flash files.

When images are exported as SWF files, ImageReady attempts to preserve dynamic text and embedded fonts. This means that non-programmers can use ImageReady to create vector shapes and text that become the basis of animations in Flash.

One of the great advantages to using Flash as opposed to multiple animated GIF and JPEG files is that one SWF Flash file contains and encapsulates all the graphics, animations, and scripts on an entire Web page.

To export an image in SWF format:

1. **In ImageReady, open the image you want export in SWF format.**

2. **Choose File⇨Export⇨Macromedia Flash SWF...**

   The Macromedia Flash (SWF) Export dialog box shown in Figure18-15 opens. This dialog box is used to select settings to preserve vector shapes and text, select a Flash background color, and enable dynamic text.

3. **Check Preserve Appearance to set ImageReady to attempt to preserve vector shapes and editable type.**

   With this options selected, ImageReady tries to keep vector shapes and editable type intact. This means that you can manipulate the shapes and edit the type in Flash. (For more about creating vector shapes, turn to Chapter 16; to find out how to create editable type, take a look at "Creating Type for the Web" later in this chapter in addition to checking out Chapter 17.)

4. **Use the SWF bgcolor drop-down list to select the background color in the Flash animation, if you know it.**

   Using this drop-down list, you can select Foreground Color, Background Color, or select a color using the Color picker.

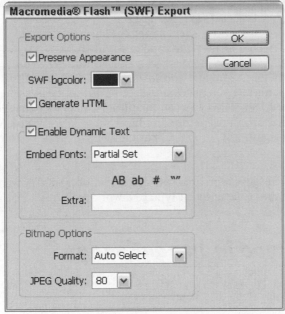

Figure 18-15:
The new Macromedia Flash (SWF) Export dialog box lets you export images directly into Flash SWF file format.

5. **Check in the Generate HTML option to have ImageReady create an HTML file.**

If you check this option, the HTML file contains information about Background color, image size, and image formatting options such as file formatting type (GIF or JPEG) and JPEG quality.

6. **If you want to ensure that any text created in ImageReady can be used in an animation in Flash, check Enable Dynamic Text.**

If you select this option, use the Embed Fonts drop-down list to select how many fonts are embedded, a Full Set, Partial Set, or None.

7. **Use the Format drop-down list in the Bitmap Options area to select how the exported image should be formatted.**

There are three Format settings: Auto Select lets ImageReady choose the formatting setting, Lossless-8 sets the image in an 8-bit format (like a GIF), Lossless-32 sets the image in a 32-bit format (like a GIF but with 32-bit format to include millions of colors) and JPEG sets the image in JPEG format. If you select JPEG, use the JPEG Quality slider to adjust the display quality (the higher the setting, the larger the file but the higher the display quality).

8. **Click OK.**

Use the Export As Macromedia SWF dialog box to name the file and select a location where you want to save the file.

Creating Type for the Web

Type in ImageReady works just like type in Photoshop. Using the Type tool (ImageReady's equivalent to Photoshop's Horizontal Type tool), you can enter type directly on the image, and format it using the Options bar, Character palette, and Paragraph palette. In addition, type appears on its own editable type layer. The type can be edited and reformatted until it is rasterized (if you wish, the type doesn't have to be rasterized). When type is optimized in ImageReady, it is automatically rasterized, becoming a part of the image.

ImageReady doesn't let you create type as a selection, place type on a path, convert type to a shape, or convert type to a work path.

Creating type in ImageReady

Using the ImageReady Type Tool, you can create horizontal or vertical text that is completely formatted as you would like it.

1. **Select the Type Tool from the Toolbox.**

2. **Click the Original tab in the image window.**

3. **Set type formatting attributes.**

   Using the Options bar, Character palette, and Paragraph palette, you can set font, style, size, anti-aliasing, alignment, and color. In addition, you can click the Change Text Orientation button on the Options bar to select whether you to create horizontal or vertical text. (For more about setting type formatting attributes, turn to Chapter 17.)

4. **Click in the image window where you want the type to start.**

   A blinking insertion marker appears in the image window.

5. **Type your text.**

6. **When you're finished entering text, click again in the image window.**

   The type appears on its own type layer in the Layers palette.

You may have noticed that the Options bar in ImageReady also offers the Warped Text option. Yes, you can create crazy, warped text in ImageReady and add it to your Web pages. To find out more about warping text, turn to Chapter 17.

Web type tips

There are a few things you should keep in mind when using ImageReady and Photoshop for creating type for the Web:

- ✔ When you jump back and forth between ImageReady and Photoshop, all type layer formatting attributes are preserved.

- ✔ Larger type works better on the Web. Because Web page resolution is a low 96 ppi, small type can appear quite dotty and be illegible. Larger type allows for a few more pixels to color each letter.

- ✔ Use Web-safe colors when creating type. If you use a color that isn't Web-safe, Photoshop or ImageReady automatically applies dithering to the edges to approximate colors when the type is optimized. Dithering makes the edges of the type look fuzzy instead of crisp and hard-edged.

- ✔ When adding type to a Web page use a color that contrasts well with the Web page. Type that is too light on a light colored Web page is almost impossible to read. The same goes for dark type on a dark-colored Web page.

Chapter 19

Slicing and Dicing Images

• •

• •

Slicing is the essential technique for creating rollovers and animations in ImageReady. (Rollovers are areas of a Web page that change when the mouse passes over them or performs some other action such as clicking.) When an image is divided into individual *slices* you can save each slice as an individual file (and file type) that contains separate color palettes, color settings, hyperlinks, rollovers and animations.

Slices are great for dealing with large images and images that contain different design elements. If an image is very large, it can be divided up into slices. The set of small slices can then be downloaded onto a Web page much faster than the entire large image would. If an image contains an area that uses a GIF animation, but the rest of the image works better as a JPEG, you can separate the GIF animation from the rest of the image as a slice and optimized as a GIF, while the JPEG area is separately optimized.

Using layers or tools in ImageReady, you can create *image maps,* separate areas that are linked to different Web addresses or URLs. When visitors arrive at your Web page and click an area in an image map, they are transported to another Web page. Image maps are an integral part of any Web page and are easy to create.

In this chapter, I show you how to use slices and image maps to take your Web graphics from ho-hum to fasten-your-seatbelt awesome. You'll find out how to create slices, slice large images for faster loading, and create image map hotspots with attached hyperlinks. In addition, you'll learn how to reshape image map hotspots and how to preview your work in ImageReady or a browser.

What's in a Slice?

A *slice* is a mechanism for dividing images for the Web. Depending what you're going to with the image, dividing an image into slices has different benefits and uses. Probably, the two most important slice applications are:

✔ **Speeding up the amount of time it takes for a large graphic to load.** By dividing the image into many smaller images, you keep the graphic from being processed by browsers as one big image. Slices enable you to put large images on the Web without making the people who visit your Web page wait too long.

✔ **Creating image maps.** Image maps allow a user to click on a portion of an image and be redirected to a specified Web location.

There are three different types of slices: user slices, layer-based slices, and auto slices. User slices are slices manually created using the Slice tool. Layer-based slices are created using layers. And auto slices are the left over areas that Photoshop or ImageReady automatically turn into slices when layer-based or user slices are created. If an area hasn't been included in a user slice or a layer-based slice, it is automatically turned into one or more auto slices.

Figure 19-1 shows an image divided into the three different types of slices. Notice that each slice is numbered and has a special icon marking it as a user slice, a layer-based slice, or an auto slice.

If you ever selected the Slice tool in Photoshop or ImageReady, you may have noticed a grayed out rectangle with number appear at the upper left corner of the image. This label indicates that ImageReady or Photoshop automatically generated an auto slice containing the entire image, as shown in Figure 19-2.

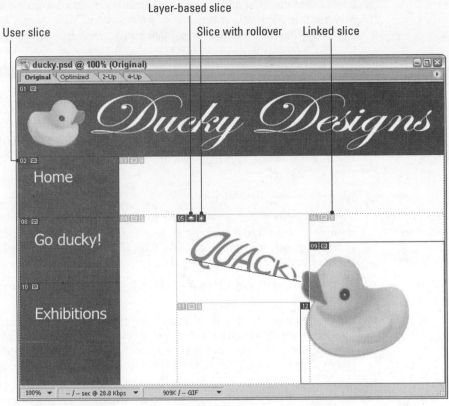

Figure 19-1:
There are three different types of slices, user slices, layer-based slices, and auto slices.

Photoshop does have the ability to create, select, and edit slices, but ImageReady offers more slice options. So, it's usually best to create and manage slices in ImageReady. But, no matter which program you use to create the slices, if you jump back and forth between the programs, all slices and slice settings are preserved.

Creating Slices

There are several ways to add slices to an image: you can let ImageReady automatically create horizontal or vertical slices, manually slice an image using the Slice tool, make slices using layers, and create slices using guides.

Letting ImageReady do the slicing

When you use ImageReady to create slices, you specify how many vertical and/or horizontal slices you want, and ImageReady does the work for you.

This method of creating slices works especially well if you have a large image that you want to slice up for quicker downloading in Web pages. To let ImageReady do all the work, follow these steps:

1. **In Image Ready, open the image to which you want to add slices.**

   ImageReady creates an auto slice containing the entire image (refer to Figure 19-2).

2. **Choose Slices⇨Promote to User Slice.**

   This menu option converts the auto slice into a user slice. Notice that the slice label changes from the grayed out auto slice label to the blue user slice label.

3. **Choose Slices⇨Divide Slice.**

   The Divide Slice dialog box opens with the Preview option selected by default. (If it isn't selected for some reason, put a check mark in the Preview check box. That way, you'll be able to see the slices as you add vertical and horizontal slices.)

4. **To create horizontal slices put a check in the Divide Horizontally Into check box.**

   Enter the desired number of horizontal slices in the Slices Down, Evenly Spaced text box, or enter a number in the Pixels per Slice text box. When you enter a value in either text box, the horizontal slices appear as a preview in the image window (see Figure 19-3).

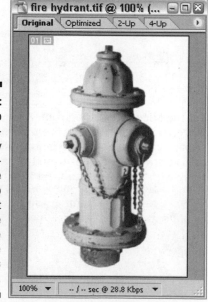

Figure 19-2: Photoshop and Image- Ready automat- ically create an auto slice that contains the entire image when the Slice tool is selected.

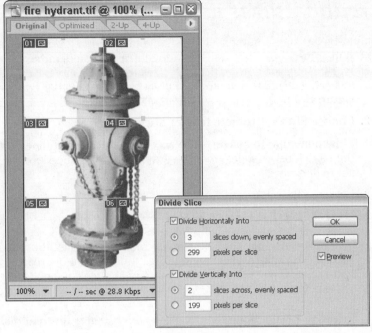

Figure 19-3:
In the Divide
Slice text
box, enter
a specific
number
of slices
or pixel
amount
per slice.

5. **To create vertical slices put a check in the Divide Vertically Into check box.**

   Enter the desired number of vertical slices in the Slices Across, Evenly Spaced text box, or enter a number in the Pixels per Slice text box.

6. **Click OK.**

   A user slice label appears in the upper left corner of each slice. The number indicates the slice number. After creating slices using the Divide Slice command, all the slices are selected.

   To select only one slice, select the Slice Select tool from the ImageReady Toolbox, and then click the slice you want to select. From here, you can reshape the slice, if necessary, or attach a URL (Uniform Resource Locator, or specific file location) to the slice as described later in this chapter in the section, "Working with Slices." If you want to publish your sliced image to the Web, save the image using the optimization directions in Chapter 18, and then upload the image and associated HTML file that ImageReady creates to your Web service provider. (Remember that the HTML file contains the code that slices the image. If you don't upload the HTML file, your image won't be sliced.)

Creating slices using layers

A layer-based slice contains all the visible pixels on a layer. If the layer is edited in some way — layer effects added, transformed, moved, and so on — the layer-based slice automatically resizes to include any new pixels. Layer-based slices work especially well for creating rollovers that contain effects, such as a bevel or drop shadow, which may increase the layer size.

Creating a layer-based slice is quite simple. In ImageReady, use the Layers palette to select the layer you want to use to create the layer-based slice. Then, choose Layer⇨New Layer Based Slice.

Manually slicing an image

The Slice tool works like the Rectangular Marquee tool in Photoshop. You drag the tool to enclose a rectangular area, but instead of creating a selection, you create a user slice. As you create user slices, ImageReady creates auto slices, dividing up the leftover area.

1. **In Image Ready, open the image to which you want to add slices.**

   ImageReady creates an auto slice containing the entire image (shown in Figure 19-2).

2. **Select the Slice tool from the ImageReady Toolbox.**

3. **Position the mouse where you want to start the slice and then drag the mouse diagonally to create the slice.**

   When you release the mouse button, a user slice label with a number appears in the upper-left corner of the slice, as shown in Figure 19-4.

4. **Continue to create as many slices as you need.**

 If you need to divide an auto slice or user slice into smaller slices, select the slice using the Slice Select tool, and then choose Slices⇨ Divide Slice. Use the Divide Slice text box to set the number of slices, and then click OK.

Working with Slices

After you create slices, you can resize them, align and distribute them, link them, put them into slice sets, and much more. In addition, you can optimize individual slices based on the needs of the image contained within the slice. For instance, one slice on a Web page could contain an animated GIF and be optimized in that file format. Another slice on the same Web page could contain a lovely photograph that is optimized as a JPEG.

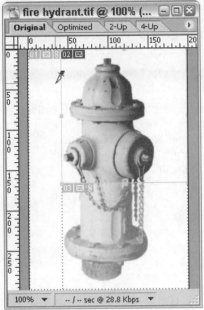

Figure 19-4: As you create user slices with the Slice tool, ImageReady automatically creates auto slices for the remaining area.

✔ **To convert an auto slice or layer-based slice to a user slice:** Choose the Slice Select tool from the ImageReady Toolbox. Select the slice you want to convert in the image window. Then choose Slices⊅Promote to User Slice.

✔ **To resize a user slice:** Select the Slice Select tool from the ImageReady Toolbox, select a slice in the image window, and then drag the slice boundary handles.

✔ **To combine auto slices and/or user slices into a larger user slice:** Use the Slice Select tool to select two or more slices in the image window. Then choose Slices⊅Combine Slices.

✔ **To assign a URL to a slice:** Use the Slice Select tool to select a slice. In the Slice palette, enter a Web address in the URL text box, as shown in Figure 19-5. When the slice is loaded on a Web page, anyone clicking the slice will be transported to that Web address.

✔ **To optimize a slice in a specific file format:** Use the Slice Select tool to select the slice in the image window. Then use the Optimize palette to select optimization settings. Turn to Chapter 18 for more about optimization settings.

✔ **To copy optimization settings from one slice to another:** Use the Slice Select tool to select the slice whose optimization settings you want to copy. Drag the Create Droplet button from the Optimize palette onto the slice in the image window that you want to copy the optimization settings to. Take a look at Chapter 18 to find out more about optimization settings.

✔ **To link slices together for optimization:** Use the Slice Select tool to select a slice in the image window. Shift+click to select the other slices that you want to link together. Choose Slices➪Link Slices for Optimization.

✔ **To unlink a slice:** Use the Slice Select tool to select the slice you want to unlink, and then choose Slices➪Unlink Slice.

✔ **To align slices:** Use the Slice Select tool to select the slices you want to align (Shift+click to select more than one slice). Click one of the align-ment buttons on the Options bar as shown in Figure 19-6. You can align slices vertically by their upper or lower edges or centers, or horizontally by their left or right edges or centers.

Only the slices move, not the images inside them.

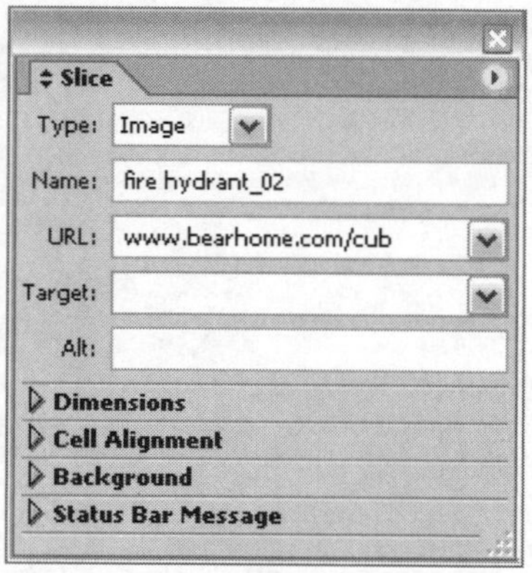

Figure 19-5:
In the Slice palette, type a Web address in the URL text box to assign a URL to a slice.

✔ **To distribute slices:** Use the Slice Select tool to select the slices you want to distribute (Shift+click to select more than one slice). Click one of the distribution buttons on the Options bar, as shown in Figure 19-6.

✔ **To delete a slice:** Use the Slice Select tool to select the slice, then choose Slices➪Delete slice.

Image Maps

An *image map* designates where specially selected areas or *hotspots* appear on an image in a Web page. Each hotspot is linked to a URL. When people browsing the Web page click the hotspot, they are transported to the URL.

Using the tools in ImageReady, you can create irregularly shaped image maps that follow the contour of an image. In addition, you can create image maps using layers.

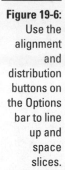

Figure 19-6:
Use the
alignment
and
distribution
buttons on
the Options
bar to line
up and
space
slices.

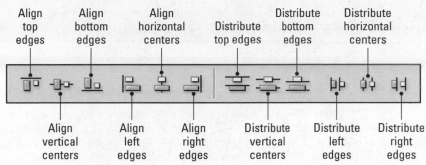

Align top edges — Align bottom edges — Align horizontal centers — Distribute top edges — Distribute bottom edges — Distribute horizontal centers

Align vertical centers — Align left edges — Align right edges — Distribute vertical centers — Distribute left edges — Distribute right edges

Creating an image map using layers

Using ImageReady, you can create an image map using the colored pixels on a layer. If you edit the layer — move it, transform it, or edit it in any way — ImageReady automatically updates the layer-based image map.

To create an image map, follow these steps:

1. **In ImageReady, use the Layers palette to select a layer.**

   The layer that you use to create a layer-based image map must contain transparent areas; otherwise, the entire layer will be one giant image map.

2. **Choose Layer⇨New Layer Based Image Map Area.**

3. **In the Image Map palette, select a shape for the hotspots.**

   Use the Shape drop-down list to create square, circular, or polygonal hotspots. Figure 19-7 shows polygonal hotspots around the dice.

4. **In the Image Map palette, enter a Web address in the URL text box.**

   When you enter the Web address in the URL text box, be sure to type **http://** before the Web address (it should look something like this: **http://www.dummies.com**). In addition, enter alternate text in the Alt text box as shown in Figure 19-8. This text will appear when someone browsing the Web page passes the mouse over the hotspot and while waiting for graphics to load.

   When the URL is entered in the Image Map palette, a tiny hand icon appears near the layer name in the Layers palette. This hand icon indicates that the layer contains a layer-based image map.

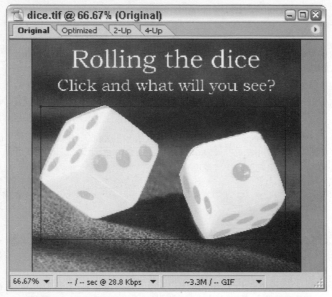

Figure 19-7:
The dice on
the dice
layer are
surrounded
by polygonal
hotspots.

5. Repeat Steps 1–4 to create image maps using any other layers.

 Preview the image in a browser by clicking the Preview in Browser button in the Toolbox. Previewing the image enables you to test out the hotspots you created. You can also optimize and save the layered image with its image map as described in Chapter 18, then upload the image and associated HTML file that ImageReady generates to your Web service provider.

Creating an image map using tools

Using the image map tools in the ImageReady Toolbox, you can create image map hotspots that are shaped around the contours of image elements.

 1. Select either the Rectangle Image Map, Circle Image Map, or Polygon Image Map tool from the Toolbox.

2. Create the hotspot around the area.

If you selected the Rectangle Image Map tool or Circle Image Map tool, drag a rectangular or circular area in the image window.

If you selected the Polygon Image Map tool, click where you want the image map boundary to start, and then continue to click around the contour of the area. When you have surrounded the area, double-click to close the image map, or click the starting point to close the shape.

Figure 19-8:
As soon as
you enter a
URL in the
Image Map
palette, a
tiny hand
icon
appears
near the
layer name,
indicating
that the
layer
contains an
image map.

Enter URL here

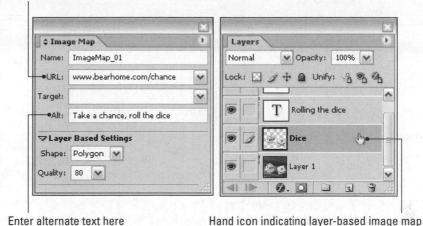

Enter alternate text here

Hand icon indicating layer-based image map

Figure 19-9 shows the Polygon Image Map tool in action, creating a polygonal hotspot around the left die.

3. In the Image Map palette, enter a Web address in the URL text box.

When you enter the Web address in the URL text box, be sure to type **http://** before the Web address. In addition, enter alternate text in the Alt text box (refer to Figure 19-8).

Figure 19-9:
Use the
image map
tools in the
Toolbox
to create
hotspots
around
Web page
elements. In
this figure,
the left die
has been
mapped.

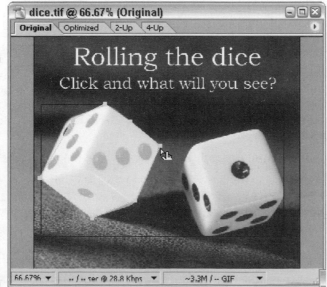

4. Repeat Steps 1–3 to create another image map hotspot.

If you preview the image in a browser by clicking the Preview in Browser button in the Toolbox, you can test out the hotspots you created. You also can optimize and save the layered image with its image map as described in Chapter 18, and then upload the image and associated HTML file that ImageReady generates to your Web service provider.

Working with image maps

You can convert layer-based image maps to tool-based image maps, change their shape, hide them if you need to edit an image or work on another aspect of a Web page, and, of course, delete them. Here are the basics:

- **To convert a layer-based image map to a tool-based image map:** Use the Image Map Select tool to select the image map you want to convert. Then, choose Promote Layer Based Image Map Area from the Image Map palette menu as shown in Figure 19-10. Only tool-based image maps can be reshaped, so it's important to know how to convert a layer-based image map if you want to reshape an image map area.

- **To reshape a tool-based image map:** Select the Image Map Select tool from the Toolbox. Select the image map you want to reshape in the image window. Drag the image map boundary handles to reshape the image map as shown in Figure 19-11.

- **To duplicate an image map:** Use the Image Map Select tool to select the image map you want to copy. Then choose Duplicate Image Map Area from the Image Map palette's menu. You can then use the Image Map Select tool to move the duplicate image map to the place where you need it.

- **To hide image maps in the image window:** Choose View➪Show➪Image Maps. Choose the Image Maps command again to view the image maps.

- **To delete an image map:** Use the Image Map Select tool to select the image map you want to delete. Then choose Delete Image Map Area from the Image Map palette's menu.

Previewing Your Image in a Browser

You can preview your Web pages right in ImageReady. This means that you can check out any image maps, rollovers, or animations you create to make sure they are working without leaving ImageReady. This is great for checking things out and making quick adjustments.

Figure 19-10:
Choose
promote
Layer Based
Image Map
Area from
the Image
Map palette
menu to
convert a
layer-based
image map
to a tool-
based
image map.

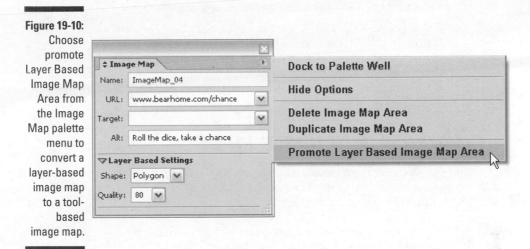

When you use ImageReady for the first time, it uses your system-default browser to generate the preview. But, if you want to view Web pages in other browsers to see how they look, you'll need to add them to the Browser List.

Figure 19-11:
Drag the
image map
boundary
handles to
reshape the
image map
area.

To add browsers to ImageReady's Browser List, choose File⇨Preview In⇨Edit Browser List. In the Edit Browser List dialog box, click the Find All button to let ImageReady find the browsers installed on your computer as shown in Figure 19-12.

Figure 19-12: Click the Find All button to let ImageReady find all browsers installed on your computer.

To set a default browser that ImageReady will automatically use to preview your Web pages, select the browser from the list of browsers at the left of the dialog box, and then click Set As Default. When you are finished adding browsers to the Browser List, click OK to close the dialog box.

After selecting a default browser, you'll notice that the Preview in Default Browser button on the Toolbox changes to the icon of the default browser you selected. Also, if you have more than one browser entered in the Browser List, a tiny arrow appears next to the button. If you position the mouse over the button and press, the entire list of browsers will be displayed on a flyout menu (see Figure 19-13).

Also notice that at the bottom of the browser flyout menu is a tiny downward pointing arrow. Drag your mouse over that arrow, and then release the mouse button. The flyout menu will turn into a mini toolbar containing the browsers (see Figure 19-13). You can use the mini toolbar for quick previews in the different browsers.

To quickly view a Web page in your default browser, just click the Preview in Default Browser button in the ImageReady Toolbox. To view a Web page in another browser, press the tiny arrow next to the Preview in Default Browser button and select a browser from the flyout menu.

If you want to view the HTML source code attached to your Web page, make sure File⇨Preview In⇨Include Source on Page is checked. When you preview the Web page, the source code appears at the bottom of the browser window, as shown in Figure 19-14.

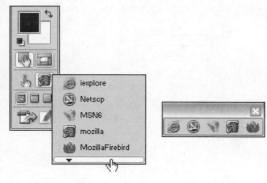

Figure 19-13:
Positioning your mouse over the tiny arrow, then pressing the mouse button lets you view a flyout menu that lists all browsers you can preview images with.

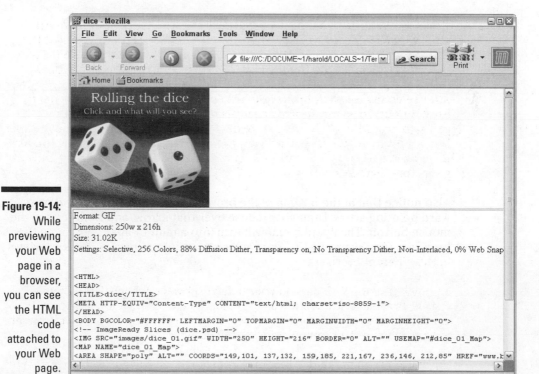

Figure 19-14:
While previewing your Web page in a browser, you can see the HTML code attached to your Web page.

Part VIII
The Part of Tens

The 5th Wave — By Rich Tennant

"Hey- let's use the Liquify command on scanned photos of ourselves and see if we can make ourselves look weird."

In this part . . .

Some say that there's magic in the number three. Bears, pigs, Musketeers, and Stooges regularly cavort about in groups of three. But I say that the real magic is in tens. Top ten lists abound in newspapers, magazines, books, and late-night TV shows. I say, why buck a trend? If everyone else is doing it, why not me?

This part contains two chapters. Chapter 20 shows you ten (or so) Photoshop filters that you can use to dramatically and easily change your images. Chapter 21 shows you ten (or so) things you can do with your image when you're finished creating it in Photoshop. Why not print your images, post them on the Web, or even create a mouse pad of a favorite photo? With Photoshop you can do all these things and more.

Chapter 20

Ten (Or So) Filters You Can Use to Create Fast Effects

*N*ewcomers to Photoshop are often very excited to find that they can create amazing image effects by simply applying a Photoshop filters — and there are almost 100 filters to play with. The good news is that power users also get plenty of bang for their buck with Photoshop filters. There are Photoshop filters that create almost any kind of effect you can think of with a few clicks of the mouse.

All the filters are available on the Filters menu. They are divided into group styles such as Artistic, Brush Strokes, Stylize, and Texture. Within each group are associated filters. (I cover filters in detail in Chapter 11.)

Although this chapter only shows you a few filter categories, I can assure you that you'll end up with well more than ten filter effects. You can use the filters shown in this chapter to create countless fast and wonderful effects.

Because these effects are visual (of course) this chapter contains a brief explanation of the filter group and samples of the filters available in that group in action.

Not all the filters are covered here. I show you a few Artistic filters including Cutout, Dry Brush, and Fresco; Sketch filters, such as Charcoal and Graphic Pen; and Stylize filters like Emboss and Solarize.

Artistic Filters

Original Image

Cutout

Dry Brush

Fresco

Neon Glow

Palette Knife

Artistic filters allow you to change your images to mimic effects that originally came from the world of art and painting. For example, the Palette Knife filter alters an image so that it resembles a painting created by dabbing paint on a canvas using an old-fashioned palette knife. If one of the effects in the group of Artistic filters meets your needs, it's hard to imagine an easier way to create such classical painterly effects.

Sketch Filters

Charcoal

Conte Crayon

Graphic Pen

Photocopy

Plaster

Stamp

The filters in the Sketch group create effects that are similar to classical drawing techniques. For example, the Charcoal filters turn images into charcoal drawings. This is not appropriate treatment for every image, but for those where it works the effect is spectacular. If you need images that look hand drawn for your project, then the Sketch filters may work for you.

Stylize Filters

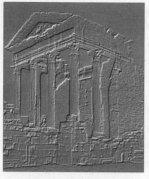

Emboss

Extrude

Find Edges

Glowing Edges

Solarize

Trace Contour

The filters in the Stylize group allow you to apply effects to an image that range from the dignified to the psychedelic. For example, the Emboss filter creates an effect that can appear like a three dimensional raised seal on a document. In contrast, the Glowing Edges and Solarize filters create images that are reminiscent of the rock-and-roll posters of the 1960s.

Chapter 21

Ten Things to Do with Your Photoshop Masterpiece

After you've edited and created a terrific image in Photoshop, there are many things you can do with it. For instance, you can print the image, export it to page layout programs such as PageMaker or InDesign, post it on the Web, and even use it in a PowerPoint presentation.

This chapter covers just a few of the ways Photoshop images can be used. Some of them cost money, and some involve the use of programs other than Photoshop, but all the following options provide food for future thought.

Printing and Dispersing

Just about everyone who has a computer also owns a printer. Desktop color printers have improved by leaps and bounds in the past couple of years. You can buy a high-quality color printer for the price of a couple nights out on the town. Epson and Hewlett-Packard have low-end printers that sell for the ridiculously low price of about $50. Both reputable manufacturers also have other printer models offering various features that cost anywhere from $100 to $1,000. My own Epson 1280 offers six color, photo-quality, border-free printing on up to 13 x 44 inch paper. And I forked over only $450 to buy it.

If you want to go one notch above a color inkjet printer, try the new personal *dye-sublimation* printers that are coming on the scene. A dye-sub printer creates images that look just like photographs — no little dots like you see in newspaper photos, just smooth-tone colors. For around $500, Olympus offers a continuous tone dye-sub printer that spits out a full-color print in 90 seconds.

Invest in some nice, glossy paper. It costs anywhere from 20 cents to $2 per sheet. Many printer manufacturers make their own paper, which is specially formulated to work well with their particular printer. Olympus offers a fantastic paper called Pictorico that sports a proprietary ceramic coating. Pictorico paper is smudge free, water resistant, and works with just about any inkjet printer. If you can't find Pictorico paper, any generic glossy paper works fine.

When printing on glossy paper, make sure that you print your image at the highest resolution your printer offers. You may want to take a look at the manual that came with your printer for settings.

Ordering Prints and Making Books

For you Mac users out there, Apple has developed a wonderful product called iPhoto 2. iPhoto 2 allows you to import photos from your digital camera, CDs, or directly from your hard drive. The program catalogs, stores, and displays the images on-screen. You can create digital photo albums, organizing them by date or event. Also, you can create custom books from your photos, choosing from several designs, and even adding a story or captions. Find iPhoto 2 at www.apple.com.

For Windows users there's Photoshop Album. A great product that let's you do everything iPhoto does. Organize your photos into catalogs, create books, calendars, and note cards. Photoshop Album can be found at www.adobe.com.

And the fun doesn't stop there. Both iPhoto 2 and Photoshop Album enable you to order Kodak prints over the Internet. You can create slide shows along with your favorite music. You can e-mail photos to family and friends. And finally, you can post your images to a personal Web page.

Placing Your Image into PageMaker or InDesign

Adobe PageMaker and InDesign are popular page layout programs. They enable you to combine text and graphics to create multipage documents such as brochures, newsletters, reports, catalogs, magazines, and even books. (For more information on these two programs, check out *PageMaker 6.5 For Dummies,* by Galen Gruman; and *Adobe InDesign For Dummies,* by Deke McClelland and Amy Thomas Buscaglia — both published by Wiley Publishing.)

Both PageMaker and InDesign allow you to import native Photoshop files, as well as TIFF files with LZW compression. (See Chapter 3 for more on file formats.) You import the file into PageMaker or InDesign by choosing File⊏>Place or by pressing Ctrl+D (⌘+D on a Mac).

InDesign 3.0 supports transparency. This means that you can import a Photoshop file that has transparent areas and place it over a background in InDesign, and you don't see a white box or hard edges as you do in programs that don't support transparency. Instead, you see the background peeking through the transparency in all the right places. This works great for importing images with soft drop shadows and placing them on solid backgrounds.

With PageMaker or InDesign, you can move the image on the page, run text around it, and print the final pages. So, unless you want to further modify the image, you have no reason to return to Photoshop. Although you can change the dimensions and rotate or skew the image in PageMaker or InDesign, it's best to do this in Photoshop rather than in a page layout program. Your file prints much faster and has less potential for snafus.

Placing Your Image into Illustrator and FreeHand

Adobe Illustrator and Macromedia FreeHand are graphics programs like Photoshop, but instead of enabling you to edit images, they let you create smooth-line *vector graphics.* Information graphics, logos, maps, architectural plans, general artwork, and single-page documents, such as flyers and ads — all these projects are ideally suited to Illustrator and FreeHand.

Both programs enable you to import images. Save your Photoshop image in the Photoshop EPS or Photoshop PSD format. In Illustrator, choose the File⊏>Place command to import your image. In FreeHand, choose the File➪Import command or Ctrl+R (⌘+R on a Mac) to import your image. Both Illustrator and FreeHand also support the TIFF format, but drawing programs work better with the EPS or PSD formats.

After placing the image, you can combine it with vector graphics or integrate it into a single-page document. The Wiley Publishing Composition Services staff used Illustrator to label the figures in this book. It's not advisable to label the figures inside Photoshop — which is where they all originated for this book. Although Photoshop has improved its text capabilities, it's best used with larger text. Likewise, PageMaker and InDesign are great for creating long text documents, but they aren't so good at handling little bits of text here and there.

Adding Your Image to a PowerPoint Presentation

Microsoft PowerPoint is a popular presentation program used for creating slides and on-screen presentations. Photoshop is a great tool for creating backgrounds for these presentations or refining head shots that may appear on the slides.

Because PowerPoint does most of its work on-screen, an easy way to transfer the image from Photoshop to PowerPoint is with the Clipboard. While inside Photoshop, just select the portion of the image you want to use, copy it by pressing Ctrl+C (⌘+C on a Mac), switch to PowerPoint, and paste the selection by pressing Ctrl+V (⌘+V on a Mac). If your image looks less than desirable, try saving the image in a file format that PowerPoint accepts, such as TIFF, and then importing the file into PowerPoint.

The transfer method recommended in the previous paragraph holds only if you're creating an on-screen presentation or plan to print the presentation on a non-PostScript printer. If you want to print overheads on a color PostScript printer, don't use the Clipboard to place the images into your presentation program. Instead, import the image into PowerPoint as a TIFF file.

As you can in page layout programs, you can move the image around, change the dimensions, and wrap text around it in PowerPoint. If you plan on displaying the presentation on-screen, you may want to give some thought to the size of the image. For example, if you intend for the image to serve as a background for a presentation that takes up an entire 17-inch monitor, the image should be 800 x 600 pixels or larger. A good size for a head shot may be 300 x 200 pixels. Experiment to find the image sizes that work best for you.

Because the boilerplate templates that ship with PowerPoint aren't the most awe-inspiring creations, you can create custom, artistic backgrounds for PowerPoint in Photoshop. Experiment with filters, the PatternMaker feature, and all the new brush options. After your background is done, save it as a TIFF and import your background image into PowerPoint.

Making a Desktop Pattern

You know that pattern or image that appears in the background behind all the icons on your Windows desktop or in the Mac Finder? You can create your own custom background using Photoshop.

For Windows XP users, here's what you do:

1. **Create your image.**

   If you want a single image to fill your entire screen, make the image the same size as the Desktop Area setting in the Windows Desktop Properties dialog box. To check the setting, right-click anywhere on the desktop, choose the Properties command to display the Display Properties dialog box, and click on the Settings tab. If the setting is 800 x 600, for example, make your image 800 x 600 pixels. Set the image resolution to 96 ppi.

2. **Save your image in the BMP, JPG, or GIF format.**

   If you save the image as a BMP file, be sure the File Format is set for Windows.

3. **Right-click anywhere on the Windows desktop to view the Display Properties dialog box.**

4. **Click the Desktop tab.**

5. **Click the Browse button.**

   Windows displays a Browse dialog box showing all your drives, folders, and files.

6. **Select your image using the Browse dialog box and click Open.**

   You see your image name selected in the Wallpaper list, along with a preview of your image.

7. **Use the Position drop-down list to set how the background is displayed.**

   You can select Tile, Center, or Stretch.

8. **Click Apply.**

   Windows applies the new wallpaper to your screen without closing the Display Properties dialog box. If you don't like what you see, you can change the Display option or choose another image to use as your wallpaper.

9. **Click OK to close the dialog box and accept your changes.**

For users of Mac OS X users, here's what you do:

1. **Click the System Preferences icon in the Dock.**

   These are the controls that affect the way your computer operates.

2. **Click on the Desktop icon in the Personal section.**

   This displays a window with a popup menu (called Collection) and a scroll bar that lets you scroll through various predefined patterns in the collection.

3. **Select the folder that contains your image from the Collection pop-up menu.**

   You can choose from other Apple desktop pattern sets or select Choose Folder and navigate to the folder that holds your images.

4. **Drag your desired image into the well.**

   Your desktop reflects your chosen image.

5. **Close the Desktop window.**

Turning Your Face into a Mouse Pad

Now that more and more folks are acquiring the ability to produce digital images, copy shops offer a plethora of products on which you can print your image. You can have your favorite Photoshop image transferred onto a mouse pad, coffee cup, T-shirt, calendar, and a whole bunch of other items that are guaranteed to be a big hit during the holiday gift-giving season. Check with your local copy shop for information on any image size, resolution, or file format requirements you need to follow when preparing your image.

Making a Slide Show

I mention earlier in this chapter (in the section "Ordering Prints and Making Books") that Mac users can use iPhoto and Windows users can use Photoshop Album to create a slide show. Both Mac and Windows users can also create one easily right in Photoshop.

Follow these steps to create a slide show in Photoshop:

1. **Open all the images you want to include in your slide show.**

2. **Shift+click on the Full Screen Mode button displayed at the bottom of your Toolbox.**

   This hides everything on your desktop.

3. **Press Tab to hide the menu bar and palettes.**

4. **Press and hold the Ctrl key and press Tab to cycle through each of your images.**

5. **When you're done, press Tab to get your menu and palettes back. Then Shift+click the Standard Screen Mode button at the bottom of your Toolbox.**

You can also use the Web Photo Gallery feature in Photoshop to create a slide show. Choose File➪Automate➪Web Photo Gallery. Select Horizontal Slide Show from the Styles drop-down list. Choose your folder of images, and Photoshop creates a slide show that you can preview in Photoshop. Then, you can post the photo gallery to the Web for others to see. Check out the details of using the Web Photos Gallery feature in Chapter 20.

Posting Your Image on the Internet or an Online Service

America Online (AOL) has Photoshop forums where members can upload images to make them available to other members. Remember, it takes time to upload and download images — so keep the images fairly small and save them in the JPEG or GIF format. (See Chapters 3 and 18 for more about these formats.)

Also, tons of Photoshop-related sites are on the Web. If you enter **Photoshop** in your favorite search engine, you'll be surprised at the number of matches you see.

If you happen to have your own Web page — or know someone who does — you can also add your image to the page, making them available to Web surfers worldwide. You can post your images easily by choosing File➪Automate➪Web Photo Gallery. (Visit www.dummies.com/go/photoshop_cs_fd to find out more.) And as I mention earlier in this chapter, Mac users can use iPhoto and Windows users can use Photoshop Album to create an easy Web page that displays Photoshop images.

Just in case you haven't gotten enough of me through the course of reading this book, by the way, you can check out my Web page at the following URL: www.dekemc.com. It offers some Photoshop tips and tricks along with a bunch of other stuff, including lots of shameless self-promotion. But hey, what's the point of having a Web page if you can't brag a little, right?

Assembling a Private Collection of Images

No one says that you have to produce artwork for public consumption. I do plenty of stuff just for my own amusement and edification. What you see in this book, for example, represents about half of what I came up with; the other images are working files, experiments, or just too hideous for publication.

So share the stuff you're proud of, keep the random experiments to yourself, and try to learn from your inevitable mistakes. Oh, yeah, and don't beat the computer when it crashes.

Index

• G •

• S •

Notes

Notes

Notes

FOR DUMMIES®

The easy way to get more done and have more fun

PERSONAL FINANCE & BUSINESS

Investing FOR DUMMIES
0-7645-2431-3

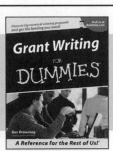
Home Buying FOR DUMMIES
0-7645-5331-3

Grant Writing FOR DUMMIES
0-7645-5307-0

Also available:

Accounting For Dummies
(0-7645-5314-3)

Business Plans Kit For Dummies
(0-7645-5365-8)

Managing For Dummies
(1-5688-4858-7)

Mutual Funds For Dummies
(0-7645-5329-1)

QuickBooks All-in-One Desk Reference For Dummies
(0-7645-1963-8)

Resumes For Dummies
(0-7645-5471-9)

Small Business Kit For Dummies
(0-7645-5093-4)

Starting an eBay Business For Dummies
(0-7645-1547-0)

Taxes For Dummies 2003
(0-7645-5475-1)

HOME, GARDEN, FOOD & WINE

Feng Shui FOR DUMMIES
0-7645-5295-3

Gardening FOR DUMMIES
0-7645-5130-2

Cooking FOR DUMMIES
0-7645-5250-3

Also available:

Bartending For Dummies
(0-7645-5051-9)

Christmas Cooking For Dummies
(0-7645-5407-7)

Cookies For Dummies
(0-7645-5390-9)

Diabetes Cookbook For Dummies
(0-7645-5230-9)

Grilling For Dummies
(0-7645-5076-4)

Home Maintenance For Dummies
(0-7645-5215-5)

Slow Cookers For Dummies
(0-7645-5240-6)

Wine For Dummies
(0-7645-5114-0)

FITNESS, SPORTS, HOBBIES & PETS

Fitness FOR DUMMIES
0-7645-5167-1

Golf FOR DUMMIES
0-7645-5146-9

Guitar FOR DUMMIES
0-7645-5106-X

Also available:

Cats For Dummies
(0-7645-5275-9)

Chess For Dummies
(0-7645-5003-9)

Dog Training For Dummies
(0-7645-5286-4)

Labrador Retrievers For Dummies
(0-7645-5281-3)

Martial Arts For Dummies
(0-7645-5358-5)

Piano For Dummies
(0-7645-5105-1)

Pilates For Dummies
(0-7645-5397-6)

Power Yoga For Dummies
(0-7645-5342-9)

Puppies For Dummies
(0-7645-5255-4)

Quilting For Dummies
(0-7645-5118-3)

Rock Guitar For Dummies
(0-7645-5356-9)

Weight Training For Dummies
(0-7645-5168-X)

Available wherever books are sold.
Go to www.dummies.com or call 1-877-762-2974 to order direct

WILEY

FOR DUMMIES®

A world of resources to help you grow

TRAVEL

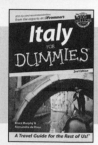

0-7645-5453-0

0-7645-5438-7

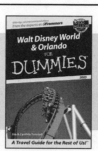

0-7645-5444-1

Also available:

America's National Parks For Dummies
(0-7645-6204-5)

Caribbean For Dummies
(0-7645-5445-X)

Cruise Vacations For Dummies 2003
(0-7645-5459-X)

Europe For Dummies
(0-7645-5456-5)

Ireland For Dummies
(0-7645-6199-5)

France For Dummies
(0-7645-6292-4)

Las Vegas For Dummies
(0-7645-5448-4)

London For Dummies
(0-7645-5416-6)

Mexico's Beach Resorts For Dummies
(0-7645-6262-2)

Paris For Dummies
(0-7645-5494-8)

RV Vacations For Dummies
(0-7645-5443-3)

EDUCATION & TEST PREPARATION

0-7645-5194-9

0-7645-5325-9

0-7645-5249-X

Also available:

The ACT For Dummies
(0-7645-5210-4)

Chemistry For Dummies
(0-7645-5430-1)

English Grammar For Dummies
(0-7645-5322-4)

French For Dummies
(0-7645-5193-0)

GMAT For Dummies
(0-7645-5251-1)

Inglés Para Dummies
(0-7645-5427-1)

Italian For Dummies
(0-7645-5196-5)

Research Papers For Dummies
(0-7645-5426-3)

SAT I For Dummies
(0-7645-5472-7)

U.S. History For Dummies
(0-7645-5249-X)

World History For Dummies
(0-7645-5242-2)

HEALTH, SELF-HELP & SPIRITUALITY

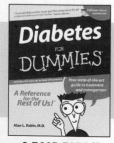

0-7645-5154-X

0-7645-5302-X

0-7645-5418-2

Also available:

The Bible For Dummies
(0-7645-5296-1)

Controlling Cholesterol For Dummies
(0-7645-5440-9)

Dating For Dummies
(0-7645-5072-1)

Dieting For Dummies
(0-7645-5126-4)

High Blood Pressure For Dummies
(0-7645-5424-7)

Judaism For Dummies
(0-7645-5299-6)

Menopause For Dummies
(0-7645-5458-1)

Nutrition For Dummies
(0-7645-5180-9)

Potty Training For Dummies
(0-7645-5417-4)

Pregnancy For Dummies
(0-7645-5074-8)

Rekindling Romance For Dummies
(0-7645-5303-8)

Religion For Dummies
(0-7645-5264-3)

Available wherever books are sold. Go to www.dummies.com or call 1-877-762-2974 to order direct

FOR DUMMIES®

Plain-English solutions for everyday challenges

FOR

DUMMIES®

Helping you expand your horizons and realize your potential

GRAPHICS & WEB SITE DEVELOPMENT

0-7645-1651-5

0-7645-1643-4

0-7645-0895-4

Also available:

Adobe Acrobat 5 PDF
For Dummies
(0-7645-1652-3)

ASP.NET For Dummies
(0-7645-0866-0)

ColdFusion MX For Dummies
(0-7645-1672-8)

Dreamweaver MX For
Dummies
(0-7645-1630-2)

FrontPage 2002 For Dummies
(0-7645-0821-0)

HTML 4 For Dummies
(0-7645-0723-0)

Illustrator 10 For Dummies
(0-7645-3636-2)

PowerPoint 2002 For
Dummies
(0-7645-0817-2)

Web Design For Dummies
(0-7645-0823-7)

PROGRAMMING & DATABASES

0-7645-0746-X

0-7645-1626-4

0-7645-1657-4

Also available:

Access 2002 For Dummies
(0-7645-0818-0)

Beginning Programming
For Dummies
(0-7645-0835-0)

Crystal Reports 9 For
Dummies
(0-7645-1641-8)

Java & XML For Dummies
(0-7645-1658-2)

Java 2 For Dummies
(0-7645-0765-6)

JavaScript For Dummies
(0-7645-0633-1)

Oracle9i For Dummies
(0-7645-0880-6)

Perl For Dummies
(0-7645-0776-1)

PHP and MySQL For
Dummies
(0-7645-1650-7)

SQL For Dummies
(0-7645-0737-0)

Visual Basic .NET For
Dummies
(0-7645-0867-9)

LINUX, NETWORKING & CERTIFICATION

0-7645-1545-4

0-7645-1760-0

0-7645-0772-9

Also available:

A+ Certification For Dummies
(0-7645-0812-1)

CCNP All-in-One Certification
For Dummies
(0-7645-1648-5)

Cisco Networking For
Dummies
(0-7645-1668-X)

CISSP For Dummies
(0-7645-1670-1)

CIW Foundations For
Dummies
(0-7645-1635-3)

Firewalls For Dummies
(0-7645-0884-9)

Home Networking For
Dummies
(0-7645-0857-1)

Red Hat Linux All-in-One
Desk Reference For Dummies
(0-7645-2442-9)

UNIX For Dummies
(0-7645-0419-3)

Available wherever books are sold.
Go to www.dummies.com or call 1-877-762-2974 to order direct